# First World War
## and Army of Occupation
# War Diary
## France, Belgium and Germany

57 DIVISION
171 Infantry Brigade
Headquarters
13 February 1917 - 31 December 1917

WO95/2980/2

The Naval & Military Press Ltd
www.nmarchive.com
Published in association with The National Archives

Published by

## The Naval & Military Press Ltd

Unit 10 Ridgewood Industrial Park,

Uckfield, East Sussex,

TN22 5QE England

Tel: +44 (0) 1825 749494

www.naval-military-press.com

www.nmarchive.com

*This diary has been reprinted in facsimile from the original. Any imperfections are inevitably reproduced and the quality may fall short of modern type and cartographic standards.*

**© Crown Copyright**
**Images reproduced by permission of The National Archives, London, England, 2015.**

# Contents

| Document type | Place/Title | Date From | Date To |
|---|---|---|---|
| Heading | WO95/2980-2 | | |
| Heading | Headquarters 171st Inf Bde (57th Div) February 1917 | | |
| Heading | War Diary Of Headquarters 171st Infantry Brigade 13.2.1917 To 29.2.1917 Volume I | | |
| War Diary | Havre | 13/02/1917 | 15/02/1917 |
| War Diary | Strazeele | 16/02/1917 | 20/02/1917 |
| War Diary | Nouveau Monde | 20/02/1917 | 22/02/1917 |
| War Diary | Fleurbaix | 22/02/1917 | 28/02/1917 |
| Miscellaneous | Move Orders Relief Orders | | |
| Miscellaneous | Instructions For Forthcoming Move No.I | 19/02/1917 | 19/02/1917 |
| Operation(al) Order(s) | 171st Brigade Order No. I | 20/02/1917 | 20/02/1917 |
| Miscellaneous | Issued With 171st Brigade Order No. I | 20/02/1917 | 20/02/1917 |
| Operation(al) Order(s) | 57th Division Order No. 1 | 19/02/1917 | 19/02/1917 |
| Miscellaneous | Table Of Reliefs | | |
| Miscellaneous | Brigade Groups 57th Division | | |
| Operation(al) Order(s) | 171st Brigade Order No. 2 | 20/02/1917 | 20/02/1917 |
| Operation(al) Order(s) | Operation Order No. 14 | | |
| Miscellaneous | 1st New Zealand Infantry Brigade. Appendix "A" To Operation Order No. 14 | 20/02/1917 | 20/02/1917 |
| Operation(al) Order(s) | 171st Brigade Relief Order No. I | 24/02/1917 | 24/02/1917 |
| Operation(al) Order(s) | 171st Brigade Relief Order No. 2 | 27/02/1917 | 27/02/1917 |
| Miscellaneous | A.G. Base | 31/03/1917 | 31/03/1917 |
| Heading | HQ 171 Infy Bde (57th Div) Vol 12 March 1917 | | |
| War Diary | | 01/03/1917 | 09/03/1917 |
| War Diary | Erquinghem | 09/03/1917 | 29/03/1917 |
| War Diary | Rue Du Bois | 30/03/1917 | 30/03/1917 |
| War Diary | Bois Grenier | 30/03/1917 | 30/03/1917 |
| Operation(al) Order(s) | Ginty Relief Order No. 3 | 04/03/1917 | 04/03/1917 |
| Operation(al) Order(s) | 57th Divisional Order No. 4 | 07/03/1917 | 07/03/1917 |
| Operation(al) Order(s) | Ginty Order No. 3 | 07/03/1917 | 07/03/1917 |
| Operation(al) Order(s) | 171st Brigade Order No. 5 | 24/03/1917 | 24/03/1917 |
| Miscellaneous | Relief Table | | |
| Operation(al) Order(s) | 57th Division Order No. 5 | 20/03/1917 | 20/03/1917 |
| Heading | Minor Operations Referred To In 171st Infantry Brigade War Diary 130217 To 300317 | | |
| Miscellaneous | Report On Raid By 2/7th K.I. Regt. 171st Brigade Night Of 24/25th March | 25/04/1917 | 25/04/1917 |
| Miscellaneous | Report By O.C. Raid | | |
| Miscellaneous | 57th Division Subject : Summer Time | 24/03/1917 | 24/03/1917 |
| Miscellaneous | H.Q. 171st Brigade | 21/03/1917 | 21/03/1917 |
| Miscellaneous | Ginty Order No. 4 | | |
| Miscellaneous | Ginty Order No. 5 | 20/03/1917 | 20/03/1917 |
| Miscellaneous | Combined Artillery And Infantry Programme | | |
| Miscellaneous | Issued With 171st Brigade Order No. 4 | | |
| Miscellaneous | 2/7th K.L.R. Order | 00/03/1917 | 00/03/1917 |
| Miscellaneous | Objective-Organisation | | |
| Miscellaneous | 2/8th K.L.R. Order No. 1 | 00/03/1917 | 00/03/1917 |
| Miscellaneous | Objectives-Organisation | | |
| Miscellaneous | O.C. Master | 14/03/1917 | 14/03/1917 |
| Map | Map | | |

| | | | |
|---|---|---|---|
| Miscellaneous | Statement Of Casualties Forwarded In conjunction with 171st Infantry Brigade War Diary 130217 To 300317 | | |
| Miscellaneous | 171st Infantry Brigade | 30/04/1917 | 30/04/1917 |
| Heading | Headquarters 171st Inf Bde (57th Div) April 1917 | | |
| Heading | War Diary Of Headquarters 171st Infantry Brigade 31.3.1917 To 30.4.1917 Volume II | | |
| War Diary | Bois Grenier Rue Du Bois Sector | 31/03/1917 | 15/04/1917 |
| War Diary | Erquinghem | 16/04/1917 | 25/04/1917 |
| War Diary | Armentieres | 26/04/1917 | 30/04/1917 |
| Miscellaneous | Minor Operations Referred To In 171st Infantry Brigade War Diary 310317 To 300417 | | |
| Miscellaneous | Combined Artillery & Infantry Programme | | |
| Miscellaneous | Issued With 171st Brigade Order No. 6 | | |
| Map | Map | | |
| Miscellaneous | 2/7th Battalion K.L.R. | | |
| Diagram etc | Raid Manceuvre Graph Hun Line | | |
| Miscellaneous | Appendix VII | | |
| Miscellaneous | Nominal Roll | | |
| Operation(al) Order(s) | 57th Divisional Artillery Operation Order No. 7 | 11/04/1917 | 11/04/1917 |
| Miscellaneous | Left Group | | |
| Miscellaneous | Machine Gun Order No. 2 | 15/04/1917 | 15/04/1917 |
| Miscellaneous | Advance Report On Raid Carried Out By detachment Of The 2/7th K.L.R. | 13/04/1917 | 13/04/1917 |
| Operation(al) Order(s) | 171st Brigade Order No. 6 | 00/04/1917 | 00/04/1917 |
| Miscellaneous | Report On Raid By 171st Infantry Brigade | 17/04/1917 | 17/04/1917 |
| Operation(al) Order(s) | 171st Brigade Order No. 10 | 27/04/1917 | 27/04/1917 |
| Miscellaneous | Report On Discharge Of Gas | 29/04/1917 | 29/04/1917 |
| Miscellaneous | Move Orders Relief Orders, Etc. Referred To In 171st Infantry Brigade War Diary 310317 To 300417 | | |
| Operation(al) Order(s) | 171st Brigade Relief Order No. 4 | 03/04/1917 | 03/04/1917 |
| Operation(al) Order(s) | 171st Brigade Relief Order No. 5 | 04/04/1917 | 04/04/1917 |
| Operation(al) Order(s) | 171st Brigade Order No. 7 | 10/04/1917 | 10/04/1917 |
| Operation(al) Order(s) | 57th Division Order No. 7 | 16/04/1917 | 16/04/1917 |
| Operation(al) Order(s) | 171st Brigade Order No. 8 | 19/04/1917 | 19/04/1917 |
| Miscellaneous | Preliminary Warning | 20/04/1917 | 20/04/1917 |
| Operation(al) Order(s) | 57th Division Order No. 8 | 20/04/1917 | 20/04/1917 |
| Operation(al) Order(s) | Machine Gun Order No. 3 | 20/04/1917 | 20/04/1917 |
| Operation(al) Order(s) | 171st Brigade Order No. 9 | 21/04/1917 | 21/04/1917 |
| Miscellaneous | Amendment To 57th Division Order No. 8 | 22/04/1917 | 22/04/1917 |
| Miscellaneous | 171st Machine Gun Company | 23/04/1917 | 23/04/1917 |
| Miscellaneous | Statement Of Casualties Forwarded In conjunction with 171st Infantry Brigade War Diary 310317 To 300417 | | |
| Miscellaneous | 171st Infantry Brigade | 30/04/1917 | 30/04/1917 |
| Heading | War Diary Of Headquarters, 171st Infantry Brigade 1.5.1917 To 30.5.1917 Volume III | | |
| War Diary | Armenticres | 01/05/1917 | 30/05/1917 |
| Miscellaneous | Move Orders Relief Orders, Etc. Referred To In 171st Infantry Brigade War Diary 010517 To 300517 | | |
| Operation(al) Order(s) | 171st Brigade Relief Order No. 6 | 01/05/1917 | 01/05/1917 |
| Operation(al) Order(s) | 171st Brigade Relief Order No. 7 | 09/05/1917 | 09/05/1917 |
| Operation(al) Order(s) | 171st Brigade Relief Order No. 8 | 21/05/1917 | 21/05/1917 |
| Operation(al) Order(s) | 171st Brigade Relief Order No. 9 | 22/05/1917 | 22/05/1917 |
| Operation(al) Order(s) | 171st Brigade Relief Order No. 10 | 27/05/1917 | 27/05/1917 |
| Miscellaneous | Minor Operations Referred To In 171st Infantry Brigade War Diary 010517 To 300517 | | |
| Miscellaneous | Report On Operations Of The 7th/8th May 1917 | 07/05/1917 | 07/05/1917 |

| | | | |
|---|---|---|---|
| Operation(al) Order(s) | 171st Brigade Order No. II | 19/05/1917 | 19/05/1917 |
| Miscellaneous | Appendix I | | |
| Miscellaneous | 171st Infantry Brigade. Full Special Report On contact with The enemy armentieres Sector | 23/05/1917 | 23/05/1917 |
| Miscellaneous | Report On Operations Of 25th/26th May 1917 | 26/05/1917 | 26/05/1917 |
| Miscellaneous | Statement Of Casualties Forwarded In conjunction with 171st Infantry Brigade War Diary 010517 To 300517 | 30/05/1917 | 30/05/1917 |
| Miscellaneous | 171st Infantry Brigade. Casualties from 010517 To 300517 | 30/05/1917 | 30/05/1917 |
| Heading | War Diary Of 171st Inf Bde Hd Qtrs For June 1917 | | |
| Heading | War Diary Of Headquarters 171st Infantry Brigade 31.5.1917 To 30.6.1917 Volume IV | | |
| War Diary | Armentieres | 31/05/1917 | 30/06/1917 |
| Miscellaneous | Relief Orders, Etc., Referred to in 171st Infantry Brigade War diary 31.5.17 To 30.6.17 | 30/06/1917 | 30/06/1917 |
| Miscellaneous | 171st Brigade Relief Order No. II | 05/06/1917 | 05/06/1917 |
| Miscellaneous | 171st Brigade Relief Order No. I2 | 09/06/1917 | 09/06/1917 |
| Miscellaneous | 171st Brigade Relief Order No. I3 | 14/06/1917 | 14/06/1917 |
| Miscellaneous | 171st Brigade Relief Order No. I4 | 22/06/1917 | 22/06/1917 |
| Operation(al) Order(s) | 171st Brigade Order No. 13 | 07/06/1917 | 07/06/1917 |
| Miscellaneous | 171st Brigade Order No. 13A | 13/06/1917 | 13/06/1917 |
| Miscellaneous | Minor Operations Referred To In 171st Infantry Brigade War Diary 310517 To 300617 | 30/06/1917 | 30/06/1917 |
| Miscellaneous | 171st Infantry Brigade-Armentieres Sector | 12/06/1917 | 12/06/1917 |
| Miscellaneous | 171st Infantry Brigade-Armentieres Sector | 13/06/1917 | 13/06/1917 |
| Miscellaneous | Report On Minor Enterprises-Night of 14th/15th June 1917 | 15/06/1917 | 15/06/1917 |
| Operation(al) Order(s) | 171st Brigade Order No. 15 | 12/06/1917 | 12/06/1917 |
| Miscellaneous | Reference Brigade Order No. 15 | 13/06/1917 | 13/06/1917 |
| Miscellaneous | Special Instructions For S.O.S. | 20/06/1917 | 20/06/1917 |
| Miscellaneous | 57th Division Report on minor Operations Carried Out in armentieres Section. | 21/06/1917 | 21/06/1917 |
| Miscellaneous | Statement Of Casualties. Forwarded in Conjunction with 171st Infantry Brigade War Diary 310517 To 300617 | 30/06/1917 | 30/06/1917 |
| Miscellaneous | 171st Infantry Brigade | 30/06/1917 | 30/06/1917 |
| Heading | Headquarters 171 Infantry Brigade (57th Division) July 1917 Vol.6 | | |
| Heading | War Diary Of Headquarters-171st Infantry Brigade 1.7.1917 To 31.7.1917 Volume V | | |
| War Diary | Armentieres | 30/06/1917 | 31/07/1917 |
| Miscellaneous | Relief Orders, Etc. Referred To In 171st Infantry Brigade War Diary 010717 To 310717 | 31/07/1917 | 31/07/1917 |
| Miscellaneous | 171st Brigade Relief Order No. 15 | 30/06/1917 | 30/06/1917 |
| Miscellaneous | 171st Brigade Relief Order No. 16 | 01/07/1917 | 01/07/1917 |
| Miscellaneous | 171st Brigade Relief Order No. 17 | 09/07/1917 | 09/07/1917 |
| Miscellaneous | 171st Brigade Relief Order No. 18 | 13/07/1917 | 13/07/1917 |
| Miscellaneous | 171st Brigade Relief Order No. 19 | 17/07/1917 | 17/07/1917 |
| Miscellaneous | 171st Brigade Relief Order No. 20 | 22/07/1917 | 22/07/1917 |
| Miscellaneous | 171st Brigade Relief Order No. 21 | 27/07/1917 | 27/07/1917 |
| Miscellaneous | Minor Operations Referred To In 171st Infantry Brigade War Diary 010717 To 310717 | 31/07/1917 | 31/07/1917 |
| Miscellaneous | Report On Enemy's Operations | 01/07/1917 | 01/07/1917 |
| Miscellaneous | 171st Infantry Brigade | 04/07/1917 | 04/07/1917 |
| Miscellaneous | Headquarters, 57th Division | 06/07/1917 | 06/07/1917 |
| Miscellaneous | Report On Discharge Of Gas From Armentieres Sector | 10/07/1917 | 10/07/1917 |

| | | | |
|---|---|---|---|
| Miscellaneous | 171st Infantry Brigade Armentieres Sector | 14/07/1917 | 14/07/1917 |
| Miscellaneous | 171st Infantry Brigade | 15/07/1917 | 15/07/1917 |
| Miscellaneous | 171st Infantry Brigade-Armentieres Sector | 16/07/1917 | 16/07/1917 |
| Operation(al) Order(s) | 171st Infantry Brigade Order No. 21 | 16/07/1917 | 16/07/1917 |
| Miscellaneous | Preliminary Programme Of Co-Operation By Left group 57 Division R.A. | | |
| Miscellaneous | Programme Of Co-Operation By 171st Machine Gun Company | | |
| Miscellaneous | Programme Of Co-Operation By 171st Light Trench Mortar Battery | | |
| Operation(al) Order(s) | 171st Brigade Order No. 18 | 03/07/1917 | 03/07/1917 |
| Miscellaneous | 171st Infantry Brigade-Armentieres Sector | 26/07/1917 | 26/07/1917 |
| Miscellaneous | Headquarters, 57th (W.L) Division | 30/07/1917 | 30/07/1917 |
| Miscellaneous | 171st Infantry Brigade-Armentieres Sector | 31/07/1917 | 31/07/1917 |
| Miscellaneous | Statement Of Casualties. Forwarded in Conjunction with 171st Infantry Brigade War Diary 010717 To 310717 | 31/07/1917 | 31/07/1917 |
| Miscellaneous | 171st Infantry Brigade | | |
| Miscellaneous | Orders, Etc., Reference C.E.P. forwarded In conjuction with 171st Infantry Brigade War Diary 010717 To 310717 | 31/07/1917 | 31/07/1917 |
| Operation(al) Order(s) | 171st Infantry Brigade Order No. 19 | 14/07/1917 | 14/07/1917 |
| Miscellaneous | Table Issued With 171st Infantry Brigade Order No. 18. | | |
| Miscellaneous | O.C. "F" Battalion | 22/07/1917 | 22/07/1917 |
| Miscellaneous | O.C. 1st Coy. 3rd Regt. C.E.P. | 23/07/1917 | 23/07/1917 |
| Heading | Headquarters 171st Inf. Bde. (57th Div) August 1917 Vol7 | | |
| Miscellaneous | Headquarters, 57th (West Lancs) Division | 01/09/1917 | 01/09/1917 |
| Heading | War Diary Of Headquarters-171st Infantry Brigade 1.8.1917 To 31.8.1917 Volume VI | | |
| War Diary | Armentieres | 01/08/1917 | 02/08/1917 |
| War Diary | Fleurbaix | 02/08/1917 | 31/08/1917 |
| Miscellaneous | Minor Operations Referred To In 171st Infantry Brigade War Diary 010817 To 310817 | | |
| Miscellaneous | 171st Infantry Brigade-Fleurbaix Sector | 14/08/1917 | 14/08/1917 |
| Miscellaneous | Report On Bombardment Of Battalion Headquarters | | |
| Miscellaneous | Headquarters 57th (West Lancs) Division | 25/08/1917 | 25/08/1917 |
| Miscellaneous | Translation Of Report On Raid | 24/08/1917 | 24/08/1917 |
| Miscellaneous | Battalion 29 | 24/08/1917 | 24/08/1917 |
| Miscellaneous | Relief Orders e.t.c Referred To In 171st Infantry Brigade War Diary 010817 To 310817 | | |
| Miscellaneous | Amendment To And Continuation Of 171st Brigade Order No. 23 | 31/07/1917 | 31/07/1917 |
| Operation(al) Order(s) | 171st Infantry Brigade Order No. 23 | | |
| Miscellaneous | Move Table | | |
| Miscellaneous | O.C. 1st Leicestershire Regt | 04/08/1917 | 04/08/1917 |
| Miscellaneous | O.C. 1st Leicester Regt | 04/08/1917 | 04/08/1917 |
| Operation(al) Order(s) | 171st Infantry Brigade Order No. 24 | 05/08/1917 | 05/08/1917 |
| Miscellaneous | March Table Issued With 171st Infantry Brigade Order No. 24 | | |
| Miscellaneous | In Continuation Of 171st Infantry Brigade Order No. 24 | 05/08/1917 | 05/08/1917 |
| Operation(al) Order(s) | 171st Infantry Brigade Order No. 25 | 05/08/1917 | 05/08/1917 |
| Miscellaneous | Amendment To 171st Infantry Brigade Order No. 26/1 | 13/08/1917 | 13/08/1917 |
| Miscellaneous | Amendment To 171st Infantry Brigade Order No. 26 | 12/08/1917 | 12/08/1917 |
| Operation(al) Order(s) | 171st Infantry Brigade Order No. 26 | 11/08/1917 | 11/08/1917 |

| | | | |
|---|---|---|---|
| Miscellaneous | March Table Issued With 171st Infantry Brigade Order No. 26 | | |
| Operation(al) Order(s) | 171st Infantry Brigade Operation Order No. 27 | 15/08/1917 | 15/08/1917 |
| Operation(al) Order(s) | 171st Infantry Brigade Operation Order No. 28 | 17/08/1917 | 17/08/1917 |
| Miscellaneous | March Table Issued With 171st Infantry Brigade O.O. No.28 | | |
| Operation(al) Order(s) | 171st Infantry Brigade Operation Order No. 29 | 22/08/1917 | 22/08/1917 |
| Operation(al) Order(s) | 171st Infantry Brigade Operation Order No. 30 | 23/08/1917 | 23/08/1917 |
| Miscellaneous | Statement Of Casualties Referred To In 171st Infantry Brigade War diary 010817 To 310817 | 01/08/1917 | 01/08/1917 |
| Miscellaneous | 171st Infantry Brigade. Casualties from 010817 To 310817 | 31/08/1917 | 31/08/1917 |
| Heading | Headquarters 171st Inf Bde (57th Div) September 1917 | | |
| Miscellaneous | Headquarters 57th (West Lancs) Division | 01/10/1917 | 01/10/1917 |
| Heading | War Diary Of Headquarters-171st Infantry Brigade 1.9.1917 To 30.9.1917 Volume VII | | |
| War Diary | Fleurbaix | 01/09/1917 | 16/09/1917 |
| War Diary | La Gorgue | 17/09/1917 | 17/09/1917 |
| War Diary | La Micquellerie | 18/09/1917 | 18/09/1917 |
| War Diary | St. Hilaire Cottes | 19/09/1917 | 30/09/1917 |
| Miscellaneous | Statement Of Casualties. Referred To In 171st Infantry Brigade War diary 010917 To 300917 | 01/09/1917 | 01/09/1917 |
| Miscellaneous | 171st Infantry Brigade. Casualties from 010917 To 310917 | 01/09/1917 | 01/09/1917 |
| Miscellaneous | Relief Orders Etc Referred To In 171st Infantry Brigade War diary 010917 To 300917 | 01/09/1917 | 01/09/1917 |
| Operation(al) Order(s) | 171st Infantry Brigade Operation Order No. 31 | 31/08/1917 | 31/08/1917 |
| Operation(al) Order(s) | 171st Infantry Brigade Operation Order No. 32 | 07/09/1917 | 07/09/1917 |
| Operation(al) Order(s) | 171st Infantry Brigade Order No. 33 | 12/09/1917 | 12/09/1917 |
| Miscellaneous | March Table To Accompany 171st Infantry Brigade Order No. 33 | | |
| Operation(al) Order(s) | 171st Infantry Brigade Order No. 34 | 17/09/1917 | 17/09/1917 |
| Miscellaneous | March Table Issued With 171st Infantry Brigade Operation Order No. 34 | | |
| Miscellaneous | All Recipients Of 171st Infantry Brigade Order No. 34 | 17/09/1917 | 17/09/1917 |
| Miscellaneous | Administrative Orders | | |
| Operation(al) Order(s) | 171st Infantry Brigade Order No. 35 | 18/09/1917 | 18/09/1917 |
| Miscellaneous | March Table Issued With 171st Infantry Brigade Order No. 35 | | |
| Miscellaneous | Minor Operations Referred To In 171st Infantry Brigade War Diary 010917 To 300917 | 01/09/1917 | 01/09/1917 |
| Miscellaneous | Report On The Circumstances Leading To The capture Of 2 prisoners | 08/09/1917 | 08/09/1917 |
| Miscellaneous | Headquarters 57th (W.Lancs) Division | 15/09/1917 | 15/09/1917 |
| Heading | HQ 171 Infy Bde (57th Div) Vol 9 October 1917 | | |
| Heading | War Diary Of Headquarters 171st Infantry Brigade 1.10.1917 To 31.10.1917 Volume VIII | | |
| War Diary | St. Hilaire Cottes | 01/10/1917 | 18/10/1917 |
| War Diary | Renescure Proven Area No.4 | 19/10/1917 | 23/10/1917 |
| War Diary | Malakoff Area | 24/10/1917 | 25/10/1917 |
| War Diary | Langemarck Area | 26/10/1917 | 31/10/1917 |
| Miscellaneous | Relief Orders e.t.c Referred To In 171st Infantry Brigade War diary 011017 To 311017 | 01/10/1917 | 01/10/1917 |
| Operation(al) Order(s) | 171st Infantry Brigade Order No. 37 | 05/10/1917 | 05/10/1917 |
| Miscellaneous | Minor Orders Attached To 171st Infantry Brigade Order No. 37 | 07/10/1917 | 07/10/1917 |

| | | | |
|---|---|---|---|
| Miscellaneous | Appendices To 171st Infantry Brigade Order No. 37 | | |
| Operation(al) Order(s) | 171st Infantry Brigade Order No. 38 | 15/10/1917 | 15/10/1917 |
| Miscellaneous | March Table Issued With 171st Infantry Brigade Order No. 38 | | |
| Miscellaneous | Amendments To 171st Infantry Brigade Order No. 38 | 16/10/1917 | 16/10/1917 |
| Miscellaneous | Administrative Orders In Connection With 171st Infantry Brigade Operation Order Number 38 | 17/10/1917 | 17/10/1917 |
| Operation(al) Order(s) | 171st Infantry Brigade Operation Order No. 39 | 19/10/1917 | 19/10/1917 |
| Miscellaneous | Administrative Orders In connection with 171st Infantry Brigade Operation Order No 59. | 30/10/1917 | 30/10/1917 |
| Miscellaneous | 171st Infantry Brigade March Table For Transport | 20/10/1917 | 20/10/1917 |
| Operation(al) Order(s) | 171st Infantry Brigade Order No. 40 | 23/10/1917 | 23/10/1917 |
| Miscellaneous | Table "A"-Attached To 171st Infantry Brigade Order No. 40 | | |
| Miscellaneous | Table "B"-Attached To 171st Infantry Brigade Order No. 40 | | |
| Miscellaneous | Table "C"-Attached To 171st Infantry Brigade Order No 40 | | |
| Miscellaneous | To All Recipients Of 171st Infantry Brigade Order No. 40 | 23/10/1917 | 23/10/1917 |
| Miscellaneous | To All Recipients Of 171st Infantry Brigade Preliminary Instruction No.1 | 24/10/1917 | 24/10/1917 |
| Miscellaneous | 171st Infantry Brigade Preliminary Instructions No.1 | 24/10/1917 | 24/10/1917 |
| Operation(al) Order(s) | 171st Infantry Brigade Order No. 41 | 25/10/1917 | 25/10/1917 |
| Operation(al) Order(s) | 171st Infantry Brigade Order No. 42 | 27/10/1917 | 27/10/1917 |
| Operation(al) Order(s) | 171st Infantry Brigade Order No. 43 | 28/10/1917 | 28/10/1917 |
| Miscellaneous | O.C. 2/5th K.L.R. | 30/10/1917 | 30/10/1917 |
| Miscellaneous | Minor Operations e.t.c Referred To In 171st Infantry Brigade War Diary 011017 To 311017 | 01/10/1917 | 01/10/1917 |
| Map | Operation Map No 1 Appendix B | | |
| Map | Operation Map No 1 Appendix A | | |
| Miscellaneous | Statement Of Casualties In connection with 171st Infantry Brigade War diary 011017 To 311017 | 01/10/1917 | 01/10/1917 |
| Miscellaneous | 171st Infantry Brigade. Casualties from 011017 To 311017 | 01/10/1917 | 01/10/1917 |
| Map | Map | | |
| Miscellaneous | Glossary | | |
| Heading | Headquarters 171st Inf Bde (57th Div) November 1917 | | |
| Heading | War Diary Of Headquarters 171st Infantry Brigade 1.11.1917 To 30.11.1917 Volume IX | | |
| Miscellaneous | Headquarters, 57th Division | 01/12/1917 | 01/12/1917 |
| War Diary | Langemarck Area | 01/11/1917 | 03/11/1917 |
| War Diary | Malakoff Area | 03/11/1917 | 05/11/1917 |
| War Diary | Nordausques | 06/11/1917 | 30/11/1917 |
| Miscellaneous | Relief Orders e.t.c. Referred To In 171st Infantry Brigade War Diary 011117 To 301117 | 01/11/1917 | 01/11/1917 |
| Operation(al) Order(s) | 171st Infantry Brigade Order No. 44 | 01/11/1917 | 01/11/1917 |
| Miscellaneous | To All Recipients Of 171st Infantry Brigade Order No. 45 | 01/11/1917 | 01/11/1917 |
| Operation(al) Order(s) | 171st Infantry Brigade Order No. 45 | 01/11/1917 | 01/11/1917 |
| Miscellaneous | Table Of Moves "A"-Issued with 171st Infantry Brigade Order No 45 | | |
| Miscellaneous | 171st Infantry Brigade Warning Order | 05/11/1917 | 05/11/1917 |
| Operation(al) Order(s) | 171st Infantry Brigade Order No. 46 for Move to Nordausques Area | 05/11/1917 | 05/11/1917 |

| | | | |
|---|---|---|---|
| Miscellaneous | Table "A"-Issued with 171st Infantry Brigade Order No. 46 | | |
| Miscellaneous | Table "B" Issued with 171st Infantry Brigade Order No 46 | | |
| Miscellaneous | Table "C" Issued with 171st Infantry Brigade Order No 46 | | |
| Miscellaneous | Administrative Orders In Connection With 171st Infantry Brigade Order No. 46 | 05/11/1917 | 05/11/1917 |
| Operation(al) Order(s) | 171st Infantry Brigade Brigade Order No. 47 | 05/11/1917 | 05/11/1917 |
| Miscellaneous | Statement Of Casualties In connection with 171st Infantry Brigade War Diary 011117 To 301117 | 01/11/1917 | 01/11/1917 |
| Miscellaneous | 171st Infantry Brigade Casualties from 011117 To 301117 | 30/11/1917 | 30/11/1917 |
| Heading | HQ 171 Infy Bde (57th Div) Vol 11 December 1917 | | |
| Heading | Headquarters 57th (West Lancs) Div | | |
| Heading | War Diary Of Headquarters, 171st Infantry Brigade 1.12.1917 To 31.12.1917 Volume X | | |
| War Diary | Nordausques | 01/12/1917 | 07/12/1917 |
| War Diary | Proosdy | 08/12/1917 | 16/12/1917 |
| War Diary | Fifteen Wood | 17/12/1917 | 25/12/1917 |
| War Diary | Boesinghe Area 2 | 25/12/1917 | 28/12/1917 |
| War Diary | Canada Area | 29/12/1917 | 29/12/1917 |
| War Diary | Goedwaer Swelve | 30/12/1917 | 30/12/1917 |
| War Diary | Steenwerck | 31/12/1917 | 31/12/1917 |
| Miscellaneous | Statement Of Casualties In connection with 171st Infantry Brigade War Diary 011217 To 311217 | 31/12/1917 | 31/12/1917 |
| Miscellaneous | 171st Infantry Brigade Casualties from 011217 To 311217 | 31/12/1917 | 31/12/1917 |
| Miscellaneous | Minor Operations Referred To In 171st Infantry Brigade War Diary 011217 To 311217 | 01/12/1917 | 01/12/1917 |
| Miscellaneous | Headquarters 57 (West Lancs) Division | 29/12/1917 | 29/12/1917 |
| Miscellaneous | Report On Enemy's Attack On Turenne Crossing 22nd Dec 1917 | 22/12/1917 | 22/12/1917 |
| Miscellaneous | Tactical & Intelligence Summaries In connection with 171st Infantry Brigade War Diary 011217 To 311217 | 01/12/1917 | 01/12/1917 |
| Miscellaneous | Tactical Situation Report | 17/12/1917 | 17/12/1917 |
| Miscellaneous | Tactical Situation Report | 18/12/1917 | 18/12/1917 |
| Miscellaneous | Patrol Report-57th Division-XIX Corps | | |
| Miscellaneous | Tactical Situation Report | 19/12/1917 | 19/12/1917 |
| Miscellaneous | Patrol Report-57th Division-XIX Corps | | |
| Miscellaneous | 171st Infantry Brigade Intelligence Summary Period 24 hours ending 6 a.m., 21.12.1917 | 21/12/1917 | 21/12/1917 |
| Miscellaneous | Patrol Report-57th Division-XIX Corps | | |
| Miscellaneous | Tactical Situation Report | 21/12/1917 | 21/12/1917 |
| Miscellaneous | Patrol Report-57th Division-XIX Corps | | |
| Miscellaneous | 171st Inf. Bde. Tactical Situation Report | 22/12/1917 | 22/12/1917 |
| Miscellaneous | 171st Infantry Brigade-Intelligence Summary 24 hours ending 6 a.m. 24.12.1917 | 24/12/1917 | 24/12/1917 |
| Miscellaneous | Patrol Report-57th Division-XIX Corps | | |
| Miscellaneous | 171st Infantry Brigade-Intelligence Summary 24 hrs ending 6 a.m. 25.12.1917. | 25/12/1917 | 25/12/1917 |
| Miscellaneous | Patrol Report-57th Division-XIX Corps | | |
| Miscellaneous | Relief Orders e.t.c Referred To In 171st Infantry Brigade War Diary 011217 To 311217 | | |
| Operation(al) Order(s) | 171st Infantry Brigade Order No. 49 | 06/12/1917 | 06/12/1917 |

| Type | Description | Date | Date |
|---|---|---|---|
| Miscellaneous | March Table for 171st Brigade Group Transport Nordausques to Lederzeele | 07/12/1917 | 07/12/1917 |
| Miscellaneous | Table "B" | | |
| Miscellaneous | Administrative Instructions | 05/12/1917 | 05/12/1917 |
| Miscellaneous | Administrative Instructions No.2 | 07/12/1917 | 07/12/1917 |
| Miscellaneous | Reference Administrative Orders No.2 | 07/12/1917 | 07/12/1917 |
| Operation(al) Order(s) | 171st Infantry Brigade Order No. 49A | 07/12/1917 | 07/12/1917 |
| Operation(al) Order(s) | 171st Infantry Brigade Order No. 50 | 15/12/1917 | 15/12/1917 |
| Miscellaneous | Table "A"-Issued with 171st Infantry Brigade Order No 50 | | |
| Miscellaneous | Table "B" Issued with 171st Infantry Brigade Order No 50 | | |
| Miscellaneous | Administrative Instructions In Connection With Brigade Order No. 50 | | |
| Miscellaneous | Addition To Table "B" Issued with 171st Inf. Bde Order No 50 | 16/12/1917 | 16/12/1917 |
| Operation(al) Order(s) | 171st Infantry Brigade Order No. 50 | 16/12/1917 | 16/12/1917 |
| Miscellaneous | Administrative Instructions In connection with Brigade Order no 5 | 14/12/1917 | 14/12/1917 |
| Operation(al) Order(s) | 171st Infantry Brigade Order Number 51 | 20/12/1917 | 20/12/1917 |
| Operation(al) Order(s) | 171st Infantry Brigade Order No. 52 | | |
| Operation(al) Order(s) | 171st Infantry Brigade Order No. 53 | 23/12/1917 | 23/12/1917 |
| Operation(al) Order(s) | 171st Infantry Brigade Order No. 54 | 23/12/1917 | 23/12/1917 |
| Miscellaneous | Relief Table Issued With 171st Infantry Brigade Order No. 53 | | |
| Operation(al) Order(s) | 171st Infantry Brigade Order No. 55 | 27/12/1917 | 27/12/1917 |
| Miscellaneous | March Table Issued with 171st Infantry Brigade Order No. 55. | | |
| Miscellaneous | Administrative Instructions | 27/12/1917 | 27/12/1917 |
| Miscellaneous | Addendum To 171st Inf. Brigade Order No. 55 | 28/12/1917 | 28/12/1917 |
| Miscellaneous | Amendment To 171st Inf. Brigade Order No. 55 | 28/12/1917 | 28/12/1917 |
| Miscellaneous | Additional Administrative Instructions | 29/12/1917 | 29/12/1917 |
| Operation(al) Order(s) | 171st Infantry Brigade Order Number 56 | 28/12/1917 | 28/12/1917 |
| Miscellaneous | March Table Issued with 171st Infantry Brigade Order No 56. | | |
| Operation(al) Order(s) | 171st Infantry Brigade Order No. 57 | 30/12/1917 | 30/12/1917 |

moss / 2g80 (2)

moss / 2g80 (1)

Vol. 1.

Headquarters
71st Inf. Bde.
(57 & 8W)
February 1917

On His Majesty's Service.

CONFIDENTIAL.

WAR DIARY

of

HEADQUARTERS, 171st INFANTRY BRIGADE.

........

13.2.1917 to 30/3/1917.

VOLUME I.

# WAR DIARY
## or
## INTELLIGENCE SUMMARY
*(Erase heading not required.)*

Army Form C. 2118

| Place | Date | Hour | Summary of Events and Information | Remarks and references to Appendices |
|---|---|---|---|---|
| HAVRE. | FEB. 13th. | 1.30 p.m. | Brigade HdQrs with Signal Section, Light T.M.B., arrived in "Manchester Importer". Disembarkation proceeded at once. Personnel of Brigade HdQrs proceeded to No.1 Rest Camp. Owing to severe wintry conditions, rendering roads like ice, great difficulty was experienced in getting wagons along, entailing a late arrival. | |
| | 14th. | 9.15 p.m. | Brigade HdQrs left. Owing to railway accident previous day, train was much delayed. One halt allowed. The controlling system of halts was bad, and no time given for men to have hot water - or for the watering of horses - or sanitary arrangements. No lavatories on train or for the necessary halts for men to go to the latrines caused quite unnecessary discomfort. Acting on the R.T.Os. Instructions at ABBEYVILLE, a 20 minutes halt was given - any further stoppage out of his control and he took no responsibility - | |
| | 15th. | | eventually waited 4 hours. Cold very intense. | |
| STRAZEELE. | 16th. | 11.30 a.m. | Arrived BAILLEUL at 11.30 a.m., Met by Staff Captain, who had proceeded in advance. Detrained at once, arrangements working quite smoothly. Marched to concentration area in MERRIS AREA. Brigade HdQrs at STRAZEELE. 2/5th and 2/6th K.L.R. already arrived, having crossed via FOLKESTONE and BOULOGNE. Arrangements for billeting already completed by Staff Captain. 2/7th and 2/8th K.L.R., arrived STRAZEELE about 8 p.m. Transport not arrived. 2/5th K.L.R. were given instruction by Divisional Gas Officer in Box Respirator. | |
| | | 8.0 p.m. | | |
| | 17th. | 3.0 a.m. | Transport of 2/7th and 2/8th K.L.R. came in. | |
| | | 10.0 a.m. | 2/6th K.L.R., given instruction in Box Respirator. | |
| | 18th. | 9.0 a.m. | Instruction and demonstration in the use of Box Respirator given by Divisional Gas Officer to 2/7th K.L.R., T.M.B., and M.G.Company. | |
| | | 10.45 a.m. | Brigade HdQrs and 2/8th K.L.R., All Units undergoing instruction of 8 hours' course. | |
| | | 6.30 p.m. | Telephone Instructions - moving up to relieve N.Z.Brigade. Issued instructions by Signals to Units as to billet parties - also to T.M.B. and M.G.Coy. to send advance parties tomorrow | |

Army Form C. 2118

# WAR DIARY
## or
## INTELLIGENCE SUMMARY
(*Erase heading not required.*)

Instructions regarding War Diaries and Intelligence Summaries are contained in F. S. Regs., Part II. and the Staff Manual respectively. Title Pages will be prepared in manuscript.

| Place | Date | Hour | Summary of Events and Information | Remarks and references to Appendices |
|---|---|---|---|---|
| | FEB. 19th. | 9.30 a.m. | Staff Captain proceeded to SAILLY. Billet Parties reported at 12 noon to him at Cross Roads, SAILLY. | |
| | | 10.15 a.m. | Advance Parties, T.M.B. and M.G.Coy. proceeded by lorry to sector of Trench Line, 1st Bde Group, N.Z.Division. Issued Movement Order No.I. | See Order I of 19th in Appendix I. |
| | | 3.0 p.m. | Brigadier-General proceeded to FLEURBAIX to see 1st Brigade Group. | |
| | | 11.40 a.m. | Received Divisional Orders for Move to Relief of Trenches. | 57th Divl. Order I. |
| | | 6.30 p.m. | Issued Orders for move of Brigade tomorrow to Billets at ESTAIRES and SAILLY. | |
| | 20th. | 10.0 a.m. | Brigade clear of STRAZEELE, and marched as per Orders for ESTAIRES and SAILLY Billet Areas. Corps Commanders, 2nd Anzac, passed Brigade. | |
| NOUVEAU MONDE. | | 12.30 p.m. | Brigade HdQrs established at NOUVEAU MONDE. | |
| | | 1.0 p.m. | All Units in their Areas. Wet day. | |
| | | 2.15 p.m. | Brigade Major proceeded with Brigadier to 1st New Zealand Brigade HdQrs, FLEURBAIX, on horseback. Made matters very late. Stopped in SAILLY Area to give brief resume of orders to 2/5th and 2/6th K.L.R., Imperative that a motor should be allotted to Brigades when a relief is made. | |
| | | 9.45 p.m. | Issued Orders for Relief of 1st New Zealand Brigade. | Order No.2 |
| | 21st. | | 2/5th and 2/6th K.L.R., with Machine Gun Coy. carried out first relief in accordance with orders. | |
| | | 2.0 p.m. | Brigadier and Brigade Major reported 1st N.Z.Bde, and proceeded round left Sector of Area held by 1st N.Z.Bde. Reliefs were reported to have worked smoothly. Staff Captain and Brigade Bombing Officer reported to learn duties at N.Z.Bde HdQrs. | |

112

Army Form C. 2118

# WAR DIARY
## or
## INTELLIGENCE SUMMARY
*(Erase heading not required.)*

Instructions regarding War Diaries and Intelligence Summaries are contained in F.S. Regs., Part II. and the Staff Manual respectively. Title Pages will be prepared in manuscript.

| Place | Date | Hour | Summary of Events and Information | Remarks and references to Appendices |
|---|---|---|---|---|
| FLEURBAIX. | FEB. 22nd. | 9.30 a.m. | Brigade HdQrs, 2/7th, 2/8th K.L.R., Wessex Field Ambulance and R.E.Coy., together with the Light T.M.B., en route for FLEURBAIX. | |
| | 23rd. | 2.0 p.m. | Relief of 1st N.Z. Bde completed and command passed to the Brigade. Brigade busy settling down and moving into Sector. Certain amount of difficulties experienced due to lack of experience on the part of Brigade. Staff Captain ill and sent to ANZAC EVACUATION CENTRE. | |
| | | 4.30 p.m. | Brigade settled in - 2/5th Right Sector, 2/6th K.L.R in Left Sector, 2/7th in Brigade Reserve with 2/8th K.L.R. in Divisional Reserve. A great deal to be done in Office. All returns, etc., The Brigadier visited Line. Nothing of any consequence to report. 171st T.M.B. made a small demonstration on enemy's front line, wire and parapets; slight retaliation by Hun - H.E. and Shrapnell Periodical bursts of Machine Gun fire. Conditions normal. | |
| | 24th | | Quiet day. Matters settling down. Sent party of 200 from 2/7th K.L.R., 200 from 2/8th K.L.R., to work under R.E.supervision. Also detailed permanent parties for Drainage and Tramways. Issued Relief Orders No.I. Brigadier visited line. Genl. Broadwood and A.D.C., C.R.E., G.S.O.I., C.R.A. Group, and Corps Counter-Batteries Commander, visited Brigade HdQrs. | See Appendix I. |
| | 25th. | | Normal situation. | |
| | 26th. | | Hun Minnies fairly active on Right Sector and Brewery. Brigade Major made reconnaissance of City Post, White City, Hudson's Bay - as regards new Support Line liason with Left Brigade. Big raid to the north at night; Huns had wind up opposite our line at night and made night into day with flares. | |
| | 27th. | | Quiet day on Sector. Normal Conditions. Divisional Commander and G.S.O.I round in the morning. Corps Commander round in the afternoon. Brigadier visited trenches with former. | |
| | 28th. | | Normal day. | |

113

APPENDIX No. I

MOVE ORDERS,

RELIEF ORDERS,

etc.,

referred to in

171st INFANTRY BRIGADE WAR DIARY,

13.2.1917 to 24th February

...

COPY NO. 12.

INSTRUCTIONS FOR FORTHCOMING MOVE NO. I.
.....

1. The Brigade Group will be known as "B" Group.

2. The Brigade will relieve a Brigade of the New Zealand Division.

3. Billeting Parties of whole Group will report at 12 noon to the Staff Captain at SAILLY, N.Z., Divl. HdQrs. - moving by shortest march route. "B" Group will be billeted in the SAILLY, ESTAIRES, Areas. The 2/5th and 2/6th K.L.R., in SAILLY Area. The 2/7th and 2/8th K.L.R., in ESTAIRES Area.

4. "B" Group will move up on the 20th instant.

5. On the relief being carried out, the distribution of "B" Group will be as per margin.

FRONT LINE.
  Right Sector,
      2/5th K.L.R.,
  Left Sector,
      2/6th K.L.R.,
RESERVE.
  Right Battn.
      2/7th K.L.R.,
  Left Battn.
      2/8th K.L.R.,

Major, Brigade Major,
171st Infantry Brigade.

19th February, 1917.

ISSUED TO :-
| | Copy No. | 1. | Brigadier-General, |
| | ,, | 2. | Brigade Major, |
| | ,, | 3. | Staff Captain, |
| | ,, | 4. | 2/5th K.L.R., |
| | ,, | 5. | 2/6th K.L.R., |
| | ,, | 6. | 2/7th K.L.R., |
| | ,, | 7. | 2/8th K.L.R., |
| | ,, | 8. | 171st Machine Gun Company. |
| | ,, | 9. | 171st Trench Mortar Battery. |
| | ,, | 10. | 171st Brigade Signal Section. |
| | ,, | 11. | War Diary |
| | ,, | 12. | War Diary. |
| | ,, | 13. | 57th Division. |

SECRET.                                          COPY NO. 2.

Reference,
Sheet 5A. I:100.000     171st BRIGADE ORDER NO.1

                              .....                            116

1.  The 171st Brigade will relieve the 1st Brigade Group
    N.Z., Division, commencing relief 20th Feb., and completing
    relief by 22nd Feb., taking over the Sector BOUTILLERIE.

2.  The sub-division of the Brigade will be as laid down
    in Instructions for Forthcoming Move Order No.1.    The
    Brigade being in the billet areas therein mentioned for
    the night of the 20th/21st Feb.,

3.  The Brigade will march tomorrow, 20th Feb., in
    accordance with the attached March Table.    Units will
    be clear of starting point at times scheduled.

4.  First and Second Line Transport will accompany Units -
    2nd Line Transport will be drawn up clear of the road on
    arrival at VIEUX BERQUIN and report to O.C. 507 Coy, A.S.C
    there and act under his instructions.

    2/8th K.L.R. and M.G.Coy 2nd Line Transport will
    report to HdQrs 507 Coy. situated at Fm.½ mile north of
    R. in VIEUX BERQUIN.

5.  The following allotment of Motor Lorries has been
    made :-

| UNIT. | No. | Time. of Arrival. | Place. | REMARKS. |
|---|---|---|---|---|
| 2/5th K.L.R. | 2 | 7.30 | Bde HdQrs. | ) |
| 2/6th  ,, | 2 | ,, | ,, | ) These will be |
| 2/7th  ,, | 2 | ,, | ,, | ) issued by Staff |
|  |  |  |  | ) Captain. |
| T.M.B., | 1 | ,, | ,, | ) |
| Bde HdQrs. | 1 | ,, | ,, | ) |
| 2/8th K.L.R. | 2 | 7.30 | Battn.HdQrs. |  |
| M.G.Coy. | 1 | 7.30 | Belle Croix Farm. |  |

    Motor Lorries will move independently of the Brigade; not
    more than 3 ranks are to accompany each Lorry.

6.  Ordinary march formations will be observed as far as

2.

ESTAIRES - after which the danger area is entered and formations of Platoons at $100^x$ interval will be observed. Dress will be marching order with packs - no blankets will be carried.

7. Units will detail one Guide to report to O.C. 507 Coy, A.S.C., at BAC - St.MAUR Railway Station at 3.0 p.m. 20th instant, to shew where Units are billeted.

8. All Units will, as far as possible, complete their training with Box Respirators in the back area before moving forward. Should any Unit have to move forward before it has completed its training, it will not be allowed to use the Box Respirator until trained with it, and until such training is completed they will depend on the P.H.G.Helmet, but the training with the Box Respirator must be carried through with the least possible delay.

9.(A) Units will report to Brigade HdQrs at NOUVEAU MONDE, ½ way between ESTAIRES and SAILLY, as soon as they have established their Battalion HdQrs.

(B) Units will furnish 2 Runners to Brigade HdQrs as soon as possible after arrival.

Lieut.Colonel,
Brigade Major, 171st Infantry Bde.

ISSUED AT 7.40.h. TO

1. War Diary.
2. G.S., File.
3. Brigadier-General.
4. Brigade Major.
5. Staff Captain.
6. 2/5th K.L.R.,
7. 2/6th K.L.R.,
8. 2/7th K.L.R.,
9. 2/8th K.L.R.,
10. 171st Machine Gun Coy.
11.    ,,   T.M.B.,
12. 507 Coy, A.S.C.,
13. 2/2nd Wessex Field Ambulance.
14. 57th Division.

SECRET.

ISSUED WITH 171st BRIGADE ORDER NO. 1

........

Reference Sheet 5$^A$. $\frac{1}{100.000}$

.....

MARCH TABLE - Feb. 20th 1917.

| TROOPS in ORDER OF MARCH. | STARTING POINT. Place. | Time of Passing. | ROUTE. | DESTINATION. | REMARKS. |
|---|---|---|---|---|---|
| 2/5th K.L.R. | | 8.15 am | | ( SAILLY ( BILLET AREA. ( | On arriving at ESTAIRES 2/5th & 2/6th K.L.R proceed via SAILLY BRIDGE to SAILLY. |
| 2/6th K.L.R., | | 8.35 am. | | | |
| 2/7th K.L.R., | Brigade Headquarters, STRAZEELE. | 8.55 am. | STRAZEELE - STRAZEELE RY. STATION VIEUX BERQUIN - NEUF BERQUIN ESTAIRES. | ESTAIRES. | |
| 171st T.M.B., | | 9.15 am. | | SAILLY. | |
| 2/2nd Wessex Fd. Ambce. | | 9.35 am. | | ESTAIRES. | |
| Bde HdQrs. | | 9.55 am. | | NOUVEAU MONDE. | |
| 2/8th K.L.R., | VIEUX BERQUIN. | 10.40 am. | VIEUX BERQUIN. NEUF BERQUIN. ESTAIRES. | (ESTAIRES. (BILLET (AREA. | Head of 2/8th KLR to remain clear of road junction until remainder of Brigade less M.G.Co. has passed |
| 171st M.G.Co. | | 10.55 am. | | | |
| 507 Co. A.S.C. | | 11. 0 am | | SAILLY. | |

Secret

Reference –
Sheet 36 1:40,000.

Copy No. 17  119

57th Division Order No. 1.

19th February, 1917.

1.     The 57th Division will relieve the New Zealand Division in accordance with the attached table.

2.     Command of the Right Sector of the Second ANZAC Corps front will pass from the NEW ZEALAND Division to the 57th Division at 12 noon 25th February at which hour 57th Division Headquarters will open at SAILLY, and Headquarters, NEW ZEALAND Division at STEENWERCK.

3.     All units will, as far as possible, complete their training with Box Respirators in the back area before moving forward.
    Should any unit have to move forward before it has completed its training, it will not be allowed to use the Box Respirator until trained with it and until such training is completed they will depend on the P.H.G. helmet, but the training with the Box Respirator must be carried through with the least possible delay.

4. Acknowledge.

CECIL ALLANSON,    Lieut-Colonel,
General Staff, 57th Division.

C.A.

Issued at 10.30 a.m. to:-
Copy No.
1.   War Diary.
2.   G.S.File.
3.   A.D.C. to G.O.C.
4.   C.R.A.
5.   C.R.E.
6.   170th Inf.Bde.
7.   171st  ,,  ,,
8.   172nd  ,,  ,,
9.   "A"
10.  "Q"
11.  O.C., Div. Train.
12.  A.D.M.S.
13.  A.P.M.
14.  D.A.D.O.S.
15.  NEW ZEALAND Division.
16.  O.C., Div. Sig. Coy.
17.  )
18.  ) Spare.
19.  )

# 57th DIVISION.

## TABLE OF RELIEFS.

| | Relieving Unit of 57th Division. | Relieved Unit of New Zealand Division. | Commence Relief. | Complete Relief. | Sector. | Remarks. |
|---|---|---|---|---|---|---|
| 1. | 170th Bde. Group. | 3rd N.Z. Rifle Brigade Group. | | 18th Feb. | CORDONNERIE | Relief already completed. |
| 2. | 285th Bde. R.F.A. | 'A' Bde. F.A. New Zealand Div. | - | - | | Supporting operations. Relief already completed. |
| 3. | 286th Bde. R.F.A. | 'B' Bde. F.A. New Zealand Div. | 21st Feb. | 23rd Feb. | BOIS GRENIER | |
| 4. | 171st Bde. Group 57th Division. | 1st Bde. Group N.Z. Division. | 20th Feb. | 22nd Feb. | BOUTILLERIE | Advanced Billetting Party to report to Staff Captain, 171st Bde. at Cross Roads SAILLY at 12 noon 19th inst. 171st Bde. Group will billet night of 20th/21st in SAILLY and ESTAIRES and relief will be carried out under arrangements to be made between Brigadiers concerned. In the march up Units may move by shortest route. |
| 5. | 172nd Bde. Group. | 2nd N.Z. Bde. Group. | 22nd Feb. | 25th Feb. 8.00 a.m. | BOIS GRENIER | Advanced billetting parties on 21st Feb. to SAILLY. Remainder of Group on 22nd to Billetts as per 171st Bde. Group. |

## N O T E S.

Field Coys. R.E. will carry out reliefs with corresponding numbers of NEW ZEALAND Division under arrangements to be made by the respective C.R.E's.

P.T.O.

Page 2.

The 2/2nd Wessex Field Ambulance will move with 171st Brigade Group.

The 2/3rd Wessex Field Ambulance will move with 172nd Brigade Group.

The Medium Trench Mortar Batteries of the New Zealand Division will stay in the line until relieved by the Medium Trench Mortar Batteries of the 57th Division. The New Zealand Division are leaving details in the line to instruct the Medium Trench Mortar Batteries of the 57th Division. Trench Mortars will NOT be exchanged between the two Divisions.

# APPENDIX I.

## BRIGADE GROUPS, 57th DIVISION.

Issued with 57th Div. Order - No. 1.

### 170th BRIGADE GROUP.

    170th Inf. Bde.
     ,,   Light T.M. Battery.
     ,,   Machine Gun Coy.
    'X' Medium T.M. Battery
    No. 1 Coy. R.E. (1/3rd Wessex)
    No. 2 Coy. A.S.C. (506th)
    3/2nd W. Lancs. Fld. Ambulance

### 171st BRIGADE GROUP.

    171st Inf. Bde. & Light T.M. Battery.
     ,,   Machine Gun Coy.
    'Y' Medium T.M. Battery.
    No. 2 Fld. Coy R.E. (1/3rd W. Lancs)
    No. 3 Coy. A.S.C. (507th)
    2/2nd Wessex Fld. Ambulance.

### 172nd BRIGADE GROUP.

    172nd Inf. Bde. and Light T.M. Battery.
     ,,   Machine Gun Coy.
    'Z' Medium T.M. Battery.
    No. 3 Fld. Coy. R.E. (2/3rd Wessex.)
    No. 4 Coy. A.S.C. (508th)
    2/3rd Wessex Fld. Ambulance

SECRET.                                                           COPY NO. 1

Reference,                    171st BRIGADE ORDER No. 2
Sheet 36, 1:40.000                      .....                              122

                                                    20th February, 1917.

1.   Relief of the 1st N.Z. Infantry Brigade - Headquarters,
FLEURBAIX - by the 171st Infantry Brigade will be carried
out as follows :-

February 21st.
(a) The 2/5th K.L.R. will relieve the 1st Bn. Wellington
Regt. on the right sector.     The head of the 2/5th K.L.R.
will report by 8.30 a.m. at FLEURBAIX to 1st N.Z. Brigade HdQrs.
(b) The head of the 2/6th K.L.R., will report at 1st N.Z.
Brigade HdQrs at 10.30 a.m., relieving 1st Bn. Auckland Regt.
in Brigade Reserve.      2/6th K.L.R. will send a Billeting
Party to report at 8.15 a.m., the 2/6th K.L.R. billeting for
the night at 21st/22nd at FLEURBAIX.
(c) The 171st Machine Gun Coy will report to 1st N.Z. Brigade
HdQrs at 9.30 a.m., and relieve 1st N.Z. M.G.Coy.
(d) 2/7th and 2/8th K.L.R., will send a Billeting Party to
report at 12 noon to 1st N.Z. Brigade HdQrs.

February 22nd.
     2/6th K.L.R., will relieve 2nd Bn. Wellington Regt.,
acting under orders from G.O.C., 1st N.Z. Infantry Brigade.
     Head of 2/7th K.L.R., will report at 10.0 a.m. to 1st
N.Z., Brigade HdQrs, relieving 2/6th K.L.R. in Brigade Reserve.
     Head of 2/8th K.L.R., will report at 12 noon to 1st
N.Z., Brigade HdQrs, and will relieve 2nd Bn Auckland Regt. in
Divisional Reserve.
     171st Trench Mortar Battery will report at 9 a.m. to 1st
N.Z., Brigade HdQrs, and relieve 1st N.Z. Light T.M.B.,

2.   Guides will be furnished for each Formation on arrival
at FLEURBAIX by 1st N.Z. Infantry Brigade.

3.   Route to be followed by Battalions from their Billets is
as follows - SAILLY - BAC-ST.MAUR - FORT ROMPU - FLEURBAIX.
Formations will move with 100$^X$ interval between Platoons.

4.   All trench stores, telescopes, log books, maps, defence
schemes, and necessary records will be handed over on relief -

2.

Receipts will be obtained in duplicate, and one copy forwarded to Brigade HdQrs.

5. Rear Parties will be left behind in compliance with 57th Divisional Orders on this subject, and hand over billets.

6. Commands will pass on completion of reliefs.

7. Transport Lines - and Quarter-masters Dumps are situated between H.13 D.5.5 and H.14 A.7.3

8. Quartermasters or their representatives must make themselves acquainted tomorrow, 21st instant, with the dumps of the respective Battalions they are relieving.

9. All Units of the Brigade will be under the orders of the G.O.C., 1st N.Z. Infantry Bde until relief is complete : when they will be duly notified.

10. HdQrs of the Brigade will be at NOUVEAU MONDE until 10 a.m., 22nd instant.

11. Acknowledge.

Lieut.Colonel,
Brigade Major, 171st Infantry Brigade.

ISSUED AT 9.45 p.m.

Copy No. 1.  War Diary.
,, 2.  G.S.File.
,, 3.  Brigade Commander.
,, 4.  Staff Captain.
,, 5.  2/5th K.L.R.,
,, 6.  2/6th K.L.R.,
,, 7.  2/7th K.L.R.,
,, 8.  2/8th K.L.R.,
,, 9.  171st M.G.Coy.
,, 10.  ,, T.M.B.,
,, 11.  507 Coy, A.S.C.,
,, 12.  2/2nd Wessex Field Ambulance.
,, 13.  57th Division.
,, 14.  1st N.Z. Brigade.
,, 15.  N.Z. Division.
,, 16.  170th Brigade.
,, 17.  No.2 Section, Divl. Signals, R.E.,

SECRET

## 1ST. NEW ZEALAND INFANTRY BRIGADE.

### OPERATION ORDER No: 14

1. The New Zealand Division is being relieved in its present area by the 57th Division.
   The 1st. N.Z. Infantry Brigade is to be relieved by the 171st. Brigade, which is arriving in the SAILLY-ESTAIRES area today.

2. Reliefs will be carried out as follows:-

   1/5 K.L.R — February 21st. 1st. Battalion Wellington Regt. will be relieved in the right of the line by "A" Battalion 171st Brigade.
   2/6 K.L.R — 1st. Battalion Auckland Regt. will be relieved in Brigade Reserve by "B" Battalion 171st. Brigade.
   1st. N.Z. Machine Gun Company will be relieved by 171st Brigade Machine Gun Company.
   2/6 K.L.R — February 22nd. 2nd. Battalion Wellington Regt. will be relieved in the left of the line by "B" Battalion 171st. Brigade, which will be
   2/7 K.L.R — replaced in Brigade Reserve by "C" Battalion 171st Brigade.
   2nd. Battalion Auckland Regt. will be relieved in Divisional Reserve by "D" Battalion 171st Brigade.
   1st N.Z. Light Trench Mortar Battery will be relieved by 171st. Brigade Light Trench Mortar Battery.
   Headquarters 1st. N.Z Infantry Brigade will be relieved by Headquarters 171st. Brigade.
   All details will be arranged between Officers Commanding Units concerned.

3. All trench stores, telescopes, log-books, maps, defence schemes and necessary records will be handed over on relief. Receipts will be obtained in duplicate, and one copy forwarded to Brigade Headqrs.

4. All billets and lines will be handed over in a clean and sanitary condition. A certificate to this effect will be rendered by each Unit to Brigade Headquarters.

5. All personnel of 171st. Brigade attached to Units of 1st. N.Z. Infantry Brigade will rejoin their own Units as these effect their respective reliefs.

6. Commands will pass on completion of reliefs.

7. Compliance with para. 2 of this Order will be reported to Brigade Headquarters by wire on completion of reliefs.

8. Each Unit on relief will march to the SAILLY-ESTAIRES area. Times, routes, and billets will be laid down in Appendix "A" to this Order, which will be issued later.

9. Billeting parties will be detailed by each Unit, and will be held in readiness to proceed to billets to be taken over in the SAILLY-ESTAIRES area, as soon on the day previous to relief, as the billets to be occupied are known.

10. Acknowledge.

T. R. Jackson
Captain.
Brigade Major.
1st. New Zealand Infantry Brigade

Issued at    p.m.
Copy No.    To.
1.  Brigade Commr.
2.  Staff Captain.
3.  Off i/c Bde. Signals
4.  1/N.Z. Machine G. Coy.
5.  1/N.Z.L.T.M.B.
6.  1/Auckland Bn.
7.  2/       "
8.  1/Wellington Bn.
9.  2/       "
10. Centre Group N.Z.F.A.
11. No. 2 Fd. Coy. N.Z.E.
12. No. 1 Fd. Ambulance.
13. No. 2 Coy. Divl. Train.
14. N.Z. Division.
15. A.D.M.S.
16. O.C. Divl. Train.
17. 170th Brigade.
18. 2/N.Z. Inf. Bde.
19. 171st. Brigade.
20. War Diary.
2q. File.

S E C R E T.                                          February 20th 1917.

## 1ST NEW ZEALAND INFANTRY BRIGADE.

### APPENDIX "A" to OPERATION ORDER No 14.

1. Reference para.2 of Operation Order No:14:-
   "A" Battalion 171st.Bde. will be 2/5 Kings Liverpool Regt.
   "B"      "        "    "    "  "  2/6     "      "      "
   "C"      "        "    "    "  "  2/7     "      "      "
   "D"      "        "    "    "  "  2/8     "      "      "

   It has not been possible for details to be arranged in advance between Commanding Officers.

2. Battalions in the line will detail guides who will be told off for each platoon of relieving Battalions, to report at Brigade H.Q. at the hours stated below. An Officer will be detailed to take charge of each Battalion party of guides. As relieving Battalions arrive at Brigade H.Q. he will at once distribute their guides to the platoons for which they have been told off, to guide them to their respective positions in posts and trenches.

3. (a) 2/5 Kings L'pool Regt. is to be at Brigade H.Q. at or before 8:30 a.m. February 21st, and will be met there by guides from 1st. Battalion Wellington Regt., who will report at Brigade H.Q. at 8 a.m.
   (b) 171st Brigade Machine Gun Company is to be at Brigade H.Q. at 9:30 a.m. February 21st. and will be met there by a guide from 1st N.Z.M.C Coy, who will report at Brigade H.Q. at 9 a.m.
   (c) Billeting parties of 2/6 Kings L'pool Regt. are to be at Brigade H.Q. at 8:15a.m. on February 21st. and will be met there by Company guides of 1st Auckland Regt. who will report at Brigade H.Q. at 8a.m. and guide them to billets they are to take over. 2/6 King's Liverpool Regt. is to be at Brigade H.Q. at 10:30 a.m., and will be guided to billets by its own billeting parties.
   (d) Guides from 2/Wellington Regt. will be detailed for each platoon of 2/6 King's Liverpool Regt. and will report to Brigade H.Q. 2/6 King's Liverpool Regt. in FLEURBAIX at 7:0 a.m on February 22nd.
   2/6 Kings Liverpool Regt. will then distribute these guides to the platoons for which each is detailed, and forthwith commence relief.
   (e) Billeting parties of 2/7 and 2/8 King's Liverpool Regt. are to be at Brigade H.Q. at 12 noon on February 21st, and will be dealt with under arrangements to be made by the Staff Captain
   (f) 171st Light Trench Mortar Battery is to be Brigade H Q. at 9 a.m. on February 22nd    1st N.Z L T M Battery will detail a guide to meet them at that hour and place.
   (g) 2/7 King's Liverpool Regt is to be at Brigade H.Q. at 10 a.m. on February 22nd, and will be met there by it's own billeting parties, who will report at Brigade H.Q at 9.30 a.m.
   (h) 2/8 Kings Liverpool Regt. is to be at Brigade H Q. at 12 noon on February 22nd, and will be met there by its own billeting parties, who will report at Brigade H.Q. at 11:30 a.m.

4. ROUTES.
   (a) All Units of 171st Brigade will arrive by way of BAC ST MAUR—PORT ROMPU—FLEURBAIX.
   (b) 2/5 Kings Liverpool Regt. will march into line on February 21st by RUE DAVID.
   (c) 2/6 Kings Liverpool Regt. will march into line on February 22nd by RUE DE LA QUENNETTE
   (d) Units of 1st N Z Infantry Brigade will march to their destinations as each is relieved, under their own arrangements.
   (e) They will not use the road FLEURBAIX—PORT ROMPU—BAC ST MAUR before noon on February 21st, nor before 1.30 p.m. on February 22nd. This restriction applies equally to troops and to transport.

(2)

5. In front of CROIX LESCORNEX–FLEURBAIX all troops will move in single file, with intervals of not less than 50 yds between sections, 100 yds between platoons and 400 yds between Companies.
   Behind CROIX LESCORNEX – FLEURBAIX intervals of not less than 200 yds will be maintained between Companies.

6. Transport lines will be handed over under arrangements to be made between Staff Captains.
   Each Unit will detail a guide to meet the transport of its relieving unit at railway crossing H 14 a 75 35 half an hour before that relieving unit is due at this Brigade H.Q.

7. Each Battalion in the line will leave one Officer and one N.C.O. per Company with the unit relieving it.
   1st.N.Z.M.G.Company & 1st N.Z.L.T.M.Battery will each leave one Officer and one N.C.O. with 171st M.G.Coy. and Light T.M.Battery respectively. All these details will report to H.Q.171st Brigade in FLEURBAIX on February 23rd. at 2 p.m. when they will be met by transport, to be arranged by Staff Captain, to take them to 1 N.Z.Inf. Brigade H.Q. at RUE DE S/C CAMP, B 3 d 9 8, (1/40,000 Sheet 36 & 1/20000 sheet 36 N.W.)

8. Destinations. Units relieved will march out to billets at the following destinations – details arranged by Staff Captain:-
   | | |
   |---|---|
   | 1/M.G.Coy | ESTAIRES. |
   | 1/ L.T.M.Bty. | SAILLY (Cross Roads) |
   | 1/Auckland Regt. | SAILLY-RUE DE LA LYS |
   | 2/ " " | ESTAIRES, |
   | 1/Wellington Regt. | SAILLY-RUE D' ENFER. |
   | 2/ " " | ESTAIRES. |

   Units will report arrival at once to Brigade H.Q.

9. Brigade H.Q. will close at FLEURBAIX and open at NOUVEAU MONDE (Billet No S602) at 12 noon February 22nd.; but reports of completion of any reliefs not complete before that hour will be received at FLEURBAIX thereafter.

T. R. Jackson
Captain.
Brigade Major
1st N.Z. Infantry Bde.

Issued at 11 p.m.
Copy No 1 Brigade Commr.
   2  Staff Captain.
   3  Off.i/c Bde.Signals
   4  1/N.Z M.G.Coy.
   5  1/N.Z.L.T.M.B.
   6  1/Auckland Bn.
   7  2/  "    "
   8  1/Wellington "
   9  2/  "    "
   10 2/5 Kings L'pool Regt.
   11 2/6  "    "
   12 No 2 Fd.Coy.N.Z.E.
   13 Centre Group N.Z.F.A.
   14 N.Z.Division.
   15 2/N.Z.Inf.Bde.
   16 170th Brigade
   17 171st Brigade
   18 War Diary.
   19 File
   20 Spare.

SECRET.                                                          COPY No. 2

171st BRIGADE RELIEF ORDER NO. 1
........
24th February, 1917.

1. The 2/7th K.L.R., will take over the left Sector from the 2/6th K.L.R., on February 26th. Arrangements as to times of relief, which should be as early as possible, is left to Battalion Commanders.

2. The 2/6th K.L.R., will take over the billets of the 2/7th K.L.R., at FLEURBAIX and go into Divisional Reserve.

3. The 2/8th K.L.R., will become Brigade Reserve but will remain in the same billets.

4. The usual report of relief complete will be forwarded to this Office.

*[signature]*

Lieut.Colonel.
Brigade Major.
171st Infantry Bde.

ISSUED AT        P.M., TO :-

Copy No. 1.   Brigadier-General.
         2    War Diary.
         3    G.S. File.
         4    Staff Captain.
         5    2/5th K.L.R.
         6    2/6th K.L.R.
         7    2/7th K.L.R.
         8    2/8th K.L.R.
         9    171st Bde T.M.B.
        10    171st Bde M.G.Coy.
        11    2/2nd Wessex R.E.
        12    Signal Section.

SECRET

COPY NO.2.

171st Brigade Relief Order No.2.

............

27th February 1917.

1. The 2/8th K.L.R. will take over the Right Sector from the 2/5th K.L.R. on March 1st.

Arrangements as to times of relief, which should be as early as possible, is left to Battalion Commanders.

2. The 2/5th K.L.R., will take over the billets of the 2/8th K.L.R., at FLEURBAIX, and go into Divisional Reserve.

3. The 2/6th K.L.R., will become Brigade Reserve, but will remain in the same billets.

4. Units will comply with previous instructions as regards precautions for march formations on relieving each other.

5. The usual report of relief complete and passing of Commands will be forwarded to this office.

(signed) G.W. GEDDES.

Lieut. Colonel, Brigade Major,
171st Infantry Brigade.

ISSUED AT 5.0.p.m. to:-

Copy.No. 1. Brigadier-General.
2. War Diary.
3. File.
4. Staff Captain.
5. 2/5th K.L.R.
6. 2/6th K.L.R.
7. 2/7th K.L.R.
8. 2/8th K.L.R.
9. 171st Bde.T.M.B.
10. 171st Bde.M.G.Coy.
11. 2/2. Wessex R.E.
12. 2/2nd Wessex Field Ambulance.
13. Signal Section.
14. 57th Division.

CONFIDENTIAL.

A.G.,
    BASE.

............

Herewith is forwarded War Diary of Headquarters, 171st Infantry Brigade, from 13.2.1917 to 30.3.1917, together with Appendices referred to therein.

*[signature]*
Brigadier-General,
Commanding 171st Infantry Brigade.

In the Field,
    31st March, 1917.

AQ 171 Infy Bde
(57th Div.)
Vol 1 #2
March 1917.

On His Majesty's Service.

Confidential

War Diary
of
The Port of Secunp.

From November 1914

to August 31st 1915

March 1911
Nint Inf Bde.

Army Form C. 2118

# WAR DIARY
## or
## INTELLIGENCE SUMMARY

*(Erase heading not required.)*

Instructions regarding War Diaries and Intelligence Summaries are contained in F.S. Regs., Part II. and the Staff Manual respectively. Title Pages will be prepared in manuscript.

| Place | Date | Hour | Summary of Events and Information | Remarks and references to Appendices |
|---|---|---|---|---|
| | MAR. 1st. | | Very quiet day on the Line. Army Commander visited Brigade HdQrs. Brigadier attended conference at Divisional HdQrs. 2/8th K.L.R. relieved 2/5th K.L.R. on Right Sector. | Appendix I. |
| | 2nd. | | Brigade Major and O.C. Field Coy. R.E., did reconnaissance for new defensive line to connect with Left Brigade, and went round Support Line. Brigadier inspected Subsidiary Line of Defence. Normal Conditions. | |
| | 3rd. | | Normal conditions. Brigade Major, with G.S.O.3 from Army HdQrs, went round Front and Support Line. Divisional Commander and G.S.O.I came to Brigade HdQrs. | |
| | 4th. | | Normal conditions. Very good visibility. Brigade Major reconnoitred strong post line of FLEURBAIX - forwarding report to Divisional HdQrs. Orders issued for relief of 2/7th K.L.R., by 2/6th K.L.R., | Appendix I. |
| | 5th. | | Normal day. Divisional Commander and Brigadier visited Right Sector - Brigade Major Left Sector. G.S.O.I came to Brigade HdQrs in the afternoon. | |
| | 6th. | 11.30 a.m. 12 noon. | Relief of 2/7th K.L.R., by 2/6th K.L.R., completed on Left Sector. Normal conditions. Our artillery very active. | |
| | 7th. | 2.0 p.m. 11.30 p.m. | Normal conditions. Conference at Divisional HdQrs re the Division taking over a more extensive line. Scheme for holding the Area with one Battalion, and Orders issued for relief by the 170th Brigade. | Order No.3 |
| | 8th. | 2.30 p.m. | Normal conditions. 2/5th K.L.R. and 2/7th K.L.R., moved to billets in ERQUINGHEM AREA. 2/6th K.L.R.; into billets at FLEURBAIX. 2/8th K.L.R., taking over the whole Sector. Advance Parties of 4/5th North Lancs. came in. Brigade Major, 170th Bde, taken round Subsidiary Line, Support Line and Strong Posts by Brigade Major. | |

Wt. W593/826  1,000,000  4/15  J.B.C. & A.  A.D.S.S./Forms/C.2118.

Army Form C. 2118

# WAR DIARY
## or
## INTELLIGENCE SUMMARY

*(Erase heading not required.)*

Instructions regarding War Diaries and Intelligence Summaries are contained in F.S. Regs., Part II. and the Staff Manual respectively. Title Pages will be prepared in manuscript.

| Place | Date | Hour | Summary of Events and Information | Remarks and references to Appendices |
|---|---|---|---|---|
| | MAR. 9th. | 10.0 a.m. | 2/6th K.L.R. moved to billets at BAC ST MAUR. | |
| | | 11.45 a.m. | 2/8th K.L.R. relieved by 4/5th Loyal North Lancs. | |
| | | 12 noon. | Handed over to 170th Brigade. | |
| ERQUINGHEM. | | | Brigade, less 2/8th K.L.R., established in billets in Reserve. | |
| | 10th | 5.30 p.m. | Brigade Major proceeded to Division to discuss subject of Raids. | |
| | 11th | | 2/8th K.L.R. moved into billets at ERQUINGHEM. Brigadier-General visited troops in billets. Brigade Major to Division for further discussion on Raids. | |
| | 12th | | All Battalions, to extent of 14 Platoons per Battalion, on Working Parties. | |
| | 13th | | All Battalions on Working Parties. Brigade Major proceeded to Divisional HdQrs and interviewed Officer of Australian Infantry regarding details for forthcoming Raid. | |
| | 14th | | All Battalions on Working Parties. O.C., M.T.Ms. discussed co-operation for Raid. Brigadier inspected Transport Lines. Brigade Major went to 170th Brigade HdQrs to discuss support for Raid. | |
| | 15th | | All Battalions away on Working Parties. Brigade Major visited 172nd Brigade HdQrs, and then proceeded to Division regarding arrangements for the Raid and questions regarding Artillery Liason; proceeding to 170th Brigade HdQrs afterwards concerning the same matter. The question of supporting Right and Left Brigades was considered. | |
| | 16th | | All Battalions away on Working Parties. Brigade Major visited Divisional School to see parties training for Raid, and then met Brigade Major, Divisional Artillery. Brigadier, with Corps and Divisional Commanders, went round Subsidiary Line Working Parties. | |
| | | | Brigadier-General visited Subsidiary Line, 172nd Brigade - i.e., Left Brigade. All Battalions on Working Parties. Brigade Major visited Divisional School and attended at Divl.HdQrs. | |

1875 Wt. W593/826 1,000,000 4/15 J.B.C. & A. A.D.S.S./Forms/C. 2118.

Army Form C. 2118

6.

# WAR DIARY
## or
## INTELLIGENCE SUMMARY

*(Erase heading not required.)*

Instructions regarding War Diaries and Intelligence Summaries are contained in F. S. Regs., Part II. and the Staff Manual respectively. Title Pages will be prepared in manuscript.

| Place | Date | Hour | Summary of Events and Information | Remarks and references to Appendices |
|---|---|---|---|---|
| | MAR. 17th | | Brigadier-General visited Divisional School. All Battalions on Working Parties. | |
| | 18th | | All Battalions out on Working Parties. Brigade Major went to 170th Bde HdQrs to arrange further details regarding a Raid - and proceeded to Divisional HdQrs to lay scheme before G.O.C., Brigadier-General visited 172nd Brigade on Left Sector. | |
| | 19th | | All Battalions on Working Parties. Brigadier-General went to 172nd Bde HdQrs. Brigade Major went to Division regarding Raid. | |
| | 20th | | All Battalions on Working Parties. | |
| | 21st | | All Battalions on Working Parties. Brigadier went round Left Sector of 172nd Brigade. | |
| | 22nd | | All Battalions away on Working Parties - which were visited by Brigadier-General. Brigade Major went round Right Sector of 172nd Brigade. | |
| | 23rd | | All Battalions away on Working Parties. Brigade Major at 172nd Bde HdQrs and 170th Bde HdQrs. Brigadier and Brigade Major visited Divisional School to see Raiding Party rehearse. | |
| | 24th | | All Battalions away on Working Parties. | |
| | | 10.0 p.m. | Orders issued for relief of 172nd Brigade. | Appendix I. |
| | 24th/25th | 12 m' night. | Brigadier-General and Brigade Major reported at 170th Bde HdQrs. All arrangements made for Raid. | |
| | | 3.20 a.m. | Zero Hour for raid. Owing to the breaking of the bridges, Raid did not take place, and Artillery was stopped as soon as possible. Details of Raid - see Appendix III. Battalions away on Working Parties. | Appendix III |

Army Form C. 2118

# WAR DIARY
## or
## INTELLIGENCE SUMMARY
(Erase heading not required.)

Instructions regarding War Diaries and Intelligence Summaries are contained in F. S. Regs., Part II. and the Staff Manual respectively. Title Pages will be prepared in manuscript.

| Place | Date | Hour | Summary of Events and Information | Remarks and references to Appendices |
|---|---|---|---|---|
| ERQUINGHEM | 25th | | Bn Battalion going on routine work. | |
| | 26th | | The Battalion duty on routine work. Reports of 2/4 K.R.R. classes arose started work on Rue du Bois sector — details received another. | Appendix I |
| | 27th | | 2/5 K.R.R. & 2/6 G.R.R. oN came off routine parties preparatory to moving up in relief of 172nd Bde. 2/7 & 2/8 K.R.R. continued Bn. Hdqrs. issued moving to relieve 172nd Bde. | |
| | 28th | | 2/5 K.R.R. & Relieved 2/6 K.R.R. in front line of Bois GRENIER Sector. 2/8 K.R.R. relieved 2/6 K.R.R. in 2nd Battalion reserve. 2/6 & 2/7 K.R.R. came into parks Fauquisart, in relief. Brigadier General Moir there at 172nd Bde. | |
| | 29th | 3.0 h | Bde Hd Qrs relieved 172nd Bn Hd Qrs | |
| | | 4.20 pm | 2/7 K.R.R. relieved 2/4 S.E.R. relief complete. Normal conditions. Some artillery some shots active in the afternoon. | |
| RUE DU BOIS BOIS GRENIER | 30th | A.M. 12.45 | Relief of 2/5 S.L.R. by 2/6 K.R.R. complete. Command passes to Brigade from 172nd Bde. Normal conditions — Slight shelling of & establishment of the Brigade in occupation of the BOIS GRENIER — 5600 yards in tautly approximately RUE DU BOIS SECTOR. G understood I find ourselves the strength Battalion Trenches line and CT's requires much attention specially drainage | |

1875 Wt. W593/826 1,000,000 4/15 J.B.C. & A. A.D.S.S./Forms/C. 2118.

SECRET                                                    COPY.NO.2.

"GINTY" Relief order No.3.          4th March 1917

1. GIPSY will take over Left Sector from GIDDY on March 6th.

   Arrangements as to times of relief, which should be as early as possible, is left to Battalion Commanders.

2. GIDDY will take over the billets of GIPSY at FLEURBAIX and go into Divisional Reserve.

3. GIRLIE will become Brigade Reserve, but will remain in the same billets.

4. The Strictest compliance as regards previous instructions for precautionary march formations on Relief will be observed.

5. Units will report by wire when relief is complete and passing of Commands.

                            (signed) G.W.GEDDES,

                              Lieut.Colonel, Brigade Major,
                                171st Infantry Brigade.

ISSUED AT 10.0.P.M., to

Copy.No.1. Brigadier-General.
2. War Diary.
3. File.
4. Staff Captain,
5. 2/5th K.L.R.
6. 2/6th K.L.R.
7. 2/7th K.L.R.
8. 2/8th K.L.R.
9. GILUMP.
10. GIGGLES.
11. GIFFEY.
12. GINGER.
13. AMBUSH.
14. SIGNALS.
15. MASTER.
16. PAPA.
17. WESLAN.

SECRET.  
Copy.No. 7.

Ref.Map.1. 10000  
Sheets : 36 NW.4  
        36 SW 1 & 2.

## 57th Divisional Order No.4.

7th March 1917.

1. The Division will take over a more extended front.

2. The 170th Brigade Group, with 171st Machine Gun Coy., attached, with Headquarters at FLEURBAIX, will take over the front now occupied by the 171st Brigade Left resting at Junction 1.31.1 to 1.31.2 (i.e. 1.31.c.5.4.) Relief, with the exception of Light Trench Mortar Battery which is to be gradual, to be complete 9.p.m. on the 9th March.

3. The 172nd Brigade Group, with 173rd Machine Gun Coy., attached, with Headquarters in the Farm H.11.a.5.4. will take over the front now occupied by the 10th Brigade of the 3rd Australian Division with the Left resting about PEAR TREE FARM.1.16.b.3.7. Relief will be complete 9.0.a.m. on the 9th March.

4. The 171st Brigade will be withdrawn to billets at BAC ST MAUR and ERQUINGHEM LYS: Locality of Headquarters to be notified to D.H.Q.

5. The Field Coys. R.E. will remain in their present positions the 421st being affiliated in addition to the 502nd to the Right Brigade Area; the 505th to the Left Brigade Area.

6. The Artillery will stand fast for the present.

7. Brigades will report to D.H.Q. when reliefs are complete.

8. The A.D.M.S. will make the Medical arrangements for the extended area.

9. ACKNOWLEDGE.

                                        CECIL ALLANSON, Lieut.Colonel,  
                                            General Staff, 57th Division.

Issued at 8.p.m. to

| Copy No. | | |
|---|---|---|
| 1. War Diary. | 12. | A.D.M.S. |
| 2. G.S.File. | 13. | A.P.M. |
| 3. G.O.C. | 14. | D.A.D.O.S. |
| 4. G.RA. | 15. | Signals. |
| 5. C.R.E. | 16. | A.D.V.S. |
| 6. 170th Bde. | 17. | D.M.G.O. |
| 7. 171st Bde. | 18. | 11 Anzac Corps.(for information) |
| 8. 172nd Bde. | 19. | 3rd Aus.Div. |
| 9. 'A' | 20. | 49th Division. |
| 10. 'Q' | 21. | Camp Commdt. |
| 11. Div.Train. | 22. | Spare. |

SECRET.  GINTY ORDER NO.3.  COPY NO.

Reference
Sheet 36 N.W. I:20000
7th March 1917.

1. GINTY is to be relieved by Master, and will go into Billets in the ERQUINGHEM Area.

2. Reliefs will be carried out as follows:-

MARCH 8th.

(a) GIRLIE will billet in the FORT ROMPU area. Billeting parties will report to the Staff Captain at FORT ROMPU- map reference H.8.c.0.2. at 9.15 a.m. "A" battalion of MASTER will move into their vacated billets during the course of the day.

GIRLIE will be clear of Brigade H.Q. by 10.15.a.m., They will furnish 8 guides who will report to Brigade H.Q. at 9.30.a.m. to guide advance parties of "A" Battalion of MASTER to their billets and to GILT H.Q.

2nd Line Transport will report at 10.0.a.m. to Battalion H.Q. - 1 Motor Lorry will report at 11.0.a.m. to B.H.Q. - a guide will be furnished to direct this Lorry, which will do more than one trip if required. Rear Parties will be detailed to load up the same.

(b) GIDDY will billet in FORT ROMPU area. Billeting parties will report to the Staff Captain at FORT ROMPU- map reference H.8.c.0.2. at 9.15.a.m.

GIDDY will be clear of B.H.Q. by 11.15.a.m.

2nd Line Transport will report at 10.0.a.m. to Battalion H.Q. 1 Motor Lorry will report at 11.a.m. to Brigade H.Q. a guide being detailed to direct this lorry - rear parties will be left to load up same, which will do more than one trip if required.

(c) GILT will commence relief of GIPSY as per GINTY'S scheme for the Defence of the Area (now held by the Brigade) by one Battalion - at 8.30.a.m.

GIPSY will move into FLEAURBAIX and occupy billets now occupied by GIDDY for the night of the 8/9th.

Billeting Parties will report to the Area Officer at
Railway Crossing, map reference G.24.c.7.7 at 11.0.a.m.
and will billet at BAC ST MAUR for the night; this
party will be rationed by its own Unit.

MARCH 9th. (a) GIPSY will move into billets at BAC ST MAUR.
2nd Line Transport will report to Battalion H.Q. at 8.0.a.m.
A guide will be detailed to meet a M.T.Lorry, which will
report at B.H.Q. at 8.0.a.m. This Lorry will do more than
one trip if required. The necessary rear parties will
( be left.

(b) GILT will be relieved by "A" Battalion of MASTER and
will detail under mutual arrangements what guides, if
any, that O.C. Advance Party of "A" Battalion may require.
Relief will take place as early as possible.
GILT will billet for the night of the 9/10th at FLEURBAIX,
occupying the billets vacated by GIPSY.

(c) GINTY will close at FLEURBAIX at 10.0.a.m. and open at
ERQUINGHEM at 12 noon.

MARCH.10th. GILT will billet at ERQUINGHEM Village. Billeting
Party will report at B.H.Q. ERQUINGHEM, at 8.30.a.m.
2nd Line Transport will report to Battalion H.Q. at 8.0.a.m.
GILT will detail a guide to meet 1 M.T.Lorry which will be
at present B.H.Q. at 8.a.m. which will do more than one
trip if necessary.

The Battalion will be clear of FLEURBAIX by 10.a.m.

3. Permanent Tramway and Drainage men will remain in the
sector and be attached for discipline and rations as and
from the 10th inst. to the 421st Field Coy.R.E.,

4. 1st Line Transport and Q.M.Stores will remain as at
present. The Refilling point will not be changed.

5. All Trench Stores,Telescopes,Log Books,Maps,Defence
Schemes, and necessary records will be handed over on
relief. Receipts will be obtained in duplicate, and
one copy forwarded to Brigade H.Q.

6. Rear Parties where concerned will be left behind in compliance with 57th Divisional Orders on this subject, and hand over billets.

7. Commands will pass on completion of Reliefs.

8. GILUMP and GIGGLES will not be relieved, but pass under the command of MASTER.

9. Strictest compliance with precautionary march formations as previously ordered, will be observed.

10. GINTY will close at FLEURBAIX at 10.0.a.m. and open at ERQINGHEM (billet 30 Rue d'Eglise) at 12 noon, 9th March; but reports of completion of any reliefs not complete before that hour will be received at FLEURBAIX thereafter.

11. <u>ACKNOWLEDGE.</u>

                                        (signed) G.W.GEDDES.
                                          Lieut.Colonel, Brigade Major,
                                          171st Infantry Brigade.

ISSUED.at 11.30.p.m.

| Copy No. 1. War Diary. | Copy No. 10. GIGGLES. |
|---|---|
| 2. File. | 11. GINGER. |
| 3. Brigade Commdr. | 12. GIFFEY. |
| 4. Staff Captain. | 13. AMBUSH. |
| 5. GIRLIE. | 14. WESLAN. |
| 6. GIPSY. | 15. MASTER. |
| 7. GIDDY. | 16. PAPA. |
| 8. GILT. | 17. O.C.SIGNALS.H.K.11. |
| 9. GILUMP. | |

SECRET.
COPY NO. 2

Ref. Map.
Sheet 36 N.W. 1:10,000
& 1:20,000.

171st BRIGADE ORDER No.5

24th March, 1917.

......

1. In accordance with 57th Divisional Order No.5 dated the 20th March, the 171st Brigade will relieve the 172nd Brigade in the BOIS GRENIER - RUE DU BOIS Sector, in accordance with the instructions below, and the attached Relief Table.

2. Advance parties of the 2/5th, 2/8th, 2/7th and 2/6th K.L.R. will report to the Battn. HdQrs of the 2/9th, 2/10th K.L.R., 2/4th and 2/5th S.L.R. respectively, 24 hours before reliefs take place, and will remain with Units they are to relieve for the night.

3. Billeting parties of the 172nd Brigade will report to the Battn. HdQrs of Battalions whose Billets they are taking over, 24 hours prior to relief - except in the case of the 2/10th K.L.R., who will report at the 2/6th K.L.R. HdQrs at 10 a.m. on the 29th, on which date the 2/6th K.L.R. will be clear of their Assembly Position by 5 p.m.

4. All Trench Stores, Telescopes, Log Books, Maps, Defence Schemes and necessary records will be handed over on relief. Receipt will be obtained in duplicate, and one copy forwarded to Brigade HdQrs.

5. Rear parties will be left behind to hand over Billets, 57th Divl. Orders on this subject being complied with.

6. Commands will pass on completion of reliefs.

7. Transport Lines and Quartermasters' Dumps will remain where they are, but Quartermasters or their representatives must make themselves thoroughly acquainted with the Dumps of the Battalions they are relieving, prior to reliefs taking place.

8. The 171st L.T.M.B. will relieve the 172nd L.T.M.B. on the night of the 28th/29th in the RUE DU BOIS Sub-Sector, and the BOIS GRENIER SUB-SECTOR on the night of the 29th/30th.
    The Transport of the 171th Brigade will take back the guns of the 172nd Brigade in the RUE DU BOIS Sub-Sector.
    The 172nd Brigade will arrange transport for the night of the 29th/30th in the BOIS GRENIER Sub-Sector.
    The 172nd L.T.M.B. will take over the Billets of the 171st Brigade L.T.M.B. at ERQUINGHEM; details of reliefs will be arranged between Os.C. L.T.M.Bs concerned.
    A proportion of the personnel of the 172nd Brigade L.T.M.B. will remain in the trenches until the 171st Brigade L.T.M.B. become acquainted with the line.

9. March formations of Units moving by day will be as previously laid down when moving in the danger area, i.e., South of the LAVENTIE - ARMENTIERES RAILWAY, and strictly adhered to. By night, platoons will keep closed up.

10. Until the relief of the whole Sector is complete, Units of this Brigade will be under the orders of the G.O.C., 172nd Brigade, and vice versa.
    Units will render routine returns, etc., to this Office, but all Operation and Intelligence Reports to the G.O.C. 172nd Brigade.

2.

II.  Relief of Brigade HdQrs will take place at 3 p.m. on the 29th instant.
    Commands will pass on the night of the 29th/30th March. Brigade HdQrs will open at 4 p.m. on the 29th instant at H.II.A.50.40.

                                    Lieut.Colonel, Brigade Major.
                                         171st Infantry Brigade.


ISSUED AT 10 P.M.,

    Copy No. 1.     War Diary.
     ,,      2.     G.S. File.
     ,,      3.     Brigade Commander.
     ,,      4.     Staff Captain,
     ,,      5.     2/5th K.L.R.,
     ,,      6.     2/6th   ,,
     ,,      7.     2/7th   ,,
     ,,      8.     2/8th   ,,
     ,,      9.     171st L.T.M.B.,
     ,,     10.     507 Coy, A.S.C.,
     ,,     11.     57th Division.
     ,,     12.     170th Brigade.
     ,,     13.     172nd   ,,
     ,,     14.     No.2 Section, Divl. Signal Co, R.E.,
     ,,     15.     172nd M.G.Co.
     ,,     16.     173rd   ,,
     ,,     17.     9th Aus. Brigade.
     ,,     18.     3/2nd West Lancs F.Ambulance.
     ,,     19.     Left Group Artillery.
     ,,     20.     505 Field Coy, R.E.,
     ,,     21.     57th Divl. Artillery HdQrs.

Ref. Map. 1:10,000; 1.20,000.
Sheet 36. N.W.,

## RELIEF TABLE.

### SECTOR — BOIS GRENIER.

| Date of Relief. | UNIT. | UNIT of 172nd BDE to be Relieved. | POSITION and BATTN. HdQrs. | RENDEZVOUS and where Guides will be. | Hour of Arrival of head of Batn. | ROUTE from BILLETS. | REMARKS. |
|---|---|---|---|---|---|---|---|
| MARCH 8th. | 2/5th K.L.R. | 2/9th K.L.R. | Right Front Battn. THE CARLTON. I.19.B.80.10 | Cross Roads – RUE DES CHARLES. BOIS GRENIER. CROMBALOT ROADS. H.30.A.90.50. | 10.0 a.m. | RUE DELETREE – MOAT FARM – PARK ROW & GREATWOOD AVENUES. | The Battn. will move less its Lewis Guns. Lewis Gun Limbers will not proceed past CANTEEN FARM. Each Gun Team will be met by a Guide. |
|  | LEWIS GUNS. |  | – do – | CANTEEN FARM. H.23.B.10.99. | 3.0 p.m. | – |  |
| 8th. | 2/8th K.L.R. less, I Coy. | 2/10th K.L.R. less, I Coy. | Right Reserve Battn. | LA ROLANDERIE. H.17.B.00.15. Bn.HdQrs. | 3.15 p.m. | RUE DU BIEZ. | One Company plus its Lewis Guns will be under the orders of O.C. 2/5th K.L.R. |
| 8th. | 2/8th K.L.R. I Coy. | 2/10th K.L.R. I Coy. | With 2/5th KLR. in Subsidiary Line. | – do – | 3.0 p.m. | – do – LIMBERS | This Company will be at the head of its Battn. Lewis Guns will not proceed past CANTEEN FARM. The Company will be under the orders of O.C. 2/5th K.L.R. |

### SECTOR — RUE DU BOIS.

| Date | UNIT. | UNIT of 172nd BDE to be Relieved. | POSITION and BATTN. HdQrs. | RENDEZVOUS and where Guides will be. | Hour of Arrival of head of Batn. | ROUTE from BILLETS. | REMARKS. |
|---|---|---|---|---|---|---|---|
| 8th. | LEWIS GUNS. 2/6th K.L.R. | 2/5th S.L.R. | Left Front Battn. I.14.B.55.75. | SANDBAG CORNER. I.1.D.70.30 | 7.0 p.m. | ERQUINGHEM – ARMENTIERES LEVEL CROSSING at B.30.c.15.05. Righthanded to LEVEL CROSSING at H.6.B.92.12. CROWN PRINCE HOUSE. | O.C.2/5th SLR. will arrange accommodation in the Subsid. Line for the night of 28th/29th March. The relief of the Lewis Guns taking place during the day of the 29th inst. under Battn. arrangements. |
| 9th. | 2/7th K.L.R. less, I Coy. | 2/4th S.L.R. less, I Coy. | Left Reserve Battn. RUE MARLE AREA. CROWN PRINCE HOUSE. I.1.c.50.50. | RAILWAY CROSSING at H.6.B.92.12. | 4.0 p.m. | ERQUINGHEM – ARMENTIERES LEVEL CROSSING at B.30.c.15.05. Righthanded to LEVEL CROSSING at H.6.B.92.12. CROWN PRINCE HOUSE. | One Coy, plus its Lewis Guns, will be under the command of O.C. 2/6th K.L.R. |
| 9th. | 2/7th K.L.R. I Coy. | 2/4th S.L.R. I Coy. | Left Front Bn. I.14.D.55.75. | 172nd BDE HdQrs. H.11.A.50.40. | 3.0 p.m. | GRIS POT – LA VESEE. | Lewis gun Limbers will not proceed East of GRIS POT. |
| 9th. | 2/6th K.L.R. | 2/5th S.L.R. | Left Front Bn. I.14.D.55.75. | SANDBAG CORNER. I.1.D.70.30. | 7.0 p.m. | As for 2/7th K.L.R. "UP" C.Ts. LEITH WALK. WINE AVENUE. |  |

Copy No..7..

SECRET.

Ref. Map 1/10,000
Sheets; 36 N.W. 3 & 4.
........

## 57th DIVISION ORDER No. 5.

.........

20th March, 1917.

1. The 171st Brigade will relieve the 172nd Brigade in the Left Sub-Sector of the Line, commencing on the 28th March.

2. Details of relief will be arranged between the Brigadiers concerned.

3. On relief, the 172nd Brigade will take over the billets in ERQUINGHEM and BAC ST MAUR vacated by the 171st Infantry Brigade.

4. The 172nd Light Trench Mortar Battery will leave a proportion of their personnel in the Line until the 171st Light Trench Mortar Battery have become acquainted with their new positions.

5. Field Companies R.E. and Machine Gun Companies will remain as they are.

6. The relief will be completed, except as regards the Light Trench Mortar Batteries, by 5 a.m., on 30th March.

7. Command will pass on completion of the Infantry relief.

8. ACKNOWLEDGE.

CECIL ALLANSON.

Lieut.Colonel, General Staff.

Issued at 12 noon to :-

| Copy No. | | | | |
|---|---|---|---|---|
| 1. | War Diary. | | 13. | A.P.M. |
| 2. | G.S.File. | | 14. | D.A.D.O.S. |
| 3. | G.O.C. | | 15. | Signals. |
| 4. | C.R.A. | | 16. | A.D.V.S. |
| 5. | C.R.E. | | 17. | D.M.G.O. |
| 6. | 170th Bde. | | 18. | II ANZAC Corps.(for informat) |
| 7. | 171st Bde. | | 19. | 3rd Aust. Div. " |
| 8. | 172nd Bde. | | 20. | 49th Division. " |
| 9. | "A" | | 21. | Camp Commdt. |
| 10. | "Q" | | 22. | D.G.O. |
| 11. | Div.Train. | | 23) | |
| 12. | A.D.M.S. | | 24) | Spare. |
| | | | 25) | |

APPENDIX No. III.

MINOR OPERATIONS

referred to in

171st INFANTRY BRIGADE WAR DIARY,

13.2.1917 to 30.3.1917

.....

REPORT ON RAID BY 2/7TH K.L.REGT.,
171ST BRIGADE - NIGHT OF 24/25TH MARCH.

Headquarters,
57th Division.

       3.20 a.m. O.C. Raid 'phoned that "enterprise could not come off as Bridge had broken over borrow ditch and requested that guns should be switched off and an attempt made in an hour's time" - on being ordered to get across at all costs - O.C. Raid reported "that they had attempted it, but men were up to their necks in water and could'nt cross".

       3.24 a.m. O.C. Searchlight was ordered to throw a beam of light upwards - signal to stop the guns. At the same time Brigade Major, 170th Bde. communicated to Brigade Major, 57th Divisional Artillery, to stop guns by 'phone.

       3.25 a.m. As guns continued to fire O.C. Searchlight was ordered to send up two rockets.

       3.27 a.m. Certain guns continuing to fire, another rocket was ordered to be sent up. O.C. Searchlight reported that this stopped the guns firing.

       3.48 a.m. Called up 57th Divisional Artillery Headquarters asking if guns could co-operate in a further attempt - answer received was in the negative.

       3.50 a.m. Ordered O.C. Raid to bring in broken bridge, Gap posts and close sally port.

       *signature* Brigadier-General,
       Commanding, 171st Infantry Brigade.

25/4/1917.

REPORT BY O.C. RAID.

## NIGHT 24TH/25TH MARCH.

1. 12.30 a.m. Advance Party under Lieut. Addy laid Bridge across borrow ditch, cut final gaps in our own wire; 3 straw mats being also laid over our own wire..

2. 2.45 a.m. Three other bridges were taken over outside our own wire, tapes and telephone wires were laid ready.

3. 2.55 a.m. Lieut. Nickels arrived with Raiding Party at point of assembly in our front line.

4. 3.9 a.m. Lieut. Nickels and the scouts proceeded through sally port to see the position of the other three bridges. The borrow ditch bridge broke and this party fell in. The depth of the water was 3 feet, but the difficulty of getting out arose from the clinging mud and was also due to the sides of the ditch being perpendicular. The distance from the ground level to the bottom of the borrow ditch was approximately 7 feet.

5. 3.15 a.m. O.C. Raid attempted to stop the guns but had to 'phone through Battalion Headquarters at FORAY HOUSE to get the Liaison Officer. The Liaison Officer who reported as ordered to the O.C. Raid at WYE FARM at zero minus two hours informed O.C. Raid that his orders were not to accompany O.C. Raid but to go to Battalion Headquarters. I left the matter of stopping the guns in the Liaison Officer's hands.

6. 3.20 a.m. I reported the matter to Brigade Major, 171st Brigade.

7. 3.22 a.m. Enemy's barrage opened with shrapnel; A minute after he opened with H.E. also, distributing his fire on front line - NO MAN'S LAND - Communication Trenches - and the supports. Barrage was not very intense. A Machine gunner opened from the direction of THE ANGLE.

8. 3.45 a.m. Hun barrage died down.

9. 4.0 a.m. Five men who had been left in NO MAN'S LAND returned and reported that the enemy were throwing up Very Lights well in rear of their front line. The shooting of our guns were very good and appeared to be landing every 10 yards in the enemy's front line. These men by the aid of a duckboard spanned across the break of the bridge, AND managed to crawl over the borrow ditch.

10. 4.10 a.m. Lieut. Cowper extemporized a new bridge with the aid of the old bridge and duckboards, and with 8 men salved the three bridges left in NO MAN'S LAND together with the broken bridge, straw mats and tapes, filled up the gap in the wire with knife rests - the sally port being closed by the engineers, so as to leave as little trace as possible of the point of departure of the raid.

11. 5.30 a.m. All parties were clear of the trenches. There were no casualties.

Brigadier-General,
Commanding, 171st Infantry Brigade.

SECRET.                                                      G.96/44.

                           57th DIVISION.
                           ..............

                    SUBJECT:- SUMMER TIME.
                    ..............

Orders have been issued that we have to take on Summer Time at 11 p.m. to-night; that means that at that hour all watches are advanced one hour.

In order to avoid the great difficulty of synchronising watches at so late an hour, all watches synchronised for the Operation to-night should be advanced one hour when the Officer who is synchronising watches brings his watch round.

Zero hour will now be for the Operation to-night 3-20 a.m. instead of 2-20 a.m.
          ACKNOWLEDGE.

D.H.Q.,                           CECIL ALLANSON, Lieut-Colonel,
  24/3/1917.                           General Staff, 57th Division.

                                              CA

ISSUED at 3.15 p.m. to:-

    C.R.A.
    C.R.E.
    H.Q., 2nd ANZAC Heavy Artillery.
      "   170th Brigade.
    O.C., 170th Light T.M.Battery.
    H.Q., 171st Brigade.
    O.C., 171st Light T.M.Battery.
    H.Q., 172nd Brigade.
    O.C., 172nd Light T.M.Battery.
    Signals.
    O.C., Divisional School.
    O.C., Raid.
    D.M.G.O.
    A.D.M.S.
    D.T.M.O.

S E C R E T.
-------------

H.Q., 171st Brigade.
Lieut. Peters (Divisional School)
2/Lieut. Manning      do.
C.R.A.
-------------

     The following minor alterations have taken place with reference to the coming Operation.

     The men commence to issue through the sally port at Zero minus 2 minutes instead of at Zero hour. The diversion will take place at Zero hour instead of at Zero hour minus 5 minutes.

     The barrage will lift at Zero plus 3 instead of at Zero plus 4. The barrage will cease at Zero hour plus 30, but at any time after Zero plus 23 will cease on the sending up of special Rockets from FLEURBAIX. If it is desired to stop the barrage before Zero plus 23, which is a most unlikely occurrence, a searchlight will be thrown up vertically at FLEURBAIX.

     The S.O.S. to be inoperative from Zero minus 35 to Zero plus 40.


D.H.Q.,
   21/3/1917.
                                   CECIL ALLANSON, Lieut-Colonel,
                                        General Staff, 57th Division.

SECRET.                                                          COPY NO. 1

                          GINTY    ORDER    NO.   4.
                          ..............

MAP REFERENCE.    RADINGHEM.  36. S.W.2.   I:I0000.
                  AUBERS.     36. S.W.I.   I:I0000.
                  BRIGADE TRENCH MAP.  AREA M.   I:I0000.
                  SPECIAL SUN-PRINT.       I:2500.
                  AEROPLANE PHOTOGRAPHS.


                  I.  On Z day at Zero hour, detachments of the 2/7th and
                  2/8th King's Liverpool Regiment will carry out raids on
                  portion of enemy's trenches - front line - and supporting
                  strong points, with the object of :-
                  (a) Killing and capturing as many of the enemy as possible.
                  (b) Capturing and destroying War Material.
                  (c) Destroying Dugouts and Machine Gun Emplacements.
                  (d) Gaining information regarding enemy's front line
                      system.


ORGANISATION.     2. "A" RAID will be carried out as a diversion at 3
                  minutes before zero on the enemy's front line trench
                  opposite N.IO.I, the enemy's front line being entered
                  between co-ordinate points N.IO.c.I7.3  to  N.IO.c.37.35.

                     "B" RAID - MAIN RAID.   The enemy's front line being
                  entered between the co-ordinates O.I.A.2.7 to O.I.A.45.7,
                  to a depth of I20 yards  -  taking in BOLTON CASTLE.


                  3. Detail of A and B Raid to be in accordance with
                  Combined Artillery and Infantry Programme, Appendix I.


                  4. A Liason Officer, R.A., will be with O.C. "A" and "B"
                  Raids.


                  5. The I70th Brigade will support the enterprise.


                  6. Os.C. I70th, I7Ist and I72nd Machine Gun Coys will
                  co-operate with flanking fire and an indirect barrage
                  fire on enemy's communications.


                  7. MEDICAL ARRANGEMENTS will be under that of the G.O.C.
                  I70th Brigade.
                      ADVANCED DRESSING STATION - JAY POST & V.C.HOUSE.

                  the evacuation from these Dressing Stations being arranged
                  by M.Os of I70th Brigade.


                  8. PRISONERS will be handed over to an Officer in charge of
* AND V.C. HOUSE  Roll Call Station at JAY POST, and who will arrange for
                  them to be sent to I70th Brigade HdQrs without delay.
COPY NO.

I. War Diary.     9. Secret Code to be used for these Operations - see
2. Brig.General.  Appendix I.
3. Brigade Major.
4. 57th Divn.
5. 57th Divl.Arty.
6. I70th Bde.     IO. ACKNOWLEDGE.
7. I72nd Bde.
8. O.C.Raid."A"
9. O.C.Raid."B"
                                              Lieut.Colonel, Bde Major,
                                                          GINTY.

SECRET.                                                          COPY NO. 1

GINTY   ORDER   No. 5

20th March, 1917.

| | | |
|---|---|---|
| Amendment to | I. | Ginty Order No.4 is amended as follows :- |
| Para.2 of | | |
| Operation Order | | The Infantry part of the Programme as regards |
| No.4. | | "A" Raid, which was partaking in the diversion, will |
| | | not now take place.   The Artillery Programme, |
| | | however, remains unaltered. |

                    2.   ACKNOWLEDGE.

Lieut.Colonel,
Brigade Major, GINTY.

COPY NO.  1.  War Diary.
  ,,      2.  Brigadier-General.
  ,,      3.  Brigade Major.
  ,,      4.  57th Division.
  ,,      5.  57th Divl. Artillery.
  ,,      6.  170th Brigade.
  ,,      7.  172nd Brigade.
  ,,      8.  O.C., Raid "A".
  ,,      9.  O.C., Raid "B".

SECRET.

## COMBINED ARTILLERY and INFANTRY PROGRAMME.

- 20 Mins Zero.  Infantry formed up ready.

- 3 Mins Zero.  "A" RAID.

  A. Intense 18 pr. barrage opens from Trenches of OWL and AN. (N.10.c.52.48) to junction of KID, IF, IS. (N.10.c.0.3) inclusive.  N.9.D.99.28.
  6" Hows. open on (a) LABIETTE. N.16.c.40.95.
  (b) CROSS ROADS at LES CLOCHERS, N.16.B.65.75. N.10.c.75.50.
  (c) DOLLS HOUSE, N.11.C.33.
  Heavy, Medium and Light T.M.Bs form box on flanks of point of entry.

  B. Infantry leave Trench at N.10.c.17.62.

- 1 Min. Zero.  18 pr. barrage lifts to the line KIT, DOG, COW, turning corners of the barrage back on IF, KID, KIT, and CALF, OWL.
  6" Hows. and Trench Mortars continue as above.

- Zero.  "A" RAID.

  A. Artillery as above.

  B. Infantry 1st, 2nd, 3rd Parties enter enemy's front line between N.10.c.25.30 and N.10.c.37.33.

- Zero.  "B" RAID.

  A. Intense 18 pr. barrage opens from the ANGLE to BRIDOUX FORT.
  4.5 Hows. (1) THE ANGLE.
  (2) ,,
  (3) BOLTON CASTLE.
  (4) ,,
  (5) JUNCTION OF FOP, FOR, FARM.
  (6) ,, FIFE, FAME, FALL.
  (7) ,, FONT, FULL, FERN.
  (8) ,, FLEA, FOP, FOG.
  (9) ,, FEUD, FALL, FADE.
  (10) ,, FED, FOIL.
  (11) ~~FISH.~~
  (12) ~~FEUD.~~

  MAP REFERENCE.
  RED CIRCLES.

  6" Hows. (1) BOLTON CASTLE. O.I.A.20.5.3.
  (2) ,, O.I.A.30.60.
  (3) BRIDOUX FORT. I.31.D.00.22.
  (4) JUNCTION OF FIZZ, FIX, FOR.
  (5) CORNER FORT, N.6.D.40.95.
  60 prs. Counter BATTERY.
  M.T.Ms. will act as (a) a diversion on the left of BRIDOUX FORT; (b) Cutting wire experimentally by night without previous registration for future operations.
  L.T.Ms. engaging enemy's Machine Guns should the opportunity arise or any diversion he may create.

  B. Infantry 1st Party leaves Sally Port for DES DAMPS.
  OBJECTIVE - ENEMY'S FRONT LINE.

Zero + ½ Min.   A. Artillery as above.

B. Infantry 2nd Party leaves Sally Port for DES DAMP.
OBJECTIVE - BLOCK at DEAL.

Zero + 1 Min.   A. 18 prs. and 4.5 Hows. as above.
6" Hows. (1) JUNCTION OF FLAY, FIT, FEEL.
         (2)      ,,       FAWN, FADE, FONT.

B. Infantry 3rd Party leaves Sally Port for DES DAMP.
OBJECTIVE - BLOCK at BREUX.

Zero + 1½ Mins.  A. Artillery continues as above.

B. Infantry 4th Party leaves Sally Port for DES DAMP.
OBJECTIVE - BLOCK 30 yards down FIFE.

Zero + 2 Mins.  A. Artillery continues as above.

B. Infantry 5th Party leaves Sally Port for DES DAMP.
OBJECTIVE - BOLTON CASTLE.

Zero + 4 Mins.  A. 18 prs. lift to BLUE LINE, i.e., FARM, ~~FLY~~ FRY, FALL, FISH
Map Ref.,       FUN, FULL.   Sides of box turned back on FEUD and ~~FIRM~~.
BLUE CIRCLES.   4.5 Hows. (3) FALL.
                          (4) FOP.
Remainder as above.
6" Hows. as above.

Zero + 5 Mins.  A. Artillery as above.

B. Infantry 1st Party enters enemy's Front Line at E.
of FEW.

Zero + 5½ Mins. A. Artillery as above.

B. Infantry 2nd, 3rd and 4th Parties enter enemy's
Front Line.

Zero + 6 Mins.  A. Artillery as above.

B. Infantry 5th Party crosses enemy's Front Line and
advances on BOLTON CASTLE.

Zero + 8 Mins.  "A" RAID.

A. Artillery continues as at ZERO.

B. Infantry withdraw if they have not already done so.


"B" RAID.

A. Artillery as above.

B. Infantry 5th Party enters BOLTON CASTLE.

Zero + 18 Mins. "A" RAID.

A. Artillery ceases fire.

B. Infantry back in Trenches.

3.

Zero + 18 Mins.   "B" RAID.

                      A. Artillery continues.

                      B. 5th Party withdraws (if they have not already done so) under cover of barrage.

Zero + 30 Mins.   A. Artillery ceases fire.

                      B. Infantry back in own Trenches.

Lieut.Colonel,
Brigade Major.
GINTY.

ISSUED WITH 171st BRIGADE ORDER NO.4.　　II.　　T I M E　　T A B L E.　　March, 1917.

| TIME. | INFANTRY. | ARTILLERY. | M.Gs. | H., M., & L., T.M.Bs. |
|---|---|---|---|---|
| | | Nil. | Nil. | Nil. |
| MINUS 20 Mins. | "A" & "B" Raiding Parties formed up in Trench. | | | |
| MINUS 5 Mins. | "A" Raid leaves Trench & advances towards enemy's Lines. | "A" Raid, Phase One commences; Lines of fire shown on special map. | "A" Raid, Phase One commences. Flanks covered & enemy's communications barraged by indirect fire. | Phase One commences; Barrage along such portions of enemy's front line on front of attack as are not under Artillery fire. |
| ZERO. | "A" Raid. Infantry enters enemy's front line. | Bombardment lifts to Phase Two. See special map. | - do - | - do - |
| PLUS ½ Min. | "B" Raid. 1st Party leaves Trench & advances towards enemy's front line. | "B" Raid, Phase One commences. Lines of fire shown on special map. | "B" Raid, Phase as above, commences. | "B" Raid, Phase as above commences. |
| PLUS 1 Min. | "B" Raid. 2nd Party leaves Trench & advances towards enemy's front line. | - do,- except 6" Hows. (1) (2) lift to Phase Two. | - do - | - do - |
| PLUS 1½ Mins. | "B" Raid. 3rd Party leaves Trench & advances towards enemy's front line. | - do - | - do - | - do - |
| PLUS 2 Mins. | "B" Raid. 4th Party leaves Trench & advances towards enemy's front line. | - do - | - do - | - do - |
| PLUS 2 Mins. | "B" Raid. 5th Party leaves Trench & advances towards enemy's front line. | - do - | - do - | - do - |
| PLUS 4 Mins. | "B" Raid. Infantry continue as above. | 1B pre. bombardment lifts to BLUE LINE, 2nd Phase. 4.5" Hows. (3) FAIL, 2nd Phase. (4) FOB. Remainder as above. | - do - | - do - |

2.

| TIME. | INFANTRY. | ARTILLERY. | M.Gs. | H., M., & L., T.M.Bs |
|---|---|---|---|---|
| PLUS 5 Mins. | "B" Raid. Infantry 1st Party enters enemy's front line. | As above. | As above. | As above. |
| PLUS 5½ Mins. | "B" Raid. 2nd, 3rd, 4th Parties enter enemy's front line. | - do - | - do - | - do - |
| PLUS 6 Mins. | "B" Raid. 5th Party crosses enemy's front line & advances on BOLTON CASTLE. | - do - | - do - | - do - |
| PLUS 8 Mins. | "A" Raid. Infantry withdraw if they have not already done so. "B" Raid. 5th Party enters BOLTON CASTLE. | | | |
| PLUS 15 Mins. | "A" Raid. Infantry back in Trenches. "B" Raid. 5th Party withdraws if they have not already done so, under cover of barrage. | "A". Artillery cease fire. "B". Artillery continues. | "A". Cease fire. "B". Continues. | "A". Cease fire. "B". Continues. |
| PLUS 30 Mins. | Infantry back in our own Trenches. | Cease Fire. | Cease Fire. | Cease Fire |

SECRET.

B. C. D. E. F. G. H. I. J. K.,          1, 2, 3, 4, 5, 6, 7, 8, 9, 0

    CIGAR.                First Line Captured.
    CIGARETTE.            BOLTON CASTLE Captured.
    WHO.                  Prisoner.
    WILL.                 Machine Gun.
    WHAT.                 Enemy Killed.
    BIT.                  All Parties have Returned.
    BAT.                  Slight Casualties.
    BIFF.                 Fairly Heavy Casualties.
    ~~BUZZ~~. BANK         Heavy Casualties.
    KIT.                  Killed.
    KICK.                 Wounded.
    KID.                  Missing.
    DIM.                  Cease Fire.
    DAMN.                 Continue your Fire.
    DIMPLE.               Heavy Enemy Fire.
    DIP.                  Enemy Fire not Heavy.
    DONE.                 All Quiet.
    QUICK.                Enemy Counter-Attacking.
    QUIET.                Raiding Party are clear of Communication Trenches.
    QUIT.                 Enemy awaiting attack and Raid abandoned.

COPY NO. 3

2/7th K.L.R., ORDER.

March, 1917

| | |
|---|---|
| Map Reference. | France. Sheet 36 S.W.2., & 36 S.W.I. I:10000.<br>Special Sun-Print. I:2500.<br>Aeroplane Photographs. |
| Intention. | 1. On Z date at Zero hour a party of the Battalion will carry out a Raid on a portion of the enemy's trenches - front line and supporting strong point. |
| Object. | 2. (a) Killing and capturing as many of the enemy as possible.<br>(b) Capturing and destroying material.<br>(c) Destroying Dugouts and Machine Gun Emplacements.<br>(d) Gaining information regarding enemy's system of defence. |
| Organisation. | 3. O.C., Raid, Captain Dorning.<br>3 Officers and 78 Other Ranks. |
| Support. | 4. 170th Brigade in the Line will act as supports. |
| Place of Assembly. | 5. Troops will assemble in our Front Line Trench at N.10.C.18.65.<br>Points of Assembly will be marked by signboards. |
| Formation. | 6. Parties will advance in column formation with intervals between columns. |
| Objective. | 7. The enemy's front line extending between the area O.A.2.7 to O.A.5.7, to a depth of 120 yards.<br>1st Party cuts wire; bridges and lays mats over wire if necessary at E of FEW.<br>2nd, 3rd and 4th Parties enter enemy's front line simultaneously:-<br>2nd Party forming block at junction of DEAL and FRONT LINE.<br>3rd ,, ,, ,, ,, ,, BREUX ,,<br>4th Party block 30 yds down FIFE.<br>5th Party (A) Party mops up front line Trench, while<br>(B) ,, assault party passes through and clears up Bolton Castle. |
| Line of Action. | 8. Artillery and M.T.Ms will cut the enemy's wire along the front to be raided prior to the date of operations. Ours will be cut the night of the operations. |
| Minus 15 Mins. | The Raiding Party will be formed up with arrangements complete, in our front line at O.I.I. |
| Minus 5 Mins. | A diversion, representing a minor raid, will be made at N.10.2 by artillery, Light T.M.Bs, and the explosion of a mine. |
| ZERO. | Artillery and T.M.Bs will bombard the enemy's front line and supports.<br><br>The 1st Party of the Infantry leave for DES DAMPS. |
| Plus ½ Min. | The 2nd ,, ,, ,, ,, |
| Plus 1 Min. | The 3rd ,, ,, ,, ,, |
| Plus 1½ Mins. | The 4th ,, ,, ,, ,, |
| Plus 2 Mins. | The 5th ,, ,, ,, ,, |
| Plus 4 Mins. | Bombardment on Sector lifts. |
| Plus 5 Mins. | 1st Party of Infantry enters the enemy's front line. |
| Plus 5½ Mins. | 2nd, 3rd, and 4th Parties enter the enemy's front line. |

2.

| | | |
|---|---|---|
| Plus 6 Mins. | | The 5th Party crosses enemy's front line and advances on BOLTON CASTLE. |
| Plus 8 Mins. | | The 5th Party enters BOLTON CASTLE. |
| Plus 18 Mins. | | Unless already withdrawn, the 5th Party will withdraw. |
| Plus 30 Mins. | | Bombardment ceases, unless otherwise ordered. Infantry back in our front line. |
| Withdrawal. | 9. | On completion of their task, B.Assault Party, by a prearranged signal between Os.C., will withdraw from BOLTON CASTLE and retire through 2nd, 3rd and 4th and A Assault Parties. As soon as they have got 50 yds into No Man's Land, the remainder will withdraw from enemy's front line. |
| Roll Call. | 10. | Roll Call Station will be established at JAY POST. Each member of the Raiding party will be provided with a luggage label bearing his number and name, to be tied round his neck On returning to our trenches all ranks will at once proceed to the Roll Call Station, hand in labels, and proceed to Billets. There must be no loitering in the front line or at Roll Call Station. |
| Casualties. | 11. | Any killed or wounded must be brought back. The M.O. detailed by G.O.C., 170th Brigade will make arrangements for the evacuation of wounded from our front line to Aid Post at JAY POST. |
| Prisoners. | 12. | Prisoners will be handed ober to Officer i/c Roll Call Station, who will arrange for them to be sent under escort to Brigade HdQrs without delay. |
| Material. | 13. | Captured Material will be handed in to O.C. Operations at JAY POST immediately on return. |
| Dress. | 14. | All ranks will be as lightly equipped as possible. Service Dress; Steel Helmets; Waistcoats; Small Box Respirators; will be worn by all ranks. Equipment to be worn by those who will be detailed for various duties is set out in a ttached table. No official or private correspondence - maps - papers, etc. - to be carried. All watches will be synchronised at on Z day. But Zero will also be the hour of the 1st Gun going off also. |
| Reports. | 15. | All reports will be sent to O.C. Operations at Signal Station, H.P.25, in Trench O.I.I, until return of Raid Parties; and thereafter to JAY POST. Officer i/c Roll Call will report to 170th Brigade HdQrs as soon as Roll Call is completed. |
| | NOTE. | Every man must know his job thoroughly, and that of every other Officer, N.C.O. Leader and man. |

H Drakeford
Capt. & Adjutant.
2/7th K.L.R.,

COPY NO. 1. File.
 ,, 2. O.C.Raid.
 ,, 3. 171st Brigade HdQrs.
 ,, 4. 57th Division.
 ,, 5. 57th Divl. Artillery.
 ,, 6. 170th Brigade.

| Unit | Party | Forming-Up Position indicated by Numbered Boards | Time to leave Sally Port | Officers | N.C.Os or Leaders | Demolition Men | Runners | Bombers | Bayonet Men | Rifle Grenade-Men | Moppers-Up | Carriers | Lewis Gunners | Telephonists | Stretcher Bearers | Bridgemen | Matmen | Scouts Wirecutters | Guard on Prisoners and Loot | OBJECTIVE | JOB | REMARKS |
|---|---|---|---|---|---|---|---|---|---|---|---|---|---|---|---|---|---|---|---|---|---|---|
| 2/7th Battalion, K.L.R. | 1 | 1 | Z | 1 | | | | | | | | | | | | 6 | 3 | 4 | | E. of FEW. | LAY BRIDGES, PLACE MATS, CUT WIRE. | |
| | 2 | 2 | Z + 1½" | | 2 | | 1 | 2 | 2 | 1 | | 1 | | | | | | | | DEAL. | CLEAR FRONT LINE FROM FILL TO DEAL & ESTABLISH A BLOCK WHERE DEAL JOINS FRONT LINE. | |
| | 3 | 3 | Z + 1" | | 2 | | 1 | 2 | 2 | 1 | | 1 | | | | | | | | BREUK. | CLEAR FRONT LINE FROM FIB TO WHERE BREUX CUTS FRONT LINE AND ESTABLISH A BLOCK. | |
| | 4 | 4 | Z + 1½" | | 2 | 2 | 1 | 3 | 3 | 1 | | | | | | | | | | FIFE. | CLEAR FIFE FOR 30 yds & ESTABLISH A BLOCK. | |
| | 5 | 5 | Z + 2" | 1 | | | | | | | | | | 2 | 4 | | | | | E. of FEW. | ESTABLISH COMMUNIC. WITH OUR FRONT LINE. FORM HdQrs OF ASSAULT PARTY. LAY OUT WHITE TAPE. | THIS PARTY FORMS UP UNDER COVER OF FRONT FACE ENEMY'S FRONT LINE. |

( 2 )

| UNIT | Party | Forming-Up Position indicated by Numbered Boards. | Time to Leave Sally Port. | Officers. | N.C.Os or Leaders. | Demolition Men. | Runners. | Bombers. | Bayonet Men. | Rifle Grenade-Men. | Moppers-Up. | Carriers. | Lewis Gunners. | Telephonists. | Stretcher Bearers. | Bridgemen. | Matmen. | Scouts; Wirecutters. | Guard on Prisoners and Loot. | OBJECTIVE. | JOB. | REMARKS. |
|---|---|---|---|---|---|---|---|---|---|---|---|---|---|---|---|---|---|---|---|---|---|---|
| 2/7th Battalion, K.L.R., | 5 (CONTINUED) | | | | | | 2 | | | | | | | | | | | | 4 | | TO TAKE CHARGE OF PRISONERS AND LOOT. | JOIN FROM 1ST PARTY BRIDGEMEN. |
| | | | | | | | | | | | | | | | 4 | | | | | | | JOIN FROM SCOUTS. |
| | | | | | 1 | 2 | | 2 | 2 | | | | | | | | | | | FRONT LINE. | CLEAR FRONT LINE. | 3 MATMEN OF 1ST PARTY JOIN IN AT E. of FEW, INCLUDED IN THIS PARTY, ONE BEING LEADER OF PARTY TO MOP UP FRONT LINE. THE OTHER 2 BAYONET MEN. |
| | | | | 1 | | | | | | | | | | | | | | | | BOLTON CASTLE. | BOLTON CASTLE. CLEAR RIGHT HALF | JOINS FROM 1ST PARTY & LEADS ASSAULT PARTY. |
| | | | | | 1 | | 1 | 2 | 2 | 1 | | 1 | | | | | | | | do. | "BOLTON CASTLE" do. LEFT HALF. | GO OVERLAND. |
| | | | | | 1 | | 1 | 2 | 2 | 1 | | 1 | | | | | | | | (a) JUNCTION of COURANT DES DAMP. (b) BREUX DES DAMPS. | (a) GUARD RIGHT FLANK. (b) LEFT FLANK AGAINST ANY ACTION OF ENEMY. | do. |
| | | | | | | | | | | | | | 8 | | | | | | | | | 2 Guns. |

| EQUIPMENT. | Revolvers. | Mills Bombs. | .450 Ammunition. | Torch. | Bomb Waistcoat. | Rifle. | Bayonet. | S.A.A., | Wire Cutters. | No.23 Rifle Grenade. | Rifle Grenade Cup. | Cartridges, Rifle Grenades. | White Tape. | Stokes Shell. | Dynamite Charge. | REMARKS. |
|---|---|---|---|---|---|---|---|---|---|---|---|---|---|---|---|---|
| OFFICERS. 2 |  | 8 |  | 2 |  |  |  |  |  |  |  |  |  |  |  |  |
| N.C.Os. 8 | 8 | 32 | 48 | 8 |  |  |  |  |  |  |  |  |  |  |  |  |
| DEMOLITION MEN. 4 | 4 | 16 | 192 |  |  |  |  |  |  |  |  |  |  | 8 | 8 |  |
| RUNNERS. 6 | 6 | 12 | 48 |  |  |  |  |  |  |  |  |  |  |  |  |  |
| BRIDGEMEN. 6 | 6 | 24 | 72 |  |  |  |  |  |  |  |  |  |  |  |  |  |
| MATMEN. 3 |  | 12 | 72 |  |  | 3 | 3 |  |  |  |  |  |  |  |  |  |
| BOMBERS. 13 |  | 130 |  | 3 | 13 |  |  |  |  |  |  |  |  |  |  |  |
| BAYONET MEN. 11 |  | 44 |  | 11 |  | 11 | 11 | 550 |  |  |  |  |  |  |  | Rifles and Bayonets with men at School – except Rifles for Rifle Grenades. |
| RIFLE GRENADE-MEN. 5 |  | 10 |  |  | 5 | 5 | 5 | 150 |  | 75 | 5 | 100 |  |  |  |  |
| CARRIERS. 4 |  | 80 | 96 |  | 4 |  |  |  |  |  |  |  |  |  |  |  |
| LEWIS GUNNERS. 8 | 6 | 32 |  |  |  |  |  |  |  |  |  |  |  |  |  |  |
| TELEPHONISTS. 2 | 2 | 4 | 24 | 2 |  |  |  |  |  |  |  |  |  |  |  |  |
| STRETCHER BEARERS. 4 | 4 | 16 | 48 |  |  |  |  |  |  |  |  |  |  |  |  |  |
| SCOUTS. 4 | 4 | 16 | 96 | 4 |  |  |  |  | 4 |  |  |  | 1000 yds |  |  |  |
| TOTALS. OFFICERS, 2; O.RANKS 78 | 40 | 436 | 696 | 30 | 22 | 19 | 19 | 700 | 4 | 75 | 5 | 100 | 1000 | 8 | 8 |  |

COPY NO. 3

"A" RAID.

2/8th K.L.R., ORDER NO. I.

March, 1917.

| | |
|---|---|
| Map Reference. | France, Sheet 36 S.W.I & 2. I:I0000.<br>Special Sun-Print, I:2500.<br>Aeroplane Photographs. |
| Intention. | I. On Z date at - 3 mins. Zero, a party of the Battalion will carry out a Minor Raid on a portion of the Enemy's Trenches, acting as a diversion to a larger Raid. |
| Object. | 2. (a) Killing and capturing as many of the enemy as possible.<br>(b) Capturing and destroying material.<br>(c) Destroying Dugouts and Machine Gun Emplacements.<br>(d) Gaining information regarding enemy's system of defence. |
| Organisation. | 3. O.C., Raid, Lieut. Tiplady.<br>I Officer and 22 Other Ranks. |
| Supports. | 4. I70th Brigade will act as Supports. |
| Place of Assembly. | 5. N.IO.C.I5.62. |
| Formation. | 6. Column formation, with intervals between columns. |
| Objective. | 7. The enemy's Front Line, extending between the area N.IO.C.26.3 and N.IO.C.36.32.<br>Ist, 2nd, 3rd, enters simultaneously.<br>Ist Party mops up Front Line.<br>2nd Party establishes a Block at Junction of ANT and FRONT LINE.<br>3rd Party establishes a Block at Junction of OR and FRONT LINE. |
| Line of Action. | 8. (i) M.T.Ms will cut the enemy's wire along the Front to be raided prior to the date of operations.<br>(ii) Zero - 20 Mins. the Raiding Party will be formed up in our Front Line with arrangements complete. |
| Zero - 3 Mins. | (iii) The Artillery bombardment commences; our Raiding Parties leave our Front Line Trench. |
| Zero. | (iv) "B" Raid commences. Our Ist, 2nd and 3rd Parties enter enemy's Trench. |
| Plus 8 Mins. | (v) Our Raiding Party withdraws. |
| Plus I8 Mins. | (vi) Our Raiding Party back in their Trenches, and Artillery bombardment ceases. |
| Roll Call. | 9. Roll Call Station will be established at V.C.HOUSE<br>Each member of the Raiding Party will be provided with a luggage label, bearing his number and name, and tied round his neck.<br>On returning to our Trenches, all ranks will at once proceed to the Roll Call Station, hand in his label, and proceed to Billets.<br>There must be no loitering in the Front Line or at Roll Call Station. |
| Casualties. | IO. Any killed or wounded must be brought back.<br>The M.O. detailed by G.O.C. I70th Brigade will make arrangements for evacuation of our wounded from our front line, and establish Advanced Dressing Station at V.C.HOUSE. |
| Prisoners. | II. Will be handed over to Officer i/c Roll Call Station, who will arrange for them to be sent under escort, vide the Orders of G.O.C. I70th Brigade. |

2.

**Material.**

12. Captured Material will be handed in to O.C. Raid at V.C.HOUSE immediately on return.

**Dress.**

13. All ranks will be as lightly equipped as possible. Service Dress; Steel Helmets; Waistcoats; Small Box Respirators; will be worn by all ranks.
Equipment to be worn by those who will be detailed for various duties is set out in attached table.
No official or private correspondence - maps - papers, etc., - to be carried.
All watches will be synchronised at          on Z day.    Zero will also be the hour of the 1st gun going off.

**Reports.**

14. All reports will be sent to O.C. Operations at          until return of Raid Parties, and thereafter to Roll Call Station at V.C.HOUSE.
Officer i/c Roll Call Station will report to 170th Brigade HdQrs as soon as Roll Call is completed.

NOTE.  Every man must know his job thoroughly, and that of every other Officer, N.C.O. and man.

Route to be followed to and from Front Line to V.C.House, via PINNEY'S AVEN., SUPPORT LINE, and V.C.AVEN.

                    Lieut.
              O.C. "B" RAID.
             2/8th Bn. K.L.R.,

COPY NO. 1. File.
" 2. O.C. Raid.
" 3. 171st Brigade.
" 4. 57th Division.
" 5. 57th Divl. Artillery.
" 6. 170th Brigade.

# ORGANISATION.    "A" RAID.

| Unit. | Party. | Time to leave Sally Port. | Officers. | N.C.Os or Leaders. | Runners. | Bombers. | Bayonet Men. | Rifle Grenadiers | Carriers. | Scouts. Wirecutters. | OBJECTIVE. | JOB. | REMARKS. |
|---|---|---|---|---|---|---|---|---|---|---|---|---|---|
| 2/8th Battalion, K.L.R. | 1 | Z. | 1 | 1 | 1 | 2 | 2 | | | 2 | AT. | Clear FRONT LINE from JUNCTION (a) IS, AT, ANT. to (b) AT, AN, OR. | |
| | 2 | Z. | | 1 | | 2 | 2 | 1 | 1 | | JUNCTION of IS, AT, ANT. | Establish a BLOCK at IS, ANT, AT. | |
| | 3 | Z. | | 1 | | 2 | 2 | 1 | 1 | | JUNCTION of AT, OR, AN. | Establish a BLOCK at AT, OR, AN. | |

OBJECTIVES

| EQUIPMENT. "A" RAID. | | Revolvers. | Mills Bombs. | .450 Ammunition. | Torch. | Bomb Waistcoat. | Rifles. | Bayonets. | S.A.A. | Wire Cutters. | No.23 Rifle Grenades. | Rifle Grenade Cup. | Cartridges, Rifle Grenade. | REMARKS. |
|---|---|---|---|---|---|---|---|---|---|---|---|---|---|---|
| OFFICERS. | 2 | | | | | | | | | | | | | |
| N.C.Os or LEADERS. | 3 | 2 | 12 | 48 | | | 3 | 3 | 150 | | | | | |
| RUNNERS. | 2 | 2 | 4 | 24 | | | | | | | | | | |
| BAYONET MEN. | 6 | | 24 | | 6 | 6 | 6 | 6 | 300 | | | | | RIFLES AND BAYONETS WITH MEN AT SCHOOL – EXCEPT RIFLES FOR RIFLE GRENADIERS. |
| BOMBERS. | 6 | | 60 | 48 | | | | | | | | | | |
| SCOUTS. | 2 | 2 | 8 | | | 2 | | | | | | | | |
| RIFLE GRENADIERS. | 2 | 4 | | | | 2 | 2 | 2 | | 2 | 30 | 2 | 40 | |
| CARRIERS. | 2 | | 40 | | | | | | | | | | | |
| TOTALS. Off. 2; O.R.23. | 25 | 8 | 152 | 120 | 6 | 10 | 11 | 11 | 450 | 2 | 30 | 2 | 40 | |

| EQUIPMENT. | Revolver. | Mills Bombs. | .450 Ammunition. | Watch. | Whistle. | Torch. | Bomb Waistcoat. | Rifle. | Bayonet. | S.A.A. | Wire Cutters. | No.23 Rifle Grenades. | Rifle Grenade Cup. | Cartridges, Rifle grenade. | White Tape. | Slabs. Guncotton. | Primers. | Knobkerry. | REMARKS. |
|---|---|---|---|---|---|---|---|---|---|---|---|---|---|---|---|---|---|---|---|
| OFFICERS. | 1 | 4 | 24 | 1 | 1 | 1 | | | | | | | | | | | | | ALL RANKS - SERVICE DRESS JACKET & TROUSERS. NO BADGES OR CHEVRONS. |
| N.C.Os LEADERS. | 1 | 4 | 24 | 1 | 1 | 1 | 1 | | | | | | | | | | | 1 | PUTTEES - STEEL HELMET - WAIST - COAT - BOX RESPIRATOR - |
| BOMBERS. | | 10 | | | | | | | | | | | | | | | | | WHITE STREAMERS - FACES ALL RANKS BLACKED. |
| BAYONET MEN. | | 4 | | | | 1 | 1 | 1 | 1 | 50 | 1 | | | | | | | 1 | |
| CARRIERS. | | 20 | | 1 | | | | | | | | | | | | | | | |
| SCOUTS. | 1 | 4 | 24 | 1 | | | | | | | | | | | | | | | OFFICERS - ONE STAR. |
| RUNNERS. | 1 | 2 | 12 | | | | | | | | | | | | | | | | N.C.Os & LEADERS - ONE STRIPE. |
| SIGNALLERS. | 1 | 2 | 12 | | | | | | | | | | | | 500 yds | | | | |
| STRETCHER BEARERS. | 1 | 4 | 12 | | | | | | | | | | | | | | | | |
| RIFLE GRENADIER. | 1 | 2 | | | | 1 | 1 | 1 | 1 | 50 | | 15 | 1 | 20 | | | | | |
| BRIDGE MEN. | 1 | 4 | 12 | | | | | | | | | | | | | | | | |
| MAT MEN. | | 4 | | | | | | | | | | | | | | | | | |
| DEMOLITION MEN. | 1 | 4 | 12 | | | | | 1 | 1 | | | | | | | 1 | 1 | | |
| LEWIS GUNNER. | 1 | 4 | 12 | | | | | | | | | | | | | | | | 1 LEWIS GUN - EACH LEWIS GUNNER 2 MAGAZINES FILLED |

SECRET.

O.C.,
    MASTER.

........

With reference to a minor enterprise which is to be carried out by this Brigade on the Sector held by the Brigade under your Command;  as it is highly probable that this Brigade may be on another Sector of the Line when this matter takes place, I shall be unable to render the necessary assistance.

I would be much obliged if you could help in this matter, under the paras. enumerated below, and as orders regarding date, time, etc., of this enterprise will not be issued until a few hours before it takes place, that matters may be so arranged that the shortest of notice will ensure their through execution.

(a) That one of the M.Os i/c Battalions makes the necessary arrangements for the evacuation of wounded from the Front Line at a point OI.I approximately to Regimental Aid Posts at JAYPOST; route to be followed - from FRONT LINE via ABBOTS LANE, and from there by arrangement with the Field Ambulance.

(b) That a certain amount of activity in the use of periscopes be made daily in future on the Sector N.IO.I to N.IO.4 inclusive.

(c) That with your approval a diversion is proposed in the Sector N.IO.2, in which it is requested that the Light T.M.Bs of this Brigade, now under your command, will participate, together with artillery and the exploding of a charge by the R.E.,

(d) That you will render the necessary support to the enterprise should the Hun attempt a counter-attack, and that should a favourable opportunity present itself, the Light T.M.Bs and Machine Guns of your Brigade engage the Hun Machine Guns.

                                    Brigadier-General,
                                    Commanding GINTY.

B.H.Q.
    14th March, 1917

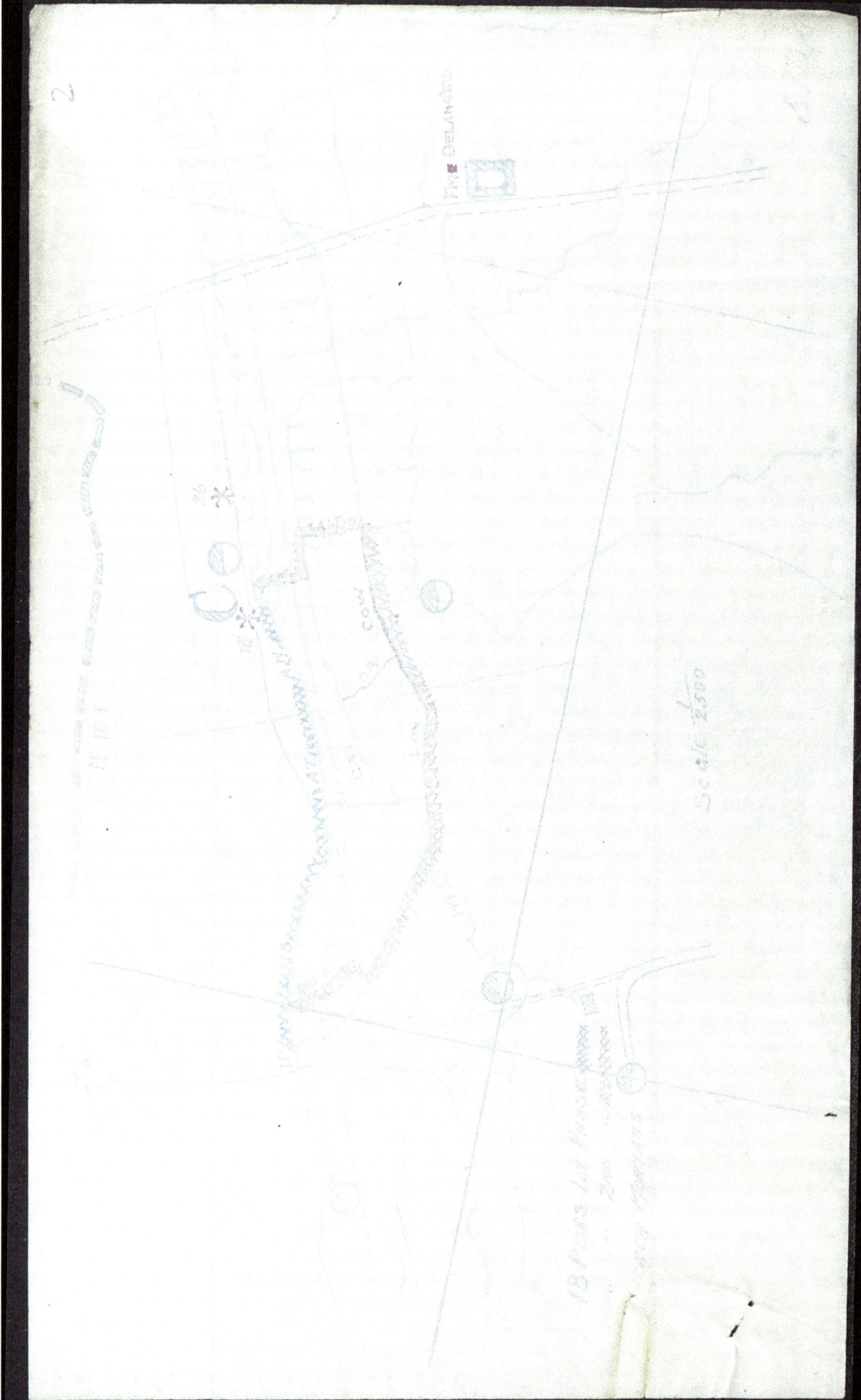

APPENDIX No. II.

STATEMENT of CASUALTIES.

.....

Forwarded in conjunction
with

171st INFANTRY BRIGADE WAR DIARY,

13.2.1917 to 30.3.1917

....

## 171st INFANTRY BRIGADE.

### CASUALTIES up to 30th MARCH, 1917.

| DATE. 24 hours ending noon :- | KILLED. Officers. | KILLED. O.Ranks. | WOUNDED. Officers. | WOUNDED. O.Ranks. | WOUNDED (ACCIDENTALLY) Officers. | WOUNDED (ACCIDENTALLY) O.Ranks. |
|---|---|---|---|---|---|---|
| 22.2.1917. | - | 1 | - | 2 | - | 1 |
| 24.2.1917. | - | - | - | 1 | - | 1 |
| 25.2.1917. | - | - | - | - | - | - |
| 26.2.1917. | - | 3 | - | 3 | - | - |
| 27.2.1917. | - | - | - | 3 | - | - |
| 28.2.1917. | - | 2 | - | - | - | 1 |
| 1.3.1917. | - | - | - | 4 | - | 2 |
| 2.3.1917. | - | 3 | - | 3 | - | - |
| 3.3.1917. | - | - | - | 5 | - | 1 |
| 4.3.1917. | - | - | - | 2 | - | - |
| 6.3.1917. | - | - | - | - | - | - |
| 7.3.1917. | - | - | - | 2 | - | 1 |
| 8.3.1917. | - | - | - | - | - | - |
| 10.3.1917. | - | - | - | - | - | - |
| 21.3.1917. | - | - | - | - | - | 1 |
| 22.3.1917. | - | - | - | 1 | - | 2 |
| 23.3.1917. | - | 3 | - | - | - | 2 |
| 29.3.1917. | 1 | 1 | - | 1 | - | 1 |
| 30.3.1917. | - | - | - | 2 | - | - |
| TOTAL. | 1 | 13 | - | 27 | - | 9 |

Lieut. C.N. Hudson, 2/5th Liverpool Regt., Killed after noon on 29.3.1917.
Includes one Wounded – Self-Inflicted, 173nd Machine Gun Co.

B.H.Q.
30.3.1917

Vol. 3.

Headquarters
171st Inf. Bde.
(57th Div.)
April 1917

On His Majesty's Service.

CONFIDENTIAL.

WAR DIARY

of

HEADQUARTERS, 171st INFANTRY BRIGADE.

31.3.1917 to 30.4.1917.

VOLUME II.

Army Form C. 2118

# WAR DIARY
## or
## INTELLIGENCE SUMMARY
*(Erase heading not required.)*

Instructions regarding War Diaries and Intelligence Summaries are contained in F. S. Regs., Part II. and the Staff Manual respectively. Title Pages will be prepared in manuscript.

| Place | Date | Hour | Summary of Events and Information | Remarks and references to Appendices |
|---|---|---|---|---|
| BOIS GRENIER RUE DU BOIS SECTOR | MARCH 31st | | Quiet day on the whole of the Brigade Sector. Occasional bursts of artillery fire from Huns. Usual French to German difficulty in patrolling owing to moon. | |
| | April 1st | | Another quiet day with only slight enemy artillery activity. Heavy snow all night. | |
| | 2nd | | Quiet except in the morning when Huns Lewis's [barked?] to a Coy. to be taking but has moved his night before. Snow continued till 11.0 a.m. when thaw set in. Patrolling & Lewis's informed same to Huns 4 [guns?]. | |
| | 3rd | | Quiet normal conditions — only very slight artillery activity. | |
| | 4th 5th 6th | | Quiet normal conditions. Quiet normal conditions. 2/8 K.L.R relieved 2/5. K.L.R without any interruption in BOIS GRENIER (R. Left In.) in accordance with Relief Order No. H. 2/5. K.L.R. going into Right Reserve Battalion. | Appendix I |
| | 6th | 10.0 | Brigadier General BRAY D.S.O. reported to take over command of Brigade from General Gilbert D.S.O. Normal day in trenches. Inspected 2/7. K.L.R. relieved 2/6 K.L.R. in RUE DUBOIS Sector. | Appendix I |
| | 7th | | General Bray took over command from Gen Gilbert proceeding home. Normal conditions. | |
| | 8th | | Normal conditions. | |

Army Form C. 2118

# WAR DIARY
or
# INTELLIGENCE SUMMARY
(Erase heading not required.)

Instructions regarding War Diaries and Intelligence Summaries are contained in F. S. Regs., Part II. and the Staff Manual respectively. Title Pages will be prepared in manuscript.

| Place | Date | Hour | Summary of Events and Information | Remarks and references to Appendices |
|---|---|---|---|---|
| BOIS GRENIER RUE-DU-BOIS Sector | 9th | | Normal condition - Heavy fall of snow | |
| | 10th | 10.25 pm | Normal condition - 172nd Bn. made a raid from BOIS GRENIER Sector - unsuccessful - 2/5. K.L.R. giving support. | Appendix I |
| | | 9.0 | Order No 7 - for relief by 172nd Bn. issued. to all concerned. | |
| | 11th | | Normal condition rather incessant artillery activity throughout. Hun trench dn. Gun of relative | |
| | | | situation in which a movement in subsidiary line | |
| | 12th | 5.30 pm | 2/5 K.L.R. relieved by 2/6 K.L.R. in right reserve. 2/5 K.L.R. moved into billets at BAC-ST-MAUR | |
| | | | 2/8 K.L.R. relieved by 2/10 K.L.R. in front line & BOIS GRENIER Sector. Relief completed without an | |
| | | 9.0 | incident - Normal condition | |
| | 13th | 3 pm | Normal condition - 2/6 K.L.R. relieved in left reserve by 2/5 S.L.R. - Relief of 2/7 K.L.R. by | |
| | | | 2/4 S.L.R. without incident. | |
| | 14th | 8.30 am | Continuous fours & sleet by 172nd Bn. completed without incident - Batln billeted between | |
| | | 2.20 | 2/5. K.L.R. BAC-ST-MAUR. 2/7. K.L.R. - The Channing | |
| | 15th | | 2/6. K.L.R. RUE-DORMOIRE 2/8. K.L.R. ERQUINGHEM. | |
| | | | The Brigadier received forward surplus push. awaiting practical, and when latter | |
| | | | has arrived | |

Army Form C. 2118

# WAR DIARY
or
# INTELLIGENCE SUMMARY
(Erase heading not required.)

Instructions regarding War Diaries and Intelligence Summaries are contained in F.S. Regs., Part II. and the Staff Manual respectively. Title Pages will be prepared in manuscript.

| Place | Date | Hour | Summary of Events and Information | Remarks and references to Appendices |
|---|---|---|---|---|
| ERQUINGHEM | April 16th | | Brigade furnished holding batts. as usual. 2/5 K.L.R. (½ Batt.) went under a Gas demonstration. Brigadier visited Transport Lines. | |
| | 17th | 1.0.a.m | A raid by 7th K.L.R. consisting of 3 Officers 68 O.R. succeeded at LA VÉSÉE - Bn. Hd. Qrs. now established at THE CHAPEL - Battn. Hd. Qrs. of the BOIS GRENIER Sector. | Appendix III |
| | | 3.20am | ½ hour artillery bombardment answered to terminate. | |
| | | 3.24am | Raid reported to have started successfully. Full details of Raid see Appendix. | |
| | | | Casualties 2 killed 9 wounded. | |
| | | 5.0 pm | Divisional Commander inspected Raiding party, and last draft of 2/7 K.L.R. Hd. Qn. Brigade furnishing holding batts. as usual - Gas demonstration for ½ Batt. 2/9 K.L.R. | |
| | 18th | 10.30 am | Conference of C.O's at Bde. Hd. Qrs. Brigadier visited Pailulé. 2/5 W.L.R. | |
| | | | Gas demonstration ½ Batt. 2/7 K.L.R. hd. at Battalion holding batts. as usual. Promotion ½ Batt. 2/9 K.L.R. Div. Commander present at Gas demonstration given to ½ Batt. | |
| | 19th | 11.0 a.m. | Brigadier visited 2/6 K.L.R. billets in afternoon. Battalion in holding batts - continued. | |
| | 20th. | | Orders received cancelling relief by 10th Brigade CORDONNERIE - BOUTILLERIE Sector - preliminary having to relieve 10th Australian Bde. in ARMENTIERES Sector. BRIGADIER & STAFF proceeded to 3rd Australian Bn. Hd. Qrs - & then to 10th A.I.B. Hd. Qn. to arrange about relief. Battalion continuing usual holding batts. w/11 Platoon per Batt. - Gas demonstration ½ Batt. 2/5 K.L.R. | APPENDIX I |

Army Form C. 2118

# WAR DIARY
## or
## INTELLIGENCE SUMMARY
*(Erase heading not required.)*

Instructions regarding War Diaries and Intelligence Summaries are contained in F.S. Regs., Part II. and the Staff Manual respectively. Title Pages will be prepared in manuscript.

| Place | Date | Hour | Summary of Events and Information | Remarks and references to Appendices |
|---|---|---|---|---|
| ERQUINGHEM | April 21st | | 57th Divn Order No. 8 - detailing relief of 10th A.I. Bde by 172nd I.B. received. Bn Major settled final arrangements. Relief at 10". A I B. 172nd Bde. Batn=Coy Commanders were met by guides & visited their relieves at HOUPLINES & EPINETTE. Brig General inspected billets of 2/8 K.L.R. | Appendix I |
| | | 3.0 A.m | Brigade Order No. 9 for relief of 10th A.I.B issued. Battalion continued in their holding posts - 2/6. K.L.R (3 Baths) given Gas demonstration. | Appendix I |
| | 22nd | | Brigadier - Brigade Major went on reconnaissance of his share of the ARMENTIERES sector, returning divne - 2/7 K.L.R Given Gas demonstration (3 Baths). Battn furnished working parties as usual - Officers reconnoitred EPINETTE & HOUPLINES sector. Brig=Major & Brigade Major reconnoitred EPINETTE sector. First southern line. | ? |
| | 23rd | | N.C.O's & Officers of Battns also reconnoitred their new sector. 2/5 & 2/8 K.L.R. furnished working parties to R.E. Brigadier, G.S.O. 1 Brig=Major made a reconnaissance of HOUPLINES sector. Officers & N.C.O's of Sector also - B.G.C. G.S.O.I B.M Major had round glance of ARMENTIERES. | ? |
| | 24th | | 2/5. K.L.R. & 172nd T.M.Y moved into billets in the right of ARMENTIERES 2/5 K.L.R relieved 37th Anzac Infantry in EPINETTE Sector 172nd L.T.M.B. - 10th A.I L.T.M.B. 2/7. K.L.R. relieved billets in ARMENTIERES as W Reserve Batn (with B.N Orders No. 9) | Appendix I |
| | 25th | | | ? |

1875 Wt. W593/826 1,000,000 4/15 J.B.C. & A. A.D.S.S./Forms/C. 2118.

Army Form C. 2118

# WAR DIARY
## or
## INTELLIGENCE SUMMARY
(Erase heading not required.)

Instructions regarding War Diaries and Intelligence Summaries are contained in F. S. Regs., Part II. and the Staff Manual respectively. Title Pages will be prepared in manuscript.

| Place | Date April | Hour | Summary of Events and Information | Remarks and references to Appendices |
|---|---|---|---|---|
| ARMENTIERES | 26th | 6.0 p.m. | Brigade command passes from 10th Australian Infantry Brigade, taking over American defences of HOUPLINES [SECTOR] - L'EPINETTE [SECTOR] | |
| | | | 2/1st K.L.R. relieves 87th A.I.Bn. in HOUPLINES Sector. | |
| | | | 2/8th K.L.R. winds relieves in Reserve Battalion Reserve. | |
| | 27th | 1.30 p.m. | Bombardment by enemy guns of ARMENTIERES an Right Battalion reserve. Inspection for his release of gas from his Boissak sector, in conjunction with that from his left or Instruction for his release of gas from his left on | |
| | | | 75th Brigade on LE TOUQUET Sector however which projector nine discharges — 173rd M.G. Coy. assists. Owing to unfavourable conditions the discharge of gas was postponed — by instruction from Special Coy. R.E. | |
| | | 11.30 p.m. | Quietness on front. Exceptionally quiet any & practical no action on the part of the enemy artillery | |
| | 28th | | Gas was discharged from his Brigade frontage in conjunction with the 75th Bde on left. | |
| | 29th | am 12.30. | who also confirm projection on FRELINGHEIM. under cover of which a patrol from his 9th Bn. Australian in party tried to enter his our private from to our by line & the flooded area at the RIVER LYS. It was intended to send out a patrol from his R.Cy Sector but on the sector shown by R.E. officer decided but to where gas as he considered horizons too slight — At 4.15 R.E. personnel rear-guards stored man by the 2/6 Mcht. R who succeeded in the attack. | Appendix III |
| | | | 6. Gas — No retaliation from his enemy receiving machine, which was wildly fired in a return amount of ordinary machine gun fire. Quiet day. Weather normal condition | |

# WAR DIARY
or
## INTELLIGENCE SUMMARY

Army Form C. 2118

| Place | Date | Hour | Summary of Events and Information | Remarks and references to Appendices |
|---|---|---|---|---|
| ARMENTIERES | April 30th | | Battn in Reserve. Commenced Special platoon training in the Offensive. Slight activity on the part of the enemy artillery. Otherwise normal. Attachment of Lewis gun detachments with returns in Appendix II | |

APPENDIX NO. III.

MINOR OPERATIONS

referred to in

171st INFANTRY BRIGADE WAR DIARY,

31.3.1917 to 30.4.1917

.......

APPENDIX I.

## COMBINED ARTILLERY & INFANTRY PROGRAMME.

......

- 30 Mins. Zero.   Infantry formed up ready at Point of Assembly, I.26.I.

- 15 Mins. Zero.   Infantry moves out in successive parties to point of
                 Deployment, 150 yds out in N.M.Land.
                 1st Party  -  Objective, Enemy's Wire.
                 2nd   ,,         ,,   Right Block at I.32.A.80.00.
                 3rd   ,,         ,,   Left Block at I.32.B.00.20.
                 4th   ,,         ,,   Mop Up enemy's front & supervision
                         Line and Dugouts.
                 5th   ,,      -  Parapet Party.

ZERO.    A. Intense 18 pr. barrage from I.32.A.68.68 to I.26.D.30.70.
            4.5" Hows on selected targets.  See Appendix 3
             and attached sketch.   6" Hows - the same.
           60 prs.   Counter Battery.
           M.T.Ms. Barraging the flanks and enemy's communications.
           L.T.Ms. Engaging enemy's Machine Guns on fixed targets.

        B. Infantry under cover of barrage move forward to 100
           yds of Hun Line to be raided.

Zero + 2 Mins.   A. 2nd Phase.
            18 Prs. lift and form a box :-
            (a) Front Line, I.26.D.19.50 to I.26.D.31.39
            (b) North Side of Box - Communication Trench I.26.D.
               25.54 to I.26.D.51.48.
           Back of Box - I.26.D.51.48 to I.32.B.08.57.
           South Side of Box - I.32.B.08.57 to I.32.A.70.68.
           (c) Front Line - I.32.A.72.70 to I.32.A.64.61.
           Remainder as in Phase One.

        B. Infantry advance on objective.

Zero + 3½ Mins.  A. Artillery as above.

        B. Infantry enter Hun Lines.

Zero + 15 Mins.  A. Artillery as above.

        B. Infantry withdraw.

Zero + 25 Mins.  A. Artillery cease fire.

        B. Infantry back in Trenches.

2.

**Casualties.** 9. First Aid Post will be established at TRAMWAY AVENUE, I.26.A.40.55.
Advanced Dressing at the BREWERY, BOIS GRENIER, I.30.b.50.99 to which all walking cases will go via SHAFTESBURY AVENUE.

**Prisoners.** 10. There will be no waiting to collect prisoners. Directly the first prisoner is taken, he will be despatched direct under escort to the junction of SHAFTESBURY AVENUE and SUBSIDIARY LINE without delay, where the Officer i/c that point will deatch the prisoner, and hand him over at once to an escort detailed by the Battn. holding the BOIS GRENIER Sector, who will, on completion of the enterprise, send under escort all the prisoners to Brigade HdQrs at H.II.A.50.40.

**Material.** 11. Captured material will be dumped at Position of Assembly and handed in to O.C.Raid. Battn. in Line will be responsible for the safe custody of same and forwarding to Brigade HdQrs at H.II.A.50.40. Dead Huns found in enemy's lines must be stripped of chevrons, etc., and well searched, before withdrawing on completion of task.

**Dress.** 12. All ranks will be as lightly equipped as possible. Service Dress, Steel Helmets, Waistcoats, Small Box Respirators, will be worn by all ranks.
Equipment worn will be that as detailed in attached Table - Appendix VII.
No official or private correspondence - maps - papers, etc. to be carried.

**Synchronising of Watches.** 13. All watches will be synchronised at       on Z day. But Zero will be the hour of the barrage falling.

**Liason.** 14. An Artillery Liason Officer will be with O.C.Raid, and one at Advanced Brigade HdQrs at the CARLTON, I.19.B.70.10.

**Communications.** 15. Brigade Signals will establish direct telephone communication between O.C.Raid and H.M.4, H.E.3.

**Emergency Signal.** 16. Should an unforeseen contingency arise which would necessitate the raid being abandoned, Golden Rain and Green Rockets will be sent up to stop the Guns firing needlessly, from Advanced Brigade HdQrs. A duplicate set of rockets will also be with O.C.Raid, who will, however, on no account use this signal unless communication with Advanced Brigade HdQrs has broken down, and he is convined that no effort whatever on his part can overcome the circumstances which render the enterprise abortive.

**Reports.** 17. All reports will be sent to O.C.Raid at I.26.I until return of Raiders; and thereafter to Advanced Brigade HdQrs at the CARLTON, I.19.B.70.10 - Battn HdQrs of the BOIS GRENIER SECTOR - where O.C.Operations will report on return with all Leaders of Parties.

18. ACKNOWLEDGE.

Lieut.Col. Brigade Major.
171st Infantry Brigade.

Copy No.
1. B.G.C.,
2. Brigade Major.
3. O.C.Raid.
4. 57th Division.
5. 170th Brigade.
6. 172nd ,,
7. 57th Divl.Artillery.
8. War Diary.
9.     ,,

Copy No.
10. D.T.M.O.
11. D.M.G.O.

AFTER ORDER. 19. From - 10 Mins.Zero to Zero + 35 Mins. the S.O.S.Signal will be only acknowledged if confirmed by telephone.

ISSUED WITH 171st BRIGADE ORDER No. 6.   TIME TABLE.   APPENDIX I. April 17.

| TIME. | INFANTRY. | ARTILLERY. | M. & L.T.M.Bs. | MACHINE GUNS. |
|---|---|---|---|---|
| Minus 30 Mins. | Raiding Party formed up at T.26.I. | Nil. | Nil. | Nil. |
| Minus 15 Mins. | Raiders leave Trenches for position of Deployment in NO MAN'S LAND. | | | |
| ZERO. | Infantry at position of Deployment in N.M.L., & creep forward under barrage. | Phase One commences - Lines of fire shown on Special Map. 18 prs barrage Hun front Line. Hows engaging selected points. 60 prs. Counter-Battery. | Barrage flanks of point of entry, & enemy's communications, and M.Guns engaged. | Vickers Guns form barrage around the area raided. Lewis Guns pushed well out affording flank protection. |
| Plus 2 Mins. | Infantry commence assault. | Phase Two commences. Lift to form Box. Remainder as in Phase One. | - do - | - do - |
| Plus 3½ Mins. | Infantry enter Hun Front Line. | - do - | - do - | - do - |
| Plus 15 Mins. | Infantry withdraw if they have not already done so, under cover of barrage. | - do - | - do - | - do - |
| Plus 25 Mins. | Infantry back in our own Trenches. | Cease Fire. | Cease Fire. | Cease Fire. |

SECRET
37041

7

I.26.B.
79.50
I.26.B.
82.75
84

I.26.D.
51.49

I.26.D.
30.70

I.26.D.
20.50

I.26.D.
36.20

I.32.B.
26.83

I.32.B.
25.82

I.32.A.
95.78

I.32.B.
13.60
I.32.B.
69.18

I.32.A.
68.68

I.32.A.
26.02

4.5" Howitzers ─────
6"    "      ─────
T.M.B's        ─────
18 Pdr. Barrage, 1st Phase
    "      "    2nd  "

APPENDIX II

| UNIT | Party | Forming-up Posn. | Time to leave Assembly Point. | Officers. | N.C.O.'s or Leaders | Demolition Men | Runners. | Barbars. | Bayonet Men. | Rifle Grenadiers. | Carriers. | Lewis Gunners. | Telephonists. | Stretcher Bearers. | Bridgemen. | Matmen. | Scouts, Wirecutters. | Guard on Prisoners and Material. | OBJECTIVE. | JOB. | REMARKS. |
|---|---|---|---|---|---|---|---|---|---|---|---|---|---|---|---|---|---|---|---|---|---|
| 2/7th Battalion, K.L.R. | 1 | 1 | 15 Mins | 1 | | | | | | | | | | | 4 | 3 | 4 | | I.26.c.90.10 | Cut wire, lay bridges & mats. | |
| | 2 | 2 | 12 Mins | | 2 | | 1 | 2 | 2 | 1 | 1 | | | | | | | | I.32.A.80.00 | Establish Right Block. | |
| | 3 | 3 | 9 Mins | | 2 | | 1 | 2 | 2 | 1 | 1 | | | | | | | | I.32.B.00.20 | Establish Left Block. | |
| | 4 | 4 | 6 Mins | 1 | 1 | 2 | 1 | 4 | 4 | 2 | 2 | | | | | | | | I.26.c.90.10 | To clear front line, supervision line & dugouts | Divide into 2 parties, moving right and left. |
| | 5 | 5 | 3 Mins | 1 | | | 3 | | | | | | 2 | 2 | | | | 4 | I.26.c.90.10 | Establish communication with OC Raid. Form HQrs of Assault Party. Lay out Telephone & white tape. | 4 of 8 Stret. Brs. are men from 1st party. This forms parapet party & remains under cover of front face of enemy's para pet. |
| | 6 | 6 | ZERO. | | | | | | | | | | 3 | | | | | | I L.Gun at I.26.c.50.25 I L.Gun at I.26.c.60.53 | To protect flanks against any action of enemy. | 2 Lewis Guns |

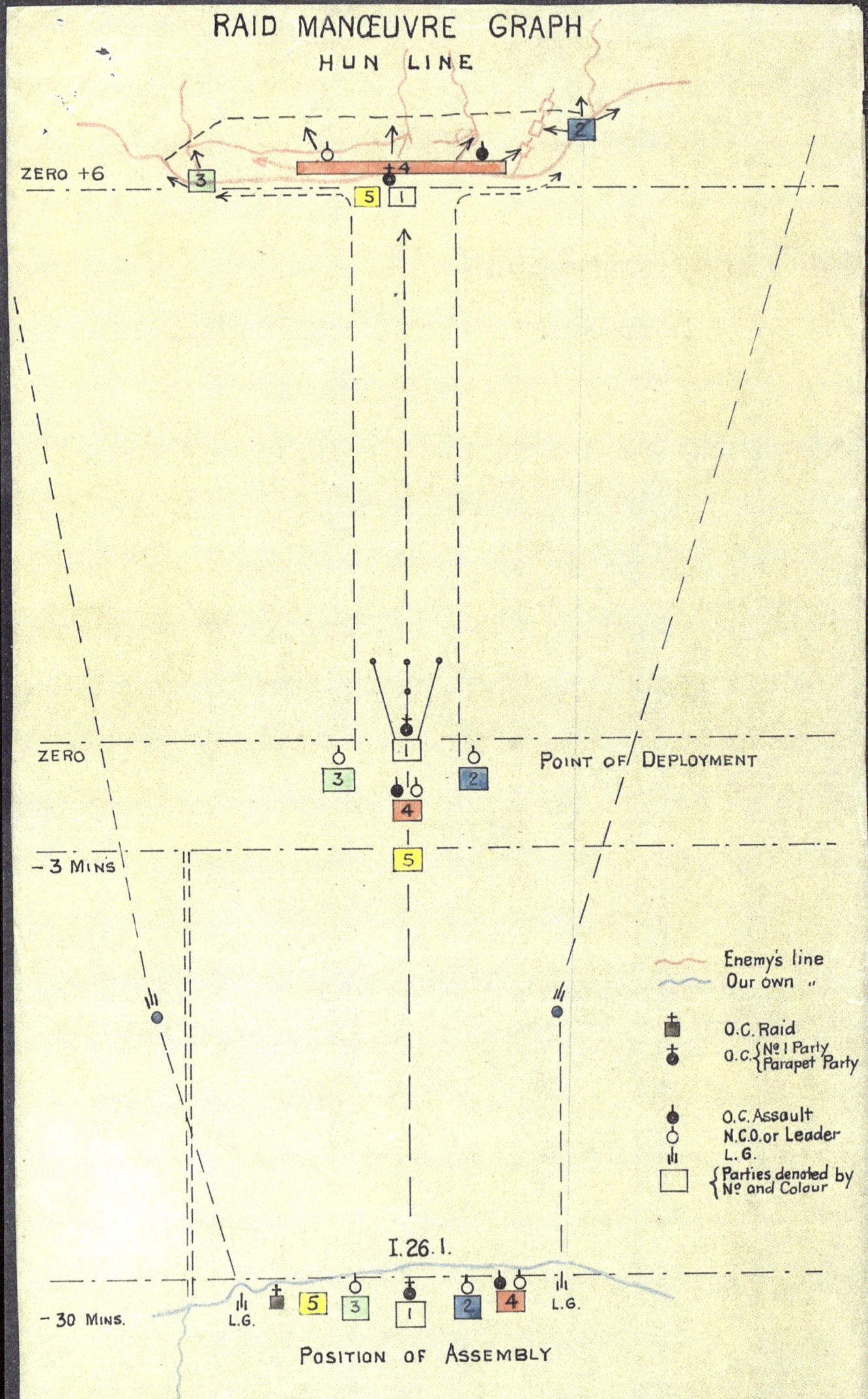

APPENDIX. VI.

SECRET CODE.
........

Q. R. S. T. U. V. W. X. W. Y.          1. 2. 3. 4. 5. 6. 7. 8. 9. 0.
                              ....

| | |
|---|---|
| KING. | HUN LINE PENETRATED. |
| QUEEN. | MACHINE GUN. |
| KNAVE. | PRISONER. |
| ACE. | ENEMY KILLED. |
| STAR. | ALL PARTIES HAVE RETURNED. |
| SLOW. | SLIGHT CASUALTIES. |
| STICK. | FAIRLY HEAVY CASUALTIES. |
| STIFF. | HEAVY CASUALTIES. |
| SAVE. | ENEMY COUNTER ATTACKING. |
| DONE. | KILLED. |
| DIDDLED. | WOUNDED. |
| DAMN. | MISSING. |
| DOUSE. | CEASE FIRE. |
| DEMAND. | CONTINUE YOUR FIRE. |
| FLOOD. | HEAVY ENEMY FIRE. |
| FEEBLE. | ENEMY FIRE NOT HEAVY. |
| FINISH. | ALL QUIET. |
| FULL. | RAIDING PARTY ARE CLEAR OF COMMUNICATION TRENCHES. |
| FOILED. | ENEMY AWAITING ATTACK AND RAID ABANDONED. |

APPENDIX VII.

| EQUIPMENT. | Revolver. | Mills Bombs. | .450 Ammunition. | Watch. | Whistle. | Torch. | Bomb Waistcoat. | Rifle. | Bayonet. | S.A.A. | Wire Cutters. | No.23 Rifle Grenades. | RIFLE GRENADE Cup. | Cartridges, Rifle Grenade. | White Tape. | Slabs, Guncotton. | Armors. | Knokkerry. | Remarks. |
|---|---|---|---|---|---|---|---|---|---|---|---|---|---|---|---|---|---|---|---|
| OFFICERS. | 1 | 4 | 24 | 1 | 1 | 1 | | | | | | | | | | | | | ALL RANKS - Service dress Jacket & Trousers. No Badges or Chevrons. Puttees - Steel Helmet - Waistcoat - Box Respirator - White streamers - Faces all Ranks blacked. OFFICERS - One Star. N.C.Os & Leaders - one stripe. |
| N.C.Os LEADERS. | | 16 | 24 | 1 | 1 | 1 | | 1 | 1 | 50 | | | | | | | | 1 | |
| BOMBERS. | | 16 | | | | | 1 | | | 50 | | | | | | | | | |
| BAYONET MEN. | | 4 | | | | 1 | 1 | 1 | 1 | | | | | | | | | | |
| CARRIERS. | | 20 | | | | | 1 | | | | | | | | | | | | |
| SCOUTS. | 1 | 4 | 24 | 1 | | 1 | | 1 | 1 | | 1 | | | | | | | 1 | |
| RUNNERS. | 1 | 2 | 12 | 1 | | | | | | | | | | | | | | | |
| SIGNALLERS. | 1 | 2 | 12 | | | | | | | | | | | | | | | | |
| STRETCHER BEARERS. | 1 | 4 | 12 | | | 1 | 1 | 1 | 1 | | | | | | | | | | |
| RIFLE GRENADIER. | | 2 | 12 | | | | | 1 | 1 | 50 | | 15 | 1 | 20 | 500 yds | | | | |
| BRIDGE MEN. | 1 | 4 | 12 | | | | | 1 | 1 | | | | | | | | | | |
| MAT MEN. | 1 | 4 | 12 | | | | | | | | | | | | | | | | |
| DEMOLITION MEN. | 1 | 4 | 12 | | | | | | | | | | | | | 1 | | | |
| LEWIS GUNNER. | 1 | 4 | 12 | | | 1 | | | | | | | | | | | 1 | | 1 Lewis Gun - Each Lewis Gunner 2 Magazines fille |

## NOMINAL ROLL.

.....

| | | |
|---|---|---|
| 265783. | L/Cpl. | Allanson. |
| 269697. | Pte. | Adlington. |
| 266406. | Sgt. | Ainslow. |
| 267475. | Pte. | Ackers, W. |
| 267525. | ,, | Bullock, F. |
| 265700. | Sgt. | Baker. |
| 265895. | Pte. | Buck. |
| 265675. | ,, | Brindle. A. |
| 266228. | ,, | Carter. E. |
| 267455. | ,, | Cookson. |
| 267724. | ,, | Cowell. J. |
| 267732. | ,, | Donnelly. |
| 265366. | ,, | Davies. |
| 266137. | ,, | Dewhurst. |
| 266348. | L/Cpl. | Eaton. |
| 265137. | Pte. | Fitzsimmons. |
| 266105. | Corpl. | Farrer. |
| 267435. | Pte. | Goulding. |
| 269552. | ,, | Grady. |
| 266226. | ,, | Glover. |
| 265882. | Corpl. | Gill. |
| 266463. | Pte. | Healey. |
| 266347. | L/Cpl. | Howard. R. |
| 265416. | Pte. | Howard. J. |
| 267445. | ,, | Harrison, J.E. |
| 267498. | ,, | Jones. F. |
| 266277. | ,, | Johnson. J. |
| 266512. | ,, | Jackson. |
| 265472. | L/Cpl. | Kevelighan. |
| 265982. | Pte. | Kirk. |
| 266536. | ,, | Kershaw. |
| 267729. | ,, | Limb. C. |
| 267514. | ,, | Lindsay. F. |
| 267575. | ,, | Llewellyn. |
| 267447. | ,, | Mizon. |
| 267494. | ,, | Mullancy. |
| 266879. | L/Cpl. | Molloy. |
| 269578. | Pte. | McHale. |
| 266279. | Sgt. | McVey. |
| 267766. | Pte. | Martlew. H. |
| 267762. | ,, | Martin. |
| 265710. | ,, | Muzik. |
| 266096. | L/Cpl. | McKay. |
| 265929. | ,, | Morgan. |
| 267400. | Pte. | Morris. T. |
| 267713. | ,, | Newton. |
| 267573. | ,, | Oates. W. |
| 266091. | Sgt. | Pryar. |
| 267421. | Pte. | Roberts. |
| 266276. | ,, | Ratcliffe. |
| 266095. | Corpl. | Rassall. |
| 265900. | Pte. | Rimmer. W.B. |

2.

| | | |
|---|---|---|
| 267418. | Pte. | Rawlinson. |
| 265934. | ,, | Stone. W.E. |
| 266102. | ,, | Smith, J.R. |
| 265902. | ,, | Spenser. |
| 266459. | ,, | Turner. |
| 267529. | ,, | Tookey. J.P. |
| ~~450661.~~ | ~~Sepr.~~ | ~~Wigmill.~~ |
| 266470. | Pte. | Wright. |
| 266639. | ,, | Wallis. E. |

.......

Captain E. S. Dorning.

Lieut. J. V. Addy.

Lieut. A. L. Cowper.


........

SECRET.  
Ref: 1/10,000 Trench Maps  
New Editions  
AUBERS 8a, RADINGHEM 8d,  
BOIS GRENIER 6d.

D.A.7/94.  
Copy No ...6....

## 57TH DIVISIONAL ARTILLERY OPERATION ORDER NO. 7.

11th April, 1917.

I.      On a date and at an hour to be notified later, a raiding party composed of -

         3 officers     )  
         59 other ranks)    171st Infantry Brigade

will raid the enemy's trenches on a front from I 28 c 80.00 to I 26 d 00.20 to a depth of 50 yards. Capt. Dorning, 2/7th King's (Liverpool) Regt., is commanding.

II.      The raid will be supported by the Left Group, 57th Divisional Artillery, specially composed as follows:-

|                | 18-pdrs. | 4.5" Hows. |
|----------------|----------|------------|
| 286th Bde. R.F.A. | 12 | 6 |
| 110th do.         | 18 | 6 |
|                   | 30 | 12 |

Lt.-Col. R. G. Drury, R.A., will command.

Certain guns and howitzers of the II Anzac Heavy Artillery are also directly supporting the raid.

III.      The II Anzac Heavy Artillery has arranged from zero onwards -  
       (a) to stand by for counter battery work with 60 pdrs.  
       (b) to engage selected points with 9-inch Hows.

IV.      Medium Trench Mortars will also take part in the raid under orders to be issued by the D.T.M.O.

V.      Communication will be established forthwith from Left Group Headquarters to the batteries under it for this operation.

VI.      A gold and silver rain rocket accompanied by one green rocket will be used as a signal to stop the artillery barrage. The place from which these rockets will be sent up will be notified to all concerned.

VII. Orders as to drawing the ammunition required will be issued later to O.C., Artillery Groups. The D.T.M.O. will be responsible for the supply of all T.M. ammunition.

VIII. O.C., Left Group, will arrange for a Liaison Officer to report to O.C., Raid, at zero minus two hours at the junction of the subsidiary line and SHAFTESBURY AVENUE. Another Liaison Officer will be at Advanced Brigade Headquarters at the CARLTON I 19 b 70.10 and will report himself there to the Brigade Major, 171st Infantry Brigade.

IX. Watches will be synchronised with R.A. Headquarters at about 10, 6 and 3 hours before zero.

X. The following tables are attached:-

    (a) Action of the Field Artillery

    (b) Table of Rates of Fire

    (c) Code to be used during the operation.

XI. ACKNOWLEDGE.

                                           Major,
                                        Brigade Major,
                                        57th Divl. Arty.

Issued at 4 PM......

    Copy No.  1, File
                  2, War Diary
                  3,    do.
                  4, Left Group, 57th Divl. Arty.
                  5, D.T.M.O., 57th Division
                  6, 171st Infantry Brigade
                  7, Headquarters, 57th Division
                  8, II Anzac Heavy Artillery
                  9, R.A., II Anzac (for information)

## LEFT GROUP.

### TIME TABLE.

| Time | Guns | Objective |
|---|---|---|
| | **18-PDRS.** | |
| Zero to zero plus 2 minutes | 28 | Front line trench    650yds<br>I 32 a 68.68 to I 26 d 30.70 |
| | 1 | Search INCOME TRENCH from I 26 b 78.50 to I 27 a 18.98 |
| | 1 | Search INCOME SUPPORT TRENCH from I 26 b 95.35 to I 27 a 46.85. |
| Zero plus 2 to zero plus 25 minutes | 3 | Front line trench    69<br>I 26 d 19.50 to I 26 d 31.50 |
| | 3 | Communication Trench I 26 d 25.54 to I 26 d 51.48 |
| | 15 | I 26 d 51.48 to I 32 b 08.57 |
| | 3 | Communication Trench I 32 b 08.57 to I 32 a 70.68 |
| | 4 | Front line trench I 32 a 72.70 to I 32 a 64.61 |
| | 1 | Search INCOME TRENCH from I 26 b 78.50 to I 27 a 18.98 |
| | 1 | Search INCOME SUPPORT from I 26 b 95.35 to I 27 a 46.85. |
| | **4.5" HOWS.** | |
| Zero to zero plus 25 minutes | 1 A. | I 26 b 84.75 |
| | 1 B. | I 26 b 79.50 |
| | 1 C. | I 26 d 30.71 |
| | 1 D. | I 26 d 20.50. |
| | 1 E. | I 26 d 51.49 |
| | 1 F. | I 26 d 36.30 |
| | 1 G. | I 32 b 25.82 |
| | 1 H. | I 32 b 36.83 |
| | 1 J. | I 32 a 95.78 |
| | 1 K. | I 32 b 15.60 |
| | 1 L. | I 32 a 68.68 |
| | 1 M. | I 32 a 36.02 |

TABLE OF RATES OF FIRE

LEFT GROUP

18-PDRS.

From Zero to zero plus 5 minutes
4 rounds per gun per minute.

From zero plus 5 minutes to zero plus 25
3 rounds per gun per minute.

4-5" HOWS.

From zero to zero plus 5 minutes
3 rounds per gun per minute.

Zero plus 5 to zero plus 25
2 rounds per gun per minute.

## C O D E.
************

| | | |
|---|---|---|
| Q.R.S.T.U.V.W.X.Y.Z. | - | 1, 2, 3, 4, 5, 6, 7, 8, 9, 0. |
| KING | - | HUN LINE PENETRATED |
| QUEEN | - | Machine Gun |
| KNAVE | - | Prisoner |
| ACE | - | Enemy killed |
| STAR | - | All parties have returned |
| SLOW | - | Slight casualties |
| STICK | - | Fairly heavy casualties |
| STIFF | - | Heavy casualties |
| SAVE | - | Enemy counter attacking |
| DONE | - | KILLED |
| DAMN | - | Missing |
| DOUSE | - | Cease fire |
| DEMAND | - | Continue your fire |
| FLOOD | - | Heavy enemy fire |
| FINISH | - | All quiet |
| FULL | - | Raiding party is clear of C.Ts |
| FOILED | - | Enemy awaiting attack and Raid abandoned. |

******

SECRET.

Reference:
Map Sheet 36 N.W.4.
1/10,000.

## MACHINE GUN ORDER NO. 2.

1. On Z day at Zero hour the 171st Infantry Brigade will raid a sector of the Enemy's Trench between I.26.c.80.00 and I.26.d.00.20 to a depth of 50 yards.

DISTRIBUTION:

170th M.G.Coy. 4 guns.
171st  "   "  10   "
172nd  "   "  10   "
173rd  "   "   8   "

2. Machine Guns will co-operate –
(a) by barraging the enemy front line on either flank of the raid for a distance of approximately 500 yards S.W'ward from I.32.a.70.70 to I.32.c.13.88 and for a distance of approximately 1300 yards N.E'ward from I.26.d.20.30. to I.27.a.00.80.
(b) by barraging the C.T's running from I.32.a.70.70 to I.32.b.30.50 and from I.26.d.20.50 to I.26.d.35.15.

3. Objectives for Guns will be as shown in Appendix I (Traces distributed to Company Commanders concerned).

4. O.C., 170th M.G. Coy. will move 1 section to the RUE DU BOIS Sector on the night previous to Z day.

5. All guns will have depression stops and traversing stops fitted before opening fire.

6. (a) Guns will open fire at Zero hour and continue to fire till Zero plus 25 minutes.
(b) They will remain in position till Zero plus 90 minutes ready to deal with emergencies.
They will in the absence of other orders take their cue from the Artillery.

7. (a) Zero hour will be communicated in due course. It will be the moment of the Artillery barrage coming down.
(b) Z day has been communicated verbally to those concerned.

8. Telephone communication will be arranged by M.G.Coy. Commanders in conjunction with O.C., Divisional Signals as verbally explained by O.C., 173rd M.G.Coy.

9. O.C., Barrage will be at BOIS GRENIER in 172nd M.G. Coy's Battle H.Q. at H.30.b.55.60.

10. O.C., M.G.Coys. will arrange for sufficient S.A.A. of K.N. or K. makes, water and oil for 1 hour's fire.

D.H.Q.,
18/4/1917.

*Mark Bellingham* Captain,
Commanding 173rd M.G. Company.

DISTRIBUTION:

O.C., 170th M.G.Coy.         —B.C., 171st Inf. Brigade.
 "    171st   do.             "    170th       do.
 "    172nd   do.            C.R.A.
 "    173rd   do.

CONFIDENTIAL.

ADVANCE REPORT ON RAID CARRIED OUT BY DETACHMENT
OF THE 2/7th K.L.R., 171st Brigade, at 3.20 a.m., on
15th April, 1917.

......

OPERATIONS.
OUR OWN.

ASSEMBLY.	Raiding Party assembled according to schedule, all correct.

Minus 15 Mins Zero.	Raiders clear of our wire in front line.

Zero.	Raiders as per programme, assembled at Point of Deployment, in their correct formation, undetected.

Under cover of our barrage, the Raiding Party crept forward to within 30 yds of the Hun wire, - the going over N.M.Land was very good up to this point.   The wire in front of the Hun Line formed no obstacle, and had been very well cut, but the going was very heavy owing to shell holes and the sodden state of the ground from the rain, for the last 60 yards to the Hun parapet.

The Hun Line between the Front Parapet and the Travel Trench was heavily wired; however, the right blocking party and Assault Party were able to make an entry 50 yds to the North of "The Lighthouse", and there came in contact with a small party of Huns.   Bombing ensued, and the Huns were forced back down the ISLAND Communication Trench. Two Huns were killed for certain; unfortunately two men in endeavouring to secure identity were both wounded. An N.C.O. bombed a dugout containing a Machine Gun, similar to a Hotchkiss, but unfortunately the two men with him were wounded, and in attending to them was unable to bring back the Machine Gun, which is stated to have been destroyed, before the withdrawal was signalled.

The Assault Party bombed half way down the Travel Trench, but were unable to complete their task as time was up.

The left blocking party were unable to enter the Trench owing to the wire between the Parapet and the Travel Trench, and bombed from the top of the trench the entrances to dugouts, but it is believed that these were unoccupied.

ARTILLERY.

The shooting of our artillery was excellent, and the Raiders were able to creep up under cover of the barrage to within 60 yds of the Hun line in perfect safety.

OPERATIONS.

ENEMY.

Enemy's resistance was light, and consisted of fighting with Bombs while they retired down Communication Trenches to the left and right.

ARTILLERY.

Plus 3 Mins. Zero.

The Hun retaliation came down before their S.O.S. went up, being directed on N.M.Land, our Front Line, and a little behind, consisting to a great extent of Howitzers, of fairly large calibre.

CASUALTIES.

OUR OWN.

Estimated at I Officer slightly wounded, i.e., 2nd Lieut Cowper.

Other Ranks - 2 killed and 5 wounded.

Everyone is reported to have been brought back.

SECRET.                                                          COPY NO. 9

                    171st BRIGADE ORDER No. 6.
                    ....
                                                        April, 1917.

MAP REFERENCE.    BOIS GRENIER, 36 N.W. 4. 1:10.000.
                  - SECRET.
                  SPECIAL MAP.
                  AEROPLANE PHOTOGRAPH.

Intention.    1.  On Z day, at Zero hour, a detachment of the 2/7th K.L.R.
                  will carry out a Raid on a Sector of the Enemy's Trenches -
                  front line and supervision trenches, with their dugouts -
                  to a depth of 50 yards.

Object.       2.  (a) To continue a harrassing policy, and prevent the enemy
                  from withdrawing troops.
                      (b) Killing and capturing as many of the enemy as possible.
                      (c) Capturing and destroying war material, Machine Gun
                  Emplacements, and Dugouts.
                      (d) Obtaining identifications and gaining information
                  regarding enemy's system of defence.

Objective.    3.  The enemy's front line situated between the co-ordinates
                  references I.26.c.80.00 to I.26.D.00.20, together with his
                  supervision line and dugouts to a depth of 50 yards.

Support.      4.  The 172nd Brigade in the line - Artillery, M. & L.T.M.Bs
                  and Machine Guns - will support the enterprise.  See
                  Appendices 3, 4 and 5 concerning co-operation.

Line of       5.  Detail of Combined Infantry and Artillery Programme, together
Action.           with Time Table - see Appendix I.
                      Objective and Organisation of Infantry Raiding Parties -
                  see Appendix II.
                      M.T.M.B will cut the enemy's wire along the front to be
                  raided prior to the date of Operations, at the same time
                  distracting attention by action elsewhere.  Ours will be
                  cut the night of the Operation.

Withdrawal.   6.  (a) At Zero plus 15 Mins, the Assault and Mopping Up
                  parties will withdraw by a pre-arranged signal, passing through
                  Parapet and Blocking Parties.  As soon as they have got 50
                  yards into No Man's Land, the remainder will withdraw from
                  enemy's front line, Lewis Guns withdrawing when last parties
                  are in.  Every party will endeavour to keep together on
                  their return.
                      (b) Officers and Leaders will work by the clock.  Two
                  long whistle blasts will also be the signal to withdraw.
                  In case the din of the artillery makes whistle sounds
                  inaudible, the Officer i/c Parapet Party will despatch runners
                  to order the withdrawal in every case.
                      (c) O.C. Parapet Party will signal the code word of
                  "Withdrawal" to O.C. Raid when the last parties are out before
                  he leaves.  As soon as all the raiders are back in our
                  Trenches, O.C. Parapet Party will report the fact to the O.C.
                  Raid.

Roll Call.    7.  Roll Call Station will be established in Subsidiary Line
                  just north of junction of SUBSIDIARY LINE and SHAFTESBURY
                  AVENUE.  Each member of the Raiding Party will be provided
                  with a luggage label bearing his number and name, to be tied
                  round his neck under his jacket.  On returning to our
                  trenches, all ranks will at once proceed to Roll Call Station,
                  hand in their labels and proceed to GUNNER FARM, where motor
                  lorries will take them to their billets.  There must be no
                  loitering in the front line or at Roll Call Station.

Routes.       8.  (a) TRAMWAY EVENUE will be used only for casualties.
                      (b) Runners and Reports for Advanced Brigade HdQrs.
                      (c) SHAFTESBURY AVENUE as a down trench for those not
                  wounded.

CONFIDENTIAL.

# REPORT ON RAID BY 171st INFANTRY BRIGADE.

**UNIT.** Carried out by Detachment of the 2/7th K.L.R., on the 17th April 1917, at 3.20 a.m., and consisting of 3 Officers and 60 O.Ranks.

**RENDEZVOUS.** The party proceeded from Billets at RUE MARLE, in lorries, and rendezvous in a house at LA VESEE, I.19.a.95.80, where they dressed and were equipped, and having been finally inspected, proceeded as follows:-

## NARRATIVE.

**1.45 a.m.** The Raiding Party left LA VESEE and proceeded via TRAMWAY AVENUE to the Front Line, according to the programme set forth in Brigade Order No.6.

**POINT OF ASSEMBLY.** The Raiders formed up in the correct order of their parties,
**2.45 am.** at I.26.I.            -            and            -

**3. 0 am.** at 3 a.m. were clear of our wire, and well away across N.M.Land to the Point of Deployment.

**ZERO.** Our barrage came down to the minute, as a blanket, the
**3.20 am.** Raiding Party, who were deployed and ready 200 yds out in N.M.Land, commenced creeping forward under its cover, eventually reaching a point about 60 yds from the enemy's front line parapet. The going in N.M.Land was good up to this point, thereafter the grond was nothing but shell holes full of water, the sodden state of the ground rendering all movements laborious; and in consequence nullifying the rapid progress to the point of entry to a very great extent; at the same time requiring great physical effort on the part of the Raiders. Much valuable time was in consequence lost in entering the enemy's trench, resulting in the loss of time for interior operations. The wire had been well cut and formed no obstacle.

**ERO + 7 Mins.** Lieut.Addy, with the Mat and Bridge Men, finding no wire or borrow ditch as an obstacle, formed up as a parapet party according to plan.

**ERO + 8 Mins.** Lieut Cowper, with the Right and Assault Parties, entered the enemy's line near ISLAND TRAVERSE COMMUNICATION TRENCH, 50 yds to the right of the main point of entry, where they encountered a group of 6 to 8 Huns, who divided at ISLAND TRAVERSE C.T. into two parties. Lieut Cowper ordered the Right Blocking Party to follow up the Huns down ISLAND TRAVERSE C.T., which they did, bombing them back some 40 yds towards the South side of the Box Barrage. - two of the enemy being accounted for by the leading Bayonet Man, who shot them. This man and one other, in an attempt to search the enemy, were wounded while doing so - in the meantime the N.C.O. i/c this party discovered in a small dugout a machine gun of Hotchkiss type, which he intended to take away with him; unfortunately, 2 more of his party were wounded, and thinking more of getting these men back, he bombed the dugout with the hope of destroying the gun. (This party had had by now 7 casualties out of a total of 10).

The Assault Party under Lieut.Cowper proceeded along the TRAVEL TRENCH, which was in excellent condition, and well duck-boarded, bombing down it to an extent of about 50 or 60 yds. and following up the small party of Huns.

The Left Blocking Party were unable to get into the enemy's trench owing to the wire between the Front Line and Supervision Line, moved over the top, bombing the Supervision Trench for 50 or 60 yds.

| | |
|---|---|
| ZERO + 20 Mins. | The artillery were requested to prolong the bombardment for further 5 minutes. |
| ZERO + 27 Mins. | The last of the Raiding Party returned. |
| ZERO + 30 Mins. | Our bombardment ceased. |
| ZERO + 40 Mins. | The enemy's retaliation ceased.   Shortly after this, 2 more men of the Raiding Party, who had been overlooked, returned from N.M.Land, where they had been taking cover in a shell hole, reporting that one of our men was lying outside near the enemy's line. Lieut.Addy and Pte Macdonald, of the 2/10th K.L.R., went out and brought this man in, though he was dead. Capt Dorning, with 2 men of the 2/10th K.L.R. at the same time bringing in a bridge and 2 stretchers. |
| CASUALTIES. | Our Casualties consisted of :- |
| | 2 Killed.     Lieut.Cowper, Slightly Wounded. and 8 O.Ranks Wounded. |

ACTION OF THE ENEMY.

| | |
|---|---|
| ZERO + 3 Mins. | Retaliation by the enemy's guns came down before their S.O.S. signal lights went up, directing their fire on N.M.Land, our Front Line, and between the Front Line and Support Line.   The shooting at first was somewhat wild, and the Raiders suffered practically no loss from it until their return journey.   The employment of Hows. of 5.9 calibre, and it is said some of a larger calibre, being the chief features of the retaliation, together with Minenwerfer from the direction of INCOMB SUPPORT. |

There was a total absence of Machine Gun and rifle fire, due, no doubt, of the close attention paid to them by the Medium and Light Trench Mortar Batteries.

The enemy's resistance was light, and consisted of covering his withdrawal to the flanks under bomb and rifle grenade fire;  it is quite probable that he suffered somewhat from our artillery, trench mortars and machine guns.

**SUMMING UP.**

The Raid, unfortunately, did not produce any identifications, of the success that was hoped for after the propitious start. Had the time taken been the same as in practice as on reaching the wire (when Mats and Bridges were laid to meet obstacles such as uncut wire or a borrow ditch, which fortunately did not exist) many valuable minutes would have been gained, and identification most surely obtained. The failure was entirely due to

(a) Inability to keep within the schedule time allowance of 12 minutes in the enemy's trenches – caused by the sodden state of the ground rendered by the rain and shell holes making it almost a quadmire, thereby frustrating all rapid movement.

(b) The thick wire entanglement between the front line parapet and Supervision Trench, which was impassable, and of a new construction.

(c) The misfortune of having those men wounded who were in a position to secure identification from the 2 enemy killed.

Except for the enemy's artillery retaliation, the withdrawal was unaffected by any other fire.

The support of the artillery throughout the enterprise was all that could be desired, and inspired the greatest support and confidence to the Raiders.

The Medium and Light T.M.Batteries cut the wire perfectly, and their laying on suspected points for Machine Guns and also their general action kept down all the fire that might have been expected from this source.

The Machine Gun barrage left nothing to be desired.

Brigadier-General,
Commanding 171st Infantry Brigade.

B.H.Q.
17.4.1917

SECRET.      171st BRIGADE ORDER NO. 10.      COPY NO. 15

Map Reference,      27th April 1917.
Sheet 1:10000.
36 N.W., 2 & 4.

**Intention.**    1. It is intended to discharge gas on the Brigade front and that of the Brigade on our left on Z night when the weather conditions are favourable. South of the River LYS, gas will be discharged by "L" and "N" Special Companies, and on the front north of the River LYS by "A" and "K" Special Companies, R.E.,

In addition to the gas cloud xxxxxxxxx attack, projectors will be fired from a position North of the River on to positions opposite the Brigade front.

**Object.**    2. The object of the release of gas is to destroy as many as possible of enemy personnel.

**Locality.**    3. Gas will be discharged by "L" Special Company, R.E., from the following points of the Brigade front :-

     I.10.b.98.80      to      I.11.a.08.82
     C.29.c.32.28      to      C.29.a.10.02
     C.29.a.25.76      to      C.23.c.18.16

Gas will be discharged by "N" Special Company, R.E., from :-

     C.23.a.15.10      to      C.23.a.20.38
     C.17.c.27.60      to      C.17.a.05.25

**Line of Action.**    4. From zero to zero plus 20 minutes, gas will be discharged. At the same time, gas will be discharged and projectors will be fired by the Brigade on our left across the Brigade front.

**Precautions.**    5. (a) The front line from which gas is to be discharged will be cleared to a distance of 250 yards on either flank of the gas, with the exception of sentries, Lewis Gunners, Bombing Squads, and one Infantry Officer per Gas Sector, all of whom will wear their Box Respirators fully adjusted from zero minus 5 minutes to zero plus 30 minutes.

     (b) The Infantry Officers remaining in the Gas Sectors will keep in touch with the Special Coy R.E. Officers in charge of their Sector.

**Code.**    6. (a) The following code will be used for giving warning of a gas discharge :-
     (1) By projectors.
     (2) From Locations North of River LYS.
     (3) From Locations South of River LYS.

(1) "Return of men not inoculated will be rendered at 11 o'clock."

(2) "Handcarts will be parked at the point referred to at 11 o'clock".

(3) "Candidates will report at 11 o'clock".

     (b) In the event of the O.C. Special Companies, R.E. finding the weather conditions unfavourable prior to zero hour, the zero hour may be postponed for one or more hours, in which case a message will be sent as follows:-

"Candidates report (1) hour later".

This will mean that zero has been delayed one hour.

2.

(c) In the event of the weather conditions being so bad as to preclude any possibility of discharge of gas, the following message will be sent :-

"Candidates will not report today".

(d) The decision as to whether conditions are suitable for a gas discharge is left entirely in the hands of O.C., "A" Special Company, R.E.,

**Artillery action.**

7. Artillery will stand by for retaliation from zero, in case the enemy replies to gas waves.

**Medical arrangements.**

8. Os.C. "G" and "H" Battalions will place Regimental Stretcher Bearers at the disposal of the Officers Commanding "N" and "L" Companies, R.E., at the following points :-

"H" Battalion.
(1) 4 Stretcher Bearers with 2 Stretchers to report to R.E. Officer in front line at top of VAUXHALL AVENUE.
(2) 6 Stretcher Bearers with 3 Stretchers at C.28.d.90.76. (Concrete dugout LONDON ROAD).
(3) 4 Stretcher Bearers with 2 Stretchers at FRYPAN.

"G" Battalion.
(1) 6 Stretcher Bearers with 3 Stretchers at junction of EDMEADS AVENUE and 2nd Support Line.
(2) 6 Stretcher Bearers with 3 Stretchers at junction of IRISH AVENUE and 2nd Support Line.

Stretcher Bearers will report minus 1 hour zero at their posts. Should casualties ensue, cases will be dealt with at Battn. Aid Posts of "E" and "F" Battns.
Advanced Dressing Station at C.26.D.50.90.
Brigade

**Synchronising of Watches.**

9. Watches will be synchronised at xxxxx HdQrs at 7 p.m. 27th instant, and if gas is not released on that day, daily at the same hour until this operation is completed.
An Officer will report to the Staff Captain with 3 watches.

**Liaison.**

10. 3 Patrols from the Brigade on our left are pushing into FRELINGHEIN - and a situation might arise which may necessitate their returning through the front held by the Brigade. The following precautions, which have been made in conjunction with the Brigade on our left, will be taken:-
(a) The challenge will be "Halt - who goes there?"; if the answer is friendly, a counter-challenge "Advance one and be recognised" will be made.
(b) A sign of our own forces returning will be 3 flashes of an electric torch - but this is not to be expected as torches may become lost.
(c) An Officer or Leader of the Patrols will stay at the first post he meets, reporting to the Officer or N.C.O. in charge - and will report when his party are in. After this report has been rendered, all others approaching will be treated as the enemy.
(d) Patrols will be dressed in ordinary Field Service Jackets and Trousers - and Steel Helmets.

11. Reports will be rendered to these Headquarters early.

12. ACKNOWLEDGE.

G.W.GEDDES.
Lieut.Colonel, Brigade Major.
171st Infantry Brigade.

P.T.O.

ISSUED AT 4.15 p.m., to :-

Copy No. 1.  B.G.C.,
2.  "E" Battalion.
3.  "F"      ,,
4.  "G"      ,,
5.  "H"      ,,
6.  57th Division.
7.  172nd Brigade.
8.  11th Australian Brigade.
9.  C.R.A.,
10. Loft Group, R.A.,
11. 171st M.G.Coy.
12. 171st L.T.M.B.
13. "L" Coy, R.E.,
14. "N"    ,,
15. War Diary.
16.          ,,
17. G.S.File.

REPORT ON DISCHARGE OF GAS
from
HOUPLINES - EPINETTE SECTOR.

April 29th 1917.

12.40 a.m., Capt. Bruce, of the Special Company, R.E., reported that the gas had been released from the Sector at zero according to programme, and also from the Division on the left, together with projectors. This is verified from the report from the Battalion holding the HOUPLINES Sector. Four localities had been previously selected for the discharge of gas, but gas was only discharged from two of these, viz :-

Localities 16 & 17. Ref. 36.c.17.c.20.80 - C.17.a.20.10
" 8 & 9. Ref. 36.c.29.c.20.50 - C.29.a.05.45

Gas was not released from the other localities by order of the R.E. Officer in charge - as he considered that there was insufficient wind, and that it would be dangerous to our own troops. The Officer in command of the Infantry at these points was warned, and the patrol which was ready to go out did not, in consequence, carry out its line of action to discover the effects of the gas cloud, and obtain, if possible, identifications in C.29.Central.

Divisional Headquarters were notified by telephone that the gas had been released.

1.11 a.m. Capt. Bruce reported that all Gas had been discharged.

1.40 a.m. Battalions holding HOUPLINES and EPINETTE Sector reported all quiet and O.K.

1.45 a.m. 57th Divisional HdQrs were notified of the situation.

Action of Enemy. The enemy appeared to be on the alert, as he immediately sent up Light Rockets and Flares, which rendered the gas quite visible. The gas cloud rose very slowly to a considerable height, and travelled towards the enemy line. The alarm was raised within 5 minutes, whistle and gongs in the front line, and syrens in rear being heard. Machine Gun and Rifle fire was opened by the enemy at once, and at zero plus 10 minutes he retaliated with Minnies and Pineapples all along the Front and Support Lines of the HOUPLINES Sector; his fire was very inaccurate and no damage done. There was a total absence of artillery retaliation.
Opposite AUSTRALIA AVENUE, Locality 8, C.29.c.32.28, he bombed his own wire, but did not retaliate in any other way.

Our Action. Instructions laid down in Brigade Order No.10 were duly carried out. A patrol which it had been intended to send out from C.29.Central did not proceed owing to the gas on this area not being discharged by order of the supervising R.E. Officer. No retaliation by our artillery was called for.

3. 0 a.m. Our heavy artillery fired, but without drawing any retaliation from the enemy.

CASUALTIES. Owing to 2 cylinders at C.17.c.25.85 and C.17.c.25.65 leaking, 4 of the R.E. personnel were gassed - one badly and 3 slightly. 1 man of "F" Battn. slightly gassed.

Brigadier-General,
Commanding G. O. 3

APPENDIX NO. I.

MOVE ORDERS,

RELIEF ORDERS,

etc.,

referred to in

171st INFANTRY BRIGADE WAR DIARY,

31.3.1917 to 30.4.1917.

COPY NO. 18

## 171st BRIGADE RELIEF ORDER NO. 4.

3rd April, 1917.

1. The 2/8th K.L.R. will relieve the 2/5th K.L.R., and take over the BOIS GRENIER or RIGHT SECTOR on the night of the 5th/6th April.

2. Reliefs will take place not earlier than 7.30 p.m., arrangements as to Reliefs being left to Battn. Commanders.

3. The 2/5th K.L.R., less 1 Company, will go into Right Reserve Battalion, taking over the billets vacated by the 2/8th K.L.R., O.C. 2/5th K.L.R. detailing one Company to remain in the Subsidiary Line; this Company coming under the orders of the O.C. 2/8th K.L.R.,

4. (a) Advanced Parties of the 2/8th K.L.R. will report to O.C. 2/5th K.L.R., 24 hours before relief of Battalions takes place, and will remain in the Trenches until the arrival of their Battn.

(b) Advanced Parties of the 2/5th K.L.R., will likewise report to O.C. 2/8th K.L.R., and arrange matters as regards the billets in Reserve.

5. Commands will pass on completion of relief, which will be reported to this Office by wire.

6. ACKNOWLEDGE.

Lieut.Colonel, Brigade Major.
171st Infantry Brigade.

ISSUED AT 8.45 P.M.,

| Copy No. | | Copy No. | |
|---|---|---|---|
| 1. | H.Q. 57th Div. "G". | 13. | 170th Inf. Bde. |
| 2. | ,, "Q" | 14. | 9th Aus. Inf. Bde. |
| 3. | Staff Captain. | 15. | Left Group, R.A., |
| 4. | Signals. | 16. | 57th Divl. Artillery, H.Q. |
| 5. | 2/5th K.L.R. | 17. | 171st L.T.M.B. |
| 6. | 2/6th ,, | 18. | War Diary. |
| 7. | 2/7th ,, | 19. | ,, |
| 8. | 2/8th ,, | 20. | File, |
| 9. | 172nd M.G.Co. | 21. | 3"2nd W.L.Field Ambce. |
| 10. | 173rd ,, | | |
| 11. | 505 Field Co, R.E. | | |
| 12. | 421 ,, | | |

SECRET.                                                                    COPY NO. 18

## 171st BRIGADE RELIEF ORDER No. 5.

4th April, 1917.

1. The 2/7th K.L.R. will relieve the 2/6th K.L.R., and take over the RUE DU BOIS or LEFT SECTOR on the night of the 6th/7th April.

2. Reliefs will take place not earlier than 8.0 p.m., arrangements as to Reliefs being left to Battn. Commanders.

3. The 2/6th K.L.R., less 1 Company, will go into Left Reserve Battalion, taking over the billets vacated by the 2/7th K.L.R., O.C., 2/6th K.L.R., detailing one Company to remain in the Subsidiary Line; this Company coming under the orders of O.C., 2/7th K.L.R.,

4. (a) Advanced Parties of the 2/7th K.L.R., will report to O.C., 2/6th K.L.R., 24 hours before relief of Battalions takes place, and will remain in the Trenches until the arrival of their Battalion.

(b) Advanced Parties of the 2/6th K.L.R., will likewise report to O.C., 2/7th K.L.R., and arrange matters as regards the billets in Reserve.

5. Commands will pass on completion of relief, which will be reported to this Office by wire.

6. ACKNOWLEDGE.

Lieut.Colonel, Brigade Major,
171st Infantry Brigade.

ISSUED AT 3.45 P.M.,

| Copy No. | | Copy No. | |
|---|---|---|---|
| 1. | H.Q., 57th Div. "G". | 13. | 170th Inf. Bde. |
| 2. | ,, ,, "Q". | 14. | 9th Aus. Inf. Bde. |
| 3. | Staff Captain. | 15. | Left Group, R.A. |
| 4. | Signals. | 16. | 57th Divl. Artillery, H.Q. |
| 5. | 2/5th K.L.R., | 17. | 171st L.T.M.B., |
| 6. | 2/6th ,, | 18. | War Diary. |
| 7. | 2/7th ,, | 19. | ,, |
| 8. | 2/8th ,, | 20. | File. |
| 9. | 172nd M.G.Co. | 21. | 3/2nd W.L.Field Ambce. |
| 10. | 173rd ,, | | |
| 11. | 505 Field Co, R.E., | | |
| 12. | 421 ,, | | |

SECRET.                                                      COPY NO. 22

                  171st BRIGADE ORDER NO. 7.
                                                    10th April, 1917.
Ref.Map.1/10.000.
Sheets 36 N.W. 3 & 4.            ........

1.   In accordance with 57th Divisional Order No.6 dated
     9th April 1917, the 172nd Brigade will relieve the 171st
     Brigade in the Left Brigade Sector.         Relief to be
     complete by 4.30 a.m., night of 13th/14th April.

2.   The 171st Brigade will take over the Billets in ERQUINGHEM
     and BAC.ST.MAUR vacated by 172nd Brigade.

3.   Reliefs will be carried out as follows :-

     April 11th/12th - Night of.

          O.C. 2/8th K.L.R., will make arrangements for the
          accommodation of Lewis Guns of the 2/10th K.L.R., who
          will move into the Subsidiary Line.     Relief of
          Lewis Guns will take place under Battalion arrangements
          during the day of the 12th instant.

     April 12th.
                         less one Company in Subsid.Line
     (a)  The 2/5th K.L.R.,^will be relieved by the 2/9th K.L.R.
          in Right Reserve.     Relief to commence at 5.30 p.m.

     (b)  1 Company, 2/5th K.L.R., in the Subsidiary Line will
          be relieved by 1 Company, 2/9th K.L.R., Relief to
          commence at 8 p.m.

     (c)  Billeting Parties, 2/5th K.L.R., to report to HdQrs,
          2/10th K.L.R., G.18.D.80.80. at 10 a.m. on 12th instant,
          and take over their billets.

     April 12th/13th - Night of.

     (a)  The 2/8th K.L.R., will be relieved by the 2/10th K.L.R.
          in the BOIS GRENIER FRONT LINE SECTOR.    The 2/10th
          K.L.R. will not cross the RUE DELETTREE before 8.30 p.m.

     (b)  Billeting Parties, 2/8th K.L.R., will report to H.Qrs.,
          2/9th K.L.R., at 10 a.m. 12th instant, at ERQUINGHEM
          (opposite back of Brigade HdQrs, H.4.D.30.70) and take
          over their Billets.

     (c)  Guides will be furnished under Battn. arrangements.

     April 12th/13th - Night of.

        O.C. 2/7th K.L.R., will arrange for the accommodation of
        the Lewis Guns, 2/4th S.L.R., in the Subsidiary Line.
        Relief of Lewis Guns will take place during the day of
        the 13th instant under Battalion arrangements.

     April 13th.

     (a)  The 2/6th K.L.R., less 1 Company, will be relieved by
          the 2/5th S.L.R., and take over their Billets at RUE
          DORMOIRE.    Relief will be arranged inter-regimentally
          but must commence by 3 p.m.,

April 13th (Contd).

 (b) Billeting Parties 2/6th K.L.R., will report to H.Qrs 2/5th
     S.L.R., H.S.B.90.30, at 10 a.m., 13th instant, and take over
     billets.

 (c) The Company of 2/6th K.L.R. in Subsidiary Line will be
     relieved by a Company of 2/5th S.L.R., who will not pass
     CROWN PRINCE HOUSE before 8 p.m.    Route to be followed
     by Company of 2/6th K.L.R. coming out will be - SUBSIDIARY
     LINE - LA VESSEE - GRISBET - RUE DESACQUETS.

April 13th/14th - Night of.

 (a) The 2/7th K.L.R., will be relieved by 2/4th S.L.R., in the
     RUE DU BOIS SECTOR.    Relief to commence at 9 p.m.

 (b) Billeting Parties, 2/7th K.L.R., will report to H.Q. 2/4th
     S.L.R. at The Laundry, H.5.A. on the 13th instant at 3 p.m. to
     take over Billets.

April 12th/13th - Night of.

   The 171st L.T.M.B. will be relieved by the 172nd L.T.M.B. in
the RUE DU BOIS SECTOR under the arrangements of Officers
Commanding, the procedure in Brigade Order No.5 dated 29th March
being reversed, and eliminating the section referring to personnel
remaining in Trenches.    Relief to take place at night (at) 9 p.m

April 13th/14th - Night of.

 (a) Relief of L.T.M.B. in BOIS GRENIER SECTOR will take place
     at 9 p.m.

 (b) The 172nd Brigade will arrange for the transport of their
     L.T.M.Bs to take away the 171st L.T.M.B. on both occasions.

4. Officers Commanding Battalions and Units will arrange inter-
   Regimentally as to Guides required.

5. All Trench Stores - Log Books - Maps - Defence Schemes - and
   necessary Records will be handed over on relief.    Receipts will
   be obtained in DUPLICATE and one copy forwarded to Brigade H.Qrs.

6. Rear Parties will be left behind in compliance with 57th Divl.
   Orders on the subject - and receipts obtained that Lines and Billets
   have been handed over to the satisfaction of Incoming Units.

7. Commands will pass on completion of Reliefs.

8. Brigade Orders regarding March Formations will be strictly
   observed in the various areas - by night, Platoons will keep closed
   up.

9. Until the Relief of the whole Sector is complete, Units of the
   172nd Brigade in this area will come under the orders of the B.G.C.
   171st Brigade; and vice versa.    Units will render routine etc.,
   returns to their own Brigade H.Qrs, but all Operation and Intelligence
   Reports to those HdQrs.

10. Relief of Brigade H.Qrs will take place at 3 p.m. on the 13th inst.
    Brigade H.Qrs will open at ERQUINGHEM, H.4.D.30.70 at 4 p.m. on 13th
    inst.    The Command will pass on the night of the 13th/14th.

11. ACKNOWLEDGE.

ISSUED AT 9.0 P.M. Copy 8. 57th Divl.H.Q."G".
Copy 1. B.G.C.         9.   "      "   "Q"               Lieut.Col. Bde Major.
     2. O.S.Fts.      10.  171st L.T.M.B.                 171st Infantry Brigade.
     3. Staff Capt.   11.  507 Co.A.S.C.    Copy 16. 173rd M.G.Co.
     4. "E" Battn.    12.  170th Brigade.        17. 2/2nd W.L.Fd Amboo.
     5.  "F"  "       13.  172nd   "             18. Left Group Arty.
     6.  "G"  "       14.  2 Sec.Div.Sigs.       19. 505 Field Co.R.E.
     7.  "H"  "       15.  172nd M.G.Coy.        20. 421   "    "   "
    21. Divl. Arty. 22. "War Diary."             23. "War Diary.

S E C R E T.

Copy No. 7

Ref. Map 1/10,000
Sheets 36 N.W.3 & 4.

## 57th DIVISION ORDER NO. 7.

16th April, 1917.

1. 171st Brigade will relieve 170th Brigade in the Right Brigade Sector - Relief to be complete by 4 a.m. night 23/24th April.

2. All Reliefs will take place by night and will be arranged between the Brigadiers concerned.

3. On Relief, 170th Brigade will take over the billets in ERQUINGHEM and BAC ST MAUR vacated by 171st Brigade.

4. Field Companies R.E. and Machine Gun Companies will remain in their present positions.

5. Command will pass at 5 p.m. on 23rd April.

6. Completion of Relief will be reported to Divisional Headquarters.

7. ACKNOWLEDGE.

CECIL ALLANSON, Lieut-Colonel,

General Staff,

Issued at 12 noon to:-

Copy No. 1. War Diary.
2. G.S. File.
3. G.O.C.
4. C.R.A.
5. C.R.E.
6. 170th Bde.
7. 171st do.
8. 172nd do.
9. 'A'
10. 'Q'
11. Div. Train.
12. A.D.M.S.
13. A.P.M.
14. D.A.D.O.S.
15. Signals.
16. A.D.V.S.
17. O.C., 173rd M.G.Coy.
18. II ANZAC Corps (for information)
19. 3rd Aust. Division do.
20. 49th Division. do.
21. Camp Commandant.
22. D.G.O.
23. )
24. ) Spare.
25. )

SECRET.                                                     COPY NO. 24

171st BRIGADE ORDER NO. 8.

                                                            19th April 1917.
Ref.Map 1/10.000.          .......
Sheets 36 N.W. 3 & 4.

1.    In accordance with 57th Divisional Order No.7 dated 16th
      April 1917, the 171st Brigade will relieve the 170th Brigade
      in the Right Brigade Sector.       Relief to be complete by
      4 a.m. night of the 23rd/24th.

2.    The 170th Brigade will take over the Billets in the
      ERQUINGHEM and BAC ST MAUR areas vacated by this Brigade.

3.    RELIEFS WILL BE CARRIED OUT AS FOLLOWS :-

Night of 21st/22nd April.

      The Lewis Guns of the 2/6th K.L.R., will move into the
Support Line of the Left or BOUTILLERIE SECTOR for the night.
They will relieve the Lewis Guns of the 2/5th "King's Own"
by day on the 22nd.

      Route to be followed from Billets  - FORT ROMPU -
FLEURBAIX., Lewis Guns of the Left and Reserve Companies using
TINBARN AVENUE C.T.,     those of the right and Centre
Companies, C.T.WATLING STREET.         Limbers can proceed as
far as WYE FARM and CROIX MARECHAL.

      FORT ROMPU will not be passed before 8.0 p.m.

Night of 22nd/23rd April.

(a) The 2/6th K.L.R. will relieve the 2/5th "King's Own" in
the Front Line, BOUTILLERIE SECTOR.         Left and Reserve
Companies will move via ELBOW FARM. TIN BARN AVENUE.
Right and Centre Companies via CROIX MARECHAL and WATLING
STREET.

      Battalion Headquarters at FORMY HOUSE.

      Transport can be taken as far as WYE FARM and CROIX
MARECHAL.

      Route to be observed from Billets as laid down for Lewis
guns.
                           to
      FORT ROMPU is not ^ be passed before 8.0 p.m.

      The 2/8th K.L.R. will relieve the 2/5th L.N.L. and
become the Battalion in Right Brigade Reserve, going into
Billets at ROUGE de BOUT.       Headquarters at G.36.D.26.67.
                billets
      Route from ^ FORT ROMPU  -  RUE RATAILLE, RUE DU QUESNOY.

      FORT ROMPU is not to be passed before 7.30 p.m.

      One Company will relieve Platoons of the 2/5th L.N.L. in
the Subsidiary Line.        Battalion will give way to the
T.M.B. if necessary.


(b) The 171st L.T.M.B. will relieve the 170th L.T.M.B. as
follows:-

      The 4 Guns for the CORDONNERIE SECTOR moving via FORT
ROMPU - PORT A CLOUS - RUE DU BIACH - ROUGE de BASSIERES -
EXX EATON HALL.     FORT ROMPU is not to be passed before
7.30 p.m.

2.

The 4 Guns for the BOUTILLERIE SECTOR moving via FORT ROMPU - FLEURBAIX - CROIX MARECHAL - TATLING STREET. FORT ROMPU is not to be passed before 8.0 p.m.

The Battery will move into the Support Line for the night, relief taking place during the day of the 23rd.

A proportion of the 170th L.T.M.B. will remain in the Line for 24 hours until the 171st L.T.M.Bs are acquainted with the Line.

Limbers can be taken as far as CROIX MARECHAL and EATON HALL.    Battery Headquarters at FLEURBAIX.

(c) The Lewis Guns of the 2/5th K.L.R. will move into the Support Line in the CORDONNERIE SECTOR for the night, and will relieve by day on the 23rd the Lewis Guns of the 2/4th L.N.L.

Route from Billets for Guns of the Right and Centre Coys - RUE DE BRUGES - RUE DE QUESNOY - ROUGE de BOUT - WINDY POST - V.C. HOUSE - V.C. AVENUE.

For Guns of Left and Reserve Coys - through H.13.C. - RUE RATAILLE - H.19.C. - H.25.B. - RUE de BASSIERES - CROIX BLANCHE - EATON HALL - CELLAR FARM.

Limbers can proceed as far as EATON HALL and V.C. HOUSE. The Cross Roads at ROUGE DE BOUT and LA CROIX LES CORNET will not be passed before 8.0 p.m.

Night of 23rd/24th April.

The 2/5th K.L.R. will relieve the 2/4th L.N.L., taking over the Front Line CORDONNERIE SECTOR.

Route from Billets and restrictions will be as that laid down for the Lewis Guns.

The 2/7th K.L.R., will relieve the 4/5th L.N.L. as Battalion in Left Brigade Reserve at FLEURBAIX, detailing one Company to relieve those of the 2/5th "King's Own" at CROIX MARECHAL. ELBOW FARM - CHAPEL FARM and SMITHS VILLA - COMMAND POST.

Route from Billets - RUE DELPIERRE - FLEURBAIX.    The level crossing at Pt.de BIEZ is not to be passed before 7.30 p.m.

4.    Officers Commanding Battalions and Units will arrange inter-Regimentally all further details as regards Reliefs and Guides required.

5.    Advance Parties will report to the Battalion HdQrs of those Battalions whom their Battalions are relieving 24 hours prior to going up on relief, and remain for the night in their future Sector.

6.    All Trench Stores - Log Books - Maps - Defence Schemes and necessary records will be taken over on Relief.    Receipts will be obtained in duplicate, and one copy forwarded to Brigade HdQrs.

7.    Billeting Parties of the 170th Brigade will report to Battn. HdQrs at 10 a.m., on the day of Relief to take over Billets.    Rear Parties will be left behind in compliance with 57th Divisional instructions on this subject - and receipts obtained that all Billets have been handed over to the satisfaction of the incoming Units.

3.

8. Commands will pass on completion of Reliefs.

9. Orders regarding March Formations, as previously issued, will be strictly adhered to. East of the LAVENTIE - ARMENTIERES railway line, the strictest precautions must be observed, except when moving by night, when Platoons will keep closed up.

10. Until the passing of the Command to this Brigade is complete, Battalions will be under the orders of the B.G.C., 170th Brigade, to whom all operation and Intelligence Reports will be rendered; Routine, etc., returns to this Office.

11. Completion of Reliefs will be reported by wire.

12. Brigade Command will pass at 5.0 p.m. on 23rd April.

   Brigade HdQrs will close at ERQUINGHEM at 4 p.m. on the 23rd April, and open at FLEURBAIX at 5.0 p.m.,

13. ACKNOWLEDGE.


                                          G. E. GEDDES.

                                    Lieut. Colonel, Brigade Major,
                                         171st Infantry Brigade.


ISSUED AT 4.0 P.M., to :-

Copy No.                                Copy No.

1. B.G.C.,                              14. H.Qrs, 172nd Brigade.
2. Staff Captain.                       15. 170th M.G. Company.
3. H.Q., 57th Div., "A"                 16. 171st      ,,
4.    ,,      ,,    "G"                 17. 505 Coy, R.E.,
5. Signals.                             18. 507 Coy, R.E.,
6. "E" Battn.                           19. 421 Coy, R.E.,
7. "F"  ,,                              20. Right Group, R.A.,
8. "G"  ,,                              21. A.D.M.S.,
9. "H"  ,,                              22. 146th Brigade.
10. Divisional Artillery.               23. Brigade Bombing Officer.
11. 171st L.T.M.B.,                     24. War Diary.
12. 507 Coy, A.S.C.,                    25.        ,,
13. H.Q., 170th Brigade.                26. G.S. File.

SECRET.                                                        G.148/12.
- - - - -

P R E L I M I N A R Y   W A R N I N G.
........  ..........

1.      171st Infantry Brigade will take over the ARMENTIERES Sector from the Right Brigade of the 3rd Australian Division on 21st April.

2.      Orders for Artillery, R.E., and M.G. Coys. will be issued later.

3.      A.D.M.S. will arrange direct with A.D.M.S. 3rd Australian Division to take over the Medical arrangements in the Sector.

4.      B.G.C. 171st Brigade will arrange to reconnoitre the ARMENTIERES Sector forthwith. Headquarters of the Brigade in this Sector is in ARMENTIERES.

5.      Further orders as to the relief will be issued as soon as received.

6.      Divisional Headquarters will probably move to CROIX DU BAC but no move will take place prior to the fresh Line being completely taken over.

7.      ACKNOWLEDGE.

D.H.Q.,                                    CECIL ALLANSON, Lieut-Colonel,
20/4/1917.                                    General Staff, 57th Division.

Issued at 8 a.m. to:-

    C.R.A.
    C.R.E.
    H.Q., 170th Brigade.
     "   171st  do.
     "   172nd  do.
    O.C., Signals.
     "  173rd M.G. Coy.
    O.C., Train.
    A.D.M.S.
    A.D.V.S.
    D.A.D.O.S.
    A.P.M.
    Camp Commandant.
    'Q'
    D.G.O.

SECRET.                                                    COPY NO. 9

### PRELIMINARY WARNING.

20th April, 1917.

1. The 171st Infantry Brigade will relieve the 10th Australian Infantry Brigade, and take over the ARMENTIERES SECTOR, the relief being complete by 4.30 a.m., on the 27th April.

2. The 2/5th K.L.R., will relieve the 37th Battn. Australian Infantry, and take over the Right or EPINETTE SECTOR, relief taking place on the night of the 25th/26th.

3. The 2/6th K.L.R., will relieve the 38th Battn. Australian Infantry, and take over the Left or HOUPLINES SECTOR, relief taking place on the night of the 26th/27th.

4. The 2/8th K.L.R., will go into Right Brigade Reserve in Billets in ARMENTIERES, the afternoon of the 26th.

5. The 2/7th K.L.R., will go into Left Brigade Reserve in Billets in ARMENTIERES, the afternoon of the 25th.

6. Lewis Guns of 2/5th and 2/6th K.L.R., will move into the Subsidiary Line of their future Sectors, 48 hours previous to reliefs by Battalions.     Advance parties consisting of 1 Officer and 1 N.C.O. for Battalion Hdqrs, and 1 Officer and 1 N.C.O. per Platoon, 24 hours previous to reliefs.

7. Commanding Officers - Company Commanders - Battalion Lewis Gun Officers - O.C. and 1 Officer 171st L.T.M.B. - xxxxxxxxxxxxxxxxxxxxxxxxxxxxxxxxxxxxxxxxxx - will report to 10th Australian Infantry Brigade Hdqrs at 9.30 a.m., tomorrow, 21st April, where guides will meet them and conduct them round their Sector.

8. The 10th Australian Infantry Brigade Hdqrs are situated in ARMENTIERES - Reference G.25.D.60.50.     Route - ERQUINGHEM - Level Crossing at H.8.B.95.62 - first turning to right - 1st to left - then straight past Church at H.30.D.70.20 - Half-past-Eleven Square G.25.D.30.70 - first to right down RUE JESUIT - Large W. on wall denotes Brigade Hdqrs.

9. Further orders as to reliefs will be issued as soon as received from Division.

10. ACKNOWLEDGE.

G.W. GEDDES.

Lieut.Colonel, Brigade Major.
171st Infantry Brigade.

ISSUED AT 3.0 p.m. to :-

Copy 1.   B.G.C.,
     2.   Staff Captain.
     3.   G.S.File.
     4.   "E" Battalion.
     5.   "F"    "
     6.   "G"    "
     7.   "H"    "
     8.   171st L.T.M.B.
     9.   War Diary.
    10.         "

SECRET.
-------

Reference Map 1/10,000
  Sheets 36 N.W.2 & 4.
  ........

Copy No...7....

20th April, 1917.

### 57th DIVISION ORDER NO. 8.
**************

1. 57th Division Order No. 7 is cancelled.

2. The 57th Division will take over the whole of the Corps front South of the RIVER LYS.

3. The 171st Brigade will consequently relieve the Right Brigade of the 3rd Australian Division by April 26th: details of relief to be arranged between B.Gs.O. concerned.

4. The Divisional Artillery with one Army Brigade F.A. will cover 57th Divisional Front under arrangements to be made by C.R.A.

5. One Field Company R.E. will be affiliated to each Brigade Sector under orders of the C.R.E.

6. A.D.M.S. will arrange with A.D.M.S. 3rd Australian Division to take over the Medical arrangements in the ARMENTIERES Sector.

7. One Brigade 25th Division (less 1 Battalion) will be billeted in the ERQUINGHEM - WATERLANDS Area from 29th April under arrangements to be made by "A". 57th Division will have a direct call on this Brigade in case of emergency.

8. The distribution of the Machine Gun Companies over the area will be notified later.

9. Separate orders will be issued as regards Administrative Boundaries.

10. 57th Divisional Headquarters will move to CROIX DU BAC at 12 noon on 1st May.

11. Completion of relief will be reported to Divisional Headquarters.

12. ACKNOWLEDGE.

Issued at ...3pm... to:-      CECIL ALLANSON, Lieut-Colonel,
                                        General Staff.
Copy No.
  1. War Diary.                16. A.D.V.S.
  2. G.S.File.                 17. O.C., 173rd M.G. Coy.
  3. G.O.C.                    18. II ANZAC Corps. (for information)
  4. C.R.A.                    19. 3rd Australian Division    do.
  5. C.R.E.                    20. 49th Division              do.
  6. 170th Bde.                21. 25th Division.             do.
  7. 171st  do.                22. Camp Commandant.
  8. 172nd  do.                23. D.G.O.
  9. 'A'                       24.)
 10. 'Q'                       25.) Spare.
 11. Train.                    26.)
 12. A.D.M.S.
 13. A.P.M.
 14. D.A.D.O.S.
 15. Signals.

PTO

In continuation of 57th Division Order No. 8 -

The M.G. Coys. will be distributed as follows:-

(1) One Coy. In each Bde. Sector ) 170th M.G.Coy. in 170th Bde.Area
                                               ) 171st   do.     171st    do.
                                               ) 172nd   do.     172nd    do.

(2) 173rd M.G.Coy. in the ARMENTIERES Defences.

The redistribution will be carried out under arrangements of O.C., 173rd M.G.Coy. in conjunction with the Brigades.

D.H.Q.,                              CECIL ALLANSON, Lieut-Colonel,
20/4/1917.                                General Staff, 57th Division.

S E C R E T.

## MACHINE GUN ORDER No. 3.

**********

1.  (a) The 57th Division will take over the whole of the Corps front South of the RIVER LIS.

    (b) The 171st Brigade will relieve the Right Brigade of the 3rd Australian Division in the ARMENTIERES Sector by the 26th April.  Details of relief to be arranged by B.Gs.C. concerned.

2.  Machine Gun Companies will be distributed as follows :-

    170th M.G.Coy. will take over the whole of 170th Bde. Sector.
    171st     ,,     ,,   ,,   ,,   ,,   ,,  ,,   171st   ,,     ,,
    172nd     ,,     ,,   ,,   ,,   ,,   ,,  ,,   172nd   ,,     ,,
    173rd     ,,     ,,   ,,   ,,   ,,   ,,  ,, defence of the town of ARMENTIERES.

3.  (a) Os.C. 170th, 171st, and 172nd M.G.Coys will at once get in touch with their respective Brigade Headquarters, and with the Os.C. outgoing M.G.Coys, reconnoitre the portion of the line new to them, and submit a scheme of defence for the whole Sector to B.Gs.C. their respective Brigades, and General Staff, (Machine Guns) 57th Division.

    (b) O.C., 173rd M.G.Coy. will receive orders as to moving from General Staff (Machine Guns) 57th Division later.

4.  Headquarters, 57th Division will open at CROIX du BAC at 12 noon, 1-5-1917.


D.H.Q.                                    *Alan Bellingham*  Captain,
20-4-1917.                                  Commanding 173rd M.G.Coy.

DISTRIBUTION:-

H.Q., 170th Brigade.
  "   171st   do.
  "   172nd   do.
O.C., 170th M.G. Coy.
  "   171st   do.
  "   172nd   do.
  "   173rd   do.
War Diary,
G.S.File
"A" and "Q"

SECRET.                171st BRIGADE ORDER NO. 9.           COPY NO. 23

Ref. Map. 1:20.000.                                21st April, 1917.
Sheet 36. N.E.

1. In accordance with 57th Divisional Order No.8, the 171st Infantry Brigade will relieve the 10th Australian Infantry Brigade and take over the ARMENTIERES SECTOR. Relief to be completed by 4.30 a.m., April 27th.

2. Point of Rendezvous for Guides will be referred to as P. of R., as regards passing times and will be the Level Crossing at H.5.B.95.82.

3. Reliefs will be carried out as follows :-

April 24th.

(a) The 2/5th K.L.R., will move into Billets in ARMENTIERES on the afternoon of the 24th - billeting there for the night of 24th/25th. P. of R. will be passed at 3.0 p.m.,

Night of April 24th/25th.

(b) Advance Parties 2/5th K.L.R., will move into the Right or EPINETTE SECTOR.

Lewis Guns 2/5th K.L.R., will move into the Subsidiary Line of the Right or EPINETTE SECTOR, reporting to Battn. HdQrs of that Sector. The relief of the Lewis Guns of the 37th Battn. Australian Infantry will take place on the day of the 25th.

The 171st L.T.M.B. will relieve the 10th Australian L.T.M.B. A proportion of the latter will remain in the line until the 171st L.T.M.B. are acquainted with the line.

P. of R. will be passed at 7.30 p.m.,

(c) The 2/7th K.L.R. will go into Billets at ARMENTIERES on the afternoon of the 25th - and form the Left Battn. in Brigade Reserve. P. of R. will be passed at 4 pm.

Night of 25th / 26th April.

(d) The 2/5th K.L.R., will relieve the 37th Battn. Australian Infantry and take over the Right or EPINETTE SECTOR. Head of the Battalion will leave Billets at 8.0 p.m.,

Advance Parties 2/6th K.L.R., will move into Left or HOUPLINES SECTOR - P. of R. to be passed at 3 pm

Lewis Guns 2/6th K.L.R., will move into the Subsidiary Line, HOUPLINES SECTOR, reporting to Battn. HdQrs. of that Sector. The relief of the Lewis Guns 38th Battn. Australian Infantry will take place on the day of the 26th. P. of R. to be passed at 7.30 p.m.

(e) The 2/8th K.L.R., will go into Right Brigade Reserve in Billets in ARMENTIERES on the afternoon of the 26th instant. P. of R. to be passed at 3.0 p.m.

Night of 26th/27th April.

(f) The 2/6th K.L.R., will relieve the 38th Battn. Australian Infantry and take over the Left or HOUPLINES SECTOR. P. of R. to be passed at 7.4 p.m.,

2.

4. Battalions in Reserve will immediately reconnoitre all Emergency Routes - and the Sector in general.

5. Battalion Commanders will arrange that their Advance Parties report to and remain with the Companies and Platoons they are relieving for 24 hours previous to relief, reporting to the Battn. HdQrs of the Battn. they are to relieve.

6. Officers Commanding Battalions and Units will arrange inter-Regimentally all further details regarding Reliefs.

7. All Trench Stores - Log Books - Maps - Defence Schemes and necessary records will be taken over on relief - and receipts exchanged.

8. Billets will be left scrupulously clean in accordance with previous orders on this subject. Small rear parties in charge of an Officer will see that these Orders have been complied with, and a report will be rendered to this Office to that effect.

9. No limbers or carts will be taken beyond a line running North and South of the Level Crossing at C.27.A.20.10.

10. Commands will pass on completion of Reliefs.

11. Previous Orders regarding March Formations will be strictly observed. A line running North and South through the Level Crossing at C.27.A.20.10 necessitates the strictest precautions.

12. Until the passing of the Command to this Brigade is complete, Battalions will be under the orders of the B.G.C. 10th Australian Infantry Brigade, to whom all operation and Intelligence Reports will be rendered; Routine etc. returns to this Office.

13. Completion of Reliefs will be reported by wire.

14. Brigade Command will pass at 6 p.m. on the 26th instant. Brigade HdQrs will close at ERQUINGHEM at 5 p.m. on the 26th, and open at RUE JESUIT, C.25.D.60.50. ARMENTIERES, at 6 p.m.

15. ACKNOWLEDGE.

G. W. GEDDES.

Lieut.Colonel, Brigade Major.
171st Infantry Brigade.

ISSUED AT 3.0 p.m., to :-

Copy No.

1. B.G.C.,
2. Staff Captain.
3. H.Q., 57th Div., "A".
4. ,, ,, "G".
5. Signals.
6. "E" Battn.
7. "F" ,,
8. "G" ,,
9. "H" ,,
10. Divisional Artillery.
11. 171st L.T.M.B.,
12. 507 Coy, A.S.C.,
13. H.Q., 170th Brigade.

Copy No.

14. H.Qrs, 172nd Brigade.
15. 173rd M.G.Company.
16. 171st ,, ,,
17. 505 Coy, R.E.,
18. 502 Coy, R.E.,
19. 421 Coy, R.E.,
20. 10th Australian Inf.Bde.
21. A.D.M.S.,
22. Brigade Bombing Officer.
23. War Diary.
24. ,,
25. G.S.Gild.
26. Spare.

SECRET.
- - - - -


AMENDMENT TO 57TH DIVISION ORDER NO. 8.
*******************

22nd April, 1917.


The Move of 57th Divisional Headquarters to CROIX DU BAC will be completed by 12 noon 2nd May and not 1st May as stated in Division Order No.8 dated 20th April.

CECIL ALLANSON, Lieut-Colonel,
General Staff.

Copies issued to all recipients of Division Order No.8.

SECRET.

O.C.,
   171st Machine Gun Company.

.....

Reference Brigade Order No.9 of the 21st instant.

The Machine Gun Company under your Command will relieve the 207th Machine Gun Company in the EPINETTE - HOUPLINES SECTOR.

The B.G.C., is desirous that the relief of the whole Company should take place, if possible, on the night of the 25th/26th April. At any rate, half the relief must be completed on that night, and the remaining half on the night of the 26th/27th April.     Arrangements for Guides and Reliefs to be arranged between Os.C. Machine Gun Companies.

Should the whole relief not take place on the night of the 25th/26th April, half of your Company will billet in ARMENTIERES for the night.

G.W.GEDDES.

Lieut.Colonel, Brigade Major.
171st Infantry Brigade.

B.H.Q.
   23.4.1917

APPENDIX No. II.

STATEMENT of CASUALTIES.

..............

Forwarded in conjunction with

171st INFANTRY BRIGADE WAR DIARY,

31.3.1917 to 30.4.1917.

......

# CASUALTIES 171st INFANTRY BRIGADE from 31.3.1917 to 30.4.1917.

| DATE. 24 hours ending noon:- | KILLED. Officers. | KILLED. O.Ranks. | WOUNDED. Officers. | WOUNDED. O.Ranks. | WOUNDED. (ACCIDENTALLY) Officers. | WOUNDED. (ACCIDENTALLY) O.Ranks. |
|---|---|---|---|---|---|---|
| 31.3.1917 | - | 1 | - | - | - | - |
| 1.4.1917  | - | - | - | 2 | - | - |
| 2.4.1917  | - | - | - | 6 | - | 1 |
| 3.4.1917  | - | 3 | - | 2 | - | - |
| 4.4.1917  | - | - | - | 1 | - | - |
| 5.4.1917  | - | 1 | - | 2 | - | 1 |
| 6.4.1917  | - | 1 | - | 1 | - | - |
| 7.4.1917  | - | - | - | 1 | - | - |
| 8.4.1917  | - | - | - | 1 | - | 2 |
| 9.4.1917  | - | - | - | 5 (inc 2 slightly at duty) | - | - |
| 10.4.1917 | - | - | - | 2 (inc.1 S.Inflicted) | - | - |
| 11.4.1917 | - | - | - | 4 (inc.3 Slightly) | - | - |
| 12.4.1917 | - | - | 1 (2nd Lt G.Davis) | - | - | - |
| 13.4.1917 | - | - | - | 1 | - | - |
| 14.4.1917 | - | - | - | 1 | - | - |
| 16.4.1917 | - | 2 | 2 (Lts Addy & Cowper) (Inc.1 Sl.at duty) | 10 (inc.1 slightly at duty) | - | - |
| 17.4.1917 | - | - | - | 1 | - | - |
| 19.4.1917 | - | - | - | 1 | - | - |
| 21.4.1917 | - | - | - | - | - | 1 |
| 23.4.1917 | - | - | - | 1 | - | 1 |
| 25.4.1917 | - | - | - | - | - | 2 |
| 28.4.1917 | TOTAL. | 1 | TOTAL. | TOTAL. | TOTAL. | - |
| 29.4.1917 | - | 2 | - | 5 | - | - |
| 30.4.1917 | - | 1 | - | 1 | - | - |
|           | - | 11 | 3 | 48 | - | 7 |

B.H.Q., 3.5.1917

CONFIDENTIAL.

WAR DIARY

of

HEADQUARTERS, 171st INFANTRY BRIGADE.

1.5.1917 to 30.5.1917.

VOLUME III.

Army Form C. 2118

# WAR DIARY
## or
## INTELLIGENCE SUMMARY
*(Erase heading not required.)*

Instructions regarding War Diaries and Intelligence Summaries are contained in F. S. Regs., Part II. and the Staff Manual respectively. Title Pages will be prepared in manuscript.

| Place | Date | Hour | Summary of Events and Information | Remarks and references to Appendices |
|---|---|---|---|---|
| ARMENTIERES | 1.5.17 | | O.C. 111th Battalion in Reserve in the billet. Ordinary activity on part of Enemy Artillery. Subsidiary line of L'EPINETTE sector having particular attention paid to it — and the Tournekuff sector also — though his trench. | |
| " | 2.5.17 | From 9.30am to 1.30pm the Tournewan flunk heavily shelled. M.R.G.G.S. q Corps visited Bn. It the Enemy artillery activity has been on whole factor. a also observer alongside found no main lines of enemy lines between trenches to subsidiaries. Activity of Enemy artillery rather less. | |
| " | 3.5.17 | 11.30am 2.30am | Officer patrol pieces Enemy of front v in fields line in Enemy's fugat - return safely without any casualties. Enemy artillery quiet today. but a considerable increase of activity night. the Town. Enemy quite heavy shelled. 2/5 K.L.R relieves 2/5 K.L.R in L'EPINETTE Sub. Sector. | Appendix I |
| | 4.5.17 | | Enemy artillery quite active. but the Tournewan man shelled at twilight. Quite active in general. minimum action in HOUPINETTE Sectors at HERRS FARM. | |
| | 5.5.17 | am 3.20 | Attempt by the enemy to raid our lines was frustrated by M/G v Lewis gun fire without artillery without A.Patrols contact with enemy. two men killed 7 wounded - however day. Enemy artillery active about artillery overnight activity his Town. 2/3 K.L.Relieves 2/6 K.L.R in HOUPINETTE Sub. Sector. | Appendix I |

Army Form C. 2118

# WAR DIARY
or
## INTELLIGENCE SUMMARY
*(Erase heading not required.)*

Instructions regarding War Diaries and Intelligence Summaries are contained in F.S. Regs., Part II. and the Staff Manual respectively. Title Pages will be prepared in manuscript.

| Place | Date | Hour | Summary of Events and Information | Remarks and references to Appendices |
|---|---|---|---|---|
| ARMENTIERES | 6.5.17 | 2.30 a.m. | Enemy Artillery fire very intense, all attack areas and the Corps front were heavily shelled, but the town & front portion of Ryes sector quiet. Normal conditions during [rest of the] day. | |
| | 7.3.17 | — | Enemy Artillery active throughout the day. On back areas & French line especially. | |
| | | 7.30 p.m. | Enemy put heavy barrage down on the North & River LYS. Whilst his barrage he brought it down on L.C & on L/I of HOUPLINES sector — which he raided 15 minutes later. A Coy. 2/7 K.L.R. held Mine his barrage further south he raided the L'EPINETTE sector at trenches 5 & 6 — held by the 2/6 K.L.R. Retaliation opened on front in Attempt — to pulverise raid. | Appendix II |
| | | 10.20 | O.K. has reported from W. sector. | |
| | 8.3.17 | 1.25 | G. Trnunomorph — Attempts Garnis & Machine Gun barrage was Shipakolley trenches between Rue du Bois sector on Attempt. | Appendix I |
| | | | On & heavy night at L'EPINETTE sector. Enemy Artillery slightly less active throughout the day. | |
| | 9.3.17 | 9.30 a.m. | Enemy Artillery commenced trench mortar scheme — ARMENTIERES a heavy fire on trenches from 8.3" to 4.2" J heard from station continued throughout the day — When shells ufd. | |
| | | A.m. 8.10 | All was quiet. | |

Army Form C. 2118

# WAR DIARY
## or
## INTELLIGENCE SUMMARY
*(Erase heading not required.)*

Instructions regarding War Diaries and Intelligence Summaries are contained in F.S. Regs., Part II. and the Staff Manual respectively. Title Pages will be prepared in manuscript.

| Place | Date | Hour | Summary of Events and Information | Remarks and references to Appendices |
|---|---|---|---|---|
| ARMENTIERES | 10.5.17 | | Nothing special to report. Enemy artillery considerably less on previous days. | |
| | 11.5.17 | | Own Airops active on counter-battery work & balloons in ARMENTIERES - and lively artillery activity shown on HOUPLINES front. Enemy battery causing annoyance was silenced. | |
| | 12.5.17 | a.m. 12.30 | Quieter - No further fire last week. 2/S.R.L.R. completed relief of 2/S.R.W.M.RR. at LEPINETTE front by relief. Brigadier General BRAY D.S.O. proceeded on leave, command of the Brigade passing to Mr. GEDDES D.S.O. | Appendix I Appendix L |
| | 13.5.17 | | Enemy artillery again somewhat active, including ARMENTIERES in his attention, searching for our batteries located in the town. Our hy. anti-aircraft in Bois(?) were directed to his posts at LA VESÉE. Enemy planes hit by anti-aircraft guns. 2/8 R.L.R. relief of 2/7 R.L.R. completed in HOUPLINES SECTOR. Very quiet day. No artillery activity. | Appendix L Appendix L |
| | 14.5.17 | a.m. 12.45 | Nothing to report of any unusual occurrence. Normal condition | Appendix L |
| | 15.5.17 | | Unusually quiet day. - Our hy. Artillery to have taken place in the enemy lines. Fine available man from Battalion in Reserve employed on Camp Paths, for the Special Coys. R.E. installed. | Appendix L |
| | - | | Rain in the front line - Strong enemy patrol sortied - | |
| | 16.5.17 | | Very quiet day again - nitro-chloric to short hand tranch police charge in the weather again to east and rain - Every available man of Reserve Battalion employed on camp paths with Special Coys R.E. Strong Covering parties held by Battalion in the line. | Appendix L |

# WAR DIARY or INTELLIGENCE SUMMARY

Army Form C. 2118

| Place | Date | Hour | Summary of Events and Information | Remarks and references to Appendices |
|---|---|---|---|---|
| ARMENTIERES | 17.5.17 | — a.m. 9.15 a.m. | Another quiet day, only slight artillery activity. Enemy attempted to raid Brigade on our left. Received report this to have been driven off. Machine gun & artillery. | — |
| | 18.5.17 | 4 | Reserve Bn employed on camp, baths & Special Coy. R.E. under orders of Strong covering parties from Bselm in this area. Camps widened with view to weather conditions. Rain had unnerved up to 9pm. | # |
| | | | Quiet day again on his Bn. Front with nothing unusual to report. Reserve Bn employed on Camps, baths & enemy Special Coy. R.E. | # |
| | 19.5.17 | | Enemy artillery, mine active, & trench mortars v trenches with French mortars. But altho' many telescoped— | |
| | | a.m. 4.0 | Normal quiet. Bn Comdrs visited Bn Hd. Qu. Reserve Bns employed on night carrying parties as usual. For Special Coy R.E. Bn Orders No. 11. Issued to discharge organ. | # Appendix II |
| | 20.5.17 | | Enemy quiet on whole sector. Nothing to report – only slight artillery activity. G.O.C. Division visited Bn Head Quarters. Lt Col. Faulkner D.S.O. commanding 2/6 K.L.R. handed over command to Major H.R. Wilson on proceeding on leave. | # |

**WAR DIARY**
or
**INTELLIGENCE SUMMARY**
*(Erase heading not required.)*

Army Form C. 2118

Instructions regarding War Diaries and Intelligence Summaries are contained in F.S. Regs., Part II. and the Staff Manual respectively. Title Pages will be prepared in manuscript.

| Place | Date | Hour | Summary of Events and Information | Remarks and references to Appendices |
|---|---|---|---|---|
| ARMENTIERES | 1917 21.5.17 | a.m. 2.30 | Patrol of the Enemy attempted to enter trench at 13. 1E. C. 23. 4. held by 2/6 K.L.R. between sector M trams, on dead, identification obtained 21st Bavarian Infantry Regiment. Our post suffered no casualties. [illegible crossed out] | |
| | | p.m. 4.0 | Quiet on the rest of the front with mk. nk. & stokes artillery activity, and a minnenwerfer shot at H.9 of London Road | Appendix F |
| | 22.5.17 | | 2/8 K.L.R. relieved 2/5 K.L.R. in L'EPINETTE Sub Sector Quiet day on Sector artillery activity to his (enemy) movement continue to what. All preparations have been made for discharge of gas, wind conditions necessitates it being cancelled. 2/7 K.L.R. relieved 2/6 K.L.R. in HOUPLINES Sub Sector. | Appendix F |
| | 23.5.17 | a.m. 1.55 | Long Gunnel Sap B.S.O. returned at night sustained commands after Barrage the enemy attempt to raid locality 16 & 17. 1E. C. 17 5. C.16.1 was probably by the Smashing of initiative of Lieut COWPER 2/7 K.L.R. on whose sector raid was attempted. Identification obtained that to Bavarian Regiment. Our casualties nil. The enemy leaves 2 dead in our hands. | Appendix F |
| | 24.5.17 | | During the day enemy activity normal. Gustav onslaught automatic fire for distance. Nothing to report. Enemy shelled Irish Avenue chiefly, but no hostile he. mm. | |
| | 25.5.17 | 3.15am | 2/7 K.L.R. captured one of the enemy identification to Bavarian Giosh day, otherwise calm | Appendix F |

# WAR DIARY or INTELLIGENCE SUMMARY

Army Form C. 2118

| Place | Date | Hour | Summary of Events and Information | Remarks and references to Appendices |
|---|---|---|---|---|
| ARMENTIERES | 1917<br>26.5.17 | a.m.<br>1.55 | Enemy put a barrage of trench gun - minnenwerfer with a machine gun barrage in the rear of forward S. post I.S.I. in the L'EPINETTE sector held by 2/8 K.L.R. & attempted to force an entrance under cover of leaving our dead enemy wire - Men to number assumed that he had been concentrated to harass subjects to show him our Fire J. ambulance proved his events blown to 21st Bavarian ... hard condition still un favorable Quiet for the rest of the day. No attempt discharge gas. | Appendix I |
| | 27.5.17 | 1.30am | False alarm of gas - Every precaution was taken & inhabitants of ARMENTIERES duly warned.<br>Quiet day on the whole sector. Enemy displaying no activity. Wind unfavourable for gas discharge.<br>Relief Order No. 10 issued.<br>Nothing to report. Weather conditions still unfavourable for gas discharge. | Memo. I<br>(appendix) |
| | 28.5.17 | | | |
| | 29.5.17 | 10.30am | C.of.F.(Commander) visited Pontvieux H.Qrs.<br>Quiet day on the whole sector<br>Discharge of gas from projectors. Weather condition unfavourable for gas discharge from cylinders<br>Trench Relief has to be postponed | |
| | 30.5.17 | 10.30pm | Quiet day on the whole sector, nothing to report. 2/5. K.L.R. relieved 2/8 K.L.R. according to Relief Order No. 10.<br>Casualties for month ending 30.5.17 shown in Appendix III | Appendix III |

Stewart<br>Bn. Maj: 197thd Bde.

APPENDIX NO. I.

MOVE ORDERS
RELIEF ORDERS,

etc.,

referred to in

171st INFANTRY BRIGADE WAR DIARY,

1.5.1917 to 30.5.1917.

.........

SECRET.                                                    COPY NO. 17

### 171st BRIGADE RELIEF ORDER No. 6.
                                                        1st May, 1917.

1. The following Reliefs will take place in L'EPINETTE - HOUPLINES SECTOR.

2. (a) <u>Night of 3rd/4th May 1917.</u>

   "H" Battalion will relieve "E" Battalion in L'EPINETTE SECTOR.

   (b) <u>Night of 4th/5th May 1917.</u>

   "G" Battalion will relieve "F" Battalion in the HOUPLINES SECTOR.

3. Reliefs to commence at 9.6 p.m., i.e., time of leaving billets.

4. Lewis Guns will move into the Subsidiary Line on the night previous to relief.

   Relief to be carried out at daylight on the day of the Battalion relief, in small parties at a time.

5. Reliefs will be arranged inter-Regimentally.

6. "E" Battalion will take over the billets of "H" Battalion, and go into Right Reserve.

   "F" Battalion those of "G" and go into Left Reserve.

7. Completion of Reliefs and passing of Commands to be reported by Signal to these Headquarters.

8. ACKNOWLEDGE.

                                            G.W.GEDDES.
                                Lieut.Colonel, Brigade Major.
                                        171st Infantry Brigade.

ISSUED AT 3.0 p.m., to

| Copy No. | | Copy No. | |
|---|---|---|---|
| 1. | B.G.C., | 11. | 171st L.T.M.B. |
| 2. | Staff Captain. | 12. | 421st Field Company, R.E. |
| 3. | "E" Battalion. | 13. | Signals. |
| 4. | "F"    ,, | 14. | 57th Divl.Artillery H.Q. |
| 5. | "G"    ,, | 15. | Left Group, R.A. |
| 6. | "H"    ,, | 16. | 9th Australian Inf.Bde. |
| 7. | 57th Division "G" | 17. | War Diary. |
| 8. | ,,    ,,    "Q" | 18. | ,, |
| 9. | 172nd Brigade. | 19. | File. |
| 10. | 171st M.G.Company. | | |

SECRET.                171st BRIGADE RELIEF ORDER NO. 7.           COPY NO. 14
                                  .....                            9th May, 1917.

1. The following Reliefs will take place in L'EPINETTE - HOUPLINES SECTOR.

2. (a) Night of 11th/12th May 1917.

   "E" Battalion will relieve "H" Battalion in L'EPINETTE SECTOR.

   (b) Night of 12th/13th May 1917.

   "F" Battalion will relieve "G" Battalion in the HOUPLINES SECTOR.

3. Reliefs to commence at 9 p.m., i.e., time of leaving Billets.

4. Lewis Guns will move into the Subsidiary Line on the night previous to relief.

   Relief to be carried out at daylight on the day of the Battalion relief, in small parties at a time.

5. Reliefs will be arranged inter-Regimentally.

6. "H" Battalion will take over the Billets of "E" Battalion, and go into Right Reserve.

   "G" Battalion those of "F" Battalion and go into Left Reserve.

7. Completion of Reliefs and passing of Commands to be reported by Signal to these Headquarters.

8. ACKNOWLEDGE.

                                                Lieut.Colonel, Brigade Major.
                                                171st Infantry Brigade.

ISSUED AT 2.30 p.m., to :-

Copy No. 1. B.G.C.,                 Copy No. 11. 171st L.T.M.B.,
         2. Staff Captain.                   12. 421st Field Coy, R.E.,
         3. "E" Battalion.                   13. Signals.
         4. "F"    ,,                        14. 57th Divl.Artillery H.Q.
         5. "G"    ,,                        15. Left Group, R.A.,
         6. "H"    ,,                        16. 9th Australian Inf.Bde.
         7. 57th Division. "G".              17. War Diary.
         8.    ,,      ,,   "Q"              18.    ,,
         9. 172nd Brigade.                   19. File.
        10. 171st M.G.Company.

SECRET.
COPY NO. 18

## 171st BRIGADE RELIEF ORDER No. 8.

21st May 1917.

1. The following Relief will take place in L'EPINETTE SUB-SECTOR.

2. <u>Night of 21st/22nd May 1917.</u>

   "H" Battalion will relieve "E" Battalion in L'EPINETTE SECTOR.

3. Relief to commence at 9.15 p.m., i.e., time of leaving Billets.

4. Lewis Guns of "H" Battalion will move into the Subsidiary Line on the night of Relief.

   Relief of Lewis Guns to be carried out at dawn on the 22nd instant.

   O.C., "E" Battalion will take such action as will ensure his Lewis Guns, on relief, marching back to Billets at an interval of at least 10 minutes between teams.

5. Relief will be arranged inter-Regimentally.

6. "E" Battalion will take over the Billets of "H" Battalion, and go into Right Reserve.

7. Completion of Relief and passing of Command to be reported by Signal to these Headquarters.

8. ACKNOWLEDGE.

Lieut.Colonel, Brigade Major.
171st Infantry Brigade.

ISSUED AT 2.30 p.m., to :-

| Copy No. | | Copy No. | |
|---|---|---|---|
| 1. | B.G.C., | 11. | 171st L.T.M.B., |
| 2. | Staff Captain. | 12. | 421st Field Co. R.E., |
| 3. | "E" Battalion. | 13. | Signals. |
| 4. | "F" Battalion. | 14. | 57th Divl. Artillery HdQrs. |
| 5. | "G" Battalion. | 15. | Left Group, R.A., |
| 6. | "H" Battalion. | 16. | 9th Australian Inf.Bde. |
| 7. | 57th Division, "G". | 17. | War Diary. |
| 8. | " "Q". | 18. | " |
| 9. | 172nd Brigade. | 19. | File. |
| 10. | 171st M.G.Company. | | |

SECRET.                                                     COPY NO. 18

171st BRIGADE RELIEF ORDER No. 9.
                                                22nd May, 1917.

1. The following Relief will take place in HOUPLINES SUB-SECTOR.

2. <u>Night of 22nd/23rd May 1917.</u>

   "G" Battalion will relieve "F" Battalion in HOUPLINES SECTOR.

3. Relief to commence at 9.15 p.m., i.e., time of leaving Billets.

4. Lewis Guns of "G" Battalion will move into the Subsidiary Line on the night of Relief.

   Relief of Lewis Guns to be carried out at dawn on the 23rd instant.

   O.C., "F" Battalion will take such action as will ensure his Lewis Guns, on relief, marching back to Billets at an interval of at least 10 minutes between teams.

5. Relief will be arranged inter-Regimentally.

6. "F" Battalion will take over the Billets of "G" Battalion, and go into Left Reserve.

7. Completion of Relief and passing of Command to be reported by signal to these Headquarters.

8. ACKNOWLEDGE.

                                        Lieut.Colonel, Brigade Major,
                                              171st Infantry Brigade.

ISSUED AT 5.0 p.m., to :-

Copy No. 1. B.G.C.,                 Copy No. 11. 171st L.T.M.B.,
         2. Staff Captain.                   12. 421st Field Coy, R.E.,
         3. "E" Battalion.                   13. Signals.
         4. "F"   ,,                         14. 57th Divl. Artillery HdQrs.
         5. "G"   ,,                         15. Left Group, R.A.,
         6. "H"   ,,                         16. 9th Australian Inf.Bde.
         7. 57th Division, (G)               17. War Diary.
         8. 57th Division, (Q)               18.      ,,
         9. 172nd Brigade.                   19. File.
        10. 171st M.G.Company.

SECRET.                171st BRIGADE RELIEF ORDER NO. 10.          Copy No. 18
                                  .....                              27th May, 1917.

1. The following Reliefs will take place in L'EPINETTE - HOUPLINES SECTOR.

2. (a) Night of 29th/30th May 1917.

   "E" Battalion will relieve "H" Battalion in L'EPINETTE SECTOR.

   (b) Night of 30th/31st May 1917.

   "F" Battalion will relieve "G" Battalion in the HOUPLINES SECTOR.

3. Reliefs to commence at 9.15 p.m., i.e., time of leaving Billets.

4. Lewis Guns will move into the Subsidiary Line on the night previous to relief.

   Relief to be carried out at daylight on the day of the Battalion Relief, in small parties at a time.

5. Reliefs will be arranged inter-Regimentally.

6. "H" Battalion will take over the Billets of "E" Battalion, and go into Right Reserve.

   "G" Battalion will take over those of "F" Battalion, and go into Left Reserve.

7. Reliefs will be subject to postponement at very short notice.

8. Completion of Reliefs and Passing of Commands to be reported by Signal to these Headquarters.

9. ACKNOWLEDGE.

                                        Lieut.Colonel, Brigade Major.
                                        171st Infantry Brigade.

ISSUED AT 2 p.m., to :-

Copy No. 1. B.G.C.,                    Copy No.11. 171st L.T.M.B.,
         2. Staff Captain.                     12. 421st Field Coy, R.E.,
         3. "E" Battalion.                     13. Signals.
         4. "F"    ,,                          14. 57th Divl.Artillery H.Q.
         5. "G"    ,,                          15. Left Group, R.A.,
         6. "H"    ,,                          16. 9th Australian Inf.Bde.
         7. 57th Division, "G"                 17. War Diary.
         8.       ,,       "Q"                 18.      ,,
         9. 172nd Inf. Brigade.                19. File.
        10. 171st M.G.Company.

APPENDIX NO. II.

MINOR OPERATIONS

referred to in

171st INFANTRY BRIGADE WAR DIARY,

1.5.1917 to 30.5.1917.

............

REPORT ON OPERATIONS OF the 7th/8th MAY 1917.

............

On the night of the 7th/8th May 1917, the L'EPINETTE - HOUPLINES SECTOR, held by the 171st Infantry Brigade, was raided by the enemy as follows :-

## NARRATIVE.

**MAY 7th.**

7.30 pm.   The enemy put a heavy barrage North of the RIVER LYS, and with great accuracy rolled his barrage on to the whole of
7.35 pm.   the Left Company Sector in the HOUPLINES SUB-SECTOR, the Front Line from the Right of HOBBS FARM to the RIVER LYS, and a box formed by CAMBRIDGE and IRISH AVENUES, with the back of the box on the Second Support Line, being particularly heavy. Gas Shells, Smoke and Dust raised a thick fog which made it well nigh impossible to see what was taking place, even in the Subsidiary Line. This probably led to the Gas Alarm being given, whereas there was no Cloud Gas but only Gas Shells.

8. 0 pm.   Communication was entirely cut with the Left Company Front Line at 8 p.m., At this hour, the enemy raided the HOUPLINES SECTOR, forcing an entry in our lines at C.17.4 and C.17.5. Making a fair estimate as to the strength of the Raiders, it may be put down from 50 to 60; a portion only of these succeeded in forcing an entry at C.17.4, who, it is presumed, captured the post including the Lewis Gun at this point, from which eleven men were afterwards found to be missing. The Lewis Gun at this point was heard to be firing until the barrage lifted off the Front Line and formed its box. Identification was found from a dead Raider left in our trenches, which showed him to belong to the Pioneer Company attached to the 21st Bavarian Regiment. The enemy retired on a whistle being blown, leaving behind the following :-
   3 Boxes of Explosives.
   20 to 30 stick grenades.
   1 Coil of Wire.
   1 Signalling Lamp.
   1 Rifle.
Handles of stick grenades were also found seventy yards down IRISH AVENUE. The enemy retired in parties of 5 and 6 in single file, enfiladed by our Lewis Guns.

8.20 pm.   At this hour, the enemy's artillery slackened a bit, and, still keeping a barrage on the HOUPLINES SECTOR, rolled down the Front Line to L'EPINETTE SECTOR.

8.45 pm.   At this hour, the enemy dropped an intense barrage like a clap of thunder on I.5.2. and I.5.3. in L'EPINETTE SECTOR. The sides of the box being formed on JAPAN and PLANK AVENUES, with the back of the box on the line S.P.X., S.P.Y., S.P.Z. The Sector raided was held by three bombing posts and three
9.20 pm.   Lewis Guns. The Right Lewis Gun was successful in holding up the main party of the enemy, and driving it off. The Centre Lewis Gun Team and Bombing Post delayed the 2nd party of the enemy, though it was reduced to a strength of only one man. The Left Lewis Gun Team, although unsuccessful in stopping the enemy from forcing an entry, killed the Officer in charge of the Raid and three others, the identity showing them to belong to the 1st Battn. 21st Reserve Bavarian Infantry.

The strength of each of the three parties of raiders is estimated at about 15 strong.

9.25 p.m.   The enemy retired on the arrival of the counter-attacking party.

9.35 p.m.   Enemy barrage slackened, and died down on the HOUPLINES SECTOR at 9.35 p.m., and 10 p.m. on L'EPINETTE SECTOR.

### 8th May.

1.25 a.m.   Heavy Machine Gun fire opened on the Right of the Brigade Sector.

1.35 a.m.   A heavy Minnie barrage was opened by the enemy on the Right of L'EPINETTE SECTOR, which rolled off on to the RUE DU BOIS SECTOR.

1.52 a.m.   O.K., was reported on the whole front.

CASUALTIES.

|  | Killed. | Wounded. | Missing. |
|---|---|---|---|
| L'EPINETTE SECTOR. | | | |
| Officers. | - | 1 | - |
| O.Ranks. | 5 | 15 | 1 |
| HOUPLINES SECTOR. | | | |
| Officers. | - | 1 | - |
| O.Ranks. | 1 | 13 | 11 |

DEDUCTIONS.   (a) The vital necessity of having defended Localities well wired.

(b) That all posts must be made up to their Night Strength fully an hour before sunset.

(c) The Counter-Attacks to be delivered at once.

NOTE.   The chief feature of the enemy's line of action was the excellent way in which the artillery was handled — its registration was perfect, and the handling of his rolling barrage, which traversed some 3,000 yards, showed a very high standard of efficiency.

Brigadier-General,
Commanding 171st Infantry Brigade.

In the Field.
    11th May, 1917

**SECRET.**   COPY NO. 17

**171st BRIGADE ORDER NO. II.**

Maps Rodoronoc,
Sheet 36 N.W.2,
& N.E.I (Parts
of) 1:10.000.

19th May, 1917.

........

**Intention.**  1. In accordance with 57th Divisional Order No.10, Gas will be discharged from Cylinders and Projectors co-ordinately on the Brigade Front in conjunction with a similar discharge from the front of the Brigade on our Left on the night of the 20th/21st May 1917, or on the first suitable occasion.

**Object.**  2. The object of the release of Gas is to destroy as many as possible of enemy personnel.

**Locality.**  3. (a) Gas has been installed in Cylinders at the following points :-

 I.10.b.98.39 to I.11.a.08.87 - termed "L" Sector. 300 capacity.
 C.29.c.28.31 to C.29.a.10.02 - termed "A" Sector. 520 capacity.
 C.29.a.21.72 to C.23.c.15.25 - termed "B" Sector. 300 capacity.

The above Sectors are manned and fought by "L" Special Company, R.E.,

 C.23.c.15.25 to C.23.c.10.70 - termed "N" Sector. 400 capacity.
 C.23.a.15.10 to C.23.a.20.40 - termed "C" Sector. 300 capacity.
 C.17.c.25.60 to C.17.c.32.95 - termed "D" Sector. 500 capacity.

The above Sectors are manned and fought by "N" Special Company, R.E.,

(b) Projectors are set in the open in C.22.D. Central and in conjunction with the above Cylinders 250 Projectors, operated by "N" Special Coy, R.E., will be fired simultaneously on to the following targets :-

 (i) C.22.c.90.55 to C.23.D.00.80 (Enemy Support Line)
 (ii) LES 4 HALLOTS, C.23.D.25.60
 (iii) BATTN.HdQrs at C.24.c.50.50

(c) The discharge of gas from South of the RIVER LYS will be synchronised, if possible, with a discharge from the North of the RIVER LYS. Should circumstances not permit of a combined discharge, however, the operations South of the RIVER LYS will be launched independently.

(d) The decision as to whether conditions are suitable for a gas discharge is left entirely in the hands of O.C., "N" Special Coy, R.E., in conjunction with O.C., "L" Special Coy, R.E.,

(e) (i) The Gas Cylinders will be discharged in one wave.
 (ii) The Projectors will be fired at Zero plus 3 minutes.

## 2.

**Artillery Action.** 4. Artillery will stand by for retaliation from zero, in case the enemy replies to gas waves.

**Patrols.** 5. Patrols, accompanied by a N.C.O. of the Special Coy, R.E., will leave our trenches at zero plus HOURS 15 minutes, or as soon after that time as is considered safe by the Officer of the Special Coy, R.E., on the spot, to investigate the effects of the gas, obtain identifications, and capture prisoners or war material.

O.C., "E" Battalion will send out a patrol under an Officer from the vicinity of Locality 3, I.10.5 - I.10.6.

O.C., "F" Battalion will send out a similar patrol or patrols, if possible, from Locality 13, C.23.4., and Gap, C.17.4.

Care must be taken that no marks of identification whatever are to be worn by patrols.

**Code.** 6. The following code will be used for warning and other messages as regards the discharge of Gas :-

(a) IT IS INTENDED TO DISCHARGE GAS.
Any message containing the word PRESENTATION - on Z day at Z hour. Ex., "Presentation of Medals took place at 12.30 p.m. on the 18th".

(b) IN THE EVENT OF A POSTPONEMENT FOR AT LEAST 2 HOURS. The message "INDENT for 'X' number of Bicycles from this Depot"; 'X' being the number of hours. Ex., "Indent for 3 bicycles from this Depot" - means, "Gas discharge postponed 3 hours".

(c) ZERO BEING CANCELLED. The following message will be sent - "Await further instructions".

(d) Time used will be "Universal Time", and hours reckoned from 0 to 24.

**Medical Arrangements.** 7. Os.C. "G" and "H" Battalions will place Regimental Stretcher Bearers at the disposal of the Officers Commanding "N" and "L" Companies, R.E., at the following points:-

"H" Battalion.
(1) 4 Stretcher Bearers with 2 Stretchers to report to R.E. Officer in front line at top of VAUXHALL AVENUE.
(2) 6 Stretcher Bearers with 3 Stretchers at C.28.d. 90.70. (Concrete dugout, LONDON ROAD).
(3) 4 Stretcher Bearers with 2 Stretchers at FRYPAN.

"G" Battalion.
(1) 6 Stretcher Bearers with 3 Stretchers at top of EDMEADES AVENUE.
(2) 6 Stretcher Bearers with 3 Stretchers at top of IRISH AVENUE.

"F" Battalion.
O.C., "F" Battn. will detail 6 Stretcher Bearers - top of WESSEX AVENUE.

3.

**Signals.**    8. Special Rocket Signals, showing triple consecutive lights – red – green – red, will be sent up from two points, one in G.22.c. and the other in I.3.d. in the event from any cause whatever of Zero hour having to be postponed or cancelled, within the period of the last warning Zero minus one hour. Confirmation of this signal will be at once sent by runner or telephone to all concerned.

**Communication.**    9. (a) In conjunction with Os.C.Battalions in the Line, the Brigade Signalling Officer will arrange for inter-communication by Fullerphone between Brigade HdQrs – the 6 Sectors mentioned in para.3, and runners should this communication break down.

    (b) Special Coy R.E.Officers in order to facilitate quick communication may use 'Urgent Priority' messages. It should be remembered, however, that these messages must be very limited, as a large number handed in will block the line.

**Precautions.**    10. (a) The front line from which gas is to be discharged will be cleared to a distance of 250 yards on either flank of the gas, with the exception of sentries, Lewis Gunners, Bombing Squads, and one Infantry Officer per Gas Sector, all of whom will wear their Box Respirators fully adjusted from Zero minus 5 minutes to Zero plus 30 minutes.

    (b) The Infantry Officers remaining in the Gas Sectors will keep in touch with the Special Coy R.E.Officers in charge of their Sector.

    (c) All other Ranks in the Brigade Area will observe precautions for Wind Dangerous.

    (d) No man will return to that part of the line from which gas has been discharged until ordered to do so by an Officer.

**Synchronising of Watches.**    11. Watches will be synchronised at Brigade HdQrs at 7 p.m. 20th instant, and if gas is not released on that day, daily at the same hour until this operation is completed. An Officer will report to the Staff Captain with 3 watches.

**Reports.**    12. Reports will be rendered to these Headquarters early.

    12. ACKNOWLEDGE.

, Lieut:Colonel, Brigade Major,
171st Infantry Brigade.

ISSUED AT 10 p.m., to :-

| Copy No. 1. B.G.C., | Copy No. 10. Left Group, R.A., |
|---|---|
| 2. "E" Battalion. | 11. 171st M.G.Company. |
| 3. "F" ,, | 12. 171st L.T.M.B., |
| 4. "G" ,, | 13. "L" Company, R.E., |
| 5. "H" ,, | 14. "N" ,, ,, |
| 6. 57th Division. | 15. War Diary. |
| 7. 172nd Brigade. | 16. |
| 8. 11th Australian Brigade. | 17. G.S.File. |
| 9. C.R.A., | 18. Spare. |

## APPENDIX I.

Reference para. 5, of Brigade Order No. II. The following Fighting Patrols will be sent out to investigate the effects of Gas, obtain identifications, and capture prisoners or war material:-

1. By O.C., Battalion in the RIGHT or L'EPINETTE SUBSECTOR:-

   (a) 1 Officer and 16 O.Ranks from the vicinity of Locality 4, I.10.6, who will reconnoitre the area bounded on the North by a line drawn through I.II.a.60.70 to I.II.a.92.70, and on the South by I.II.a.36.12 to I.II.a.86.II.

   (b) A Patrol from Locality 8, C.29.2. (working in conjunction with the Battalion holding the HOUPLINES SUBSECTOR) between the boundaries,
   Northern, C.29.c.76.42 to C.29.d.02.00
   Southern, C.29.d.10.15 to C.29.d.31.15

2. Fighting Patrols of 1 Officer and 14 O.Ranks will be sent out by O.C. Battalion in the LEFT or HOUPLINES SUBSECTOR, from the vicinity of GAP J. and Locality 9, i.e., C.29.3., C.29.4.

   (a) Between the Boundaries,
   Northern, C.29.a.48.29 to C.29.a.80.28
   Southern, C.29.a.39.85 to C.29.c.78.89

   (b) Between the Boundaries,
   Northern, C.23.b.10.57 to C.23.b.25.55
   Southern, C.23.b.10.00 to C.23.b.29.00

   (c) Between the Boundaries,
   Northern, C.17.a.38.45 to C.17.a.52.45
   Southern, C.17.c.83.61 to C.17.d.02.68

3. O.C., "L" and "N" Special Companies will detail an N.C.O. or Sapper to accompany each Patrol. Patrols will leave immediately the R.E. Officer of the Special Company from whose Sector patrols are leaving decides it is safe to do so, and not before.

4. The S.O.S. will become inoperative by Signal Rockets from Zero until Battalion Commanders have reported to Brigade Headquarters and their Artillery Liason Officer that patrols are in. The S.O.S., during this period, will only be acknowledged by telephone.

Ref. Map.
36 N.W., 2
& N.E.I (parts of)
1:10.000

## 171st INFANTRY BRIGADE.

### FULL SPECIAL REPORT ON CONTACT WITH THE ENEMY
### - ARMENTIERES SECTOR.

........

Night of 23rd/24th May 1917.

I. A. At 11.55 p.m. Lieut. A.L.Cowper, of the 2/7th K.L.R. with Corpl Kevelighan, and 4 others, went out from C.17.a.05.20, to reconnoitre the best route into the CHICKEN RUN.

The patrol had not proceeded 10 yards when they perceived a party of the enemy estimated at from 20 to 30, assembled in NO MAN'S LAND, as if in a preparatory formation for the attack. The patrol had escaped detection by the enemy - and immediately attacked the enemy, each member of the patrol throwing two Mills Grenades into the middle of the enemy, and opening rapid fire with their rifles. The enemy at once retired, showing no fight, round the edge of the Pond, to a point marked 'D' on the attached sketch map, which appeared to be a sap head, and from whence lights were seen to go up. Lieut Cowper and his patrol returned to our trenches, and Left Bombing Post.

As previously reported, there was every indication that the enemy suffered heavily; unfortunately, the nature of the ground, and the fact that it was entirely new country to our patrol, prevented the patrol from following up the enemy with the rapidity that was desired, and which would no doubt have secured further identification.

Lieut Cowper, on his return to our trenches, moved the extreme Left Lewis Gun still further to the left, and was at this time fired at by one of the enemy in rear of our trenches.

1.30 a.m.,

Lieut.Cowper again took out his patrol, and made a thorough search without avail, to secure any wounded from the enemy who had been driven off. He proceeded towards the sap through which the enemy appeared to have re-entered their trenches, but found it to be strongly held, and his bomb attack could make no progress, as he was outranged.

He then returned and searched the ground in rear of our trenches for the enemy who was seen, until 4.45 am. but found no one.

12 Midnight.

B. A small party of the enemy, estimated strength 10, attempted to enter our trench at Locality 15, C.17.3. - C.17.4. at the point where a Lewis Gun is in position. The Corporal in charge of the Lewis Gun fired with his revolver at the two leading men of the enemy's party, one of whom was left dead on our parapet. The other is claimed to have been hit, but his body was not secured. This attack was driven off by rifle fire; the Lewis Gun in question jammed and did not fire.

Action of the Enemy.

After the attack was beaten off, the enemy were very quiet, and sent over only a few rifle shots. There was a total absence of Machine Guns, Pineapples and Minenwerfers.

2.

CASUALTIES.          Our Own.           NIL.

                    Enemy.     One dead left in our hands.


Morning of 25th
  May 1917.

  3.15 a.m.,    2.    A man was seen by the double-sentries at RIVER POST C.I5.b.75.05 — where there is a detached Lewis Gun Post at night — moving along the Right Bank of the RIVER LYS. They crawled along the bank, and, getting between him and our lines, on seeing he was a German, covered him with their rifles and held him up. The enemy threw up his hands, and shouted "Kamerad" several times. They held him there until the Lance-Corporal in charge of the Post arrived, who had him marched down to the Company HdQrs, from whence he was despatched to Battalion HdQrs, where he was given food, and then despatched to Brigade HdQrs.


CASUALTIES.          Our Own.           NIL.

                    Enemy.             One Prisoner.


                                        Lieut.Colonel, Brigade Major.
                                           17½st Infantry Brigade.

B.H.Q.,
  25.5.1917

REPORT ON OPERATIONS of 25th/26th MAY, 1917.

...........

On the Night of the 25th/26th May 1917, the enemy attempted to force an entry into our Lines on L'EPINETTE SUBSECTOR, held by the 2/8th (Irish) Battn. K.L.R., as follows:-

NARRATIVE.

May 26th 1917.

1.55 a.m.,   The enemy barraged with Whizzbangs and Minenwerfer, Locality 5, i.e., Point I.5.I, in L'EPINETTE SUBSECTOR, forming a box on the Support Line and Communication Trenches leading to this Locality, the flanks being swept by Machine Gun fire.

2.10 a.m.,   The enemy, at an estimated strength of 12, attempted to force an entry, but were driven off by Lewis Gun and rifle fire without obtaining a footing in our Lines.

One of the enemy was left dead on our wire, but it can be reasonably assumed that his losses were heavier. Identification obtained from the dead body shows the man to have belonged to the 3rd Battalion, 21st Bavarian Infantry Regiment.

2.25 a.m.,   The enemy's fire ceased, and the situation was reported quiet.

Lieut.Colonel, Brigade Major.
171st Infantry Brigade.

B.H.Q.
27.5.1917

APPENDIX No. III.

STATEMENT of CASUALTIES.

..........

Forwarded in Conjunction with

171st INFANTRY BRIGADE WAR DIARY

1.5.1917 to 30.5.1917.

......

## 171st INFANTRY BRIGADE.

### CASUALTIES from 1.5.1917 to 30.5.1917.

| DATE. 24 hours, ending :- | KILLED. | | WOUNDED. | | MISSING. | |
|---|---|---|---|---|---|---|
| | Officers. | O.Ranks. | Officers. | O.Ranks. | Officers. | O.Ranks. |
| 1.5.17 | - | 1 | - | 2 | - | - |
| 2.5.17 | - | 1 | Lieut. Dickinson J. | 4 | - | - |
| 3.5.17 | - | 1 | - | 1 | - | - |
| 4.5.17 | - | - | - | 1 | - | - |
| 6.5.17 | - | 4 | - | 7 | - | - |
| 7.5.17 | - | - | - | 4 | - | - |
| 8.5.17 | - | 7 | 2nd Lts. Sampson. P.R. Whiting. R.C. Lieut. Boak.G.B. Capt. Mayhew A.H. | 33 | - | 12 |
| 9.5.17 | - | 2 | - | 6 | - | - |
| 10.5.17 | - | - | - | 5 | - | - |
| 11.5.17 | - | - | - | 6 | - | - |
| 13.5.17 | - | - | 2nd Lt. Periton. R.C. | 3 | - | - |
| 14.5.17 | - | - | - | 4 | - | - |
| 16.5.17 | - | - | - | 3 | - | - |
| 17.5.17 | - | - | - | 1 | - | - |
| 18.5.17 | - | - | - | 5 | - | - |
| 19.5.17 | - | 1 | - | 3 | - | - |
| 20.5.17 | - | - | Lieut. Alcock P.F. | 4 | - | - |
| 21.5.17 | - | - | - | 6 | - | - |
| 22.5.17 | - | - | - | 1 | - | - |
| 23.5.17 | Lieut. Keith.N. | - | - | 1 | - | - |
| 24.5.17 | - | - | - | 3 | - | - |
| 25.5.17 | - | 3 | - | 3 | - | - |
| 26.5.17 | - | 1 | 2nd Lt. Little. J.H.M. | 10 | - | - |
| 27.5.17 | - | - | - | 5 | - | - |
| 28.5.17 | - | - | - | 3 | - | - |
| 30.5.17 | - | - | 2nd Lt. Stainton. H.H. | 4 | - | 1 |
| TOTAL. | 1 | 21 | 9 | 128 | - | 13 |

Vol 5

War Diary
of
141st Inf. Bde. Hd. Qtrs.
for
June 1914

CONFIDENTIAL.

WAR DIARY

of

HEADQUARTERS, 171st INFANTRY BRIGADE.

............

31.5.1917    to    30.6.1917.

.........

VOLUME IV.

..

# WAR DIARY or INTELLIGENCE SUMMARY

Army Form C. 2118

| Place | Date | Hour | Summary of Events and Information | Remarks and references to Appendices |
|---|---|---|---|---|
| ARMENTIERES | 31.5.17 | | Quiet normal day on Brigade Front. Nothing to report. | |
| | 1.6.17 | | 2/6. K.L.R. relieved 2/7 K.L.R. in HOUPLINES Sector. No activity displays by enemy. Brigade Front quiet. Great aerial activity on our part. Nine shewn on this part of the Enemy. | |
| | 2.6.17 | | Quiet normal day on Brigade front. Brigade H.Qrs. moved at 5.0 pm from 3 RUE des JESUITES to 95 Sq, Canal. | App/A |
| | 3.6.17 | | Quiet on the right subsector of Brigade Front. Enemy artillery rather more active than usual on our left. One of our aeroplanes attacked by five enemy machines & brought down at L.30 km at approximated C.12. Central. East of FRELINGHIEN. | App/A |
| | 4.6.17 | | Enemy artillery active on our Battalions in ARMENTIERES and HOUPLINES in reply to Trench Mortars on targets N. of R. LYS. | App/A |
| | 5.6.17 | | Continued artillery activity - increasing on both sides towards midnight. Italian very quiet in the line. | App/A |
| | 6.6.17 | | Artillery very active on both sides. 100 - 77mm into our trench Eyglin - ARMENTIERES was again shelled about 140 15cm falling in C.26.b.d. From an infantry point of view the day was quiet. G.O.C. day relief. | App/A |
| | 7.6.17 | | Intense Artillery bombardment on our left in which our artillery co-operated commenced 3.10. a.m. Enemy artillery retaliated at first very slight - in the afternoon particular between 2.0 & 4.0. HOUPLINES km. shelled and our left subsector was searched with more than the normal quantity of shells. No incident to report as regards infantry. | App/A |
| | 8.6.17 | | Continued artillery activity - particularly great in early hours of the morning and in response. Enemy artillery put about 600 - 77; 10 5 9 -15 cm shells into ARMENTIERES and HOUPLINES. | |

H.M.E. L'ATTARGETTE - known enemy mort. Our extreme left Sector of trenches was heavily shelled.

1875. Wt. W593/826 1,000,000 4/15 I.B.C. & A. A.D.S.S./Forms/C. 2118.

**Army Form C. 2118**

# WAR DIARY
## or
## INTELLIGENCE SUMMARY
*(Erase heading not required.)*

II

Instructions regarding War Diaries and Intelligence Summaries are contained in F.S. Regs., Part II. and the Staff Manual respectively. Title Pages will be prepared in manuscript.

| Place | Date | Hour | Summary of Events and Information | Remarks and references to Appendices |
|---|---|---|---|---|
| ARMENTIERES | 8.6.17 (contd) | | No serious damage was caused. Otherwise a quiet day from the Infantry. 2/gr returned 2/5 KRR in the EPINETTE sector. | togH. Appendix I |
| | 9.6.17 | | Quieter than preceding days – Artillery confined to counter battery work. 2/gr relieved 2/6 KRR in the HOUPLINES sector. | togH. Appendix I |
| | 10.6.17 | | Artillery on both sides showed more than normal activity. On the Enemy's system PLANK AVENUE and the whole of the left portion - IRISH & CAMBRIDGE AVENUES – of the left subsector were shelled during the day. Factory N of ARMENTIERES - approx C.19 - was set on fire by incendiary shells. This area was heavily shelled which the fire was in progress. The ERQUINGHEM road was shelled from H.6.a.o.8 to B.30.B.6.o. A deserter from 17.BAV.IR. surrendered to our sentry group on the extreme left. | togH. |
| | 11.6.17 | | Artillery active on both sides – chiefly on back areas. The prisoner captured yesterday gave information as to times & places of intended German raid which he still attempted at 9.25pm. Immediately our barrage descended and repulsed any assault of exploitation of the raid. Our trenches were not entered. 5 dead Germans of 14.BAV.IR. were found outside – | togH. Appendix II |
| | 12.6.17 | | ARMENTIERES was shelled persistently but not heavily by day & night. A small silent raid was carried out by 2/8 KRR. Enemy wire entered at 11.0 a. No enemy found. G.O.C. Div. called during morning on his way up Div. O.P. to the fact 111 square. | togH. Appendix II |
| | 13.6.17 | | less shelling of ARMENTIERES & other back areas. Normal artillery activity on Frenchsystem – Unsuccessful released GAS at 11.0 pm & 12.30 am (14th). Enemy retaliation practically nil. | togH. Appendix I |
| | 14.6.17 | | Normal shelling of back areas, rather more activity of trenches. Owing to successful raid of operations N of Rue LYS enemy withdrew from FRELINGHIEN was reported to South of operations. Aire activity on left Company sector provided that his front line was still held – During night 2 patrol attempts to enter his lines. OU INANE TRENCH was encountered returned after 2½ hours. Rain in left another | togH. Appendix II |

1875 (Wt. W593/826 1,000,000 4/15 J.B.C. & A. A.D.S.S./Forms/C. 2118.

# WAR DIARY or INTELLIGENCE SUMMARY

Army Form C. 2118

| Place | Date | Hour | Summary of Events and Information | Remarks and references to Appendices |
|---|---|---|---|---|
| | 14.6.17 | | Patrol knocked out by him more that down the enemy - F.O.C. Sent across round points of our front system - | 20/11 |
| | 15.6.17 | | Very quiet from an infantry point of view. During the evening - when recent of NW rose that FRELINGHIEN was increasingly being the Brigade on our left - 7 NZ R.B. Three new craters were created opposite the enemy at 6.30pm to free creep hours the rescues his presence. Apatrol went along R.L.L.S on left down the line getting to within 50 yards of the BREWERY. Enemy trenches opposite our left appear to be held lightly. 3rd Auckland Bn on our left were relieved by 3rd Wellington Bn - | 20/11 |
| | 16.6.17 | | Artillery guiks on both sides. Close observation kept on enemy trench system in front of FRELINGHIEN which is understood held. A patrol attempted to get round by the river LYS and capture enemy in to BREWERY. they were led up by M.G. fire which in emery mine. Enemy patrol over Quesnoy was brought down in flames at 6 p.m. 2/5 K.S.R. relieved 3/8 K.L.R. in EPINETTE subsector | 30/11 Appendix I |
| | " | | A Quiet day in the line - ARMENTIERES was shelled intermittently - more activity at night. An enemy aeroplane opened fire on our line at EPINETTE without result. Movement observed in enemy trenches in front of FRELINGHIEN. 1/6 K.L.R. relieved 2/5 K.L.R. in HOUPLINES. | 30/11 Appendix I |
| | 17.6.17 | | | |
| | 18.6.17 | | Messages from NZ Bn. on our left received 6.45am stating intention to recon patrols out to line of R. LYS - Enemy aircraft & artillery were particularly active - the latter was chiefly engaged in shelling Battery positions - Enemy movements normal - Large fire at Quesnoy was burning all the afternoon | 30/11 |
| | 19.6.17 | | A quiet day in the line - Continued aeroplane activity. Enemy artillery slightly less active though Combes Battery area was still in trouble - several direct hits on main roads were observed & him | 30/11 |

# WAR DIARY or INTELLIGENCE SUMMARY

Army Form C. 2118

| Place | Date | Hour | Summary of Events and Information | Remarks and references to Appendices |
|---|---|---|---|---|
| | 20.6.17 | | Enemy artillery still active. Damage done to trenches in ARMENTIERES PORTUPINE is extraordinarily small in proportion to the number of shells fired into the town. Battery at 36 B 30 & was heavily shelled and shells are distributed over the SPINETTE subsector apparently in reprisal shoots. Enemy aeroplane again active, & succeeded in bringing down 2 of our Observation Balloons. Normal day in the trenches. | 20/ft |
| | 21.6.17. | | Enemy artillery continued their programme of shelling Battery positions in ARMENTIERES itself fewer shells fell hit in the 9 pm. C.20 'C.21 he hrs. particularly oppressive. Several direct hits on railway bridge where G.O.C. Div & O.C. Left Coys R.A. were both seriously wounded: the subsequently died. Normal movement observed behind enemy lines. | 20/ft |
| | 22.6.17. | A 1.0 a.m. | a raiding party of 3 off. 100 O.R. divided into 3 parties left in trio & entered enemy trenches at CENTAUR - town enemy-filled. Our casualties 1 off. wounded 3 O.R. killed 1 Missing. 6 Wounded. 10 king of infantrymen achieved. Enemy artillery active - wire was cut as far as NORMS FARM & IRISH AVE locality no heavily shelled. Shelling of trench area no less. | 8/ft Appendix II |
| | 23.6.17. | | Artillery again active on left sector. Normal shelling of ARMENTIERES. Two exploded at ONESSY and the explosion at FRELINGHIEN. Enemy aircraft less active than ours for | 4/ft |
| L'EPINETTE | 24.6.17. | AM 2.10. | Several gas had. Enemy fired from a machine barrage on L'EPINETTE Sector & attempted to raid - Raid was driven off no info made by our trench Mortars. Enemy artillery again active, scheme left of sector receiving considerable attention. IRISH AVENUE being almost completely destroyed. Ammunition shelves at ration limit throughout his day and night. | ft |

L'EPINETTE

2/8. R.L.R. relieved 2/5. R.L.R. in HOURAINE Sector vide Re Order.

Appendix I

# WAR DIARY
## or
## INTELLIGENCE SUMMARY

*(Erase heading not required.)*

Army Form C. 2118

Instructions regarding War Diaries and Intelligence Summaries are contained in F. S. Regs., Part II. and the Staff Manual respectively. Title Pages will be prepared in manuscript.

| Place | Date | Hour | Summary of Events and Information | Remarks and references to Appendices |
|---|---|---|---|---|
| ARMENTIERES | 25.6.17 | | Various Artillery activity by the enemy. Armentieres being heavily shelled during the night. In the line the enemy confined his attention to the HOUPLINES Sub-Sector. 2/7 K.R.R. relieved 2/6 K.R.R. in the HOUPLINES Sector without Orders. | |
| | 26.6.17 | | Heavy Artillery activity throughout the day and night — ARMENTIERES and HOUPLINES Sub-Sector receiving much attention. Mines died shells exploded in the L'EPINETTE Sector. | Appendix I |
| | 27.6.17 | | Our attention has been given to attention to ARMENTIERES area. The day — the whole of the front areas were subjected to an increased activity. ARMENTIERS and shelled at night. Thin movement than usual in enemy's lines. | |
| | 28.6.17 | | Enemys artillery activity on our front line has been marked. Quite a little has been brought to the Intlian line. ARMENTIERES again received considerable attention during the night. | |
| | 29.6.17 | | The whole sector was subjected to considerable activity on the part of the enemy, which has greatly increased. Armentieres received attention during the day, & was heavily shelled during the night. | |

**Army Form C. 2118**

# WAR DIARY
## or
## INTELLIGENCE SUMMARY
*(Erase heading not required.)*

VI

| Place | Date | Hour | Summary of Events and Information | Remarks and references to Appendices |
|---|---|---|---|---|
| ARMENTIERES | 30.6.17 | | Continued enemy artillery activity directed on to back area. ARMENTIERES, and HOUPLINES were heavily shelled & so also the area immediately in rear of the Subsidiary (line.) No incidents of importance reported from the Infantry in the line. | So/ft. |
| | | | Casualties for the month ending June 1917 are contained in APPENDIX III | |

Spruce
Major
6th Major
171st Infantry Bde.

APPENDIX No. I.

RELIEF ORDERS,

etc.,

Referred to in

171st INFANTRY BRIGADE WAR DIARY,

31.5.1917 to 30.6.1917.

.......

SECRET.

## 171st BRIGADE RELIEF ORDER NO. II.

COPY NO. 14
5th June 1917.

1. The following Reliefs will take place in L'EPINETTE - HOUPLINES SUBSECTORS.

2. (a) Night of 7th/8th June, 1917.

    "H" Battalion will relieve "E" Battalion in L'EPINETTE SUBSECTOR.

   (b) Night of 8th/9th June, 1917.

    "G" Battalion will relieve "F" Battalion in the HOUPLINES SUBSECTOR.

3. Reliefs to commence at 9.30 pm., i.e., time of leaving Billets.

4. Lewis Guns will move into the Subsidiary Line on the night previous to relief, leaving Billets not before 9.30 p.m. Relief to be carried out at daylight on the day of the Battalion Relief, in small parties at a time.

5. Reliefs will be arranged inter-Regimentally.

6. "E" Battalion will take over the Billets of "H" Battalion and go into Right Reserve.

    "F" Battalion will take over those of "G" Battalion, and go into Left Reserve.

7. Reliefs will be subject to postponement at very short notice.

8. Completion of Reliefs and Passing of Commands to be reported by Signal to these Headquarters.

9. ACKNOWLEDGE.

*G J Huntley*

Lieut. Acting Brigade Major.
171st Infantry Brigade.

ISSUED AT 2 p.m., to :-

Copy No. 1.  B.G.C.,
       2.  Staff Captain.
       3.  "E" Battalion.
       4.  "F"    ,,
       5.  "G"    ,,
       6.  "H"    ,,
       7.  57th Division. "G"
       8.    ,,       ,,   "Q"
       9.  172nd Inf.Brigade.
      10.  171st M.G.Coy.

Copy No. 11.- 171st L.T.M.B.,
      12.- 421st Field Co, R.E.
      13.- Signals.
      14.  57th Divl. Artillery H.
      15.- Left Group R.A.,
      16.- 57th Divl. Detachment.
      17.  War Diary.
      18.    ,,     ,,
      19.  File.

SECRET.                                                                    COPY NO. 17
                    171st BRIGADE RELIEF ORDER No. 12.
                                                                           9th June, 1917.
                              ......

       Owing to the Operations proposed in Divisional Order No.17,
the following modifications to Brigade Relief Order No.11 are
made :-

1.     On the receipt of message "BARRELS NOT YET ARRIVED", the
relief will proceed normally.

2.     If the Operations take place at 9.45 p.m., reliefs will be
postponed for one hour.

3.     On receipt of code word "TUBS"  -  (it is hoped to send
this by 8.45 p.m.) - indicating that the Operations are
postponed from 9.45 p.m. to 11.30 p.m., the Company of "G"
Battalion in the Subsidiary Line will move up and relieve one
Company of "F" Battalion, who will take their place in the
Subsidiary Line.

       The Right Company of "F" Battalion will be relieved by a
Company of "G" Battalion.    This latter Company will move up
via BUTERNE AVENUE  -  SUBSIDIARY LINE  -  SPAIN AVENUE.
These Local Reliefs to be complete by 11.0 p.m.,    The
Company of "F" Battalion which has been relieved will proceed
direct to Billets.

4.     The remaining two Companies and Headquarters will proceed
via route in para.3, or GLOUCESTER AVENUE, as directed by C.O.,
and take up a convenient position in the Subsidiary Line North
of SPAIN AVENUE, to facilitate relief.          If gas is
discharged at 11.30 p.m., these Companies will relieve when the
situation is quiet (but not before midnight).

       If the gas discharge is timed to take place at 1.15 a.m.,
the above Companies will relieve before that hour, and MUST have
completed reliefs by 12.45 a.m.,

5.     The Commanding Officer of ingoing Battalion will take proper
steps to ensure that there is no relief in progress during the
half-hour preceding the hour for the discharge of gas.

6.     The Right Battalion ("H" Battalion) will send 4 Guides to
"G" Battalion HdQrs, and report to Adjutant by 7.30 p.m.,   These
Guides must know their way to the Sector, via BUTERNE AVENUE.

7.     ACKNOWLEDGE.

                                                  Lieut. Acting Brigade Major.
                                                  171st Infantry Brigade.

ISSUED AT 3 p.m., to :-

   Copy No.  1.  B.G.C.,                    Copy No. 11.  171st L.T.M.B.,
             2.  Staff Captain,                      12.  421st Field Co, R.E.
             3.  "E" Battalion.                      13.  Signals.
             4.  "F"   ,,                            14.  57th Divisional Arty.
             5.  "G"   ,,                            15.  Loft Group, R.A.,
             6.  "H"   ,,                            16.  57th Divl. Detachment.
             7.  57th Division. "G"                  17.  War Diary.
             8.         ,,      "Q"                  18.       ,,
             9.  172nd Infantry Bde.                 19.  File.
            10.  171st M.G. Company.                 20.  Spare.

SECRET.   171st BRIGADE RELIEF ORDER NO. ~~1~~    COPY NO. 17

14th June, 1917.

1. The following Reliefs will take place in L'EPINETTE – HOUPLINES SUBSECTORS.

2. (a) Night of 16th/17th June 1917.

   "E" Battalion will relieve "H" Battalion in L'EPINETTE SUBSECTOR.

   (b) Night of 17th/18th June 1917.

   "F" Battalion will relieve "G" Battalion in the HOUPLINES SUBSECTOR.

3. Reliefs to commence at 9.30 p.m., i.e., time of leaving Billets.

4. Lewis Guns will move into the Subsidiary Line on the night previous to Relief, leaving Billets not before 9.30 p.m., Relief to be carried out at daylight on the day of the Battn. Relief, in small parties at a time.

5. Reliefs will be arranged inter-Regimentally.

6. "H" Battalion will take over the Billets of "E" Battalion and go into Right Reserve.

   "G" Battalion will take over those of "F" Battalion, and go into Left Reserve.

7. Reliefs will be subject to postponement at very short notice.

8. Completion of Reliefs and passing of Commands to be reported by Signal to these Headquarters.

9. ACKNOWLEDGE.

2nd Lieut. Acting Brigade Major.
171st Infantry Brigade.

ISSUED AT 12 Noon, to :-

| Copy No. | 1. | B.G.C., | Copy No. | 11. | 171st L.T.M.B., |
|---|---|---|---|---|---|
| | 2. | Staff Captain, | | 12. | 421st Field Co, R.E., |
| | 3. | "E" Battalion. | | 13. | Signals. |
| | 4. | "F" " | | 14. | 57th Divl. Artillery H.Q. |
| | 5. | "G" " | | 15. | Left Group, R.A., |
| | 6. | "H" " | | 16. | 4th N.Z.Inf.Bde. |
| | 7. | 57th Division, "G". | | 17. | War Diary. |
| | 8. | " " "Q" | | 18. | " |
| | 9. | 172nd Inf.Brigade. | | 19. | File. |
| | 10. | 171st M.G.Company. | | 20. | File. |

SECRET.    171st BRIGADE RELIEF ORDER No. 14.    COPY NO. 18
                                                22nd June 1917.

1. The following Reliefs will take place in L'EPINETTE - HOUPLINES SUBSECTORS.

2. (a) Night of 24th/25th June 1917.

"H" Battalion will relieve "E" Battalion in L'EPINETTE SUBSECTOR.

(b) Night of 25th/26th June 1917.

"G" Battalion will relieve "F" Battalion in the HOUPLINES SUBSECTOR.

3. Reliefs to commence at 9.45 p.m., i.e., time of leaving Billets.

4. Lewis Guns will move into the Subsidiary Line on the night previous to relief, leaving Billets not before 9.45 p.m., Relief to be carried out at daylight on the day of the Battn. relief, in small parties at a time.

5. Reliefs will be arranged inter-regimentally.

6. "E" Battalion will take over the Billets of "H" Battalion and go into Right Reserve.

"F" Battalion will take over those of "G" Battalion, and go into Left Reserve.

7. Reliefs will be subject to postponement at very short notice.

8. Completion of Reliefs and passing of Commands to be reported by Signal to these Headquarters.

ACKNOWLEDGE.

                                    2nd Lieut. Acting
                                     Brigade Major,
                                    171st Infantry Brigade.

ISSUED AT 3 p.m., to :-

Copy No. 1. B.G.C.,                 Copy No. 11. 171st L.T.M.B.,
        2. Staff Captain.                    12. 421st Field Co. R.E.,
        3. "E" Battalion.                    13. Signals.
        4. "F"   ,,                          14. 57th Divl. Artillery.
        5. "G"   ,,                          15. Left Group R.A.,
        6. "H"   ,,                          16. 4th New Zealand R.Bde.
        7. 57th Division. "G"                17. 173rd M.G. Company.
        8.     ,,         "Q"                18. War Diary.
        9. 172nd Inf. Brigade.               19.      ,,
       10. 171st M.G. Company.               20. File.

SECRET.                    171st BRIGADE ORDER No. 13.           Copy No. 16
Map of.                                                          7th June, 1917.
Sheet 36 N.W.2.
& N.E.I (Parts of)
1:10.000.

INTENTION.    1. In accordance with 57th Divisional Order No.13, Gas
              will be discharged in conjunction with 3rd Australian
              Division on our Left, at a time to be notified later.

OBJECT.       2. To destroy as many as possible of enemy personnel.

LOCALITY.     3(a) Cylinders are installed at the following points :-
                I.10.b.98.39  to  I.11.a.08.87  termed "L" Sector.
                                                Capacity 300.
                C.29.c.29.31  to  C.29.a.10.02  termed "A" Sector.
                                                Capacity 520.
                C.29.a.21.72  to  C.23.c.15.25  termed "B" Sector.
                                                Capacity 300.
              Above Sectors are manned and fought by "D" Special Co, R.E.

                C.23.c. 2. 2  to  C.23.c. 2. 7  termed "N" Sector.
                                                Capacity 400.
                C.23.a. 1. 1  to  C.23.a. 2. 4  termed "C" Sector.
                                                Capacity 300
                C.17.c. 3. 6  to  C.17.a. 2. 1  termed "D" Sector.
                                                Capacity 500
              and more are being installed at other places.
              Above are manned and fought by "M" Special Co, R.E.

              (b) Projectors (if received in time) will be discharged on
              the following points at the same time as the gas cloud :-
              (1) Trench System opposite MUSHROOM, I.11.C.
              (2) Trenches above CENTAUR, C.29.A.
              (3) CELT system of Trenches, C.23.B. and C.17.A.
              (4) FRELINGHIEN.

              (c) The decision as to whether conditions are suitable for
              the discharge of gas is left entirely in the hands of
              O.C., "D" Special Coy R.E., in conjunction with O.C., "M"
              Special Coy, R.E.,    The final decision for the
              discharge will rest with the Special Coy R.E. Officer in
              the Trenches.    The discharge may be cancelled
              irrespective of the 3rd Australians, or may be discharged
              at the hours laid down if the wind is favourable, even if
              the Australians are unable to.

PROGRAMME.    4. The discharge will be silent.   The projectors
              will be fired at zero plus 3 minutes.   Valves of
              cylinders will be turned off at zero plus 30 minutes.

ARTILLERY.    5. Artillery will stand by for retaliation from zero.

CODES.        6. The following will be employed, and messages marked
              URGENT:-

              Wind is favourable,   CANADA.      No discharge from
              Wind unfavourable,    BERLIN.       my Sector.        COLOGNE.
              All ready,            LILLE.       Zero hour is
              Discharge proceeding, HAVRE.        confirmed.        AMIENS.
              Discharge completed)               Discharge cancelled,
              Line may be         ) BRUSSELS.     return.           BETHUNE.
              reoccupied.         )              Zero postponed,    ARRAS,
                                                  followed by number of
                                                  hours.

2.

**MEDICAL ARRANGEMENTS.** 7. Os.C. Right and Left Battalions in Line will place Regimental Stretcher Bearers at the disposal of Os.C. "D" and "M" Special Coys, R.E., at the following points :-
RIGHT BATTN.
(1) 4 Stretcher Bearers with 2 Stretchers in front line at top of VAUXHALL AVENUE.
(2) 6 Stretcher Bearers with 3 Stretchers at C.28.d.90.70 (Concrete dugout LONDON ROAD).
(3) 4 Stretcher Bearers with 2 Stretchers at FRY-PAN.
LEFT BATTN.
(1) 6 Stretcher Bearers with 3 Stretchers at top of EDMEADS AVENUE.
(2) 6 Stretcher Bearers with 3 Stretchers at top of IRISH AVENUE.
LEFT RESERVE BATTN. O.C. will detail :-
6 Stretcher Bearers with 3 Stretchers at top of WESSEX AVENUE.

**SIGNALS.** 8. Special Rocket signals, showing triple consecutive lights - Red - Green - Red, will be sent up from 2 points, one in C.23.C., the other in I.3.D., in the event, from any cause whatever, or zero hour having to be postponed or cancelled within the period of the last warning Zero minus one hour. Confirmation of this signal will at once be sent by runner or telephone to all concerned.

**COMMUNICATION.** 9. (a) In conjunction with Os.C. Battalions in the Line, the Brigade Signalling Officer will arrange for inter-communication by Fullerphone between Brigade HdQrs - the 6 Sectors mentioned in para.3, and runners should this communication break down.

(b) Special Company R.E. Officers, in order to facilitate quick communication, may use 'URGENT PRIORITY' messages. It should be remembered, however, that these messages must be very limited, as a large number handed in will block the line.

**PRECAUTIONS.** 10. (a) The front line from which gas is to be discharged will be cleared to a distance of 250 yards on either flank of the gap, with the exception of sentries, Lewis Gunners, Bombing Squads, and one Infantry Officer per Gas Sector, all of whom will wear their Box Respirators, fully adjusted, from Zero minus 5 minutes, to zero plus 30 minutes.

(b) The Infantry Officers remaining in the Gas Sectors will keep in touch with the Special Company R.E. Officers in charge of their Sector.

(c) All other ranks in the Brigade Area will observe precautions for Wind Dangerous.

(d) No man will return to that part of the line from which gas has been discharged until ordered to do so by an Officer.

**SYNCHRONISING OF WATCHES.** 11. Watches will be synchronised at Brigade HdQrs at 7 p.m. on the day upon which the code word FLETCHER is received by wire, an Officer reporting to the Staff Captain for that purpose with 3 watches, and, if gas is not released on that day, daily at the same hour until this operation is completed.

3.

REPORTS. 12. Reports will be rendered to these Headquarters early.

13. ACKNOWLEDGE.

*[signature]*
Lieut. Acting Brigade Major.
171st Infantry Brigade.

ISSUED AT 6 p.m., to :-

```
Copy No.  1   B.G.C.,
          2   "E" Battalion
          3   "F"      "
          4   "G"      "
          5   "H"      "
          6   57th Division.
          7   172nd Brigade.
          8   57th Divl. Detachment.
          9   C.R.A.,
         10   Left Group, R.A.,
         11   171st M.G. Company.
         12   173rd    "
         13   171st L.T.M.B.,
         14   "D" Company, R.E.,
         15   "M"     "
         16   War Diary.
         17          "
         18   G.S. File.
         19.) Spare.
         20.)
```

SECRET.                                                                COPY NO. 16

Ref. Map
36 NW 2 &          171st BRIGADE ORDER NO. 13 A.          13th June, 1917.
NE I (Parts of)
1:10,000.
                        (In continuation of Brigade Order No.13).


1. The Gas Cylinders now South of the RIVER LYS in this Brigade Area, will be discharged on the first favourable opportunity, under the orders of the B.G.C., It is improbable that any discharge will take place North of the River LYS, but from now onwards, our discharge will in any case be entirely independent of any other.

2. The final decision for the discharge will rest with the Special Company R.E. Officer in the Trenches.

3. Units will be notified the hour it is intended to release the Gas, by the following code :-

   Count the hours from 1 to 24, and give the time of the discharge in minutes with the prefix "MEN AVAILABLE". Thus, if the discharge is to be at 9.25p.m., = 21 hours 25 minutes = 1285. Code message "MEN AVAILABLE 1285". Or 3 a.m., = 3 hours = 180. Code message "MEN AVAILABLE 180".

4. In the event of the discharge being subsequently cancelled, the telegraphic number of the telegram only will be used, stating "MY NO. so-and-so CANCELLED".

5. ACKNOWLEDGE.

                                                    Lieut. Acting Brigade Major.
                                                    171st Infantry Brigade.


ISSUED AT 3 p.m., :-

| Copy No. | | Copy No. | |
|---|---|---|---|
| 1. | B.G.C., | 11. | 171st M.G.Company. |
| 2. | "E" Battalion. | 12. | 173rd " |
| 3. | "F" " | 13. | 171st L.T.M.G., |
| 4. | "G" " | 14. | "D" Company, R.E., |
| 5. | "H" " | 15. | "M" " |
| 6. | 57th Division. | 16. | War Diary. |
| 7. | 172nd Brigade. | 17. | " |
| 8. | 4th New Zleand Inf.Bde. | 18. | G.S.File. |
| 9. | C.R.A., | 19. | Spare. |
| 10. | Left Group R.A., | 20. | " |

APPENDIX NO. II.

MINOR OPERATIONS

Referred to in

171st INFANTRY BRIGADE WAR DIARY,

31.5.1917 to 30.6.1917.

..........

CONFIDENTIAL.

## 171st INFANTRY BRIGADE — ARMENTIERES SECTOR.

### REPORT on CONTACT with the ENEMY.

### Night of 11th June, 1917.

* * * * *

At 9.23 p.m., on the 11th June 1917, the enemy put down a heavy barrage from the right of HOBBS FARM to the North of the RIVER LYS.

Thanks to the information received from XI Corps, through a prisoner taken by this Brigade on the night of the 10th / 11th, it was made possible to arrange with the Left Group Commander, and through him with the Heavy Artillery, to respond at once.

Within a few seconds our guns dropped like a blanket on the enemy's lines, concentrated on the line HOBBS FARM — FRELINGHEIN.

Under cover of their barrage, the enemy attempted to raid our lines — held by the 2/7th Battn. King's Liverpool Regt. — between 0.17.c.25.68 and 0.17.c.20.10. He failed to obtain identification, and left     dead in our hands —    and must have suffered still more heavily from the prompt and excellent retaliation given by our Artillery.

Our Brigade Observers report two explosions at 9.29 p.m., South of FRELINGHEIN, and, 7 minutes later, two more to the North of QUESNOY.

IDENTIFICATION:-


CASUALTIES.   Our Casualties  —  3 O.R. Wounded, 2/7th K.L.R.

                                 1 Officer killed.) "D"
                                 2 O.R. Wounded.  ) Special
                                                    Coy, RE.



Brigadier-General,
Commanding 171st Infantry Brigade.

B.H.Q.
12.6.1917

CONFIDENTIAL.

## 171st INFANTRY BRIGADE - ARMENTIERES SECTOR.
### REPORT ON CONTACT WITH THE ENEMY - NIGHT OF 12th/13th June, 1917.

......

A party of one Officer and 150. Ranks of the 2/8th Battn. K.L.R., entered Salient in Enemy's Lines at Point I.II.a.35.25, at 11 p.m.,

The trench was found unoccupied and in a very bad condition.

Movement was heard in the Travel Trench, some 50 yards in rear. Wire prevented Patrol encountering Enemy here. Patrol, after searching for enemy about half-an-hour, withdrew.

Conclusion - Enemy occupying trench in rear, and patrol was in one of the gaps similar to our own.


Brigadier-General,
Commanding 171st Infantry Brigade

B.H.Q.,
13th June, 1917.

CONFIDENTIAL.

CONFIDENTIAL.

REPORT
on
MINOR ENTERPRISES - NIGHT of 14th/15th JUNE, 1917.

. . . . .

2/8th Battalion, K.L.R.,

2nd Lieut. Smaridge and 16 O.Ranks left our lines from point 15.c.50.58 at 11.5p.m., and entered the enemy trench between points 15.c.92.26 and 15.c.98.40, with the object of obtaining identification and encountering enemy. The trench on entrance was found to be in a bad state of repair and unoccupied.

The party proceeded to examine trench, when gongs, bells, and rattles, presumably a gas alarm, were heard. On these sounding, 4 enemy were observed to come in from No Man's Land some 50 yds to left of party and continue up trench away from party. The latter dashed off to encounter them, but their progress was impeded in consequence of the bad state of the trench, and on their reaching the point where the enemy appeared to have come in, no sign of the enemy could be seen. The party continued along the trench to 15.d.02.48, without any sign of enemy. The party then, about 12.10 a.m., withdrew from enemy trench, and took up a position on enemy parapet to await the appearance of a trench patrol; still no sign of the enemy, however, and the party returned to our lines at 12.45 a.m., Large working parties were heard about 70 yds in rear of front line, hammering and shouting.

There were no Casualties.

. . . . . . . . . . . .

2/7th Battalion, K.L.R.,

2nd Lieut. Nickel and 16 O.R., left our trenches at 10.30 p.m. as arranged to enter the enemy's trench at C.17.C.9.4. Half-way across No Man's Land the enemy sounded an alarm with horns and bells and shouted "GAS". A large amount of movement was then heard in the trench. The patrol waited for the excitement to die down. Arrived at enemy outer belt of wire and cut a gap through, and reached sap leading from CELL TRENCH north to CELL LANE; sap filled with wire. Reached a point where there is another belt of wire, which was about 6 yds thick, and could find no gap. Located German Post of about 8 men at top of CELL LANE, and sentries at intervals of about 25yds. The total number of Germans observed was about 25. The patrol was not detected, although it lay guiding tapes, and brought them back. The patrol returned at 2.20 a.m., having failed to get into the trench.

The lookout on the part of the enemy appears to be indifferent. The wire had been cut about the place of entry, and also in other places on the front, but the long grass at present makes it very difficult to see where it is cut.

There were no Casualties.

The object of both Patrols, was :-

(1) Ascertain definitely if enemy is holding line.

(2) Obtain Identification.

(3) Encounter and kill the Enemy.

Brigadier-General,
Commanding 171st Infantry Brigade.

B.H.Q.
15.6.1917

SECRET.                                                         COPY NO. 7

Map Ref.                                                        June 12th 1917.
36 N.W.2 &                 171st  BRIGADE  ORDER  No. 15.
N.E.I (Parts of).
1:10.000.                          ......

INTENTION.      1.      On Z. day at Zero hour, a detachment of the
                2/6th K.L.R., will carry out a Raid on a Sector of
                the Enemy's Trenches - front line and support line -
                between the following points, approximately C.29.a.38.
                08 and C.29.a.70.50.

OBJECT.         2. (a) To continue a harrassing policy, and prevent
                the enemy from withdrawing troops.
                   (b) Killing and capturing as many of the enemy as
                possible.
                   (c) Capturing and destroying war material.
                   (d) Obtaining identifications, and gaining
                information regarding the enemy's system of
                defence.

ARTILLERY.      3.      The Raid will be supported by the Left Group,
                57th Divisional Artillery.

ORDERS.         4.      O.C., 2/6th K.L.R., will render to these
                HdQrs., six days prior to the Minor Enterprise, his
                Raid Orders and Programme.

                5.      ACKNOWLEDGE.

                                                    [signature]

                                                Major, Brigade Major.
                                                171st Infantry Brigade.

ISSUED AT 3 p.m., to :-

        Copy No. 1. B.G.C.,
              2. Brigade Major.
              3. 57th Division.
              4. Left Group Artillery Commander.
              5. 2/6th K.L.R.,
              6. 57th Divisional Artillery.
              7. War Diary.
              8.      ,,
              9. File.
             10.      ,,

SECRET.

..........

Reference Brigade Order No. 15 dated 12th instant.

Delete para "5", and substitute para "6".

Add after para 4 :-

Para. 5. The O.C., 2/6th K.L.R., will send an Officer to Brigade Headquarters with 4 or more watches to synchronise at 9.30 a.m., and at 7 p.m., on Zero day.

The Left Group Commander and B.G.C., 171st Infantry Brigade will synchronise watches. Should any discrepancy of time arise, the Infantry will remember to take Artillery time, and must work by the Artillery barrage.

ACKNOWLEDGE.

B.H.Q. 13.6.1917.

Lieut. Acting Brigade Major.
171st Infantry Brigade.

SECRET.                                            COPY NO. 14

### SPECIAL INSTRUCTIONS for S.O.S.,
### – Night of 21st/22nd June, 1917 –

1. From 12.00 midnight on the 21st/22nd June 1917, until completion of Raid, i.e., when Artillery have been notified "FINISHED", the S.O.S. will only be acknowledged by request on telephone, or by written message.

2. O.C., 2/6th Liverpool Regiment will be responsible for notifying Units in the Line that Operations are completed.

ACKNOWLEDGE.

G. Huntley

2nd Lieut. Acting
Brigade Major.
171st Infantry Brigade.


ISSUED AT 9 p.m., 20.6.1917, to :–

```
Copy No.  1.  B.G.C.,
          2.  Brigade Major.
          3.  57th Division.
          4.  Left Group Artillery Commander.
          5.  2/6th K.L.R.,
          6.  57th Divisional Artillery.
          7.  2/5th K.L.R.,
          8.  2/7th   "
          9.  2/8th   "
         10.  O.C. Raid.
         11.  171st L.T.M.B.
         12.  171st M.G.Coy.
         13.  173rd      "
         14.  War Diary.
         15.    "
         16.  File.
```

## 57th DIVISION.

### REPORT ON MINOR OPERATIONS CARRIED OUT IN ARMENTIERES SECTION.

on the night of 21/22nd June 1917.

by 2/6th K.L.R.  Lt.Col. W.A.L.Fletcher, Commanding.

STRENGTH OF PARTY.  3 Off. 100 Other ranks.

POINT OF EXIT.  C.29.a.25.80. - C.28.b.96.34.
C.29.a.42.17. - C.29.a.62.41.

TIME.  1.6.a.m.

OBJECT.  To kill and capture as many as possible of the enemy destroy War Material, obtain identification and generally to harass the enemy and prevent him from withdrawing troops.

NARRATIVE.  After a preliminary barrage of two minutes on the enemy front line, the raiders, who were divided into three parties arrived at enemy's wire and in doing so followed the barrage too closely and suffered a few casualties. The Right party found the wire well cut and experienced no difficulty in entering enemy trench. As was anticipated, a strong dug-out was found in the front line at about C.29.a.42.10 built of concrete with iron doors; in this 3 men were found. These men - wearing blue uniform, with Red cross brassards - probably stretcher bearers - refused to surrender and so a bomb was thrown into the dug-out, whereupon the door was shut from the inside, the occupants were then fired upon through a loop-hole. During this encounter, fire was opened upon our raiders from behind the next traverse. Much valuable time having thus been spent this party did not reach its final objective.

The Centre party enetered enemy trench after some difficulty in getting through his wire and got into touch with the Right party. Two enemy were bombed and killed in a dug-out but as identifications were being obtained some more of the enemy came down the trench with their hands up shouting "SURRENDER", but without apparently any intention of doing so. General confusion ensued, the enemy got clear away, and identifications were not picked up.

The Left party found the first rows of wire cut, but were hung up by the final rows. They failed to get into the enemy trench.

GENERAL.  Enemy Artilery retaliation was unexpected light. It developed gradually, N.M.Land being lightly barraged with shrapnel and our front and Support Lines with H.E. The only signal seen being one green light and one golden rain which were some twenty minutes after operations commenced. Little hostile M.G.fire was encountered. All the parties withdrew according to time-table and with the exception of three missing returned to our lines. At Zero hour a Rifle Grenade barrage was fired on the Right flank as a diversion, and the 171st L.T.M.B. fired 165 rounds in co-operation on enemy Support Line. Further points are being enquired into and will be forwarded later.

CASUALTIES.  Killed 3 O.R. Wounded 1 Off. 5 O.R. Missing 3 O.R.

IDENTIFICATION.  NIL.

APPENDIX No. III.

STATEMENT of CASUALTIES.

............

Forwarded in Conjunction with

171st INFANTRY BRIGADE WAR DIARY,

31.5.1917 to 30.6.1917.

.....

# 171st INFANTRY BRIGADE.

CASUALTIES from 31.5.1917 to 30.6.1917.

| DATE. 24 hrs ending noon:- | KILLED. | | WOUNDED. | | MISSING. | |
|---|---|---|---|---|---|---|
| | Officers. | O.Ranks. | Officers. | O.Ranks. | Officers. | O.Ranks. |
| 1.6.1917 | - | 6 | - | 5 | - | - |
| 2.6.1917 | - | 1 | - | 10 | - | - |
| 3.6.1917 | - | - | - | 3 | - | - |
| 4.6.1917 | - | 2 | - | 4 | - | - |
| 5.6.1917 | - | - | - | 5 | - | - |
| 6.6.1917 | - | - | - | 6 | - | - |
| 7.6.1917 | - | 2 | - | 8 | - | - |
| 8.6.1917 | - | 1 | - | 12 | - | - |
| 9.6.1917 | - | 1 | Rev.,M.J. ELAND. | 11 | - | - |
| 10.6.1917 | - | - | - | 6 | - | - |
| 11.6.1917 | - | - | 2nd Lt.AL. COWPER. | 2 | - | - |
| 12.6.1917 | - | 3 | 2nd Lt.TC. SHAFTO. | 20 | - | - |
| 13.6.1917 | - | - | - | 22 | - | - |
| 14.6.1917 | - | 1 | 2nd Lt N. CREEDON. 2nd Lt.EL SHUBART. | 14 | - | - |
| 15.6.1917 | - | 1 | - | 6 | - | - |
| 16.6.1917 | - | - | - | 4 | - | - |
| 17.6.1917 | - | - | - | 12 | - | - |
| 18.6.1917 | - | - | - | 6 | - | - |
| 19.6.1917 | - | - | 2nd Lt. T. TIMMONS. | 5 | - | - |
| 20.6.1917 | - | - | 2nd Lt.WJP. MAXWELL-STUART. | 4 | - | - |
| 21.6.1917 | - | 1 | - | 4 | - | - |
| 22.6.1917 | - | 5 | Capt.H.C. WRIGHT. Lieut.PGF. PARKER. | 17 | - | 1 |
| 23.6.1917 | - | - | - | 6 | - | - |
| 24.6.1917 | 2nd Lt CEJ. HOLMES. | 2 | 2nd Lt.JN. BLAKE. | 15 | - | - |
| 25.6.1917 | - | - | - | 4 | - | - |
| 26.6.1917 | - | 3 | - | 12 | - | - |
| 27.6.1917 | - | 1 | - | 10 | - | - |
| 28.6.1917 | - | 1 | - | 7 | - | - |
| 29.6.1917 | - | - | - | 12 | - | - |
| 30.6.1917 | - | 2 | - | 9 | - | 1 |
| TOTALS. | 1 | 33 | 10 | 261 | - | 2 |

Vol. 6

Headquarters
171 Infantry Brigade
(57th Division)
July 1917

CONFIDENTIAL.


WAR DIARY

of

HEADQUARTERS - 171st INFANTRY BRIGADE.

....

1.7.1917 to 31.7.1917.

..

VOLUME V.

# WAR DIARY
## or
## INTELLIGENCE SUMMARY

*(Erase heading not required.)*

Army Form C. 2118

Instructions regarding War Diaries and Intelligence Summaries are contained in F.S. Regs., Part II. and the Staff Manual respectively. Title Pages will be prepared in manuscript.

| Place | Date | Hour | Summary of Events and Information | Remarks and references to Appendices |
|---|---|---|---|---|
| ARMENTIERES | 30.6.17 | | Major G.W. GEDDES D.S.O. Brigade Major handed over to CAPT. G.L. ALEXANDER on the former's appointment to G.S. 8th Division. | |
| | 1.7.17 | | At 2.10 am after heavy artillery preparation enemy raided our front line at a point NORTH of EPINETTE coxheat. He was immediately driven out by the garrison troops leaving one Lt/Sy wounded prisoner in our hands. His artillery activity on ARMENTIERES, HOUPLINES and la CHAPELLE d'ARMENTIERES continued. | Appendix II |
| | 2.7.17 | | Artillery and aeroplane activity on the enemy's part were very marked. One Aeroplane flew over our lines at a low altitude and was fired on with Machine rifle Grenades. His artillery shelled back areas fairly heavily but the line was quiet. Our artillery replied by shelling PERENCHIES and knocked out the Water Tower - 2/5 K.L.R. relieved 2/8 K.L.R. in the EPINETTE subsector. | Appendix I left |
| | 3.7.17 | | Artillery activity continued. The front and support lines of our trenches were intermittently shelled. By night ARMENTIERES and back areas were fired upon - 2/5 K.L.R. relieved 2/7 K.L.R. in the HOUPLINES subsector. | Appendix I left |
| | 4.7.17 | | The enemy artillery continued to shell ARMENTIERES vigorously during the early hours and at intervals. CITE BON JEAN on fire - Between 8.0 pm and 11.0 pm HOUPLINES and between 10.0 pm and midnight ARMENTIERES were heavily shelled. Quiet on the line. A small encounter between patrols took place in N.M's ground at 12.50 am. Enemy artillery continued very active; still directed on to ARMENTIERES, HOUPLINES and back areas. | Appendix I left |
| | 5.7.17 | | A patrol from 2/5 K.L.R. consisting of 1 Officer, 1 O.R. encountered an enemy party of 20 in No Man's land north of L'EPINETTE Salient. The enemy were driven back to their line & which 4 came thro' in our party. The officer 2/Lt E.S.M. HARDING & one O.R. being killed and 2 O.R. wounded. | Appendix II left |

# WAR DIARY
## or
## INTELLIGENCE SUMMARY

*(Erase heading not required.)*

Army Form C. 2118

Instructions regarding War Diaries and Intelligence Summaries are contained in F.S. Regs., Part II. and the Staff Manual respectively. Title Pages will be prepared in manuscript.

| Place | Date | Hour | Summary of Events and Information | Remarks and references to Appendices |
|---|---|---|---|---|
| ARMENTIERES | 6.7.17 | | Considerable aerial activity on both sides — several combats in the air took place to our south. Observed that our enemy aeroplane was forced down — In the trench system our left are was subjected to heavy shelling the Communication trenches being badly damaged. The enemy barrage on RUE du BOIS — the sector held by Brigade on our right — coincides with heavy shelling of the S. and SW parts of ARMENTIERES. At least 9 bombs were dropped from aeroplanes on the town — | 50 ft |
| | 7.7.17 | | A comparatively quiet day in the line — ARMENTIERES and HOUPLINES were again shelled during the evening — A fire was burning in PERENCHIES from dawn till midnight — | 90 ft |
| | 8.7.17 | | Enemy artillery again active on Font, Subsectors and Subsy Bay Lugos. HOUPLINES was shelled — ARMENTIERES on the other hand was quieter than it has been for over a month — Our right subsector received some retaliation to our barrage on RUE du BOIS sector. | 50 ft |
| | 9.7.17 | | Enemy appeared to be registering on our left subsector. His artillery — chiefly 77 mm — activity in reply to our 6.2.M. was very marked. Shelling of ARMENTIERES and HOUPLINES was rather less but our shelling of his trenches with 18 Pdrs was considerably heavier — Rain and haze made observation poor and few aeroplanes were up from either side. | 50 ft |
| | 10.7.17 | | Battery positions were again shelled, and a factory set on fire. In the line the Scheme left sector was heavily shelled otherwise no incident of importance occurred — 2/8 K.R.R. relieved 2/5 K.R.R. in L'EPINETTE subsector. At 1.33 am Gas was successfully discharged from cylinders and projectors. Enemy retaliation chiefly confined to rifle & M.G. fire. | Appendix I. Appendix II etc. |

1875 Wt. W593/826 1,000,000 4/15 I.B.C. & A. A.D.S.S./Forms/C. 2118.

Army Form C. 2118

# WAR DIARY
## or
## INTELLIGENCE SUMMARY
(Erase heading not required.)

Instructions regarding War Diaries and Intelligence Summaries are contained in F. S. Regs., Part II. and the Staff Manual respectively. Title Pages will be prepared in manuscript.

| Place | Date | Hour | Summary of Events and Information | Remarks and references to Appendices |
|---|---|---|---|---|
| ARMENTIERES | 11.7.17 | | Enemy artillery active especially on the left subsector — Ohenne his attitude very quiet — 2/7 KLR relieved 2/4 KLR in HOUPLINES subsector. | Appendix I. SofA |
| | 12.7.17. | | Increased hostile shelling from Left subsector — IRISH AVENUE practically destroyed and during the afternoon shelling of CAMBRIDGE AVENUE — The real communication trench on the SOUTH — commenced. Enemy aeroplanes fell out of control, just NORTH of ARMENTIERES. He ADS wounded, and Observer unhurt, being taken prisoner. | SofA |
| | 13.7.17 | | Artillery on both sides showed increased activity — The L'EPINETTE sector was quiet, but the left portion of the HOUPLINES subsector, HOUPLINES itself, NOUVEL HOUPLINES and ARMENTIERES were heavily shelled — Our casualties were very light considering the weight and intensity of hostile artillery fire — | SofA |
| | 14.7.17 | | L'EPINETTE subsector again very quiet — Enemy artillery activity on ARMENTIERES, HOUPLINES and the left subsector was continued and at times reached considerable intensity — at 8.43 pm + 10.50 pm concentrated fire was directed on Front and Support lines a entire Left — A small party of the enemy no doubt took flare from our line by Lewis guns and hand grenade. Early in the morning bombs were Dropped on ARMENTIERES. 2/5 KLR relieved 2/6 KLR in the EPINETTE subsector. | Appendix II. Appendix I. SofA |
| | 15.7.17 | | At 1.5 am and 3.30 am the same section so on night of 9/14/15 were barraged — No attempt to raid our trenches followed but the damage to our trenches and communication trenches has been very considerable. Only 8 casualties reported — | SofA |
| | 16.7.17 | | After heavy artillery preparation an enemy raiding party 2 Officers 95 OR of 1st Res. BAV. I.R. raided our front line on the extreme left — just SOUTH of R.245 — at 2.10 am | |

# WAR DIARY or INTELLIGENCE SUMMARY

Army Form C. 2118

| Place | Date | Hour | Summary of Events and Information | Remarks and references to Appendices |
|---|---|---|---|---|
| ARMENTIERES | 16.7.17 (contd) | | They were immediately exposed leaving Pioneers and 6 dead in our hands. Our casualties 7 killed 29 wounded. 2 Stokes guns damaged one beyond repair. The day was quieter than recently but at night enemy artillery resumed activity and formed heavy concentrates fire on the front & supports lines of the left subsection at 8.50 pm and again at 10.50 pm. The reply of our artillery to hostile barrage was prompt and efficient. | Appendix II Sop/it |
| | 17.7.17 | | A further barrage was put down on our extreme left by enemy artillery at 3.30 am but no infantry attack followed. The enemy's intention to prevent the repair of our trenches in this area is obvious but work progressed satisfactorily. To the knowledge of the 24 hours the line was quiet. In ARMENTIERES a battery position was heavily shelled and 3 guns were damaged. The Coy 4th Bde CEF attached to HOUPLINES & the Coy 16 HOUPLINES | Appendix 4 50pt |
| | 18.7.17 | | A comparatively quiet day. The line being for less shelling lots of the town itself and the trenches than recently. Ours & O matters there was less aeroplane activity. Observation support | 50pt |
| | 19.7.17 | | The line was fairly quiet. Parts of ARMENTIERES were very heavily shelled including billets of Right Recog. Batt. (2/5) and Brigade H.Q. which received 7 direct hits. H.Qs were hurriedly during the afternoon. At our line 5 Batteries were firing salvoes at the rate of 32 a minute into the area between RUE SADI CARNOT and the RAILWAY. At 11.40 pm the Henny shelling recommenced. Gas shells being fired as well as shrapnel and HE 2/5 KLR wearing 27 kill into HOUPLINES. | Appendix |
| | 20.7.17 | | The hostile shelling continued until 2.45 am. HOUPLINES - battery positions at the LUNATIC ASYLUM in particular - being more heavily shelled than ARMENTIERES. The number of gas shells falling is estimated at 5000 - a low figure - consequently relief was hindered and though | 20pt/it |

# WAR DIARY or INTELLIGENCE SUMMARY

Army Form C. 2118

**Place:** ARMENTIERES

| Date | Hour | Summary of Events and Information | Remarks and references to Appendices |
|---|---|---|---|
| 20.7.17 (contd) | | Our casualties were rather heavy. 4 killed 58 wounded. Many of these have been very slightly affected by Gas. 200 Corps 4th Rifle CEP relieved to two Corps CEP in L'EPINETTE and HOUPLINES respectively. | Appendix 4 to 7/A. |
| 21.7.17 | | The front & support line on the extreme left of HOUPLINES subsection and IRISH AVENUE were shelled during the day - otherwise the line was quiet - the area round ARMENTIERES RAILWAY STATION was heavily shelled during the afternoon and the killed of 2/8 K.L.R. hit. Casualties 1 killed 17 wounded. | 7/A. |
| 22.7.17 | | A quiet day so far as the Infantry in the line was concerned - Considerable aerial activity on both sides the enemy having a large number of observation Balloons up - his artillery was active at intervals shelling ARMENTIERES. Our artillery - in conjunction with New Zealand Rifle Brigade on our right flank - concentrated heavy fire on enemy trenches in front of FRELINGHIEN. Enemy retaliation about 400 77 mm on our extreme left causing no casualties. | 7/A. |
| 23.7.17 | | Hostile shelling continued on Battery positions in ARMENTIERES - 2 farms were damaged. At 9.30 pm on Divisional line HOUPLINES and parts of ARMENTIERES was shelled with H.E. and Gas Shells - a fire resulted in RUE NATIONALE. Casualties 1 killed 12 wounded. Inn Corps 4th Rifle CEP returned to ARMENTIERES from L'EPINETTE and HOUPLINES subsections respectively. The 5th Coy did not go into the line through outbreak of measles 2/8 K.L.R. manned two Coys relieved 2/5 K.L.B. - manned two Corps - in L'EPINETTE subsection. | Appendix 4 to 7/A. Appendix 1 to 7/A. |

Army Form C. 2118

# WAR DIARY
## or
## INTELLIGENCE SUMMARY
*(Erase heading not required.)*

Instructions regarding War Diaries and Intelligence Summaries are contained in F.S. Regs., Part II. and the Staff Manual respectively. Title Pages will be prepared in manuscript.

VI

| Place | Date | Hour | Summary of Events and Information | Remarks and references to Appendices |
|---|---|---|---|---|
| ARMENTIERES | 24.7.17 | | Hostile shelling of ARMENTIERES resumed early in the morning and a horse set on fire in RUE NATIONALE. Quieter by day. In the line the situation was quieter. Tonight HOUPLINES was shelled with Gas shells and H.E. | 30/fA |
| | 25.7.17 | | Beyond the shelling of ARMENTIERES the day was quiet & particularly in the trenches. | 30/fA |
| | 26.7.17 | | At 2.0 a.m. a raid party of 3 Officers 122 O.R. of 2/8 K.L.R. carried out a raid on the enemy lines SOUTH of L'EPINETTE salient. Only few of our men succeeded in entering the enemy front line as our parts were late in forming up and the enemy barrage descended on his front line before our men reached there. HOUPLINES was again heavily shelled at night. | Appendix 2. 30/fA |
| | 27.7.17 | | The L'EPINETTE sector was quiet. Enemy artillery exceptionally active on the HOUPLINES sector both on the line and on back areas. The HOUPLINES-ARMENTIERES road was very heavily shelled during the 24 hours - during the afternoon the vicinity of ARMENTIERES RAILWAY station and the RUE de LILLE was heavily shelled. The billets of Left H.Q. and 2/8 K.L.R. were in the shelled area but very few casualties were sustained. Remainder of 2/6 K.L.R. rehearsed 2 Corps e/s K.L.R. in the L'EPINETTE subsector. | appendix 1. 30/fA |
| | 28.7.17 | | A comparatively quiet day in the line. L'EPINETTE subsector being quieter than HOUPLINES. Hostile shelling of ARMENTIERES continued intermittently - a good deal of damage was done to the Q.M. stores of 2/5 % or 2/7 K.L.R. Preparations were made to move these to the | 30/fA |

# WAR DIARY or INTELLIGENCE SUMMARY

Army Form C. 2118

VII

| Place | Date | Hour | Summary of Events and Information | Remarks and references to Appendices |
|---|---|---|---|---|
| ARMENTIERES | 28.7.17 (contd) | | Lt. Col. G.H. NORTH. D.S.O. assumed command of 17th Inf. Bde. in Brig-Gen. R.N. BRAY D.S.O. going on leave. 2/7 K.R.R. relieved 2/6 K.R.R. in the LISPINETTE sub-sector. | |
| | 29.7.17 | | Commencing at midnight 28/29th the enemy shelled ARMENTIERES with extreme violence until 1.30 a.m. Thousands of GAS shells were fired into the town chiefly on to the RUE de LILLE, the Quai de Madere stretch of 2/5, 2/6 & 2/7 K.R.R. was developed, on to Billeting area RUE STRASSBURG and RUE BAYARD and RUE SADI CARNOT. One Company 2/5 K.R.R., two Companies 2/6 K.R.R. as well as the headquarters of both these Battalions were gassed and evacuated during the day. The enemy mixed his Gas shells with H.E. and it was extremely difficult to detect the presence of Gas in sufficient time to take necessary precautions. A large number of civilians in addition to our troops were gassed and evacuated. The casualties were most efficiently handled at the A.D.S. Institut S. Vaast where Capt CREEGAN - R.A.M.C. and his small staff did most excellent work, ably assisted by Capt S.R. GIBBS - R.A.M.C. In the day rather unnatural noises entered by Capt S.R. GIBBS - R.A.M.C. The damage was confined to ARMENTIERES and immediate surrounding; the troops in the line suffered no serious casualties, and the day for an infantry point of view passed quietly. The command of 2/5 K.R.R. devolved upon Capt H.A. READ as Lt. Col. S.S.G. COHEN and Major H.N.K. QUICK were gassed and evacuated - Major P.M. GILES being absent on leave. Command of 2/6 K.R.R. devolved upon Major N.K. WILSON as Lt.Col. W.A.L. FLETCHER was gassed and evacuated. | Appendix I. Appendix I. Appx. Appx. |
| | 30.7.17. | | Major N.K. WILSON gassed and evacuated. Capt. C.E. WURZBURG absent on leave, Capt A.G. ECCLES acting 2/6 K.R.R. gassed. Command devolved upon Capt. J.C. BOWRING | |

Army Form C. 2118

# WAR DIARY
or
# INTELLIGENCE SUMMARY
(Erase heading not required.)

VIII

Instructions regarding War Diaries and Intelligence Summaries are contained in F. S. Regs., Part II. and the Staff Manual respectively. Title Pages will be prepared in manuscript.

| Place | Date | Hour | Summary of Events and Information | Remarks and references to Appendices |
|---|---|---|---|---|
| ARMENTIERES | 30.7.17 (contd) | | The shelling of ARMENTIERES and HOUPLINES continued throughout the day and from 3.30 p.m. to 5.0 p.m. assumed proportions of great intensity. Areas RUE MARLE, RAILWAY STATION, and ST VAAST PLACE particularly damaged. Several fires caused. Some the morning & early afternoon Brigade HQrs in RUE SADI de la REPUBLIQUE and NOTRE DAME Cathedral were bombarded, Brigade HQrs in RUE SADI CARNOT left had no casualties to personnel. GAS shell hinged in diffusion of the Armoryards made in cellars but rain fell harsh and dissipated the large proportion. Sector due it will relieve 170th Bde — The 170th Bde will move into ARMENTIERES — Contact with the enemy on LLAPINATI outpost line place at 9.15 a.m. | So/M. Appendix I & II |
| | 31.7.17 | | Heavy shelling of ARMENTIERES continued, but not with same intensity as on previous days. Considerably quieter during the evening. Owing to two small parties of the enemy attempted to raid our line, on the left subsector north of HOBBS FARM. They were easily repulsed by rifle & M.G. fire. The two recce companies 2/5 and 2/6 K.L.R. were relieved during night 31/7/17 - 1/8/17 by H/S LOYAL NORTH LANCS and 6 2/5 KINGS OWN R. LANCS. hights were very dark and mist. | Appendix III |

Appendix III. Casualties for month July 1917 are attached hft.

APPENDIX No. I.

RELIEF ORDERS,

etc.,

Referred to in

171st INFANTRY BRIGADE WAR DIARY,

1.7.1917 to 31.7.1917.

......

SECRET.

171st BRIGADE RELIEF ORDER No.15.

COPY NO. 19

30th June 1917.

1. The following Relief will take place in the HOUPLINES SUBSECTOR.

2. <u>Night of the 3/4th July 1917.</u>

"F" Battalion will Relieve "G" Battalion in the HOUPLINES SUBSECTOR.

3. Relief to commence at 9.30.p.m.,i.e.,time of leaving billets.

4. Lewis Guns will move into the Subsidiary line on the night previous to Relief, leaving Billets not before 9.30 p.m., Relief to be carried out at daylight on the day of the Battalion Relief, in small parties at a time.

5. Details of Relief will be arranged inter-Regimentally.

6. "G" Battalion will take over the billets of "F" Battn. and go into Left Reserve.

7. Relief will be subject to postponement at very short notice.

8. Completion of Relief and passing of Command to be reported by wire to these Headquarters.

ACKNOWLEDGE.

*Alexander*
Captain, Brigade Major,
171st Infantry Brigade.

ISSUED AT 8 p.m., to :-

| Copy No. | | Copy No. | | |
|---|---|---|---|---|
| 1. | B.G.C., | 11. | Signals. | |
| 2. | Staff Captain. | 12. | 57th Div. "G". | ) |
| 3. | "E" Battalion. | 13. | ,, "Q" | ) For |
| 4. | "F" ,, | 14. | 57th Divl.Arty. | ) information. |
| 5. | "G" ,, | 15. | Left Group, R.A. | ) |
| 6. | "H" ,, | 16. | 4th N.Z.Inf.Bde. | ) |
| 7. | 171st M.G.Company. | 17. | 172nd Inf.Bde. | ) |
| 8. | 171st L.T.M.B., | 18. | War Diary. | |
| 9. | 173rd M.G.Company. | 19. | ,, | |
| 10. | 421st Field Co. R.E., | 20. | File. | |

SECRET.

171st BRIGADE RELIEF ORDER No. 16.

COPY NO. 19

1st July, 1917.

1. The following Relief will take place in L'EPINETTE SUBSECTOR.

2. <u>Night of 2nd/3rd July 1917.</u>

"E" Battalion will relieve "H" Battalion in L'EPINETTE SUB-SECTOR.

3. Relief to commence at 9.30 p.m., i.e., time of leaving Billets.

4. Lewis Guns will move into the Subsidiary Line on the night previous to Relief, leaving Billets not before 9.30 p.m., Relief to be carried out in daylight on the day of the Battalion Relief, in small parties at a time.

5. Details of Relief will be arranged inter-Regimentally.

6. "H" Battalion will take over the billets of "E" Battalion, and go into Right Reserve.

7. Relief will be subject to postponement at very short notice.

8. Completion of Relief and passing of Command to be reported by wire to these Headquarters.

ACKNOWLEDGE.

E. Alexander

Captain, Brigade Major.
171st Infantry Brigade.

ISSUED AT 12.30 p.m., to :-

| Copy No. 1. | B.G.C., | Copy No. 11. | Signals. | |
|---|---|---|---|---|
| 2. | Staff Captain. | 12. | 57th Divn. "G". | ) |
| 3. | "E" Battalion. | 13. | ,, "Q" | ) |
| 4. | "F" ,, | 14. | 57th Divl. Arty. | ) For |
| 5. | "G" ,, | 15. | Left Group, R.A. | ) Information. |
| 6. | "H" ,, | 16. | 4th N.Z.Inf.Bde. | ) |
| 7. | 171st M.G.Company. | 17. | 172nd Inf.Bde. | ) |
| 8. | 171st L.T.M.B. | 18. | War Diary. | |
| 9. | 173rd M.G.Company. | 19. | ,, | |
| 10. | 421st Field Co, R.E., | 20. | File. | |

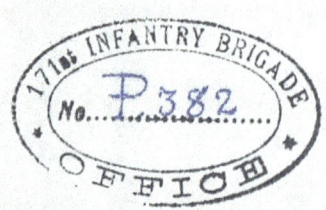

SECRET.  COPY NO. 19

## 171st INFANTRY BRIGADE
### RELIEF ORDER No. 17.

9th July, 1917.

1. Reliefs will take place according to the following table :-

| Date. JULY:- | UNIT. | From. | To. | REMARKS. |
|---|---|---|---|---|
| 10/11th. | "H" Bn. | RIGHT RESERVE. | L'EPINETTE SUB-Sector. | |
| ,, | "E" Bn. | L'EPINETTE SUB-Sector. | RIGHT RESERVE. | Takes over billets vacated by "H" Bn. |
| 11/12th. | "G" Bn. | LEFT RESERVE. | HOUPLINES SUB-Sector. | |
| ,, | "F" Bn. | HOUPLINES SUB-Sector. | LEFT RESERVE. | Takes over billets vacated by "G" Bn. |

No Reliefs to start before 9.30 p.m., - i.e., time of leaving Billets.

2. Details will be arranged inter-Regimentally.

3. Lewis Guns will move to the Subsidiary Line on the night previous to Battalion Reliefs. The relief will be carried out in daylight the next day in small parties at a time.

4. Reliefs will be subject to postponement at very short notice.

5. Completion of relief and passing of command will be reported to this Office in B.A.B.Code.

ACKNOWLEDGE.

*E. Alexander.*
Captain, Brigade Major.
171st Infantry Brigade.

ISSUED AT 12 Noon, to :-

Copy No. 1. B.G.C.,  Copy No. 11. Signals.
2. Staff Captain.  12. 57th Divn. "G"  )
3. "E" Battalion.  13.   ,,    "Q"    )
4. "F"    ,,       14. 57th Divl. Arty. )
5. "G"    ,,       15. Left Group, R.A.  ) For
6. "H"    ,,       16. 4th N.Z. Inf.Bde  ) information.
7. 171st M.G.Company.  17. 172nd Inf. Bde.  )
8. 171st L.T.M.B.,     18. War Diary.
9. 173rd M.G.Company.  19.    ,,
10. 421st Field Co. R.E.,  20. File.

SECRET.                                           COPY NO. 16

                    171st INFANTRY BRIGADE
Ref. Map.                                         13th July, 1917.
36 N.W.4.           RELIEF ORDER NO. 18.
1:10,000.
                         .......

1. The following Relief will take place tomorrow night, 14th/15th July 1917:-

   "E" Battalion will relieve "H" Battalion in the RIGHT SUBSECTOR.

2. Details will be arranged between Battalion Commanders concerned.    Reliefs not to start before 9.30 p.m., i.e., time of leaving Billets.

3. "H" Battalion on relief will take over the Billets of "E" Battalion, and go into RIGHT RESERVE.

4. Lewis Guns of "E" Battalion will move to the Subsidiary Line tomorrow night, and relieve by daylight on the 15th instant.    Lewis Guns of "H" Battalion will remain in the Line till after 6 p.m. on the 15th instant.

5. Completion of Relief will be reported to this Office in B.A.B. Code.

ACKNOWLEDGE.

                                    U Alexander.
                                    Captain, Brigade Major,
                                    171st Infantry Brigade.

ISSUED AT 10.0 p.m., 13.7.1917, to :-

Copy No. 1. Staff Captain.          Copy No. 9. Signals.
         2. "E" Battalion.                  10. 57th Divn. "G" )
         3. "F"     ,,                      11.    ,,      "Q" )
         4. "G"     ,,                      12. Left Group R.A.)  For
         5. "H"     ,,                      13. 4th N.Z.Inf.Bde)  Infrmn
         6. 171st M.G.Company.              14. 172nd Inf.Bde. )
         7. 171st L.T.M.B.                  15. War Diary.
         8. 421st Field Co, R.E.            16.    ,,

S E C R E T.

Ref.Map.
36 N.W.4.
1:10.000.

171st INFANTRY BRIGADE

RELIEF ORDER No. 19.

COPY NO. 16

17th July, 1917.

.....

1. The following Relief will take place on the night of the 19th/20th July :-

"F" Battalion will relieve "G" Battalion in the Left Subsector.

2. Details will be arranged between Battalion Commanders concerned. Relief not to start from billets before 9.15 p.m.,

3. "G" Battalion, on relief, will take over billets vacated by "F" Battalion, and go into Left Reserve.

4. Lewis Guns will be relieved the same night as the Battalion relief. Battalion Commanders will arrange that Guns are not relieved at the same time as Companies.

A minimum of 40 drums per gun will be taken in by relieving teams, and a similar number brought out by those relieved.

5. Completion of relief will be reported to this Office in B.A.B. Code.

ACKNOWLEDGE.

E.C.Alexander

Captain, Brigade Major.
171st Infantry Brigade.

ISSUED AT 10 p.m., 17.7.1917 to :-

Copy No. 1. Staff Captain.　　Copy No. 9. Signals.
　　　　 2. "E" Battalion.　　　　　　10. 57th Divn. "G"　)
　　　　 3. "F"　 ,,　　　　　　　　　11.　　 ,,　　"Q"　) For
　　　　 4. "G"　 ,,　　　　　　　　　12. Left Group, R.A.) infomation.
　　　　 5. "H"　 ,,　　　　　　　　　13. 4th N.Z.Inf.Bde. )
　　　　 6. 171st M.G.Company.　　　　14. 172nd Inf.Bde.　 )
　　　　 7. 171st L.T.M.B.　　　　　　15. War Diary.
　　　　 8. 421st Field Coy, R.E.　　 16.　　 ,,

SECRET.

Map. Ref.
BOIS GRENIER.
1:10.000.

171st INFANTRY BRIGADE

RELIEF ORDER No. 20.

COPY NO. 15

22nd July, 1917.

....

1. Reliefs will take place as follows :-

    (a) "H" Battalion, Less 2 Companies, will relieve "E" Battalion less 2 Companies, on night of 23/24th July, in HOUPLINES SUBSECTOR.

    (b) The Left and Left Centre Companies of "E" Battalion will remain in the Line, and will be relieved by the 2 remaining Companies of "H" Battalion on night of 26/27th July.

2. Details will be arranged between Battalion Commanders concerned. Reliefs will not start from Billets before 9.15 p.m.

3. "E" Battalion on relief will take over Billets of "H" Battalion, and move into Right Reserve.

4. Lewis Guns will be relieved the same night as half Battalions, Os.C. Battalions will arrange that guns are not relieved at the same time as Companies.

   A minimum of 40 drums per gun will be taken in by relieving teams, and a similar number brought out by those relieved.

5. Completion of these Reliefs will be reported to this Office by wire.

ACKNOWLEDGE.

Captain, Brigade Major.
171st Infantry Brigade.

ISSUED AT 5 p.m., to :-

Copy No. 1. Staff Captain.
        2. "E" Battalion.
        3. "F"   ,,
        4. "G"   ,,
        5. "H"   ,,
        6. 171st M.G.Company.
        7. 171st L.T.M.B.,
        8. 421st Field Co, R.E.,

Copy No. 9. Signals.
        10. 57th Division. )
        11. Left Group R.A.) For
        12. 4th N.Z Inf.Bde)Informn
        13. 172nd Inf.Bde. )
        14. War Diary.
        15.    ,,
        16. File.

SECRET.

Map. Ref.
BOIS GRENIER.
1:10,000.

171st INFANTRY BRIGADE

RELIEF ORDER No. 21.

COPY NO. 15

27th July, 1917.

1. The following Relief will take place on the night of the 28/29th July 1917 :-

   "G" Battalion will relieve "F" Battalion in HOUPLINES SUBSECTOR.

2. Details will be arranged between Battalion Commanders concerned.

   Reliefs will not start from Billets before 9.15 p.m.,

3. "F" Battalion, on relief, will take over Billets and Bivouacs vacated by "G" Battalion, and go into Left Reserve.

4. Lewis Guns will be relieved the same night as Battalions, care being taken that guns are not relieved at same time as Companies.

   A minimum of 40 drums per gun will be taken in by the relieving teams, and a similar number brought out by those relieved.

5. Completion of relief to be reported to this Office in B.A.B. Trench Code.

ACKNOWLEDGE.

Captain, Brigade Major.
171st Infantry Brigade.

ISSUED AT 12 Noon, to :-

Copy No. 1. Staff Captain.
       2. "E" Battalion.
       3. "F"    ,,
       4. "G"    ,,
       5. "H"    ,,
       6. 171st M.G.Co.
       7. 171st L.T.M.B.,
       8. 421st Field Co, R.E.

Copy No. 9. Signals.
      10. 57th Division.   )
      11. Left Group RA.   )   For
      12. 4th N.Z. Inf.Bde. ) Information.
      13. 172nd Inf.Bde.   )
      14. War Diary.
      15.       ,,
      16. File.

APPENDIX No. II.

MINOR OPERATIONS,

Referred to in

171st INFANTRY BRIGADE WAR DIARY,

1.7.1917 to 31.7.1917.

......

SECRET.

## REPORT ON ENEMY'S OPERATIONS
## on
## Night of 30th June/1st July,
## 1917.

..........

**JULY 1st.**

2.10 a.m.,  Enemy put down a box barrage on L'EPINETTE SECTOR, of Artillery, T.Ms and M.Gs, on front line in I.5.A., along AUSTRALIA AVENUE, WILLOW WALK, QUALITY STREET, PLANK AVENUE and JAPAN AVENUE.

A light barrage was placed at the same time on front line, I.5.C. and I.H.B.,

2.15 a.m.  An enemy Raiding party, about 40 strong, entered our trenches at about I.5.a.5.7.  The party was divided into 3 squads.

On entrance, two Bombing Posts of 2/8th K.L.R. were encountered.  These Posts, on being called on to surrender, replied vigorously with bombs, and the enemy was driven off, leaving one wounded man on our parapet.

2.35 a.m.  Enemy barrage ceased.  Patrols went out immediately and searched NO MAN'S LAND.  No enemy were seen, but track taken was clearly visible. Muh blood was seen.

3.10 a.m.  Left Battalion reported O.K., - No contact - no casualties.

3.15 a.m.  Right Battalion reported situation becoming normal.

The wounded prisoner was wearing the ribbon of the Iron Cross, and had "6" on the shoulder strap. This, and his identity disc, are being forwarded.

60 or 70 stick bombs, and 3 Rifles, were found in our trenches and in NO MAN'S LAND.

Our Casualties were -  5 O.R. killed.
                       7 O.R. wounded.

Enemy Casualties not known.

Considerable damage has been done to our front line, and communication trenches.

.......

SECRET.

### 171st INFANTRY BRIGADE — ARMENTIERES SECTOR.
#### Report on Contact with the Enemy,
#### Night of 3rd/4th July, 1917.

......

This affair on investigation does not appear to be very important.

12.30 a.m.,  Our patrol, of 5 O.R., encountered an enemy patrol, approximately 16 strong, in NO MAN'S LAND about I.5.c.2.2.

Our patrol was not detected by the enemy till it opened rapid fire on them. The enemy replied with bombs and rifle fire, but subsequently withdrew or were driven off.

12.50 am.  Our patrol returned to our lines, and a stronger patrol was taken out to clear up the situation, but found no trace of the enemy.

One of our original patrol was wounded near our parapet, when coming in the first time.

Brigadier-General,
Commanding 171st Infantry Brigade.

B.H.Q.
4th July, 1917

Report on contact
with the enemy on the night
5/6th July 1917.
(L'EPINETTE SUBSECTOR)

Headquarters,
57th Division.

A patrol of 1 Officer, one N.C.O. and 8.O.R. of the 2/5th K.L.R. left our lines at 11.15.p.m. 5/7/17 at a point just North of the L'EPINETTE SALIENT (C.29.c.3.3.) with the intention of dispersing and if possible obtaining identification from a small enemy working party located at C.29.C.63.30.

The patrol followed the ditch that runs N.E. across N.M. Land, and lay up at this place for about 20 minutes when they were about 50 yards in front of our wire. Nothing was heard so the patrol advanced, but on doing so was fired on with rifles and bombs, and two men were hit. The N.C.O. took these two men into the sap leading into our trench and then returned for the remainder of the patrol.

Meantime, the latter had opened rapid fire with rifles and bombs. It was now apparent that the enemy patrol consisted of at least 20 men divided into parties. The Officer and N.C.O. were in front of our patrol at this moment. The latter saw the enemy centre party attempting to close with them, and killed one man who was advancing with fixed bayonet. At this point, the patrol leader was killed, being shot in the head.

Though the enemy had retired, the N.C.O. decided to withdraw. This he did successfully, bringing the dead body in with them, covering the withdrawal with rapid fire.

He then returned to the scene of the encounter and threw bombs and opened rapid fire in the direction of the enemy. On returning, one man of the patrol was found to be missing, so the N.C.O. again went out with the same 2 men and found the missing man, who was mortally wounded, and brought him in. During his search for this man, he also searched for any of the enemy casualties, but failed to find any remaining traces of them. The patrol were all in our lines by 1.15 a.m.,

CASUALTIES.  Killed - 1 Officer (2nd Lieut.E.S.M.Harding, 2/5th K.L.R)

1 O.Rank.

Wounded, 2 O.Ranks.

N.C.Os name - Corpl MacArthur.

(Signed) R. N. BRAY.

Brigadier-General,
Commanding 171st Infantry Brigade.

B.H.Q.
6th July, 1917

SECRET.

Report on Discharge of Gas
from ARMENTIERES SECTOR,
on the Night of 9th/10th July, 1917.

..........

1. The Gas was successfully discharged from Cylinders and Projectors at about 1.33 a.m., 10th July, with certain exceptions as shewn in the report of Capt.Gilliat, O.C., "D" Special Company, R.E.,

2. (a) Immediately after the discharge, horns and gongs were heard in the enemy's lines.

(b) No special signals were discerned, and no unusual number of Very Lights were sent up.

(c) A considerable amount of retaliation took place immediately by Machine Gun and Rifle fire, chiefly from the flanks of the areas attacked. The enemy also bombed his own wire at intervals along the whole front, and threw a considerable number of pineapples on to our front line in the Left Subsector. This quieted down about 2 a.m.,

A slight retaliation by Artillery took place from about 1.40 a.m., chiefly on Reserve Lines - whizzbangs and small H.E., being distributed along the Sector.

3. Two projectiles fell short in our own lines and several more in NO MAN'S LAND; 3 men of this Brigade were slightly gassed.

All precautions regarding clearing the areas in the line of fire had been observed, and it is not at present quite clear as to how these men became gassed.

A diagrammatic explanation is being prepared, and will be forwarded in due course.

B.H.Q.,
10.7.17

Brigadier-General,
Commanding 171st Infantry Brigade.

SECRET.

## 171st INFANTRY BRIGADE — ARMENTIERES SECTOR.

Report on Enemy Activity.
Night of 14/15th July, 1917.

| | |
|---|---|
| 10.52 p.m., | Enemy barrage reported by 2/7th Battn. in HOUPLINES SUBSECTOR to have come down N. of the RIVER. |
| 10.56 p.m., | S.O.S. reported from Locality 16. (C.17.c.3.9) |
| 10.59 p.m., | One Company of Left Reserve Battalion was ordered to stand to arms. |
| 11. 3 p.m., | 2/7th Battn. reported O.K., and barrage ceased. |
| 11. 5 p.m., | Our artillery were told that our barrage was no longer required. |
| 11.19 p.m., | O.K., reported from L'EPINETTE SUBSECTOR. |
| 11.44 p.m., | 2/7th Battn. reported all quiet, but enemy artillery still firing North of the RIVER. Lines from HdQrs to two Left Companies were broken, and runners had been sent for reports. A few Minenwerfer were coming over only. |

Later reports state that enemy barrage was on front and Support line in Locality 16; field guns on the front line and heavies on the support line.

Contact with the enemy is reported, but no identification obtained at present.

Our Casualties were one wounded — no missing.

Communication with detached post has been very difficult, and a further report may follow.

All lines forward from Battalion HdQrs to two Left Companies were broken soon after the barrage started.

Brigadier-General,
Commanding 171st Infantry Brigade.

B.H.Q.
15th July, 1917

SECRET.

## 171st INFANTRY BRIGADE.

.....

Further report on Enemy Operation - Night of
14/15th July 1917, in continuation of this
Office P.452 of 15th instant.

.....

I. 5 a.m.,   Enemy put down a barrage on our front and
support lines, in Localities I5 and I6 (C.17.A.
and C.17.C).   No S.O.S. was sent up.
Artillery were warned to stand by.

I.17 a.m.,   Enemy barrage ceased.

Immediately previous to this barrage, a
patrol of 6 men was seen approaching our trenches
at C.17.c.40.89, from S.E.,   This patrol
was driven to take cover by L.G.fire, and when
enemy barrage came down it disappeared.

3.30 a.m.,   Very heavy enemy barrage was put down on
our trenches in C.23.A., C.17.C., and C.17.A.
Battalion reported all wires cut to two Left
Companies.

Artillery were asked to continue steady
fire, no S.O.S., having been sent up.

3.52 a.m.,   Enemy barrage ceased.

This barrage was the heaviest during the
night, and considerable damage to trenches has
been caused.

No contact is reported.

Our total casualties in these three barrages
are reported as:-
        I O.R. Killed.
        2 O.R. Wounded.


                    Brigadier-General,
            Commanding 171st Infantry Brigade.

B.H.Q.,
    15th July, 1917

CONFIDENTIAL.

## 171st INFANTRY BRIGADE - ARMENTIERES SECTOR.

........

Preliminary Report on Contact with
the Enemy, on the Night of 15/16th July,
HOUPLINES SUBSECTOR.
....

2.10 a.m.,     Enemy put down a very heavy barrage on Localities I5 and I6 (W.I7.C) Support Line. S.O.S. was sent up, and our guns opened immediately.

2.20 a.m.,     Barrage reported to be decreasing.

2.34 a.m.,     Barrage reported stopped.

2.40 a.m.,     Enemy party about 20 strong entered our trenches in Locality I6 between No.I and No.3 Posts.

No.I Post was attacked in rear; Nos.2 and 3 Posts in front.

Both sides bombed vigorously, and enemy were finally driven off leaving 2 prisoners and I dead in our hands. One of the prisoners is badly wounded.

Others are suspected to be still in shell holes in rear of our lines, and search is being made.

Our casualties are reported to be slight.

All communication with two Left Companies was cut at the beginning of the bombardment.

3.12 a.m.,     Barrage opened again on Locality I6 and TISSAGE DUMP was fairly heavily shelled.

3.25 a.m.,     Situation reported quiet again.


Full report will follow when received from the Battalion holding the Subsector concerned - the 2/7th K.L.R.,


                                         Brigadier-General,
                            Commanding 171st Infantry Brigade.

B.H.Q.
    16th July, 1917

SECRET.
Ref Map.
BOIS GRENIER.    171st INFANTRY BRIGADE ORDER No. 21.       COPY NO. 19
36 N.W.4.)
HOUPLINES,)  1:10,000      ......      16th July, 1917.
36 N.W.2.)
~~SPECIAL MAP - 1:5,000.~~

1. On "Z" Day at Zero hour, a Detachment of the 2/8th Battn. K.L.R., will carry out a raid on the enemy trench system in L'EPINETTE SUBSECTOR.

OBJECT.
2. (a) To harrass the enemy and assist Operations elsewhere.
   (b) To inflict casualties.
   (c) To destroy war material, dugouts and M.G.Emplacements.
   (d) To obtain prisoners for purposes of information and identification.

INTENTION.
3. Under cover of an artillery and Stokes Mortar barrage, the party will raid INANE TRENCH between :-
     I.5.c.86.28   and   I.5.d.27.60
and will penetrate as far as INANE SUPPORT between :-
     I.5.d.10.20   and   I.5.d.40.43,
inflicting as much damage as possible in a limited time.

STRENGTH of PARTY.
4. The raid will be carried out by approximately one and a half Companies, the party being detailed by LT.COLONEL O.H.NORTH, D.S.O., Commanding.

DIVERSION.
5. In order to mislead the enemy and draw his fire from the area to be raided, a diversion will be made in front of FRELINGHEIN, as follows :-
   3rd N.Z.Brigade Artillery will carry out a shoot, according to programme which will be issued later, on enemy trenches about C.IV.A., starting at Zero minus 5 mins.
   2 Bangalore Torpedoes will be placed in the enemy wire and fired at Zero minus 5 minutes, under arrangements to be made by O.C., 2/6th K.L.R., in consultation with O.C., 421st Field Company, R.E.,
   171st L.T.M.Battery will co-operate with 2 guns.

WIRECUTTING.
6. Wire-Cutting is being carried out under orders of O.C., Left Group Artillery, by Medium T.Ms.
   O.C., 171st Machine Gun Company will operate in consultation with M.T.M.Battery, in order to keep open the gaps made.
   The completion of the wire-cutting will be carried out by means of bangalore torpedoes. Arrangements for these being placed in position and fired will be made by O.C., 2/8th K.L.R., in consultation with O.C., 421st Field Company, R.E.,

ARTILLERY.
7. The Left Group, 57th Divisional Artillery, are co-operating in accordance with attached programme - APPENDIX "A".

MACHINE GUN COMPANY.
8. The 171st Machine Gun Company will co-operate in accordance with attached programme - Appendix "B".

L.T.M.B.,
9. The 171st Light Trench Mortar Battery will co-operate according to attached programme - Appendix "C".

R.E.,
10. The 421st Field Co.R.E., will provide a Detachment of Sappers for attachment to Raiding Party, and will assist in marking and preparing Assembly Position.
    They will provide, (a) Bangalore Torpedoes.
                      (b) Bridges for crossing Ditches.
                      (c) Mobile Charges for Demolition.

- 2 -

**MEDICAL.** 11. 57th Division R.A.M.C., are co-operating. Arrangements will be notified later.

**COMMUNICATION.** 12. O.C., 171st Brigade Signal Section will arrange for communication between HdQrs of O.C., Raid, Battn. HdQrs and Brigade HdQrs.
Communication forward from HdQrs of O.C., Raid will be arranged by O.C., 2/8th K.L.R.,

**CODES and SIGNALS.** 13. (a) This Operation will be referred to as "TOGO".
(b) "Z" Night will be notified to all concerned by the following code:-
Multiply the numerals indicating the night by 2, and precede them by TOGO.
Thus, night of 20/21st would be encoded as "TOGO 4042".
(c) Zero hour will be notified by the following method:-
Universal time expressed in minutes, and preceded by words "TOTAL STRENGTH".
Thus, Zero hour 11.30 p.m. would be encoded "TOTAL STRENGTH 1410".
(d) Should it be necessary to postpone zero hour from, for example, 11.30 p.m. to 12.30 a.m., message will be sent "CANCEL MY B.M.... TOTAL STRENGTH NOW 30".
(e) O.C., 2/8th K.L.R., will arrange a signal with the Artillery, in case it is necessary to postpone Operations at the last moment. Care will be taken that such postponement allows time for Raiding Party to return to our trenches before daylight.

**SYNCHRONIZATION.** 14. O.C., 171st Brigade Signal Section will obtain correct time from 57th Division Signal Company.
A watch will be sent for synchronization, leaving this HdQrs at 5 p.m., on "Z" day, to O.C., Left Group R.A., O.C. 421st Field Company, R.E., O.C., 171st M.G. Company, O.C.171st L.T.M.Battery, in the order named.
O.C., Left Group R.A., will be responsible for synchronization with 3rd N.Z.Brigade Artillery, and 2/8th K.L.R.,
O.C., 2/8th K.L.R., will be responsible for synchronization with all others concerned.

**DETAILS.** 15. O.C., 2/8th K.L.R., will issue orders regarding all further details.

16. This Order cancels 171st Brigade Order No.18, issued 3rd July, 1917.

ACKNOWLEDGE.

*E. Alexander*

Captain, Brigade Major.
171st Infantry Brigade.

ISSUED TO :-

Copy No.1. B.G.C.,
2. O.C."B" Battn.
3. ,, ,,
4. O.C."E" Battn.
5. O.C."F" ,,
6. O.C."G" ,,
7. O.C.171st M.G.Co.
8. O.C.173rd ,,
9. O.C.171st L.T.M.B.
10. 421st Field Co R.E.

Copy No.11. Staff Captain,
12. O.C.Signals.
13. O.C.Left Group R.A.
14. O.C.M.T.Ms.(thro' Left Group)
15. HdQrs 3rd N.Z.Bde.
16. HdQrs 172nd Bde. ) For
17. HdQrs 57th Div. )information.
18. War Diary.
19. ,, ,,
20. File.
21. HdQrs, 57th Divl.Arty.

APPENDIX "A".

PRELIMINARY PROGRAMME of Co-Operation by LEFT GROUP, 57th DIVISION R.A.;

| TIME. | GUNS. | TARGETS. | RATE of FIRE. |
|---|---|---|---|
| Zero to Plus 2. | 10. 18 pdrs., 10. 18 pdrs., 6. 4.5" Hows. | Front Line.     I.5.c.90.35 to I.5.d.25.50<br>Support Line.  I.5.d.10.20 to I.5.d.40.40<br>I.5.b.65.02; I.5.d.48.60; I.5.d.35.44;<br>I.5.d.12.27;  I.5.d.13.08; I.11.b.01.96; | Intense. |
| Zero plus 2 to plus 3. | 10. 18 pdrs.<br>6. 4.5" Hows. | Standing Barrage on SUPPORT LINE. | Intense. |
| Zero plus 2 to plus 5. | 10. 18 pdrs.<br>6. 4.5" Hows. | Creeping Barrage to back of box, as under :-<br>I.5.b.65.02; I.5.d.60.75; I.5.d.37.05.<br>I.11.b.01.96; I.5.b.96.48;※ I.6.a.40.00.※ | Intense. |
| Zero plus 5 to Cease Fire. | 20. 18 pdrs.<br>6  4.5" Hows. | Box Barrage as follows :-<br>I.11.b.02.87 to I.5.d.80.70<br>I.11.b.02.87 to I.5.c.68.13<br>I.5.d.80.70 to I.5.d.35.82 | Two rounds per Gun per minute |
| Zero to plus 25. | 2. 6" Hows. | Switch line from I.6.c.45.70 to I.6.c.80.20 | |
| Zero plus 25 to Cease Fire. | 2. 6" Hows.<br>2. 4.5" Hows marked ※. | Assist in Counter Battery Work. | |
| | MEDIUM | TRENCH MORTARS. | |
| Zero to Cease Fire. | 4. T.M.<br>3  ,,<br>1  ,, | I.5.b.40.60 to I.5.b.15.48<br>I.11.a.55.30 to I.5.c.65.00<br>I.11.a.45.28 | Assisted by Stokes L.T.Mortars - per Appendix "C". |

## APPENDIX "B".

### Programme of Co-Operation by
### 171st MACHINE GUN COMPANY.

| GUN POSITION. | TARGET. | GUNS EMPLOYED. |
|---|---|---|
| I.5.c.30.30 | E.F.L., I.II.a.40.30 to I.5.c.65.15 | 2 Reserve Guns of 171st M.G.Company. |
| I.9.b.40.65 | INANE ) I.12.a.15.80 AVENUE.) to I.12.a.45.80 | Nos.1 and 2 Guns of 171st M.G.Company. |
| I.10.a.05.80 | RAILWAY,) I.II.a.35.30 E.F.L., ) to & E.S.L.) I.II.a.80.30 | No.13 Gun of 171st M.G.Company. |
| I.3.d.67.52 | INANE DRIVE - I.5.b.85.05 | Nos.3 & 4 Guns of 171st M.G.Company. |
| C.28.c.65.55 | INANE ) I.12.a.20.60 ALLEY ) to I.12.a.35.45 | Subsection, 173rd M.G.Company. |
| C.28.c.60.70 | E.S.L., I.II.a.95.80 to I.II.a.80.40 | Nos.5 & 6 Guns of 171st M.G.Company. |
| C.28.c.60.72 | I.II.a.85.55 to I.II.a.85.60 | Subsection, 173rd M.G.Company. |
| C.22.c.70.83 | INANE ) I.5.b.20.40 TRENCH.) & I.5.b.25.20 | Subsection, 173rd M.G.Company. |
| C.22.c.70.88 | I.5.b.30.15 & I.5.b.40.05 | Subsection, 173rd M.G.Company. |
| C.22.a.80.35 | ENEMY ) I.5.d.50.75 STRONG ) & POINT. ) I.5.d.57.80 | Nos. 5, 7 & 8 Guns of 171st M.G.Company. |

APPENDIX "C"

Programme of Co-Operation by
171st LIGHT TRENCH MORTAR BATTERY

SCHEME.  On "Z" Day at Zero hour, the Battery will support Raid by Infantry on INANE TRENCH SYSTEM.

The Guns of the L.T.M.B. will fire on the following targets :-

| GUN. | OBJECT. | TARGET. | RATE of FIRE. |
|---|---|---|---|
| No. 1 | Suspected M.G., | I. 5.b.15.50 | |
| No. 2 | To thicken barrage on Front Line. | I. 5.b.45.60 | Zero to Plus 2. 20 per minute. |
| No. 4 | Strong Point. | I. 5.d.60.85 | Plus 2 to Plus 30. 10 per minute. |
| No. 5 | ,,   ,, | I. 5.d.45.76 | Plus 30 to Plus 35 20 per minute. |
| No. 3 | Blocking C.T., | I. 5.d.45.80 | |
| No. 7 | ,,   ,, | I.II.a.80.85 | |
| No. 6 | M.G., | I. 5.c.75.20 | Zero to Plus ½ 20 rounds. |
| | Front Line Block. | I. 5.c.65.15 | Zero plus 2 to 35. 10 per minute. |
| No. 8 | To thicken Barrage. | I.II.a.60.62 | Zero to plus 35. 10 per Minute. |

COPY NO. 11

171st BRIGADE ORDER NO. 18.

Ref. Map.
36 NW.B & NE (part of)
„  4.  1:10,000.                                              3rd July, 1917.

**SUBJECT.** 1. A Raid upon the enemy's Trench System in L'EPINETTE SUBSECTOR will be carried out by the 2/8th Battn. K.L.R.

**INTENTION.** 2. At Zero on "Z" day The Raid will be carried out in order to :-
(a) Effect a demonstration to assist Operations elsewhere.
(b) Inflict Casualties.
(c) Destroy war material, and damage enemy trenches.
(d) Obtain Identification.

**GENERAL IDEA.** 3. Under cover of an Artillery Barrage, the Raiding Party will enter the enemy's lines between :-
I.5.c.93.34  -  I.5.d.25.60
and penetrate as far as the Support Line, inflicting as much damage as possible in a limited time.

**DETAIL.** 4. The Raid will be carried out by approximately 3 Officers and 100 Other Ranks.

**ARTILLERY.** 5. O.C., Left Group Artillery will draw up a programme for Wire-Cutting and the support of this Enterprise, on the lines indicated in this Office No. P.370 of 29.6.1917.

**L.T.M.Bs.** 6. O.C., 171st L.T.M.B., will prepare Orders in co-operation with Artillery scheme.

**M.G.COMPANY.** 7. O.C., 171st M.G.Company will draw up M.G. programme to suit scheme.  O.C., 173rd M.G.Company will place guns at his disposal.

**R.E.,** 8. O.C., 421st Field Company, R.E., will assist in preparing the necessary 'jumping-off' place.  'Jump-Off' either from our line or from a tape line.  Arrangements for parties of Sappers with Mobile Charges to blow in dugouts, demolish M.G.Emplacements, etc., are to be made.

**COMMUNICATION.** 9. 171st Brigade Signal Officer will arrange special communication between 'Jumping-Off' place, Battalion HdQrs and Brigade HdQrs.

**CODE NAME.** 10. This Operation will be referred to in future as TOGO.

ACKNOWLEDGE.

                                                 E. Alexander
                                                 Captain, Brigade Major.
                                                 171st Infantry Brigade.

ISSUED AT 6 p.m., to :-

Copy No. 1. B.G.C.,              Copy No. 9. M.T.M.Commander (through Left
         2. Brigade Major.                      Group Commander)
         3. Staff Captain.              10. 421st Field Co, R.E.,
         4. 2/8th K.L.R.,                11. War Diary.
         5. 171st L.T.M.B.,              12.    „
         6. 171st M.G.Company.           13. Brigade Signalling Officer.
         7. 173rd    „                   14. 57th Division.  ) For
         8. Left Group, R.A.,            15. C.R.A., 57th Divn.) information.

CONFIDENTIAL.

## 171st INFANTRY BRIGADE - ARMENTIERES SECTOR.

### Preliminary Report on Minor Operation "TOGO" carried out on Night of 25/26th July 1917.

......

This Operation was unsuccessful, chiefly owing to the wire not being cut.

Details have been hard to obtain owing to the constant breakages in the forward lines — both during the afternoon previous to the raid, and during the operation itself.

### DIVERSION.

1.55 a.m. — Two Bangalore Torpedoes fired successfully in enemy wire in front of FRELINGHEIN. Our barrage opened at the same time, and worked as per programme.

2.0 a.m. — Enemy opened a barrage on front line and N.M.Land along whole of Left Subsector, and this lifted to Support Line at 2.20 a.m. and lasted till about 2.45 am.
This diversion appears to have drawn most of the enemy artillery fire, as intended.

### RAID.

2.0 a.m. — Bangalores in raid area were unsuccessful (no details of this are yet to hand) and the wire was not sufficiently cut.
One small party only are reported to have got through the wire, and the Officer leading them was immediately wounded (2nd Lt. A.E.Anderson).
No party apparently succeeded in entering the enemy trenches, and no identification was obtained.
Our estimated Casualties are reported as :-

|  | Officers. | O.Ranks. |
|---|---|---|
| Killed. | - | 5 |
| Wounded. | I | 4 |
| Missing. | - | - |

Our artillery barrages appear to have been successfully carried out.
The enemy retaliation was slight, and consisted almost entirely of Minnies.

3.0 a.m. — Situation was becoming quiet.

....

Full report will be rendered when received from Battalion Commander.

Brigadier-General,
Commanding 171st Infantry Brigade.

B.H.Q.,
26.7.1917

CONFIDENTIAL.

171st INFANTRY BRIGADE - ARMENTIERES SECTOR.

Report on Minor Operation "TOGO",
Carried out on Night of 25/26th July 1917.

*****

After a personal interview with O.C., 2/8th (Irish) Battn. K.L.R., Captain Smitham the O.C., Raid, and some of the Raiding Party, I have come to the conclusion that the Raid attempted by the above Regiment early this morning failed for the following reasons.

The bridges to be placed in position to enable the party to form up on the forming-up line, were not in position in sufficient time. Consequently, the party got a bad start, and were disorganised from the commencement, which resulted in only a few getting into the first line trenches.

It might have succeeded had not the enemy Minnied his own front line; this, added to the disorganised state of the party, completely upset the raid.

The previous report regarding wire not being cut was an error — the two Officers with the Raid state that the wire was cut.

The Bangalore Torpedoes were not used owing to disorganisation. I have not been able to get definite information on this point until I hear from the O.C., Field Company R.E.,

Regarding the placing of the bridges, the 421st Field Company R.E., were responsible for this. They were to have been ready in position one hour before zero. The O.C., Raid sent two Officers down to see that everything was ready, but failed to give them a definite order to report to Battalion HdQrs that the bridges were in position or not. When these two Officers discovered that the bridges were not ready, instead of reporting to Battn.HdQrs — which would have enabled the O.C., Battn. to postpone the raid for half-an-hour — they endeavoured, by their assistance, to get everything ready in time; notwithstanding this, they failed.

I am calling for a report from the Field Company as to the cause of delay in putting up the bridges.

I think the whole failure may be attributed to the fact that an Officer was not detailed with definite instructions to report that the bridges were ready.

As far as I can gather, everybody worked very hard, and endeavoured to right what they knew to be going wrong, instead of reporting and asking for a postponement.

..

There was no excessive Machine Gun fire, but the enemy replied with a heavy Minnie barrage, which he either put down by accident on his own front line, meaning it for NO MAN'S LAND, or intentionally. He Minnied NO MAN'S LAND, our front and our support lines.

Brigadier-General,
Commanding 171st Infantry Brigade.

B.H.Q.,
26th July, 1917

CONFIDENTIAL

Headquarters,
    57th (W.L.) Division.

.....

At 9.15 a.m. a party of the enemy, estimated at about 7 men entered our trenches at Locality 5, I.5.A. The presence of these men was first indicated by the firing of rifle shots. The men on Nos. 8 and 9 posts, hearing the rifle shots, proceeded at once to the spot, and found that the enemy had retired.
Lewis Gun fire was immediately opened on to N.M.L.

A bomber of No. 9 Post, who was proceed-ing to No.8 Post, was killed, but the enemy secured no identifications.

The enemy had apparently taken advantage of L'EPINETTE SALIENT to cover his approach and retreat.

None of the hostile party have, as yet, been found.

B.H.Q.
30th July 1917.

Lieut-Colonel,
Commanding 171st Infantry Brigade.

CONFIDENTIAL.

## 171st INFANTRY BRIGADE - ARMENTIERES SECTOR.

Report on Contact with the enemy, Night of
30th/31st July, 1917.

### L'EPINETTE SUBSECTOR.

At 2.30 a.m., enemy placed a heavy barrage of Minnies on our Front Line, I.5.C., Gap "F", and Nos.5. and 6 Localities, and formed a box with shrapnel and H.W. along JAPAN AVEN. I.4.B. WILLOW WALK, PLANK AVEN. I.5.C. and the SUBSIDIARY LINE, I.4.C.

The S.O.S. was sent up at 2.45 a.m., Enemy barrage ceased at 3 a.m., and as far as can be ascertained, no hostile party approached our lines.

Very considerable damage was done to our Front Line, and communication with the Front Line was cut off.

Our casualties amount to :-

15 Wounded.

No identification secured.

### HOUPLINES SUBSECTOR.

At 2.30 a.m., enemy put down a barrage between Gap "P" C.17.C. and Gap "J" C.28.D. Barrage consisted for the most part of Minnies and Pineapples, and the majority of shells dropped behind our front line.

Two hostile parties approached under cover of this barrage and attempted to enter our lines at Gap "M", C.23.C., and No.2 Post, C.23.a.15.02. Each party consisted of about 10 men.

They were driven off by bombs and Lewis Gun fire.

At 3.10 a.m., everything was reported quiet.

Our casalties have not yet been ascertained.

No identifications were secured.

Lieut.Colonel,
Commanding 171st Infantry Brigade.

B.H.Q.
31st July, 1917

APPENDIX No. III.

STATEMENT of CASUALTIES.

..........

Forwarded in Conjunction with

171st INFANTRY BRIGADE WAR DIARY,

1.7.1917 to 31.7.1917.

......

## 171st INFANTRY BRIGADE.

### CASUALTIES from 1.7.1917 to 31.7.1917.

| DATE 24 hrs ending noon:- | KILLED. | | WOUNDED. | | MISSING. | |
|---|---|---|---|---|---|---|
| | Officers. | O.Ranks. | Officers. | O.Ranks. | Officers. | O.Ranks. |
| 1.7.1917 | - | 7 | - | 16 | - | - |
| 2.7.1917 | - | 1 | - | 4 | - | - |
| 3.7.1917 | - | - | - | 3 | - | - |
| 4.7.1917 | - | - | - | 10 | - | - |
| 5.7.1917 | 2nd Lt.ESM. HARDING. | - | - | 8 | - | - |
| 6.7.1917 | - | 1 | - | 9 | - | - |
| 7.7.1917 | - | 1 | 2nd Lt.WH. DELAMERE. | 8 | - | - |
| 8.7.1917 | - | 1 | - | 7 | - | - |
| 9.7.1917 | - | 1 | - | 2 | - | - |
| 10.7.1917 | - | 1 | - | 10 | - | - |
| 11.7.1917 | - | - | - | 18 | - | - |
| 12.7.1917 | - | 9 | - | 10 | - | - |
| 13.7.1917 | - | 1 | - | 6 | - | - |
| 14.7.1917 | - | - | Lt.T.H. SUTHERLAND. | 6 | - | - |
| 15.7.1917 | - | 1 | - | 9 | - | - |
| 16.7.1917 | - | 8 | 2nd Lt.WH. DELAMERE. 2nd Lt.JH. ROWLANDSON. 2nd Lt.G. FROUDE. Capt W.J. OATFIELD. | 35 | - | - |
| 17.7.1917 | - | - | - | 3 | - | - |
| 18.7.1917 | - | - | - | 5 | - | - |
| 19.7.1917 | - | - | - | 1 | - | - |
| 20.7.1917 | - | 1 | Lt.H.O. HOPKINS. | 11 | - | - |
| 21.7.1917 | - | 1 | 2nd Lt.AJ PUMFREY. 2nd Lt.CA. MACKENZIE. 2nd Lt.WJP MAXWELL-STUART. | 16 | - | - |
| 22.7.1917 | - | 2 | - | 61 | - | - |
| 23.7.1917 | - | 5 | - | 19 | - | - |
| 24.7.1917 | - | 2 | - | 19 | - | - |
| 25.7.1917 | - | - | - | 27 | - | - |
| 26.7.1917 | - | 6 | 2nd Lt.A.E. ANDERSON, MC. | 37 | - | - |
| 27.7.1917 | - | - | - | 3 | - | - |
| 28.7.1917 | - | 2 | - | 13 | - | - |
| 29.7.1917 ) 30.7.1917 ) | - | 4 | 32* | 620 | - | - |
| 31.7.1917 | - | 2 | - | 48 | - | - |
| | 1 | 57 | 43 | 1,044 | - | - |

*See List Attached.

| RANK | NAME |
|---|---|
| Lt-Col. | S.S.G.COHEN. |
| Major. | H.H.K.QUACK. |
| Lieut. | A.A.TAYLOR. |
| Lt&Adj. | L.L.STOTT. |
| 2nd Lt. | F.A.DEARDEN. |
| 2nd Lt. | G.RIMMER. |
| 2nd Lt. | W.H.LEES. |
| HonyLt. & Qr.Mr. | J.E.B.ANDERSON. |
| Capt. | P.AMBLER. |
| Lt-Col. | W.A.L.FLETCHER.D.S.O. |
| Major. | H.K.WILSON. |
| Capt. | A.G.ECCLES. |
| Capt. | C.T.STEWARD. |
| 2nd Lt. | J.R.PAUL. |
| Capt. | ROBINSON. R.A.M.C. |
| 2nd Lt. | W.J.PEGGE. |
| 2nd Lt. | J.ROTHWELL. |
| 2nd Lt. | C.V.MOSELEY. |
| 2nd Lt. | E.E.PAUL. |
| 2nd Lt. | F.E.EVANS. |
| 2nd Lt. | H.H.E.ROYLE. |
| 2nd Lt. | W.R.COLLINGE. |
| 2nd Lt. | P.F.ALCOCK. |
| 2nd Lt. | C.T.A.WYATT. |
| 2nd Lt. | J.H.M.LITTLE. |
| 2nd Lt. | J.N.DUNCAN. |
| 2nd Lt. | W.GOLLAND. |
| 2nd Lt. | S.T.BURFIELD. |
| HonyLt. &Qr.Mr. | A.E.BOLTON. |
| Lieut. | J.LAURIE. |
| Lieut. | E.B.FLETCHER. |
| 2nd Lt. | W.F.FISHER. |

---o---

APPENDIX No. IV.

ORDERS, etc., Reference

C.E.P.,

Forwarded in Conjunction with

171st INFANTRY BRIGADE WAR DIARY,

1.7.1917 to 31.7.1917

.....

SECRET.                                                          COPY NO. 17

### 171st INFANTRY BRIGADE ORDER No. 19.            15th July, 1917.

1. Companies of the 4th Brigade, C.E.P., will be attached to this Brigade in accordance with the annexed Location Table.

2. Company Officers, N.C.Os and Specialists of the 4th Brigade C.E.P., will reconnoitre Subsectors as under :-

| JULY. | L'EPINETTE. | HOUPLINES. |
|---|---|---|
| 16th. | No.1 Coy, "B" Battn. | No.1 Coy, "C" Battn. |
| 17th. | No.2 Coy, "B" Battn. | No.2 Coy, "C" Battn. |
| 18th. | No.3 Coy, "B" Battn. | |

O's.C. L'EPINETTE and HOUPLINES Subsectors will arrange that every facility is given to these Officers, N.C.Os and men. They will send 1 Officer and Runner to report at these HdQrs at 9.30 a.m., on the dates mentioned to guide members of the C.E.P. to respective Battalion HdQrs.

3. The 4th C.E.P., have no experience of Trench routine. They will be split up in the proportion of half a Platoon to one British Platoon. Each man of the C.E.P. will be definitely attached to a man of similar rank, by whom he will be informed and instructed as to the duties that are required of him.

4. A brief summary of Trench Orders should be prepared for translation by the Interpreters.

5. Companies of the C.E.P. will be employed in the Front and Support Lines.

6. The Staff Captain, 171st Infantry Brigade, will arrange for guides to meet Billeting Parties of C.E.P. at Railway Crossing, H.5.a.0.9, at 10.30 a.m., on the days of their arrival in ARMENTIERES.

7. Companies will be approximately 150 strong, and will have one interpreter per Company.

8. Companies will be rationed by the C.E.P. up to and including the day after their arrival in the 171st Brigade Area. They will then be rationed by the 171st Brigade up to and including the day after their move to the 1st Division C.E.P. Area.

Companies of "B" Battn. will be attached for rations to 2/6th K.L.R.,
    ,,    ,,    "C"    ,,     ,,    ,,    ,,    ,, 2/7th K.L.R.

ACKNOWLEDGE.

E. Alexander.
Captain, Brigade Major.
171st Infantry Brigade.

ISSUED AT 5 p.m., to :-
  Copy No.1. Staff Captain.        Copy No.10. Signals.
       2. "B" Battalion.                 11. 57th Divn."G"( )
       3. "C"     ,,                     12.   ,,    ,, "Q"( ) For
       4. "G"     ,,                     13. Left Group R.A.) information.
       5. "E"     ,,                     14. 4th H.A.R.Bde.)
       6. 171st M.G.Company.             15. 172nd Inf.Bde.)
       7. 171st L.T.M.B.                 16. War Diary.
       8. 421st Field Co, R.E.           17.
       9. 1st Divn. C.E.P.               18. File.
          (Thro' 57th Divn)

LATRINE TABLE Issued with 111st INFANTRY BRIGADE ORDER No. 18.

| NIGHT Night of Jul. 1917. | LEFFRINCKS. | L'EPINETTE. | LA NG. HOUPLINES. | ARMENTIERES. | 1st DIV., C.E.P., AREA. |
|---|---|---|---|---|---|
| 14/15th. | No.1 Coy. "B" Bn.<br>No.1 Coy. "C" Bn. | | | | |
| 15/16th. | | No.1 Coy. "D" Bn. | | | |
| 16/17th. | | | No.1 Coy. "D" Bn. | | |
| 17/18th. | No.2 Coy. "B" Bn.<br>No.2 Coy. "C" Bn. | | | | |
| 18/19th. | | No.2 Coy. "D" Bn. | No.2 Coy. "C" Bn. | | |
| 19/20th. | | | | No.1 Coy. "B" Bn.<br>No.1 Coy. "C" Bn. | |
| 20/21st. | No.3 Coy. "D" Bn. | | | | |
| 21/22nd. | | No.3 Coy. "D" Bn. | | | |
| 22/23rd. | | | | No.2 Coy. "B" Bn.<br>No.2 Coy. "C" Bn. | No.1 Coy. "B" Bn.<br>No.1 Coy. "C" Bn. |
| 23/24th. | | | | | No.2 Coy. "B" Bn.<br>No.2 Coy. "C" Bn. |
| 24/25th. | | | | No.3 Coy. "D" Bn. | |
| 25/26th. | | | | | No.3 Coy. "D" Bn. |
| 26/27th. | | | | | |
| 27/28th. | | | | | No.3 Coy. "D" Bn. |

SECRET.

O.C. "F" Battalion.
　　 "E"　,,　　(for information)
　　 "H"　,,　(　　,,　　)

........

Reference Brigade Order No.19 dated 14.7.1917, and Amendments P.458 and O.108, the following troops of C.E.P. will be attached to "F" Battalion for training in Trench Warfare from night 23/24th July to night 25/26th July.

1. No.1.Coy, 3rd Regt. C.E.P. will move into the HOUPLINES SUBSECTOR on night 23/24th July.

2. 2 Sections, i.e. approx.40 men, will be attached to each British Company.

3. O.C.Subsector, will detail 1 N.C.O. and 8 guides to report at 171st B.H.Q., at 9.0.p.m. on the 23rd instant to lead Troops of the C.E.P. to the positions in the Subsidiary Line selected by him.

4. March Formation. First Section will leave B.H.Q. at 9.15.p.m., followed by Sections at intervals of at least 200 Yards.

5. In the training of the C.E.P., the points to which attention has already been drawn should be kept in mind.

　　　　　　　　　　　　(sd) G.L.Alexander,

　　　　　　　　　　　　　Captain, Brigade Major,
　　　　　　　　　　　　　　　171st Infantry Brigade.
B.H.Q.
　22nd July 1917.

SECRET.

O.C. 1st Coy. 3rd Regt., C.E.P.
   "G" Battalion.
Staff Captain,
Headquarters, 57th (West Lancs) Division.

........

1. No.1.Coy,3rd Regt., C.E.P., will not proceed to the Line to-night as arranged previously.

   They will move to-night, 23rd/24th July, to bivouac at ERQUINGHEM in a field about H.5.b.1.2., starting at 9.15.p.m.

2. An N.C.O. and 4 guides who know the road will be detailed by O.C. "G" Battalion to report to these Headquarters at 9.p.m. to lead the Company to this field. They will afterwards return to their Unit.

3. Movement will be by Sections at intervals of 200 yds.

4. Blankets will be carried, and to-morrows rations. Rations for 25th instant will be drawn by separate Lorries from Q.M.Stores sometime to-morrow.

5. A Lorry will pick up blankets from bivouac ground at H.5.b.1.2. to-morrow morning between 9 and 10 a.m.

6. The Company will move to First Division C.E.P. area to-morrow, after blankets have been loaded up.

                              (sd) G.L.Alexander,

                                 Captain, Brigade Major,
B.H.Q.                              171st Infantry Brigade.
   23rd July 1917.

Vol. 2.

Headquarters
171st Inf. Bde.
(52d Div)
August 1917.

On His Majesty's Service.

CONFIDENTIAL.

[Stamp: H.Q. 171st INFANTRY BRIGADE. No. BM/543/1 Date......]

Headquarters,

    57th (West Lancs) Division.

......

    Herewith War Diary - and accompanying Appendices - of these Headquarters for period 1.8.1917 to 31.8.1917.

                                Brigadier-General,
                            Commanding 171st Infantry Brigade.

B.H.Q.
  1st September, 1917.

CONFIDENTIAL.

WAR DIARY

of

HEADQUARTERS - 171st INFANTRY BRIGADE.

.....

1.8.1917 to 31.8.1917.

...

VOLUME VI.

...

Army Form C. 2118

# WAR DIARY
or
## INTELLIGENCE SUMMARY
(Erase heading not required.)

Instructions regarding War Diaries and Intelligence Summaries are contained in F. S. Regs., Part II. and the Staff Manual respectively. Title Pages will be prepared in manuscript.

| Place | Date | Hour | Summary of Events and Information | Remarks and references to Appendices |
|---|---|---|---|---|
| ARMENTIERES | 1.8.17. | | The day passed much more quietly than of late. Normal shelling of HOUPLINES by day and night. ARMENTIERES quiet by day - slight hostile artillery activity by night. The 2/5 K.L.R. and 2/6 K.L.R were relieved in Brigade Reserve by 2/5 L.N. LANCS and 2/5 K.O.R.L. respectively and moved into billets at BAC ST MAUR - the relief being accomplished without incident. | Appendix II 7a/h |
| | 2.8.17 | | A very quiet morning both in the line and in ARMENTIERES. Advanced parties of 2/4 and 7/5 L.N. LANCS reconnoitred the line and billets. 171st Brigade H.Qrs. closed at ARMENTIERES and opened at MARES NEST, FLEURBAIX. One Coy + One Platoon of each 2/5 and 2/6 K.L.R. moved into subsidiary line CORDONNERIE and BOUTILLERIE respectively. 2/4 and 7/5 L.N. LANCS marched from FLEURBAIX to ARMENTIERES. | Appendix II 7a/h. |
| FLEURBAIX | 12 noon | | | |
| | 3.8.17 | | At midnight 2/3rd the 2/7 and 2/8 K.L.R. moved into Brigade Reserve and subsidiary line BOUTILLERIE and CORDONNERIE respectively. During the evening 1/7 cheshire 1st LEICESTER REGT in left subsector, and 2/8 cheshires 9th NORFOLK REGT in right subsector. The 1st LEICESTER and 9th NORFOLK REGTS moved to billets SAILLY sur la LYS and BAC ST MAUR. Remainder of 2/5 and 2/6 K.L.R. moved into Right and Left Brigade Reserve. A very quiet period both in the line & in | Appendix II 7a/h. |

**Army Form C. 2118**

# WAR DIARY
## or
## INTELLIGENCE SUMMARY
*(Erase heading not required.)*

II

Instructions regarding War Diaries and Intelligence Summaries are contained in F. S. Regs., Part II. and the Staff Manual respectively. Title Pages will be prepared in manuscript.

| Place | Date | Hour | Summary of Events and Information | Remarks and references to Appendices |
|---|---|---|---|---|
| FLEURBAIX | 4.8.17 | | Apart from slight enemy T.M activity which was satisfactorily dealt with by our artillery the day passed very quietly. | 2/Lt. |
| | 5.8.17 | | Quiet in the line. At about 10.0 p.m. hostile aeroplane dropped 5 bombs in close vicinity of MARES NEST— considerable damage to huts. One fragment penetrated the hut occupied by CAPT G. L. ALEXANDER — Brigade Major and killed him instantaneously. Brigade runner was also killed, 1 General O.R. slightly wounded. | 2/Lt. |
| | 6.8.17 | | At 4.45 a.m. a minenwerfer fell on one of our Front line posts killing 3, wounding 4 O.R. Advance posted CE.P. — 4th Bde 1st Div — went out to the BOUTILLERIE trenches — during the afternoon the extreme left of left subsector was heavily bombarded by minenwerfer — 2/LT P.A. SEGRAVE 2/7 K.L.R. was wounded — 2 O.R. killed. 2 O.R. wounded. | 2/Lt. |
| | 7.8.17 | | Very quiet on whole sector. "A" Bttn 4/5 Bde C.E.P. relieved 2/7 K.L.R. in the left subsector — the operation taking place without incident. 2/6 2/7 K.L.R. marched into left Brigade reserve. 2/6 K.L.R. moved into billets near RUE de BRUGES. | appendix II 2/Lt. |
| | 8.8.17 | | Infantry very quiet. Enemy artillery shows slight activity. 2/5 K.L.R. marched 2/6 K.L.R. in CORD ONNERIE Subsector Corps. — Plan 2 Corps 2/6 K.L.R. relieved 2/8 — 2/7 K.L.R. in CORD ONNERIE Subsector. | appendix II 2/Lt. |

# WAR DIARY
## or
## INTELLIGENCE SUMMARY

*(Erase heading not required.)*

Army Form C. 2118

III

| Place | Date | Hour | Summary of Events and Information | Remarks and references to Appendices |
|---|---|---|---|---|
| FLEURBAIX | 9.8.17 | | Enemy artillery shelled Battery positions S.E. of FLEURBAIX. Aeroplanes were very active. No movement of activity. Capt R.W. PATTISON - 1st NORFOLK REGT reported to Bn. On it. Aeroplane activity of Brigade MAJOR. | top.fl. |
| | 10.8.17 | | Continued aeroplane activity. Hostile artillery quieter. A few large calibre intermittently fires on back areas. Bombs were dropped & night in direction of SAILLY. | top.fl. |
| | 11.8.17 | | Between midnight & 1.0 am. enemy heavily bombarded our extreme right but no infantry action followed. Quiet during remainder of morning. | top.fl. |
| | 12.8.17 | | Slightly increased artillery activity along the whole front; infantry very quiet. | top.fl. |
| | 13.8.17 | | A quiet day. At 10.15 pm enemy attempted to raid no. 4 of our posts No 1 and 2 on the right. Hostile parties were immediately repulsed. B. Ratn. 4/5 Bde CEP Relieved "A" Bn. in COR SOMMERIE ambrabri. | appendix I appendix II |
| | 14.8.17 | | At 12.15 am enemy made further attempt to raid no 1 post but was driven off by LEWIS GUN FIRE. At 4.45 am. he put down a barrage on our front line to which our artillery replied on S.O.S. lines. One prisoner was brought in from N.M. Land being the afternoon. He belongs to 101st Regt. 219 F.Div. One enemy aeroplane was shot down by enemy A.A. gun & fell behind enemy lines completely wrecked. | app I top.fl. |

Army Form C. 2118

# WAR DIARY
## or
## INTELLIGENCE SUMMARY
*(Erase heading not required.)*

| Place | Date | Hour | Summary of Events and Information | Remarks and references to Appendices |
|---|---|---|---|---|
| FLEURBAIX | 15.8.17 | | At 12.30 p.m. - midday - enemy raiding party, strength approximately 25 men attacked a post at junction of ABBOTS LANE and FRONT LINE held by the C.E.P. The attack was easily repulsed, none of the enemy obtaining even a footing in our line. O'Flaherty to-day passed quietly. | So.y.A. |
| | 16.8.17 | | Very quiet. 2/5 K.L.R. relieved 2/5 K.L.R. less 2 Companies plus 2 Companies 2/6 K.L.R. The relief being successfully carried out in daylight - the relieving Battn. commenced to leave their billets at 2.0 p.m. | Appendix II 9/A |
| | 17.8.17 | | At 4.15 a.m. the enemy shelled our front and support lines on extreme right of CORDONNERIE sector with shrapnel, Gas, and H.E. to which our artillery replied effectively. At 10.50 p.m. a hostile patrol of 10 men approached our wire & were driven off by Lewis gun fire. Enemy artillery fired 250 rounds chiefly 5.9. on Battery near ROUGE de BOUT. | So.y.A. |
| | 18.8.17 | | Hostile aircraft showed some activity - otherwise his attitude was very quiet. | So.y.A. |
| | 19.8.17 | | Normal conditions prevailed - "C" Battn. 4th Bde CEP relieved "B" Battn 4th Bde in the BOUTILLERIE sector - the relief taking place at night. | Appendix II 9/A |
| | 20.8.17 | | Very quiet. Hostile aeroplanes active by night. 5 bombs were dropped on DEAD DOG | |

# WAR DIARY or INTELLIGENCE SUMMARY

Army Form C. 2118

| Place | Date | Hour | Summary of Events and Information | Remarks and references to Appendices |
|---|---|---|---|---|
| FLEURBAIX | 20.8.17 (Cont) | | NIL P. but no casualties were caused. | 20 Aft. |
| | 21.8.17 | | Quiet on the CORDONNERIE sector - FORAY HOUSE - the H.Qrs of the C.E.P. Baker in the BOUTILLERIE sector was shelled all day. Between 10.30 am & 11.30 am this was particularly heavy and HQrs staff moved to 1st Coy H.Q. in the support line | 21 Aughlist 21 Aft. |
| | 22.8.17 | | Quiet in the line - Hostile aircraft active during the night when bombs were dropped on BAC St MAUR and FLEURBAIX. In the afternoon a small balloon drifted across our lines scattering copies of the GAZETTE des ARDENNES | 22 Aft. |
| | 23.8.17 | | heavy artillery rather more active - a quiet day from the infantry point of view | 2 Aft. |
| | 24.8.17 | | Just after 12.0. midnight a heavy bombardment commenced on our right and STOMBES LANE and BOUTILLERIE AVENUE and the hop line opposite these points. Four men were wounded. To gas was detected on this front. At 1.10 am. ARTISTS bombarded - At 1.15 the barrage lifted onto the support line and crept through to the rear - stirring to 2 officers so OR - entered our line & pushed through to the support line - this proper was checked by the intensity of our A.G. fire and he was forced to withdraw, leaving 3 prisoners in our hands. The C.E.P. sustained 28 casualties but no identification was obtained by the enemy. | 24 Aughlist 24 Aft. |

# WAR DIARY
## or
## INTELLIGENCE SUMMARY

*(Erase heading not required.)*

Army Form C. 2118

| Place | Date | Hour | Summary of Events and Information | Remarks and references to Appendices |
|---|---|---|---|---|
| FLEURBAIX | 24.8.17 (cont) | | 2/5 K.L.R. relieved 2/8 K.L.R. in the CORDONNERIE sector. | Appendix II 2/A. |
| | 25.8.17 | | A quiet day. 2/7 K.L.R. relieved 'C' Battn. 4th Bde C.E.F. in the BOUTILLERIE sector and 2/6 K.L.R. moved into left Bde reserve. | Appendix II 2/A. |
| | 26.8.17 | | Normal conditions prevailed. Enemy A.A. guns actively engaged our aeroplanes but without success. | 2/A |
| | 27.8.17 | | Enemy's attitude still quiet. At 11.15pm enemy party of 8/15 men were seen advancing towards our front line on the left of BOUTILLERIE. Lewis guns & snipers fire on them. They retired leaving no trace. | 2/A. |
| | 28.8.17 | | Very quiet. Firing both artillery and infantry standpoint. Weather conditions rainfall, heavy rain and a gale 2 winds continued to the greater part of the day. Normal conditions prevailed. | 2/A. |
| | 29.8.17 | | | 2/A |
| | 30.8.17 | | Quiet in the line & in back areas. Slight increase in enemy artillery activity. Our Battery position near FLEURBAIX was shelled during the evening. | 2/A. |
| | 31.8.17 | | Quiet all day. Brig Gen R.N. BRAY. DSO returned from leave and resumed Command of 171 Inf Bde.<br><br>STATEMENT of CASUALTIES — Appendix III | 2/A.<br><br>App |

A.N. Bray Brig Gen

APPENDIX No. I.

MINOR OPERATIONS,

Referred to in

171st INFANTRY BRIGADE WAR DIARY,

1.8.1917

to

31.8.1917.

SECRET.

## 171st INFANTRY BRIGADE — FLEURBAIX SECTOR.

### Report on Operations on night of August 13/14th.

10.15p.m.,      The enemy attempted to raid our NO.1 POST, N.8.d.50.95, and NO.2 POST, N.8.d.95.95. simultaneously.

     <u>No.1 Post</u>. The enemy party about 12 in number, entered our trenches just North of EXETER AVENUE, between the two Posts. No.1 Post immediately opened rifle and Lewis Gun fire and also bombed them. The enemy at once withdrew.

     <u>No.2 Post</u>. A party of the enemy, about 20 strong, advanced towards this Post, but were driven off by Lewis Gun fire. Only one man reached our parapet, and was immediately shot. A patrol was at once sent out to try and get an identification. After a careful search, his rifle equipment and entrenching tool were found, and are being forwarded to you. The equipment was shot through in places.

12.0 midnight.      The enemy again advanced towards our No.1 Post, N.8.d.50.95, but were at once driven off by Lewis Gun fire.

12.15 a.m.      The enemy patrols advanced up to the wire in front of No.2 Post, N.8.d.95.95, but were driven off by rifle and Lewis Gun fire.

4.40 a.m.      The enemy opened a barrage on our front line between BROMPTON ROAD and MINE AVENUE, with artillery and heavy and medium Trench Mortars.

     S.O.S. was put up by the Officer on duty in No.5 Post. Our artillery at once opened fire.

4.45 a.m.      The enemy artillery lifted on to the Communication Trenches and Support Line in rear of No.4 and No.5 Posts. This continued till 5.15 a.m., From 5.15 a.m. onwards the fire considerably decreased, and finally stopped at 5.30 a.m.

DAMAGE.      One Fire Bay blown in.
     MINE AVENUE is impassable in two places - also BROMPTON AVENUE.

OUR CASUALTIES      1 Killed.      4 Wounded (2 Slightly).

     Capt. for Lieut.Colonel,
     Commanding 171st Infntry Brigade.

B.H.Q.
14.8.1917

copy

Translation.

## REPORT ON BOMBARDMENT OF BATTALION HEADQUARTERS WHEN THIS BATTALION OCCUPIED A SUB-SECTION OF the 171st BRIGADE FRONT ON THE 21st inst.

An intense hostile artillery bombardment began at 7-0 am. falling within 100 m. short or over, and on communication trenches near the H.Q.

By observations made, it seems that the chief object of the hostile artillery was to disorganize the Batt. staff for future operations, and this object was abtained by 10-0 am. at which hour the Orderly Room, Kitchen and orderlies dugouts were damaged.

The bombardment continued from 7 am. to 9 pm. slackening the severity between 10-30 and 11-30 am. and between 3 and 4 pm.

About 11-30 am. the heavy artillery began to make itself felt, and as a result of this fact and acting on the request of the English interpreter, I gave orders for all the personnel which occupied that neighbourhood to move to the H.Q. of the 1st Coy. situated in the Support Line, remaining only the Adjutant and Signallers so as to form the central place for communications.

At 3-30 pm. it was reported to me that an English Officer had appeared at the extinct H.Q., I went there again and as the shelling had stopped gave orders that all the Battalion H.Q. staff should return to their posts and should get on with the most pressing repairs; and also that in the case of further bombardment, Battalion H.Q. should move to the 1st Coy. H.Q. temporarily, since from there connection with the other Coys. in the 1st and 2nd lines would be very easy.

At 4-0 pm. the bombardment violently recommenced, and Battn. H.Q. moved as previously ordered to the 1st Coy.

I remained in my dugout writing impressions of the day with 2/Lt. Guerreiro, attached to Battn. H.Q. and as the bombardment became denser, destroyed everything round my dugout, I decided that this Officer should go and get news of the Adjutant in the old Orderly Room, when the sentry - the only one still at his post - informed us that the Adjutant had shortly before moved to the 1st Coy.  This being so, I left my dugout with 2/Lt. Guerreiro, who seizing two portmanteaus of mine, followed me in the direction of the trenches leading to the 1st Coy., which trenches were completely blown in by the violence of the shells.  Just then we became separated, owing to a shell which fell between us, and I continued my way toe the 1st Coy. under an intense bombardment which was now falling on the C.Ts. round the extinct H.Q.

On reaching the 1st Coy. I told them that I was going to place myself with the reserve to which all communications were to be forwarded, and I immediately then went to the H.Q. of the centre company where I said the same thing and also wrote a note to identically the same effect to the left company.  Then after having visited and given the message to the Aid Post and the reserve platoon, I went to take up my position with the reserve Coy.   When I visited the 1st Coy. I found there the Adjutant and Orderly Room sergeant who accompanied me on all my rounds until my ultimate return to the reserve company.

IN THE FIELD.........August, 1917.

(sd) FRANCISCO ANTONIO BAPTISTA.

Commanding battalion.

CONFIDENTIAL.

Headquarters,
57th (West Lancs) Division.                    B.M/

. . . . .

The following report is forwarded on the enemy raid on the BOUTILLERIE SECTOR on the night of August 23/24th.

This report is written from information gained from the men holding No.3 and No.4 Posts, which were the only two Posts concerned.

At I a.m., the enemy put down a heavy barrage of Artillery and T.Ms. on our front line between ABBOTS LANE and BOUTILLERIE AVENUE.

At I.5 a.m. the Centre Company Commander sent up the S.O.S., Our Artillery and Stop Guns at once opened fire. About this time the enemy barrage lifted from our front line to the Support Line, except for slight shelling near No.3 and No.4 Posts, and heavy shelling on TIN BARN AVENUE, which was much damaged.

The enemy apparently all entered our trenches at the same point, at about N.6.C.25.95, which is about 75 yards from No.4 Post. They were not heard entering by the Posts at all. Apparently he pushed straight forward towards our Support Line, most probably making use of the TIN BARN TRAMLINE as a guide. The enemy was evidently checked by the heaviness of our M.G.fire from the stop guns and by the grenades thrown from the Support Line, and withdrew again by the same way as he had entered our lines. No.4 Post heard them withdrawing, as there were many cries from the wounded.

During the withdrawal, 3 of the enemy apparently lost their way, and two (I wounded and I unwounded) wandered into the back of No.3 Post, and I unwounded wandered into No.4 Post.

Everything had quietened down by I.45 a.m.

The chief points of note in the raid are :-

1. Apparently the enemy had realised the position of our Posts, and hence hoped to get through between them and raid our Supports.

2. No attack was made on our front line posts.

3. The enemy used tape to mark his line of retreat - which has been collected.

4. Our stop guns seemed to have been entirely successful, and must have caused him serious casualties. There are many signs of blood in the neighbourhood of the point of entry.

I also attach the report forwarded by O.C., 29th Regt., C.E.F.,

B.H.Q.
25.8.1917
                R.Pattison Capt
                /o/ Lieut.Colonel, Commanding
                    171st Infantry Brigade.

Translation of Report on Raid made on 29th Battn.
C.E.P., 24.8.1917. BOUTILLERIE SECTOR.

.....

At 12.30 a.m., a bombardment started on our Sector, being strongest on Centre Company. This took the form of a barrage, attempting to prevent reserves approaching from the flanks. A raid followed, the raiders consisting of especial storming troops and numbering 80 men, 4 sergeants and 2 Officers of the 77th, 78th and 79th Regiments. They attempted to reach our line while their artillery surrounded the Centre Company. They came in 3 groups, the first group being composed of 40 men and 1 M.G., and the other two groups being of 20 men also with a Machine Gun on either flank. The Platoon Commanders brought with them 2 telephones - one to connect directly with the artillery, the other with the Batt. H.Q.,

This attack was at once repulsed energetically by our men by means of hand grenades, M.Gs and rifle fire, and also by the artillery in consequence of the Centre and Left Company Commanders having sent for S.O.S., No.3 Post took 3 German prisoners, one of them being wounded.

During this attack there were several gas alarms owing to gas shells exploding.

From information received from prisoners, the attacking parties felt thwarted directly they saw our men in the 2nd line receive the first part so courageously, and this put them in confusion, so that they retired in disorder with several wounded.

Of our men, up to the present moment, we know of 8 killed and 15 wounded, including 2nd Lt. MANUEL de FREITAS of the 3rd Company.

(Sgd) M.A.GRANJO.

Battn. Intell. Officer, 29th Batt. C.E.P.,


Translated by

R.C.G.DARTFORD, Capt.,

attd. 4th Bde. A.Q., C.E.P.,

copy

TRANSLATION.        P. E. F.        4th Inf. Bde.

## Battalion 29.

Received.                                    On the 24.8.17.
                                              At 2 pm.

To/ O.C., 4th Inf. Bde.

### REPORT ON OPERATION WHICH TOOK PLACE IN THE EARLY MORNING OF 24th AUGUST FROM 11 PM (23rd) to 4-0 AM (24th AUGUST)...

I. **HOSTILE SITUATION.**

(a) **Before the engagement.** - The enemy prepared the attack with a light bombardment of gas shells fired chiefly on the advanced line, which began about 11 pm. and lasted until 11-15 pm., apparently intending by it merely to disorganize the defence. Following on this he attacked the whole front with infantry, machine-guns and bombs, putting an intense barrage on the centre Coy. (2nd Coy.) having as its objective the centre of the sub-section. At the same time an intense bombardment by heavy trench mortars took place on the left of our sub-section.

(b) **After the engagement.** - Repulsed to his own lines, leaving three prisoners.

II. **POSITION OCCUPIED AT END OF ENGAGEMENT.**

We maintained all our positions without reinforcements, though they were asked for.

III. **TIME FIRING BEGAN & ENDED.**

Began 11 pm. and ended 2-0 am. From dawn till 9-30 am. perhaps as retaliation, the enemy put up an intense and continuous bombardment with H.T.Ms. which destroyed many dugouts in the front line.

IV. **LOSSES SUSTAINED.**    Personnel :- 1 Officer & 27 O.Rs.

Material :- Being investigated.

V. **WOUNDED TO EVACUATE.**

19.

VI. **URGENT NECESSITIES.**

Fresh supply of ammunition. Make up specialist squads to strength, especially machine gunners.

.....

IN THE FIELD......24th August, 1917.

(sd) FRANCISCO ANTONIO BAPTISTA,

Commanding the Battalion.

APPENDIX No. II.

RELIEF ORDERS,

etc.,

Referred to in

171st INFANTRY BRIGADE WAR DIARY,

1.8.1917

to

31.8.1917.

.....

SECRET.

O.C., "E" Battalion.
     "F"    ,,

P542

* * * * * * * *

Amendment to, and Continuation of,
171st Brigade Order No. 23.

1.  Guides for incoming Battalions, night of 31st July/
    1st August, will be as follows and not as in Move Table
    issued with the above Order :-

| UNIT. | GUIDES. | TO MEET. | RENDEZVOUS. | TIME. |
|---|---|---|---|---|
| "E" Battn. | 1 N.C.O. & 4 Guides. | 2/5th L.N.L., | Level Crossing, H.6.a.05.90. | 9.30 p.m. |
| "F"   ,, | ,,          ,, | 2/5th King's Own R.L.R., | ,,         ,, | 9. 0 p.m. |

2.  These Guides will report to Officers Commanding the
    Billeting Parties of the respective Battalions, and assist
    in guiding the Companies to the Subsidiary Line and
    Billets.

3.  The 2/5th L.N.L. are taking over Right Reserve, and
    the 2/5th King's Own R.L.R. the Left Reserve.

4.  "E" Battalion and "F" Battalion, on relief, will
    move via ERQUINGHEM to B.E.F.Canteen, BAC ST MAUR, where
    they will be met by their respective Billeting Parties.

5.  "E" Battalion will move out via BRICKSTACKS, and "F"
    Battalion via GLOUCESTER.

    These routes may be altered at discretion of O.Cs.

6.  March formations will be by Platoons, at intervals
    of 100 yards.

7.  Trench Stores, Defence Schemes, Maps, etc., will be
    handed over on relief, and a receipt obtained for them.

8.  Completion of relief is to be reported to this Office
    by wire.

ACKNOWLEDGE.

(Sd) G L Alexander.
                          Captain, Brigade Major.
                          171st Infantry Brigade.

B.H.Q.
     31st July, 1917

Copy No......

- 171st Infantry Brigade Order No.23 -

Map Reference sheet 36 N.W. 1/40,000

1. The 170th Infantry Brigade will relieve the 171st Infantry Brigade in the left(Armentieres) Sector between 31st July and 4th August, the 171st Infantry Brigade taking over the Right(Fleurbaix) Sector at the same time.

2. Moves will take place according to the attached table.

3. At 12 noon on 2nd August the command of the Armentieres Sector will pass to the 170th Infantry Brigade and that of the Fleurbaix Sector to the 171st Infantry Brigade.

4. Machine Gun Companies, Field Companies R.E., Field Ambulances and Artillery Groups will remain in their present positions.

5. Stokes Gun Batteries will be relieved gradually by Sections. Separate orders will be issued shortly for these Reliefs.

6. Billeting Parties from 2/5th K.L.R. and 2/6th K.L.R. will be at B.E.F.Canteen, Rac St Maur at 1 p.m. on 31st inst: and will be met by 171st I.B. Interpreter.

7. Details of subsequent moves will be issued later.

Acknowledge.
Issued at 9-30 am. 31st July to
Copy No 1    War Diary
       2    E Battalion
       3    F Battalion
       4    G Battalion
       5    H Battalion
       6    171st L.T.M.B.
       7    171st M.G.Coy.
       8    57th Division.
       9    170th I.B.
     10    172nd I.B.
     11    4th N.Z. Bde.
     12    Staff Captain 171st I.B.
     13    File.


                (sd).G.L.Alexander,    Captain.
        Brigade-Major, 171st Infantry Brigade.

# MOVE TABLE.

| DATE. | UNIT. | FROM. | TO. | GUIDES. |
|---|---|---|---|---|
| 31st July) 1st Aug. ) | 2/5th KLR. 2/6th KLR. | ARMENTIERES & SUBSID.LINES. | BAC.ST MAUR, SAILLY. | 1 N.C.O. and 2 guides from each of 2/5th and 2/6th KLR, to meet Advance Parties of 170th Brigade at Bd.gade HdQrs, 171st Bde, at 10 a.m., |
| | 2 Battns. 170th Bde. | FLEURBAIX. | L'EPINETTE, HOUPLINES, SUBSID.LINE & ARMENTIERES. | 1 N.C.O. and 4 guides from 2/5th and 2/6th KLR respectively will be at Level Crossing, ERQUINGHEM ROAD - H.6.a.05.90 - at 9.15 p.m., 31st July, to assist in guiding Battns. of 170th Bde to Billets and Subsidiary Line. |
| 1/2nd Aug. | 2 Battns. 170th Bde. | L'EPINETTE, HOUPLINES, SUBSID.LINES & ARMENTIERES. | FRONT LINE, L'EPINETTE & HOUPLINES. | Guides to be arranged inter-Regimentally. 2/7th and 2/8th K.L.R., will take over billets vacated by 2 Battns. 170th Bde. |
| | 2/7th KLR. 2/8th KLR. | FRONT LINE. L'EPINETTE & HOUPLINES. | SUBSID.LINES. L'EPINETTE, HOUPLINES & ARMENTIERES. | |
| 2/3rd Aug. | 2 Battns. 170th Bde. | FLEURBAIX. | L'EPINETTE HOUPLINES SUBSID.LINES & ARMENTIERES. | |
| | 2/7th KLR. 2/8th KLR. | L'EPINETTE, HOUPLINES, SUBSID.LINES & ARMENTIERES. | FLEURBAIX, ROUGE de BOUT RESERVE. | |
| 3/4th Aug. | 2/7th KLR. 2/8th KLR. | FLEURBAIX, ROUGE de BOUT RESERVE. | FRONT LINE. | |
| | 2/5th KLR. 2/6th KLR. | BAC ST MAUR. SAILLY. | RESERVE. FLEURBAIX, ROUGE de BOUT. | |

O.C. 1st. Leciestershire Regt;

--------

Please note that buses for your Batt.,
will be at the SAILLY CROSS ROADS at 9.0 a.m. to-morrow.
Instructions have been received for
you to de-bus at MAGNICOURT. It is assumed that no guides
will be required.
Please acknowledge.

(s) G. L. ALEXANDER
Captain.
Brigade-Major, 171st Infantry Bde.,

B.H.Q.,
4th August 17.

SECRET.

O.C. 1st Leicester Regt.,
" " 9th Norfolk Regt.,
No.3 Coy, Divisional Train.
Staff Captain, 171st Brigade.
HdQrs, 57th Division ("G")
" " " ("A")

......

1. The 1st Leicester Regt., and 9th Norfolk Regt., will rejoin their Division tomorrow, 5th instant.

2. Busses will be at SAILLY SUR LA LYS cross roads at 9 a.m.,

3. Transport of both Battalions will move this afternoon as soon as possible after rations are drawn, and will stay the night at VENDIN, rejoining their Division tomorrow.

4. Both Battalions will be rationed for 5th and 6th inst. by the 171st Infantry Brigade.

5. Details as to times of embussing, etc., to be arranged between Os.C. 1st Leicester Regt. and 9th Norfolk Regt.

ACKNOWLEDGE.

Captain, Brigade Major.
171st Infantry Brigade.

B.H.Q.
4th August, 1917

SECRET.

171st INFANTRY BRIGADE ORDER No.84.

COPY NO.

5th August, 1917.

Map.Ref.
Sheet 36.
1:10,000

1. The 4th Brigade, C.E.P., will be attached, one Battalion at a time, to the 171st Infantry Brigade.

2. "A" Battalion, 4th Brigade CEP. will take over the BOUTILLERIE SUBSECTOR on August 7th, and will come under the orders of the B.G.C., 171st Infantry Brigade. It will be relieved on the night of 13/14th August by "B" Battalion CEP.
    The Brigade Commander, C.E.P., will be attached to HdQrs 171st Infantry Brigade.
    The 2/7th K.L.R. on relief, will go into Brigade Reserve BOUTILLERIE SECTOR.

3. Moves will take place according to attached March Table.

4. The following Signal Personnel will be left in the Line by the 2/7th K.L.R., on relief :-
    1. N.C.O. per Battalion HdQts;   2 Signallers per Station.

5. 1 Officer of 2/7th K.L.R. will be left in the line and attached to Battalion HdQrs. This Officer should speak French, if possible.

6. 6 Battalion Observers under a selected N.C.O. will be left in the line, and will be attached to the C.E.P. Observers and render them all possible assistance.

7. 1 Lewis Gun per Company will probably have to be lent to "A" Bn. C.E.P. by the 2/7th K.L.R., Details regarding this will be issued later.

8. Details of all reliefs will be arranged inter-Regimentally.

9. Battalions of 4th Brigade C.E.P. will be rationed by 1st Division, C.E.P. up to and including the day after that on which they arrive in the 57th Division area.
    They will then be rationed by the 171st Infantry Brigade up to and including the day after their return to the C.E.P. Area.

10. Completion of reliefs will be reported to this Office by wire.

ACKNOWLEDGE.

(Sd) G L ALEXANDER

Captain, Brigade Major.
171st Infantry Brigade.

ISSUED TO :-

Copy 1. "E" Battalion.
     2. "F"   ,,
     3. "G"   ,,
     4. "H"   ,,
     5.) 4th Bde. C.E.P. (Thro' 57th
     6.) Divn. - 1 copy to "A" Bn.)
     7. 171st M.G.Company.
     8. 170th L.T.M.B.,

Copy No. 9. 57th Division.    )
        10. 172nd Brigade.    ) For
        11. 3rd Bde. C.E.P.   ) Informn.
        12. Right Group, R.A. )
        13. Signals.
        14. Staff Captain.
        15. War Diary.
        16. File.
        17. 421st Field Co, R.E.

MARCH TABLE issued with 171st INFANTRY BRIGADE ORDER NO. 24.

| DATE. | UNIT. | FROM. | TO. | ROUTES. | RELIEVING. | RENDEZVOUS Where Guides will meet Incoming Troops. | REMARKS. |
|---|---|---|---|---|---|---|---|
| Aug 5th. | "A" Battalion. C.E.P. | 1st Division. CEP Area. | SAILLY SU LA LYS. | | Nil. | Cross roads, SAILLY SU LA LYS. | Billeting Party of "A" Bn. C.E.P. Billeting Party will be met by Staff Capt. 171st Inf.Bde at 10 a.m. at SAILLY G OSS ROADS. |
| 6th. | Advance Party of "A" Bn. C.E.P. | SAILLY SU LA LYS. | Line - BOUTILLERIE SECTOR. | BAC ST MAUR Level Crossing at H.13.c.6.8. Road Junctn. at H.19.b.05.90. Road junctn. at H.20.c.90.05. | Nil. | HdQrs, 171st Inf. Bde. MARES NEST. 5 p.m. | IOffice & 4 Guides of 2/7th K.L. (a) Advance Party will consist of I Office & I NCO. from Bn H.Q.; I Office & 3 NCOs pe Coy. Signalling Office. Bombing Office. (b) This party will be attached to 2/7th KL. & will await arival of Bn. on night of 7th Aug. (c) Coy. Officers will meet the Companies on arival in Subsidiary Line. |
| 7/8th. | "A" Bn. C.E.P. | SAILLY SU LA LYS. | Line - BOUTILLERIE SECTOR. | BAC ST MAUR Level Crossing at H.13.c.6.8. (Remainder of oute to be arranged Inter-regimentally). | 2/7th K.L. | Level Crossing at H.13. c.6.8. 7 p.m. | Guides from 2/7th K.L. (Number of Guides to be arranged Inter-mentally). (a) Garrison of Subsidiary Line will be relieved as early as possible by Platoon of 2/7th KL. (b) 2 Companies of 2/6th KL will remain in E EU BAIX till the 8th inst. They will come under the odes of 2/7th KL. till they move on the 8th to be attached to the 2/5th KLT. |
| 7/8th. | 2/7th K.L. | Line - BOUTILLERIE SECTOR. | Bde ESE VE. BOUTILLERIE SECTOR. | To be arranged Inter-regimentally. | To be arranged 2/6th KL. | To be arranged Guides Inter-regimentally. | |
| 7/8th. | 2/6th K.L. (less 2 Coys) | BDE ESE VE. BOUTILLERIE SECTOR. | BAC ST MAUR. FORT OMPU. | Nil. | Nil. | To be arranged by OC 2/6th KL. & Staff Capt, 171st Brigade. | |

In continuation of 171st Infantry Brigade order No.24.
dated 5th August 1917.

*******

1. Battalion and Company Commanders of "A" Battalion.
4th Brigade,O.E.F. will reconnoitre the line to-morrow,
6th inst.
This party will report at these Headquarters at
10.0.a.m. where they will be met by an officer and an
orderly of "C" Battalion,who will guide them to Battalion
Headquarters.
Further guides will then be provided to show them
round the line.

2. One Lewis Gun and detachment per Company of "C"
Battalion will be left in the line and attached for duty
to "A" Battalion,4th Brigade, C.E.F.

(Sd) L ALEXANDER
Captain, Brigade Major,
171st Infantry Brigade.

B.M.:
5.8.1917.

Issued to all recipients of 171st Infantry Brigade order No.24

SECRET. COPY NO.

5th August 1917.

171st INFANTRY BRIGADE ORDER NO. 25.

........

1. The 2/5th K.L.R. (less 2 companies) plus 2 companies of 2/6th K.L.R. (attached) will relieve the 2/8th K.L.R. in CORDONNERIE Sector on night of 8/9th August 1917.

2. (a) The 2/8th K.L.R. on relief will move into Brigade Reserve CORDONNERIE Sector at ROUGE DE BOUT.
   (b) On relief the garrison of the Subsidiary Line will be constituted as in appendix "B" of Defence Scheme.
   It will be noted that each Company of the Reserve Battalion provides one platoon for the garrison of the Subsidiary Line.

3. Details will be arranged between Battalions concerned. Relief will not start from ROUGE DE BOUT before 8.0.p.m.

4. O.C. 2/5th K.L.R. will arrange with O.C. 2/8th K.L.R. for sufficient signallers to be left in the line to make up deficiencies.

5. (a) Battalion and Company Commanders of 2/5th K.L.R. will reconnoitre the line on the 7th inst.
   (b) The following will go into the line on the evening of the 7th and await the arrival of their Unit:-
        1 Officer and 1 N.C.O. per Battalion Headquarters,
        1 Officer per Company,
        1 N.C.O. per Platoon,
        Bombing Officer,
        Signalling Officer.
   Guides for these parties will be arranged inter-regimentally.

6. Lewis Gun detachment will move into the line on the night of 7/8th August and will relieve by daylight on 8th inst in small parties. A minimum of 40 drums per gun will be carried in and brought out.

7. Completion of reliefs will be reported to this Office by wire.

ACKNOWLEDGE.

E.J.Alexander

Captain, Brigade Major,
171st Infantry Brigade.


ISSUED at 3.0pm to:-

```
COPY No. 1  "E" Battalion.
         2  "F"    ,,
         3  "G"    ,,
         4  "H"    ,,
         5  "A"    ,,        CEP.
         6  421st Field Coy. R.E.
         7  171st M.G.Company.
         8  171st L.T.M.B.
         9  57th Division.        )
        10  172nd Infantry Brigade.)  for
        11  3rd Brigade C.E.P.    )  information.
        12  Right Group R.A.      )
        13  Staff Captain.
        14  Signals.
        15  War Diary.
        16  File.
```

SECRET.   B.M./519.   COPY NO. 16

13th August, 1917.

AMENDMENT to

171st INFANTRY BRIGADE ORDER

NO. 26/1.

****

Guides of 3rd Portuguese Regiment will now be at the Rendezvous at H.13.c.6.8. at 5-0 p.m. to-day, at which hour the head of "B" Battn. 4th Bde. C.E.P. will reach the Rendezvous.

"B" Battalion 4th Bde. C.E.P. will then proceed to the trenches with platoons at 150 yards interval.

~~ACKNOWLEDGE.~~

Bde. H. Q.,
13. 8. 17.

R.W.Patterson
Captain, Brigade Major,
171st Infantry Brigade.

ISSUED to all recipients
of Brigade Order No.26/1.

SECRET.

COPY NO 16

12th August, 1917.

AMENDMENT to

171st INFANTRY BRIGADE ORDER

No. 26.

* * * *

Para. 5 of the above Order is cancelled and the following substituted:-

5.  6 Lewis Guns and detachments will be lent by 2/7th K.L.R. to "B" Battn. 4th Brigade, C.M.P.

ACKNOWLEDGE.

R Watson

Captain, Brigade Major,
171st Infantry Brigade.

Bde. H. Q.,
12. 8. 1917.

ISSUED to all recipients
of Brigade Order No. 26.

SECRET.                                                                COPY NO. 16

## 171st INFANTRY BRIGADE ORDER NO. 26.    11th August, 1917.

--------oOo--------

1. "B" Battalion 4th Brigade C.E.P. will be attached to 171st Brigade from to-day, August 11th 1917.

2. "B" Battalion will relieve 3rd Regiment C.E.P. in the BOUTILLERIE SUBSECTOR on the night of August 13th/14th and will come under orders of B.G.C., 171st Infantry Brigade.
    The 3rd Regiment C.E.P. will, on relief, withdraw to billets at SAILLY-SUR-LA-LYS.

3. Moves will take place according to attached March Table.

4. The following personnel will be attached to "B" Battn. C.E.P. while they are in the line by 2/7th K. L. R. :-
    1 Officer at Battn. Hd.Qrs. who should speak French if possible.
    1 Signalling N.C.O. for Battn. Hd.Qrs.
    2 Signallers per Station.
    1 N.C.O. and 6 Battalion Observers who will be attached to C.E.P. Observers.
    Bombing Officer and 2 Sections of Bombers who will remain at Battalion Headquarters.

5. 1 Lewis Gun and detachment per Company will be lent by 2/7th K. L. R. to "B" Battn. 4th Brigade, C.E.P.

6. "B" Battn. of 4th Brigade C.E.P. will be rationed by 171st Brigade from 13th instant up to and including the day after their return to the C.E.P. Area.

7. Completion of reliefs will be reported to these Headquarters by wire.

8. ACKNOWLEDGE.

                                            Captain, A/ Bde.Major,
                                            171st Infantry Brigade.

ISSUED TO :-

Copy No.1. Hd.Qrs. 57th Divn. "G".   Copy No.10. 172nd Inf. Bde.
        2. Hd.Qrs. 57th Divn. "Q".           11. B. G. C.
        3. O.C., 2/5th K.L.R.                12. Bde.Major.
        4. O.C., 2/7th K.L.R.                13. Staff Captain.
        5. O.C., 2/8th K.L.R.                14. Signals Off.
        6. O.C., 171st M.G.C.                15. Int. Off.
        7. O.C., 171st L.T.M.B.              16. War Diary.
        8. O.C., Right Group, R.A.           17. War Diary.
        9. O.C., 421st Fd.Coy.R.E.           18. File.
                                             19. File.

MARCH TABLE issued with 171st INFANTRY BRIGADE ORDER

| DATE. | UNIT. | FROM. | TO. | ROUTES. | Relieving. | Rendezvous where Guides will meet Incoming Troops. | To be met by:- | REMARKS. |
|---|---|---|---|---|---|---|---|---|
| Aug. 12th. | Advance Party, "B" Bn, C.E.P. | SAILLY SUR LA LYS. | Line - BOUTILLERIE SECTOR. | BAC ST MAUR. Level Crossing at H.13.c.6.8. Road Junctn. at H.20.c.60.05. | Nil. | Hdqrs, 171st Inf.Bde., MARES NEST, 5 p.m. | 1 Officer & 2 Guides 2/7th KLR. | (a) Advance Party will consist of 1 Officer & 1 N.C.O. from Bn.H.Q. & 3 NCOs per Coy. Signalling Officer. Bombing Officer. (b) This party will be attached to 3rd Regt. C.E.P. & will await arrival of their Bn. on night of Aug.13th. (c) Coy Officers will meet their Coys on arrival in Subsid. Line. |
| Aug. 13/14th. | "B" Bn. 4th Bde, C.E.P., | SAILLY SUR LA LYS. | Line - BOUTILLERIE SECTOR. | BAC ST MAUR. Level Crossing at H.13.c.6.8. Remainder of Route to be arranged inter-Regimentally. | 3rd Regt. 4th Bde. C.E.P., | H.13.c.6.8. 7 p.m. | Guides from 3rd Regt. CEP. Number to be arranged inter-Regimentally. | |
| Aug. 13/14th. | 3rd Regt. C.E.P., | Line - BOUTILLERIE SECTOR. | SAILLY SUR LA LYS. | Level Crossing at H.13.c.6.8. BAC ST MAUR. | Take over billets vacated by "B" Bn CEP. | | | |

SECRET.                                                    COPY NO 17

## 171st INFANTRY BRIGADE OPERATION
## ORDER NO. 27.

.....

1.    The 2/8th K.L.R. will relieve the 2/5th K.L.R. (less two companies) plus two companies of 2/6th K.L.R. (attached) in CORDONNERIE SECTOR, during the afternoon of August 16th.

2.    (a) The 2/5th K.L.R. (less 2 companies) plus 2 companies 2/6th K.L.R. (attached) will move into Brigade Reserve - CORDONNERIE SECTOR, at ROUGE DE BOUT.

(b) Each Company of the Reserve Battalion provides one platoon for the garrison of the Subsidiary Line posts.

3.    Details will be arranged between Battalion Commanders concerned.
      Relief will commence at 2-0 pm. All troops will move at 100 yards interval between platoons.

4.    All defence schemes and programmes of work will be handed over.

5.    Completion of reliefs will be reported to this office by wire "No rations required".

Bde. H.Q.,                                    Captain, Brigade Major,
15. 8. 1917.                                    171st Infantry Brigade.


ISSUED to:-

Copy No. 1. 2/5th K.L.R.
        2. 2/6th K.L.R.
        3. 2/7th K.L.R.
        4. 2/8th K.L.R.
        5. 171st M.G.Coy.
        6. 171st L.T.M.B.
        7. 421st Fd. Coy. R.E.
        8. "B" Bn. 4th Bde. C.E.P.
        9. 57th Division "G".
       10. 57th Division "Q".
       11. Right Group R.A.
       12. 3rd Bde. C.E.P.
       13. Brigade Commander.
       14. Brigade Major.
       15. Staff Captain.
       16. Signals Officer.
       17. War Diary.
       18. War Diary.
       19. File.

SECRET.   COPY NO. 22

## 171st INFANTRY BRIGADE OPERATION ORDER NO. 28.

1. "C" Battalion 4th Bde. C.E.P. will be attached to 171st Infantry Brigade from to-day, August 17th.

2. "C" Battalion will relieve "B" Battalion C.E.P. in the BOUTILLERIE Subsector on the night of August 19th/20th, and will come under orders of B.G.C., 171st Infantry Brigade.

   "B" Battalion 4th Bde. C.E.P. will, on relief, withdraw to billets at SAILLY-SUR-LA-LYS.

3. Moves will take place according to the attached March Table.

4. The following personnel will be attached to "C" Battn. C.E.P. while they are in the line, by 2/7th K.L.R.:-

   1 Officer at Battalion Hd.Qrs. who should speak French, if possible.
   1 Signalling N.C.O. for Bn. Hd.Qrs.
   2 Signallers per Station.
   1 N.C.O. and 6 Battn. Observers, who will be attached to Observers of C.E.P.
   1 N.C.O. and 2 Sections of Bombers, with the Reserve Company at ELBOW FARM.
   Number of Lewis Guns and detachments to be attached will be notified later.

5. "C" Battalion of 4th Bde. C.E.P. will be rationed by 171st Infantry Brigade from August 19th up to, and including, the day after their return to C.E.P. Area.

6. Troops should keep well closed up and should move at 100 yards interval, between - half-platoons.

7. Completion of relief will be reported to these Hd.Qrs. by "Rations all up".

8. ACKNOWLEDGE.

Bde. H.Q.   Captain, Brigade Major.
17.8.17.    171st Infantry Brigade.

COPY NO. 1  57th Division "G".
       2    57th Division "Q".
       3    2/5th K.L.R.
       4    2/6th K.L.R.
       5    2/7th K.L.R.
       6    2/8th K.L.R.
       7    171st M.G.C.
       8    171st L.T.M.B.
       9    Right Group R.A.
      10    421st Fd. Coy. R.E.
      11    172nd Infantry Brigade.
      12    "B" Bn. 4th Bde. C.E.P.
      13    "C" Bn. 4th Bde. C.E.P.
      14.   H.Q. 4th Bde. C.E.P.
      15.   57th Divnl. Liaison Officer with Portuguese.
      16.   B. G. C.
      17.   Brigade Major.
      18.   Staff Captain.
      19.   Signals Officer.
      20.   Intelligence Officer.
      21.   War Diary.
      22.   War Diary.
      23.   File.
      24.   File.

MARCH TABLE issued with 171st INFANTRY BRIGADE O.O. No. 28.

| DATE. | UNIT. | FROM. | TO. | ROUTES. | RELIEVING. | RENDEZVOUS for GUIDES AND HOURS. | GUIDES. |
|---|---|---|---|---|---|---|---|
| Aug. 19th/20th. | "C" Battalion 4th Bde. C.E.P. | SAILLY-SUR -LA-LYS. | Line - BOUTILLERIE SECTOR | BAC ST MAUR. Level Crossing H.13.c.6.8. Remainder of Route to be arranged Inter-Regimentally. | "B" Battalion. 4th Bde. C.E.P. | H.13.c.6.8. 7-0 pm. | Guides from "B" Bn. C.E.P. Number to be arranged Inter-Regimentally. |
| Aug. 19th/20th. | "B" Battalion 4th Bde. C.E.P. | line BOUTILLERIE SECTOR. | SAILLY-SUR -LA-LYS. | Level Crossing at H.13.c.6.8, BAC ST MAUR. | Take over Billets vacated by "C" Batin. C. E. P. | | |

SECRET.  COPY NO. 16.

171st INFANTRY BRIGADE OPERATION ORDER NO. 29.

---------------------oOo---------------------

1. The 2/5th Bn. K.L.R. will relieve the 2/8th Bn. K.L.R. in the CORDONNERIE SECTOR, during the afternoon of August 24th.

2. The 2/8th Bn. K.L.R. on relief will withdraw into Brigade Reserve, CORDONNERIE SECTOR, at ROUGE DE BOUT.

    Each Company in the Reserve Battalions provide 1 platoon in the subsidiary line posts.

3. All details will be arranged between Battalion Commanders concerned.

    Relief should not commence before 2-0 pm.

4. All defence schemes and programmes of work will be handed over.

5. Completion of reliefs will be reported to this Office by "Not required".

Bde. H.Q.  
22. 8. 17.

Captain, Brigade Major,  
171st Infantry Brigade.


COPIES TO:-
1 2/5th K.L.R.
2 2/6th K.L.R.
3 2/7th K.L.R.
4 2/8th K.L.R.
5 171st M.G.C.
6 171st L.T.M.B.
7 421st Fd. Coy. R.E.
8 "C" Bn. 4th Bde. C.E.P.
9 3rd Brigade, C.E.P.
10 57th Division "G".
11 Right Group, R.A.
12 Brigade Commander.
13 Brigade Major.
14 Staff Captain.
15 Signals Officer.
16 War Diary.
17 War Diary.
18 File.

SECRET.   COPY NO. 18

## 171st INFANTRY BRIGADE OPERATION ORDER NO. 30.

———— oOo ————

1. On the night of August 25th/26th, the following reliefs will take place.

    2/7th K.L.R. will relieve "C" Battalion 4th Brigade C.E.P. in the BOUTILLERIE SECTOR.

    2/6th K.L.R. will relieve 2/7th K.L.R. in Brigade Reserve to the BOUTILLERIE SECTOR.

2. On relief "C" Battalion 4th Brigade C.E.P. will withdraw to billets at SAILLY-SUR-LA-LYS.

3. 2/6th K.L.R. should complete the reliefs of the Posts in the SUBSIDIARY LINE by 7-30 pm. so as to enable 2/7th K.L.R. to move up to relieve at that hour.   The 2/6th K.L.R. should not leave their billets before 6-15 pm.

4. All details should be arranged between Battalion Commanders concerned.

5. All troops should move at 100 yards interval between platoons.

6. On completion, Battalion Headquarters of the BOUTILLERIE SECTOR will re-open at FORAY HOUSE.

7. The completion of the relief will be reported to this Office by "NO ALLOTMENT REQUIRED".

Bde. H. Q.   Captain, Brigade Major,
23. 8. 17.   171st Infantry Brigade.

COPIES TO :-

| | | | | |
|---|---|---|---|---|
| 1 | 57th Division "G". | | 11 | 172nd Infantry Brigade. |
| 2 | 57th Division "Q". | | 12 | Right Group, R.A. |
| 3 | 2/5th K. L. R. | | 13 | 421st Field Coy. R.E. |
| 4 | 2/6th K. L. R. | | 14 | Brigade Commander. |
| 5 | 2/7th K. L. R. | | 15 | Brigade Major. |
| 6 | 2/8th K. L. R. | | 16 | Staff Captain. |
| 7 | 171st M. G. C. | | 17 | Signals Officer. |
| 8 | 171st L. T. M. B. | | 18 | War Diary. |
| 9 | 4th Bde. C. E. P. | | 19 | War Diary. |
| 10 | "C" Bn. 4th Bde. C.E.P. | | 20 | File. |

APPENDIX No. III.

STATEMENT of CASUALTIES,

referred to in

171st INFANTRY BRIGADE WAR DIARY,

1.8.1917

to

31.8.1917.

.....

171st INFANTRY BRIGADE.

CASUALTIES from 1.8.1917 to 31.8.1917.

| DATE. 24 hours ending noon:- | KILLED. Officers. | KILLED. O.Ranks. | WOUNDED. Officers. | WOUNDED. O.Ranks. | MISSING. Officers. | MISSING. O.Ranks. |
|---|---|---|---|---|---|---|
| 1.8.1917. | - | - | Rev. W.J. GALLAGHER. 2nd Lt.A.J. GOLDSPINK. | 13. | - | - |
| 2.8.1917. | - | - | - | 5. | - | - |
| 3.8.1917. | - | - | - | 1. | - | - |
| 4.8.1917. | - | - | - | 6. | - | - |
| 5.8.1917. | Capt. G.L. ALEXANDER. | 1 | - | 7. | - | - |
| 6.8.1917. | - | - | - | - | - | - |
| 7.8.1917. | - | 2 | 2nd Lt. P. SEGRAVE. | 1. | - | - |
| 8.8.1917. | - | - | Major F.H. BOWRING. Capt. A.H. FAULKNER. | 1. | - | - |
| 9.8.1917. | - | - | - | - | - | - |
| 10.8.1917. | - | - | - | 3 | - | - |
| 11.8.1917. | - | - | - | - | - | - |
| 12.8.1917. | - | - | - | - | - | - |
| 13.8.1917. | - | - | - | 1 | - | - |
| 14.8.1917. | - | 1 | - | 6 | - | - |
| 15.8.1917. | - | - | - | - | - | - |
| 16.8.1917. | - | 1 | - | - | - | - |
| 17.8.1917. | - | - | - | 3 | - | - |
| 18.8.1917. | - | 4 | - | 3 | - | - |
| 19.8.1917. | - | - | - | 1 | - | - |
| 20.8.1917. | - | - | - | 1 | - | - |
| 21.8.1917. | - | - | Lt.Col. O.H. NORTH, D.S.O. | 1 | - | - |
| 22.8.1917. | - | - | - | 2 | - | - |
| 23.8.1917. | - | - | - | - | - | - |
| 24.8.1917. | - | 1 | - | 1 | - | - |
| 25.8.1917. | - | - | - | 1 | - | - |
| 26.8.1917. | - | - | - | 1 | - | - |
| 27.8.1917. | - | - | - | - | - | - |
| 28.8.1917. | - | - | - | - | - | - |
| 29.8.1917. | - | - | - | - | - | - |
| 30.8.1917. | - | - | - | 1 | - | - |
| 31.8.1917. | - | - | - | 2 | - | - |
| | 1 | 10. | 6. | 58. | - | - |

Headquarters
171st Inf. Bde.
(57th Division)
September 1917

On His Majesty's Service.

CONFIDENTIAL.

Headquarters,
   57th (West Lancs.) Division.

......

            Herewith War Diary - and accompanying Appendices - of these Headquarters for period 1.9.1917 to 30.9.1917.

                    Brigadier-General,
         Commanding 171st Infantry Brigade.

B.H.Q.
  1st October, 1917.

CONFIDENTIAL.

WAR DIARY

of

HEADQUARTERS - 171st INFANTRY BRIGADE.

............

1.9.1917 to 30.9.1917.

..........

VOLUME VII.

...

Army Form C. 2118

# WAR DIARY or INTELLIGENCE SUMMARY
*(Erase heading not required.)*

Instructions regarding War Diaries and Intelligence Summaries are contained in F.S. Regs., Part II. and the Staff Manual respectively. Title Pages will be prepared in manuscript.

| Place | Date | Hour | Summary of Events and Information | Remarks and references to Appendices |
|---|---|---|---|---|
| FLEURBAIX | 1.9.17 | | Attitude of enemy infantry very quiet. At 4.30 pm Heavy, Medium and Light Trench Mortars brought concentrated fire to bear on enemy front & support line opposite the left flank of BOOTILLERIE. 2/8 K.L.R. in the CORDONNERIE subsection. | Appendix II to S.R. |
| | 2.9.17 | | Quiet. Slight increase in hostile artillery fire. 2/6 K.L.R. relieved 2/7 K.L.R. in the BOOTILLERIE subsection | Appendix II to S.R. 2/S.R. |
| | 3.9.17 | | Very quiet - hostile artillery very quiet | 2/S.R. |
| | 4.9.17 | | No incident of note. Fair to moderately bright of views. Slight activity of enemy artillery directed onto the rest of embarkation line. | 2/S.R. |
| | 5.9.17 | | A patrol of 2/8 K.L.R. observed each with enemy having located enemy post opposite PINNEY'S AVENUE - arrangements made & sent 2 patrols out at 9.0 pm to capture prisoners. | 2/S.R. |
| | 6.9.17 | | Two prisoners 101 R.I.R. were captured & brought in to our lines about 2.0.am. No casualties to our patrols. Enemy artillery shelled Battery position near FLEURBAIX continuously from 2.0 pm until a heavy thunderstorm burst on the locality at 5.30 pm. | Appendix III 2/S.R. |
| | 7.9.17 | | Quiet from both artillery and infantry standpoint. No incident of interest taking place | 2/S.R. |

1875 Wt. W593/826 1,000,000 4/15 T.R.C. & A. A.D.S.S./Forms/C. 2118.

# WAR DIARY or INTELLIGENCE SUMMARY

Army Form C. 2118

| Place | Date | Hour | Summary of Events and Information | Remarks and references to Appendices |
|---|---|---|---|---|
| BEURBAIX | 8.9.17 | | Artillery very quiet so far as the enemy was concerned. Normal on our part. Patrol of 4 men of KKR encountered hostile patrol in No Man's Land. Efforts our front AVENUE near enemy wire. All our patrol returned safely. Three out of the four being wounded. | |
| | 9.9.17 | | A very quiet day. Large explosion caused by our HOWITZER fire at ERDMONCOURT opposite W. SEC. 95 K.R.R. relieved 3/6 K.R.R. in the CORDONNERIE section. | |
| | 10.9.17 | | Enemy has shewed nothing near SOUSA. Patrol engaged & took larger fire usually observed. 9 K.R.R. relieved 96 K.R.R. in BOUTILLERIE section | |
| | 11.9.17 | | Normal artillery duels prevailed — Orders from 59 Div received that he would be relieved and that 17 Bde would move into to-morrow even on 12.9.17. | |
| | 12.9.17 | | B.G.C. 11th Infbde came to reconnoitre our line. Visited bn to bn Coln HQ's in the Enemy's artillery quiet all day. | |
| | 13.9.17 | | Very quiet all day | |
| | 14.9.17 | | Enemy's attitude & K. artillery infantry very quiet | |

Army Form C. 2118

# WAR DIARY
or
# INTELLIGENCE SUMMARY
(Erase heading not required.)

III

Instructions regarding War Diaries and Intelligence Summaries are contained in F.S. Regs., Part II. and the Staff Manual respectively. Title Pages will be prepared in manuscript.

| Place | Date | Hour | Summary of Events and Information | Remarks and references to Appendices |
|---|---|---|---|---|
| FLEURBAIX | 15.9.17 | | At 4.25 am enemy barraged pont stuffed line near DEVONS AVENUE and a raiding party left traces in front of our line. Steel helmet & bombs were found in front of the head of MINE AVENUE. Our casualties 1 killed 3 wounded. | Appendix III 9/9/17. |
| | 16.9.17 | | 14th Inf Bde relieved 171 Inf Bde in the FLEURBAIX sector. 171 Bde moved back to LA GORGUE. Relief being completed 10.20 pm | 9/9/17 Appendix II 9/9/17. |
| LA GORGUE | 17.9.17 | | Brigade halted. | 9/9/17. |
| LA MICQUELERIE | 18.9.17 | | Brigade marched to BUSNES area. Bde HQ established at LA MICQUELERIE | 9/9/17 Appendix II 9/9/17. |
| ST HILAIRE COTTES | 19.9.17 | | Brigade marched to ST HILAIRE area. Bde HQ established at COTTES | 9/9/17. |
| | 20.9.17 | | Period spent by all Units in cleaning up, repairing billets etc. | 9/9/17. |
| | 21.9.17 | | Cleaning up continued. Brig. Gen. R.N. BRAY D.S.O. was accidentally thrown from his horse & sustained injuries - broken collar bone - 3rd in Rotherm. Lt. Col. D.H. NORTH D.S.O. assumed command 9/17. Inf Bde | 9/9/17. |
| | 22.9.17 | | Brigade commenced Training Program | 9/9/17. |

1875 Wt. W593/826 1,000,000 4/15 J.B.C. & A. A.D.S.S./Forms/C. 2118.

Army Form C. 2118

# WAR DIARY
or
# INTELLIGENCE SUMMARY
(Erase heading not required.)

Instructions regarding War Diaries and Intelligence Summaries are contained in F. S. Regs., Part II. and the Staff Manual respectively. Title Pages will be prepared in manuscript.

IV

| Place | Date | Hour | Summary of Events and Information | Remarks and references to Appendices |
|---|---|---|---|---|
| ST HILAIRE COTTES | 23.9.17 | | SUNDAY. Training Suspended. BRIG. GEN. J.C. LINGBORNE appointed to command 171 | |
| | 24.9.17 | | Bde and arrived during the evening. Training continued | |
| | 25.9.17 | | ditto | |
| | 26.9.17 | | ditto | |
| | 27.9.17 | | ditto | |
| | 28.9.17 | | ditto | |
| | 29.9.17 | | ditto | |
| | 30.9.17 | | SUNDAY. Training Suspended. Statement of Casualties for period | Appendix I |

—J. Longbourne.
Brig. Gen!
O.C. 171st Inf Bde.

APPENDIX No. I.

STATEMENT of CASUALTIES,

referred to in

171st INFANTRY BRIGADE WAR DIARY,

1.9.1917
to
30.9.1917.

## 171st INFANTRY BRIGADE.

### CASUALTIES from 1.9.1917 to 31.9.1917.

| DATE. 24 hours ending noon - | KILLED. | | WOUNDED. | | MISSING. | |
|---|---|---|---|---|---|---|
| | Officers. | O.Ranks. | Officers. | O.Ranks. | Officers. | O.Ranks. |
| 1.9.1917. | - | - | - | - | - | - |
| 2.9.1917. | - | - | - | 1 | - | - |
| 3.9.1917. | - | - | - | - | - | - |
| 4.9.1917. | - | - | - | - | - | - |
| 5.9.1917. | - | - | - | 1 | - | - |
| 6.9.1917. | - | 1 | - | - | - | - |
| 7.9.1917. | - | - | - | 2 | - | - |
| 8.9.1917. | - | 1 | - | 2 | - | - |
| 9.9.1917. | - | - | - | 3 | - | - |
| 10.9.1917. | - | - | - | 1 | - | - |
| 11.9.1917. | - | - | - | - | - | - |
| 12.9.1917. | - | - | - | 1 | - | - |
| 13.9.1917. | - | - | - | - | - | - |
| 14.9.1917. | - | - | - | - | - | - |
| 15.9.1917. | - | 1 | - | 5 | - | - |
| 16.9.1917. | - | 1 | - | 1 | - | - |
| 17.9.1917. | - | - | - | - | - | - |
| 18.9.1917. | - | - | - | - | - | - |
| 19.9.1917. | - | - | - | - | - | - |
| 20.9.1917. | - | - | - | - | - | - |
| 21.9.1917. | - | - | - | - | - | - |
| 22.9.1917. | - | - | - | 1 | - | - |
| 23.9.1917. | - | - | - | - | - | - |
| 24.9.1917. | - | - | - | - | - | - |
| 25.9.1917. | - | - | - | - | - | - |
| 26.9.1917. | - | - | - | - | - | - |
| 27.9.1917. | - | - | - | - | - | - |
| 28.9.1917. | - | - | - | - | - | - |
| 29.9.1917. | - | - | - | - | - | - |
| 30.9.1917. | - | - | - | - | - | - |
| TOTAL. | - | 4 | - | 18 | - | - |

APPENDIX No. II.

RELIEF ORDERS, etc.,

referred to in

171st INFANTRY BRIGADE WAR DIARY,

1.9.1917
to
30.9.1917.

SECRET.                                                        COPY NO. 16

## 171st INFANTRY BRIGADE OPERATION ORDER NO. 31.

---------------------------oOo---------------------------

1. The following reliefs will take place as under:--

    (a)   September 1st.   2/8th K.L.R. will relieve the 2/5th K.L.R. in the CORDONNERIE SECTOR.   The 2/5th K.L.R. will, on relief, withdraw into Brigade Reserve CORDONNERIE SECTOR at ROUGE DE BOUT.

    (b)   September 2nd.   2/6th K.L.R. will relieve the 2/7th K.L.R. in the BOUTILLERIE SECTOR.   The 2/7th K.L.R. will, on relief, withdraw into Brigade Reserve BOUTILLERIE SECTOR near FLEURBAIX.

2. All details will be arranged between Battalion Commanders concerned.

    Reliefs should not commence before 2-0 p.m.

3. The BOUTILLERIE SECTOR Battalions should not use the Road running from Road junction H.21.d.8.4. to road junction H.28.d.65.65. for the relief, but should use the RUE DES GRAMBIONS.

4. Completion of Reliefs will be reported to this Office by "Stores arrived."

ACKNOWLEDGE.

                                            R W Watterson

Bde. H. Q.                                  Captain, Brigade Major,
31. 8. 17.                                  171st Infantry Brigade.


COPIES TO:-
No. 1   2/5th K.L.R.
    2   2/6th K.L.R.
    3   2/7th K.L.R.
    4   2/8th K.L.R.
    5   171st M.G.C.
    6   171st L.T.M.B.
    7   421st Fd. Coy. R.E.
    8   172nd Inf. Brigade.
    9   3rd Brigade, C.E.P.
   10   57th Division "G".
   11   Right Group, R.A.
   12   Brigade Commander.
   13   Brigade Major.
   14   Staff Captain.
   15   Signals Officer.
   16   War Diary.
   17   War Diary.
   18   File.

SECRET.                                                        Copy No. 17

## 171st INFANTRY BRIGADE OPERATION ORDER No. 32.

* * * * * *

1. The following Reliefs will take place as under :-

   (a) **September 9th.**
   2/5th K.L.R. will relieve 2/8th K.L.R. in the CORDONNERIE SECTOR. The 2/8th K.L.R. will, on relief, withdraw into Brigade Reserve, CORDONNERIE SECTOR, at ROUGE DE BOUT.

   (b) **September 10th.**
   2/7th K.L.R. will relieve 2/6th K.L.R. in the BOUTILLERIE SECTOR. The 2/6th K.L.R. will, on relief, withdraw into Brigade Reserve, BOUTILLERIE SECTOR, near FLEURBAIX.

2. All details will be arranged between Battalion Commanders concerned.

   Reliefs should not commence before 2.0 p.m.

3. The BOUTILLERIE SECTOR Battalions should not use the Road running from Road junction, N.21.d.8.4. to Road junction, N.23.d.65.65, for the Relief, but should use the RUE DES CHARDONS.

4. Completion of Reliefs will be reported to this Office by "WHISKY FINISHED".

ACKNOWLEDGE.

                                            for    [signature]
                                            Captain, Brigade Major.
                                            171st Infantry Brigade.

B.H.Q.
    7th September, 1917.

ISSUED TO:-
        Copy No. 1.    2/5th K.L.R.,
                2.    2/6th      ,,
                3.    2/7th      ,,
                4.    2/8th      ,,
                5.    171st M.G. Company.
                6.    171st L.T.M.B.
                7.    421st Field Co, R.E.,
                8.    172nd Inf. Bde.
                9.    2nd Brigade, C.E.F.,
               10.    57th Division, "G".
               11.        ,,         "Q".
               12.    Right Group, R.A.,
               13.    Brigade Commander.
               14.    Brigade Major.
               15.    Staff Captain.
               16.    Signals, 171st Bde.
               17.    War Diary.
               18.    War Diary.
               19.    File.
               20.    File.

SECRET.                                                         COPY NO. 25.

Map Ref.                    171st INFANTRY BRIGADE ORDER No. 33.
1/10.000. 36 N.W.3.
1/100.000. HAZEBROUCK, 5A.          ........          12th September, 1917.


RELIEF.         1.   The 114th Infantry Brigade will relieve the 171st
                Infantry Brigade in the FLEURBAIX SECTION on Sept.16th
                1917, and the night of Sept. 16/17th, in accordance
                with the March Table attached.

GUIDES.         2.   One Officer per Battalion, Machine Gun Company and
                Trench Mortar Battery, will accompany the Guides
                detailed to meet the Relieving Units, and will be
                responsible that the Relieving Units get the right
                Guides, that the Guides know the route and destination
                of the Parties they are leading.

                     Os.C. Battalions, M.G.Company and T.M.B., she will
                make arrangements for further Guides to be picked up
                on the way up, so that there is at least a Guide for
                each Post in the Front Line, and one for each Platoon,
                Machine Gun and Lewis Gun.

BILLETING       3. (a)  The Billeting Parties - consisting of one
PARTIES.        Officer and 15 O.Ranks - of the Battalions going to
                NEUF BERQUIN, and the 171st M.G.Company going to LA
                GORGUE, should report to their respective Relieving
                Units by 7 p.m., Sept. 15th, so as to avoid these
                Units having to leave Rear Parties behind to hand
                over billets.           They will be accommodated
                for the night by the 114th Infantry Brigade.

                (b)  Os.C. Battalions and T.M.B., moving to LA GORGUE,
                will arrange to send on Billeting Parties to take
                over Billets vacated by their respective Relieving
                Units, who should report there by 2 p.m. on Sept. 16th.

                4.   Command of the Brigade Section will pass to G.O.C.
                114th Infantry Brigade, on completion of Relief.

                5.   Completion of Reliefs will be reported to Brigade
                HdQrs by reference to the Serial Numbers laid down in
                the attached March Table. (Viz., "No.1 Correct")

                6.   An interval of 100 yds will be maintained between
                Platoons on the march while on the South-West side of
                the LAVENTIE-ERQUINGHEM Railway.

                     Transports of 2/5th K.L.R., and 2/7th K.L.R., will
                move independently to LA GORGUE, under the orders of
                their respective C.Os.

                     Other Transports will move with their Units.


                7.   All maps, aeroplane photographs, defence schemes
                and trench stores will be handed over to the incoming
                troops.    Receipts will be forwarded to this office
                in duplicate.

2.

8. All other details will be arranged between C.Os concerned.

Please ACKNOWLEDGE.

*R W Patteson*
        Captain, Brigade Major.
        171st Infantry Brigade.

DISTRIBUTION :-

- Copy No. 1. B.G.C.,
- 2. Brigade Major.
- 3. Staff Captain.
- 4. 57th Division, "G".
- 5. ,, "Q".
- 6 - 13. 114th Infantry Brigade.
- 14. 2/5th K.L.R.,
- 15. 2/6th ,,
- 16. 2/7th ,,
- 17. 2/8th ,,
- 18. 171st L.T.M.B.,
- 19. 171st M.G.Company.
- 20. 421st Field Company, R.E.
- 21. Right Group, R.A.,
- 22. Signals, 171st Bde.
- 23. 3rd Brigade, C.E.P.,
- 24. 172nd Infantry Brigade.
- 25. War Diary.
- 26. War Diary.
- 27. 2/2ⁿᵈ WESSEX Fᴰ AMBᶜᵉ
- 28.)
- 29.) Spare.
- 30.)

MARCH TABLE to accompany 171st INFANTRY BRIGADE ORDER No. 33.

| Serial No. | Date. | UNIT. | From. | To. | Replacing. | Who Proceed to. | Route Taken by Unit on Relief. | No. of Guides & by whom provided. | Place and Hour. | REMARKS. |
|---|---|---|---|---|---|---|---|---|---|---|
| 1. | 16th. | 14th Bn. Welsh Regt., | NEUF BERQUIN. | BDE RIGHT RESERVE, FLEURBAIX. CORDONNERIE SUBSECTION. | 2/8th K.L.R., | NEUF BERQUIN. | RUE de la LYS. ESTAIRES. | 1 Officer. 2 Guides per Coy, 2/8th KLR. | 11am, Road Junction, RUE de la LYS. G.27.d.3.8. | Relief to be completed by 4 p.m. |
| 2. | 16th. | 15th Bn. Welsh Regt., | NEUF BERQUIN. | BDE LEFT RESERVE, FLEURBAIX. BOUTILLERIE SUBSECTION. | 2/6th K.L.R., | NEUF BERQUIN. | RUE QUESNOY. RUE de la LYS. ESTAIRES. | 1 Officer. 2 Guides per Coy, 2/6th KLR. | 11am, Road Junction, BAC ST MAUR. H.13.c.50.95. | Relief to be completed by 4 p.m. |
| 3. | 16th. | 114th M.G. Coy. | LA GORGUE. | LINE - FLEURBAIX SECTION. | 171st M.G.Co. | LA GORGUE. | RUE de la LYS. LA GORGUE. | 1 Officer. 4 Guides, 171st M.G. Coy. | 10am, SAILLY SUR-LA-LYS Cross-Roads, G.22.b.20.85. | Relief to be completed by 4 p.m. |
| 4. | 16th. | 114th L. T.M.B., | LA GORGUE. | LINE and BILLETS, FLEURBAIX SECTION. | 171st L.T.M.B., | LA GORGUE. | SAILLY. BAC ST MAUR. | 1 Officer. 4 Guides, 171st L. T.M.B., | 1.30 pm, Road Junction, BAC ST MAUR. H.13.c.50.95. | Relief to be completed by 4 p.m. |

| Serial No. | Date. | UNIT. | From. | To. | Replacing. | Who Proceed to. | Route taken by Unit on Relief. | No. of Guides & by whom provided. | Place and Hour. | REMARKS. |
|---|---|---|---|---|---|---|---|---|---|---|
| 5 | 16th | H.Q. 114th Inf.Bde. | LA GORGUE. | MARES NEST, FLEURBAIX. | H.Q. 171st Inf. Bde. | LA GORGUE. | RUE QUESNOY. RUE de la LYS. | 2 Guides. | 12 noon, Road Junction, BAC ST MAUR, H.13.c.50.95. | H.Qrs will open at LA GORGUE on completion of Relief. |
| 6 | 16/17th | 13th Bn. Welsh Regt., | LA GORGUE. | LINE - RIGHT, FLEURBAIX. CORDONNERIE SUBSECTION. | 2/5th K.L.R., | LA GORGUE. | ROUGE DE BOUT. SAILLY SUR LA LYS. ESTAIRES. LA GORGUE. | 1 Officer. 2 Guides per Coy, 2/5th KLR. | 6.30 pm. SAILLY SUR LA LYS CROSS-ROADS G.22.b.20.85. | Lewis Guns will relieve in daylight, their relief to be completed by 5 p.m. Guides; 4 per Battalion, will meet L.G.Teams at 1 pm.at same Rendezvous as the Guides for the Bns. |
| 7 | 16/17th | 10th Bn, Welsh Regt., | LA GORGUE. | LINE - LEFT, FLEURBAIX. BOUTILLERIE SUBSECTOR. | 2/7th K.L.R., | LA GORGUE. | FORT ROMPU. BAC ST MAUR. SAILLY SUR LA LYS. ESTAIRES. LA GORGUE. | 1 Officer. 2 Guides per Coy, 2/7th KLR. | 6.45 pm. Road junction, BAC ST MAUR, H.13.c.50.95 | |

SECRET.   171st INFANTRY BRIGADE ORDER No. 34.        COPY NO. 16

                       ....                          17th Sept. 1917.

Ref. Map.
Sheet 36,
1/40.000.

1.   On Tuesday, September 18th 1917, the BRIGADE GROUP will move
from LA GORGE and NEUF BERQUIN Area to BUSNES Area No.2 (Distance
10½ miles).

2.   Units will pass the Starting Point at the Road Junction, Q.5.b.
5.5. as per attached March Table.

3.   A Horse Ambulance will follow in rear of each, 2/5th, 2/6th
and 2/7th K.L.R.,   These will join the Units at the Starting
Point.

4.   One Officer to command the Rear Party will be detailed by O.C.
2/7th K.L.R.   This party will be formed at the Starting Point.

5.   All Units will report their arrival in their Billets at
once, giving the location of HdQrs.

6.   The Brigade Signal Officer will arrange to synchronise
watches by 7.30 a.m. September 18th.

ACKNOWLEDGE.

                                    Captain, Brigade Major.
                                    171st Infantry Brigade.

        ISSUED AT 2 p.m. to :-

              Copy No. 1.     B.G.C.,
                      2.      Brigade Major.
                      3.      Staff Captain.
                      4.      57th Division "G".
                      5.         ,,        "Q"
                      6.      2/5th K.L.R.,
                      7.      2/6th    ,,
                      8.      2/7th    ,,
                      9.      2/8th    ,,
                     10.      171st L.T.M.B.
                     11.      171st M.G.Co.
                     12.      421st Field Co, R.E.
                     13.      Signals, 171st Bde.
                     14.      2/2nd Wessex Field Ambce.
                     15.      No.3 Coy, 57th Divl. Train.
                     16.      War Diary.
                     17.         ,,  .
                     18)
                     19)      Spare.
                     20)

MARCH TABLE ISSUED WITH 171st INFANTRY BRIGADE OPERATION ORDER No. 34.

| SERIAL NUMBER. | UNIT. | FROM. | TO. | PASS STARTING POINT at Q.5.b.5.5. | ROUTE. | REMARKS. |
|---|---|---|---|---|---|---|
| 1. | 171st Inf.Bde H.Qrs. | LA GORGUE. | LA MIQUELLERIE. | 9.20 a.m. | | - |
| 2. | 2/8th K.L.R. | ROBERMETZ. | CANTRAINNE. | 9.30 a.m. | | From ROBECQ Bn. will move via L'ECLEME. |
| 3. | 2/5th K.L.R. | LA GORGUE. | L'ECLEME. | 9.41 a.m. | ROBECQ. | From ROBECQ direct to L'ECLEME. |
| 4. | 2/6th K.L.R. | NEUF BERQUIN. | ,, | 9.51 a.m. | | ,, ,, ,, |
| 5. | 2/7th K.L.R. | CHAPELLE DUVELLE. | LA PIERRIERE. | 10. 2 a.m. | | From ROBECQ via BUSNES. |
| 6. | 171st M.G.Co. | ,, | BUSNES. | 10.12 a.m. | CALONNE SUR LA LYS. | - |
| 7. | 171st L.T.M.B. | LA GORGUE. | ,, | 10.19 a.m. | | - |
| 8. | 421st Field Co R.E. | CHAPELLE DUVELLE. | ,, | 10.21 a.m. | | - |
| 9. | 2/2nd Wessex Fd.Ambce. | LA GORGUE. | ,, | 10.30 a.m. | | - |
| 10. | No.3 Coy,57th Divl.Train. | CHAPELLE DUVELLE. | ,, | 10.37 a.m. | | - |

SECRET.

To/

All RECIPIENTS of 171st Infantry Brigade Order No. 34.

. . . . . . . . . . . . . . . .

Reference March Table attached to 171st Infantry Brigade Order No. 34 - Times in Column 5 should be amended as under :-

Line 4 for 9-51 am. read 10.1 am.
"    5  "  10-2 am. read 10.12 am.
"    6  "  10.12 am. read 10.22 am.
"    7  "  10.19 am. read 10.29 am.
"    8  "  10.27 am. read 10.31 am.
"    9  "  10.30 am. read 10.40 am.
"   10  "  10.37 am. read 10.47 am.

500 yards interval will be maintained between Units except as under :-

Brigade HdQrs and 2/8th K.L.R.,
171st L.T.M.B., and 421st Field Co, R.E.,

ACKNOWLEDGE.

Captain, Brigade Major.
171st Infantry Brigade.

B.H.Q.
17.9.1917

## ADMINISTRATIVE ORDERS.

1. Units will be billetted in BUSNES AREA as follows :-

| | |
|---|---|
| Brigade Headquarters | - LA MIQUELLERIE. |
| 2/7th K.L.R. | - LA PERRIERRE. |
| 2/8th K.L.R. | - CONTRAINNE. |
| 2/6th K.L.R. ) | - ECLEME. |
| 2/5th K.L.R. ) | - ,, |
| 2/2nd Wessex F.Amb. | - BUSNES - RUE BRASSERIE. billets - 85 to 90, 72,76,78. |
| 507 Coy. A.S.C. | - BUSNES - RUE DELALLEAU billets - 61,63 (Offcrs.only),92. |
| 171st M.G.Coy. | - BUSNES - billets 13,14,16,17,26, 31,32,33,53. |
| 421st Fd.Coy.R.E. | - BUSNES - billets 1-9. |
| 171st L.T.M.Bty. | - BUSNES - RUE BRASSERIE. |

Billetting Parties from all Units (in case of Bns: consisting of 5 N.C.Os.) will report to STAFF CAPTAIN on 18th instant at 8-0 am. prompt at BUSNES CHURCH.

2. **POSTAL ARRANGEMENTS.**

18th instant - BUSNES AREA. POST OFFICE-LA MIQUELLERIE.
Units may draw mail and post letters at 7-0 pm.

19th instant - ST HILAIRE. POST OFFICE - BRIGADE HEADQUARTERS.

3. **VACATION OF BILLETS.**   Units will take necessary steps to ensure that billets are left thoroughly clean.

4. **BUSSES.**   ---   Instructions will be issued later.

(sd) J.G.BEAZLEY, Captain,
Staff Captain,
171st Infantry Brigade.

SECRET.

Ref.Map.
Sheet 36 A.
1/40,000.

COPY No. 17

171st INFANTRY BRIGADE ORDER No.35.

18th Sept. 1917.

1. On Wednesday, September 19th 1917, the Brigade Group will move from BUSNES Area to ST HILAIRE Area.

2. Units will pass the Starting Points as per attached March Tables "A" and "B".

3. A Horse Ambulance will follow in rear of 2/6th K.L.R., 2/8th K.L.R., and 2/7th K.L.R. These will join their Units at their respective Starting Points.

4. Units in Table "B" will march under the command of Lieut.Colonel C.S.Baines, D.S.O., 2/7th K.L.R.,

5. One Officer to command the rear party of Units mentioned in Table "A" will be detailed by O.C., 2/6th K.L.R., This party will be formed at the Starting Point.

6. All Units will report their arrival in their Billets at once, giving the location of Headquarters. Units will also report the number of men fallen out.

ACKNOWLEDGE.

Captain, Brigade Major.
171st Infantry Brigade.


ISSUED AT 6 p.m., to :-

Copy No. 1.  D.G.C.,
2.  Brigade Major.
3.  Staff Captain.
4.  37th Division, "G".
5.     "       "Q".
6.  2/5th K.L.R.,
7.  2/6th K.L.R.,
8.  2/7th K.L.R.,
9.  2/8th K.L.R.,
10. 171st L.T.M.B.,
11. 171st M.G.Co.,
12. 421st Field Co, R.E.,
13. Signals, 171st Bde.
14. 2/2nd Wessex Field Ambce.
15. No.3 Coy, 37th Divl. Train.
16. R.E., LINES.
17. War Diary.
18.    "
19. Spare.
20. File.

MARCH TABLE issued with 171st INFANTRY BRIGADE ORDER No.35.

| Serial No. | UNIT. | FROM. | TO. | Pass Starting Point. U.11.c.15.80. | ROUTE. | REMARKS. |
|---|---|---|---|---|---|---|
| | | | TABLE "A". | | | |
| 1. | 171st Bde H.Q. | LA MIQUELLERIE. | COURCQ. | 9.35 a.m. | | From BOURCQ via ST HILAIRE and NOTRE ST PORCIEN. |
| 2. | 2/8th K.L.R. | CANTRAINES. | PONTES. | 9.36 a.m. | LILLERS. BOURCQ. | |
| 3. | 2/5th K.L.R. | LOCKERS. | ST HILAIRE. | 9.47 a.m. | | |
| 4. | 2/6th K.L.R. | " | " | 10. 8 a.m. | | |
| 5. | 171st L.T.M.B. | BURNES. | MAREUIL. | 10.19 a.m. | | Branch off at Cross Roads U.I.c.20.55. |
| 6. | 421st Fd.Co R.E. | " | " | 10.20 a.m. | | " |
| 7. | 2/2nd Essex Rd Labcc. | " | BOURCQ. | 10.28 a.m. | | " |
| 8. | No.5 Co 57th Divl.Train. | " | " | 10.33 a.m. | | |

| Serial No. | UNIT. | FROM. | TO. | Pass Starting Point. 0.30.c.15.50. | ROUTE. | REMARKS. |
|---|---|---|---|---|---|---|
| | | | TABLE "B". | | | |
| 9. | 2/7th K.L.R. | LA HERRIERE. | MAISON BLANCHE. | 10. 5 a.m. | Via LE CORNET BOURBOIS - HAM EN ARTOIS - Road Junction, 0.21.c.2.0. | PORTES - Cross Roads N.34.c.55.70. LINGHEM - Cross Roads N.25.c.70.25. Cross Roads M.30.b.85.95. |
| 10. | 171st M.G.Co. | BUSNES. | " | 10.15 a.m. | | |

APPENDIX No. III.

MINOR OPERATIONS,

Referred to in

171st INFANTRY BRIGADE WAR DIARY,

1.9.1917
to
30.9.1917,

..

CONFIDENTIAL.

Headquarters,
57th Division.
................

Report on the Circumstances leading to the
capture of 2 prisoners - 101-R.I.R. - by
2/8th Bn. K.L.R. on night 5th/6th Sept. 1917.

---

2 Patrols - (a) Lt. W.Ross & 22 Other Ranks, and
(b) 2/Lt. J.A. Free, M.C. and 23 O.Ranks.
working in conjunction with one another left the
CORDONNERIE Sector at 9-20 pm. amd 8-55 pm. respectively.

'A' Patrol had instructions to follow the RIVER LAIES
from N.9.c.58.72. - the point where our parapet crosses
the river - to N.14.b.85.93, thence to N.15.a.2.6. At
this point they were to 'lie up' for any enemy party and,
if succesful in finding any, to capture prisoners.
This patrol reached their objective and laid up for
some hours but found no trace of any enemy and returned on
the agreed signal. Enemy trenches were derelict and
uninhabitable; the tramline immediately behind his front
line is destroyed.

'B' Patrol left our lines at the same place and
proceeded to enemy front line N.9.d.25.10. The road
behind the front line is completely obliterated and progress
was slow. Point N.15.b.35.83. was reached. Here sounds
of a working party to the West of the patrol were heard.

2nd Lieut. Free retained one N.C.O., Cpl. Edwards,
with him, and split the remainder into two parties, each
under an N.C.O. and ordered them to approach the working
party from either flank, while he and Cpl. Edwards advanced
towards the working party from their rear. Apparently
too little time was allowed for the flanking parties to
reach their positions with the result that 2nd Lt. Free and
Cpl. Edwards attacked the working party - strength 15 - alone
2nd Lieut. Free fired 6 rounds from his revolver, Cpl.
Edwards 10 rounds from his rifle, killing one German and
inflicting wounds on five others (estimated). The enemy
party fled leaving 2 prisoners, who were brought into our
lines. The signal to withdraw was then sent.

We sustained no casualties.

Bde. H.Q.,
8. 9. 1917.

Brigadier-General,
Comdg. 171st Infantry Brigade.

Confidential.

War Diary.

Headquarters,
    57th (W.Lancs.) Division.

H.Q.,
171ST
INFANTRY BRIGADE.
No. BM/550
Date............

At 4-25 am. the enemy opened a barrage on the support line from N.9.a.9.4. to N.10.a.9.4. This barrage was composed chiefly of shrapnel and 4.2 Howitzers.

At 4-30 am. The barrage lifted on to the front line from N.9.c.9.6. to N.10.c.8.6. This barrage was composed chiefly of shrapnel, Trench Mortars and Pineapples.

The S.O.S. was sent up at 4-35 am. This was carried out by rocket from the support line to the Artillery whose barrage came down at 4-40 am. This S.O.S. was not repeated to Brigade Headquarters and hence was not forwarded to you. On the firing being heard the Battalion was rung up from here and stated that with the exception of shelling of the centre company all was correct.

At 5-0 am. the firing diminished.

No enemy were seen but whistles were heard in the German Lines and Golden Rain lights were sent up from his Support Line.

On investigation this morning the enemy appears to have cut a gap in our wire in front of No. 6 Post (N.10.5.). Whether this was in conjunction with the barrage it is difficult to say as he has cut a gap in a different place to the area where he put down the barrage.

Information has just been received that enemy egg and stick bombs, also enemy steel helmet, have been found in front of No.5 Post at the top of MINE AVENUE.

A track through the wire has also just been discovered here which shows evidence of someone having been dragged through it.

Bde. H. Q.,
15. 9. 17.

Brigadier-General,
Commanding, 171st Infantry Brigade.

AQ171 Supp 86
(51st dw.)
of 9.
October 1917

On His Majesty's Service.

CONFIDENTIAL

War Diary
—of—
18 Casualty Clearing Station
(Column 3)

From - 1.10.17
To - 31.10.17

WAR DIARY

of

HEADQUARTERS, 171st INFANTRY BRIGADE,

1.10.1917

to

31.10.1917.

.....

VOLUME VIII.

...

Army Form C. 2118

# WAR DIARY
## or
## INTELLIGENCE SUMMARY
*(Erase heading not required.)*

Instructions regarding War Diaries and Intelligence Summaries are contained in F.S. Regs., Part II. and the Staff Manual respectively. Title Pages will be prepared in manuscript.

| Place | Date | Hour | Summary of Events and Information | Remarks and references to Appendices |
|---|---|---|---|---|
| ST. HILAIRE COTTES | 1.X.17 | | Training continued by all Units | |
| | 2.X.17 | | do | |
| | 3.X.17 | | do | |
| | 4.X.17 | | do | |
| | 5.X.17 | | do | |
| | 6.X.17 | | Inspection by C in C near ESTRÉE BLANCHE — Very wet. | |
| | 7.X.17 | | Sunday. Training suspended | |
| | 8.X.17 | | Brigade practised the attack in BOMY MANOEUVRE area | |
| | 9.X.17 | | Training continued by all Units. | |
| | 10.X.17 | | do | |
| | 11.X.17 | | do | |
| | 12.X.17 | | do | |
| | 13.X.17 | | do | |
| | 14.X.17 | | Sunday. Training suspended | |
| | 15.X.17 | | Training continued by all Units | |
| | 16.X.17 | | do | |

# WAR DIARY or INTELLIGENCE SUMMARY

Army Form C. 2118

(Erase heading not required.)

Instructions regarding War Diaries and Intelligence Summaries are contained in F.S. Regs., Part II. and the Staff Manual respectively. Title Pages will be prepared in manuscript.

| Place | Date | Hour | Summary of Events and Information | Remarks and references to Appendices |
|---|---|---|---|---|
| ST. HILAIRE COTTES | 17.X.17 | | Training continued by all Units. | S.g.f. S.g.f. |
|  | 18.X.17 | | All units cleaning billets, refitting and making preparations for move. | S.g.f. |
| RENESCURE | 19.X.17 | | Brigade moved to RENESCURE area, by march route. Head of column arriving at 1.30 p.m. | appendix I S.g.f. |
| PROVEN area No 4 | 20.X.17 | | Brigade moved to PROVEN area N.4. Infantry in Busses. Transport by road. Camps were reached early in the afternoon. | appendix II S.g.f. |
|  | 21.X.17 | | Sunday. Brigade halted | S.g.f. |
|  | 22.X.17 | | Brigade halted in billets. Weather wet — Camps very muddy + dirty. | S.g.f. |
|  | 23.X.17 | | Brigade halted in camps, completing arrangements for move to MALAKOFF area | S.g.f. |
| MALAKOFF area | 24.X.17 | | Brigade moved to MALAKOFF area — Entraining commenced at PROVEN at 12.0 noon. completed by 4.0 p.m. All units reported arrived in Camps by 7.0 p.m. Bde H.Qrs. at ULM FARM | appendix II S.g.f. |
|  | 25.X.17 | | Brigade H.Qrs. remained at ULM FARM — 2/8 K.L.R moved up to EAGLE TRENCH: Its support line in LANGEMARCK sector — 2/5 K.L.R moved into MARSOUIN FARM area. Trenches &/or Bivouacs to all units | appendix II S.g.f. |
| LANGEMARCK area | 26.X.17 | | Brigade relieved 170 Inf. Bde in the line in LANGEMARCK sector, relief being completed early in the morning of 27/X. Advanced Bde. H.Qrs established at STRAY FARM. Rear H.Qrs. at FUSILIER HOUSE in the CANAL BANK. The front line held by the Bde extends from REQUETE FARM on the right to BROEMBEEK on the left having in front of it BESACE FARM, BOWER HOUSE and GRAVEL FARM. The ground is waterlogged and the digging of trenches impossible. The line consequently consists of consolidated shell holes with advanced posts in shell holes in front of the line. Party brought corps reserve and ammunition to support line EAGLE TRENCH. 2/5 K.L.R in support. 2/6 K.L.R & 2/7 K.L.R being in reserve | appendix II S.g.f. |

# WAR DIARY or INTELLIGENCE SUMMARY

Army Form C. 2118

(Erase heading not required.)

| Place | Date | Hour | Summary of Events and Information | Remarks and references to Appendices |
|---|---|---|---|---|
| LANGEMARCK 0180 | 27.X.17 | | Hostile artillery consistently active on front line — Cross roads at LANGEMARCK were heavily shelled during the evening by H.E. and some Gas shells. 2/5 KLR relieved 2/8 KLR in front line; 2/6 KLR moved up into support - EAGLE TRENCH - 2/8 KLR withdrew to HOBBLESTON CAMP. | a few |
| " | 28.X.17 | | Continued hostile artillery activity which interfered with relief and with working parties. Large numbers of GAS shells were employed by the enemy and the presence of GAS was spoken of generally N.E. of LANGEMARCK. 2/6 KLR relieved 2/5 KLR in front line, 2/7 KLR moving up into support. EAGLE TRENCH. | |
| " | 29.X.17 | | Sniping activity still confined to artillery fire. This was directed onto our front line and the approaches — particularly LANGEMARCK - POELCAPELLE road. One working party sustained 30% casualties chiefly from GAS. | |
| " | 30.X.17 | | The farms in rear of our line and the front line itself were heavily harassed in reply to our artillery preparation for the attack on our right flank. One prisoner of 2nd Regt MARINE INFANTRY and one enemy M.G. were captured. The 2/7 KLR relieved 2/6 KLR in front line. The 2/8 KLR moving up into support line EAGLE TRENCH. | |

1875  Wt. W593/826  1,000,000  11/15  T.P.C. & A.  A.D.S.S./Forms/C. 2118.

Army Form C. 2118

# WAR DIARY
## or
## INTELLIGENCE SUMMARY  IV
(Erase heading not required.)

Instructions regarding War Diaries and Intelligence Summaries are contained in F.S. Regs., Part II. and the Staff Manual respectively. Title Pages will be prepared in manuscript.

| Place | Date | Hour | Summary of Events and Information | Remarks and references to Appendices |
|---|---|---|---|---|
| LANGEMARCK area | 31-X-17 | | Hostile activity still confined to artillery fire and Gas Shells - though his aeroplanes dropped bombs lots on front line and back areas. A few casualties being inflicted. On hereonly of transport by R.E.'s whose billets are at BRIDGE junction. Support line EAGLE TRENCH was heavily shelled for an hour during the evening & sustained about 20 casualties. No relief took place in our sector. | S.J.t. |
| | | | Note. From 26 - 31 whilst Brigade was in LANGEMARCK sector 50th Division have been operating on our left and 58th Division on our right. | |

Montgomerie, Brig. Genl.
Comdg. 171st
Bde.

1875  Wt. W593/826  1,000,000  4/15  T.P.C. & A.  A.D.S.S./Forms/C. 2118.

APPENDIX I.

RELIEF ORDERS, etc.,

referred to in

171st INFANTRY BRIGADE WAR DIARY,

1.10. 1917

to

31.10. 1917

.....

SECRET.

171st INFANTRY BRIGADE ORDER No.37.

COPY NO. 14

8th October, 1917.

GENERAL SITUATION.
1. The First Army has been ordered to attack on Zero Day, the main objective being the track from DELETTE to R.22.b.9.4 - M.19.b.55 - M.15.d.8.0.
    The 171st Infantry Brigade has been ordered to attack on Zero Day from our trenches R.11.a.30.05 - R.11.b.45.10.    The Brigade has been given two objectives:-
    (1) The line R.17.a.10.75 - R.17.b.20.70.
    (2) The road R.22.b.75.50 - R.23.a.90.20.
    The 170th Infantry Brigade is attacking on our left, and the 1st Brigade, 1st Division, on our right.    The 172nd Infantry Brigade is in reserve.

OBJECTIVES and BOUNDARIES.
2. These are shown on the attached Map - Appendix "A". Both objectives will be consolidated, covered by Lewis Gun Sections pushed out 50 to 100 yards in front of the line to be consolidated.
    Enemy strong points shown on the attached Map will be consolidated by Moppers-Up.

METHOD of ATTACK.
3. At Zero, the 2/5th K.L.R., and 2/6th K.L.R., will move forward, capture and consolidate the first objective, BLUE LINE, 2/5th K.L.R., on the right, 2/6th K.L.R. on the left.
    The 2/8th K.L.R. and 2/7th K.L.R. will be formed up on W. and E. side respectively of the road running N. and S. through R.5.B.
    At Zero, these Battalions will move forward and occupy the positions vacated by the 2/5th and 2/6th K.L.R. respectively.
    At Zero plus 30 mins. they will start to move forward, and will pass through the 2/5th K.L.R. and 2/6th K.L.R. respectively and get up to the barrages, moving forward ~~with the same~~ at Zero plus 56 mins, to capture and consolidate the 2nd objective, GREEN LINE.

    Each Battalion will attack on a frontage of 300 yards with 3 Companies each on a Platoon frontage; the 2nd and 4th Platoons will be Moppers-Up, and will be allotted definite areas.
    Each Battalion will have one Company in reserve.
    In every case, the barrage must be followed as closely as possible.

LOCATION of HdQrs.
4.  2/5th K.L.R.,   Right Battn.              )
    and 2/8th K.L.R., Right Battn.(taking     )  R.11.a.60.70
                      final objective).       )

    2/6th K.L.R., Left Battn. (taking         )
                      first objective)        )  R.11.b.40.60
    and 2/7th K.L.R., Left Battn. (taking     )
                      final objective).       )

    The Battalion HdQrs of the Battalions taking the final objective will, when it has been taken and the situation permits, move forward to the sunken road in R.17.A. having previously established a forward Command Post there.
    Brigade HdQrs in OLD QUARRY, G.31.b.5.8.
    Advanced Brigade HdQrs at R.5.b.4.9.
    Brigade Forward Station, R.11.a.9.1.

3.

**CONTACT AEROPLANES.**   11. An aeroplane will fly over the Brigade front between zero (12.30 p.m.) and zero plus 3 hours (3-0 p.m.)
Flare will be lit :-
(a) When called for.
(b) About zero plus 40 mins. (1.10 p.m.) (when called for).
(c) About zero plus 145 mins. (2.55 p.m.) (when called for).
Reference (b) and (c), at these hours the Infantry will be on the lookout for the contact aeroplanes.
Flare will only be lit by the leading line of troops.

**DRESS.**   12. Fighting Order.

13. Prisoners of War will be sent back via Brigade HdQrs to Divisional Cage at L.30.a.5.3.

14. Watches will be synchronised at Advanced Brigade HdQrs at 10 a.m. on October 8th.

15. Zero Day will be October 8th.
Zero hour, 12.30 p.m.
Battalions will be in position by 12 noon on Zero Day.

**NOTES**   16. (a) All men made casualties by the Umpires will take off their helmets and remain where they are, but will continue to watch the operations.
(b) Barrage will be represented by a line of men carrying flags.
(c) Ground signal sheets will be laid out at all Battalion and at Brigade HdQrs, and communication by panel with the contact aeroplane will be practised.
(d) Battalions will forward their orders by 7.30 p.m. tomorrow, October 7th.

17. Further Appendices re Communications, Dumps, etc. will be forwarded later.

18. ACKNOWLEDGE.

Captain, Brigade Major.
171st Infantry Brigade.

ISSUED TO :-

Copy No. 1. B.G.C.,
2. Brigade Major.
3. Staff Captain.
4. Intelligence Officer.
5. HdQrs, 57th Division.
6. O.C., 2/5th K.L.R.,
7. 2/6th ,,
8. 2/7th ,,
9. 2/8th ,,
10. 171st L.T.M.B.,
11. 171st M.G.Coy.
12. 421st Field Co., R.E.
13. R.F.C.,
14. War Diary.
15. ,,
16.)
17.)

SECRET.

MARCH ORDERS attached to 171st INFANTRY BRIGADE
ORDER No. 37.

Sheet 36A.
1:40,000.
THEROUANNE.
1:40,000.

......

For tomorrow's Attack Scheme, Units will assemble as under :-

2/7th & 2/8th K.L.R.)
42lst Fd.Co, R.E.,    )    Place of Assembly,    R.5.B.
171st L.G.Coy.        )

2/5th & 2/6th K.L.R.)
171st L.T.M.B.,       )         ,,         ,,      R.5.D.

Battalions will be at Point of Assembly by 10 a.m. and will be clear of Railway Bridge, M.22.d.4.3. by the times stated below :-

  2/7th K.L.R.,   8.25 a.m.    2/5th K.L.R.,   8.55 a.m.
  2/8th   ,,      8.35 a.m.    171st L.G.Co.   9. 0 a.m.
  2/6th   ,,      8.45 a.m.    171st L.T.M.B.  9. 5 a.m.
    42lst Field Co, R.E.,  9.10 a.m.

and will march on THEROUANNE road to M.8.Central, thence via ENGUINEGATTE, N.7.D.

......

At the conclusion of Operations - at about 3.30 pm - "Stand Fast" will mean that Units close, and Umpires assemble at road junction, R.23.a.3.2.

The "No Parade", followed by "Officer's Call" will mean, Units march home under dismounted Officers.

Mounted Officers will assemble at road junction, R.23.a.3.2.

......

O.C., 2/8th K.L.R. will provide a Bugler, who will report at R.II.d.4.7 at II a.m.,

      R W Patterson
      Captain, Brigade Major,
      171st Infantry Brigade.

ISSUED at 2 p.m., 7.10.1917, to all Recipients of
  171st Brigade Order No.37.

....

SECRET.

APPENDICES to 171st INFANTRY BRIGADE ORDER No.37.
..............

## APPENDIX "C".

BARRAGE.
Barrages will move by bounds — each bound 100 yds.
The signal to move forward will be given by the Brigade Intelligence Officer, who will be in charge of the creeping barrage.

When the barrage moves forward to the next position, barrage flags will be lowered, and the men will double forward and raise the flags again on reaching the next barrage line.

Posts have been placed in position on both flanks in depth at 100 yds interval, to mark the bounds made by barrage.

After crossing the GREEN LINE, barrage men will occupy and take cover in a line of pits, which have been dug about 200 yds beyond the GREEN LINE.

When 3 "G's" are sounded to signal the "Commence Fire" for Lewis Guns and Rifles, barrage men must keep well down in their pits, and remain so until fire has been stopped by sounding 4 "G's".

8 Stretcher Bearers will report from each Battalion to Lieut. Harkby at 11 a.m., 8th instant, at R.11.d.4.7, where barrage flags will be issued.

## APPENDIX "D".

COMMUNICATIONS.
Advanced Signal Station at R.11.a.9.1. This will be pushed forward to a point near R.17.b.1.7 when the situation allows.

Power Buzzer.
One Set (sending) will be taken forward and established by 2/8th and 2/7th K.L.R. at their Forward Command Post.

Wireless.
Will be established between Brigade HdQrs (Advanced) and Divisional HdQrs. (Imaginary).

Runners.
As soon as the first objective has been taken, O.C., 2/5th K.L.R. will establish a chain of Runner Posts to R.17.a.10.80.

Pigeons.
One pair of Pigeons will be given to each 2/7th and 2/8th K.L.R., who will arrange for same to accompany Advance Party to Forward Command Post.

Central Visual Receiving Station, at R.11.d.4.6
Sending Station, will be established by the Brigade at Forward Signal Station, R.17.b.1.7.   2/8th K.L.R. will establish Sending Station near R.23.a.2.5.   This Station will send direct to the Brigade Advanced Signal Station.

3.

## APPENDIX "G".

**DUMPS.**

Dumps, each containing 40 Boxes S.A.A., 600 Boxes Mills' No.5, 600 Boxes Rifle Grenades No.23 & No.24, S.O.S. Rockets, and Very Lights, have been established at :-
(1) Advanced Brigade HdQrs.
(2) Vicinity of Battn. HdQrs at R.II.a.60.70.

The Brigade will be responsible for keeping No.(2) Dump Supplied. The Battalions will be responsible for establishing Forward Dumps in the area of Operations, drawing on No.2 Dump for this purpose.
Battalions will tell off Carrying Parties, ready to go forward as soon as the situation allows.

## APPENDIX "H".

**MEDICAL ARRANGEMENTS.**

Advanced Dressing Station at R.5.b.6.0.
Main Dressing Station at L.28.b.5.2.
Battalion Aid Posts will be established in vicinity of front line. After GREEN LINE has been captured, Battalion Aid Posts will be moved forward under orders of Os.C. Units.

## APPENDIX "I".

**FIRE ARRANGEMENTS.**

The following Signals will be used to open and cease fire :-

1. Stokes Mortars.
Open Fire, 1 "G". Cease Fire, 2 "Gs"

2. Rifles & Lewis Guns.
Open Fire, 3 "Gs". Cease Fire, 4 "Gs".

3. (a) Stokes Mortars will be used for rapid fire on enemy Support Line from Zero to Zero plus 2 minutes.
O.C. 171st L.T.M.B. will put out lookout men on both flanks previous to Zero hour.
(b) Rifle and Lewis Gun fire will only be used after reaching GREEN LINE against a line of disappearing targets which are situated 200 yds beyond the 2nd Objective (GREEN LINE).

When 3 "Gs" sound and the targets, representing an enemy counter-attack, appear, the front line of sections only will open fire immediately to their front, and cease fire as soon as the targets disappear again, or on 4 "Gs" being sounded. The firing should be steady, and every shot carefully aimed. Section Leaders are responsible for controlling the fire of their sections, and will not fire themselves.

Dummy Rifle Grenades will be used in attacking Strong Points, etc., but every care will be taken to prevent their fire being dangerous, especially with reference to the men representing the barrage.

..................

SECRET.                                               COPY NO. 16

### 171st INFANTRY BRIGADE ORDER NO. 38.

OCTOBER 15th, 1917.

Map.
HAZEBROUCK.
Sheet 5.c.
1/100,000.

1. 171st Brigade Group will move from ST. HILAIRE AREA to the RENESCURE AREA on October 19th, 1917.

2. Units will pass the starting point, MAZINGHEM Cross Roads, in accordance with the attached March Table.

3. A distance of 100 yards will be maintained between each Company and Battalion Transport, and 500 yards between each Battalion, 2/2nd Wessex Field Ambulance and 421st Field Company, R.E.

4. Billeting parties will proceed by bus on the morning of October 19th, under arrangements to be made by Staff Captain.

ACKNOWLEDGE.

*R W Watters*

Captain, Brigade Major,
171st Infantry Brigade.

DISTRIBUTION -

1. 57th Division "G".
2. 57th Division "Q".
3. 2/5th K.L.R.
4. 2/6th ,,
5. 2/7th ,,
6. 2/8th ,,
7. 171st M.G.Coy.
8. 171st L.T.M.B.
9. 421st Fd. Coy. R.E.
10. 2/2nd Wessex Fd. Amb.
11. No. 3 Coy. A.S.C.
12. B.G.C.
13. Brigade Major.
14. Staff Captain.
15. 171st Bde. Signals.
16. War Diary.
17. War Diary.
18. Spare.

MARCH TABLE issued with 171st INFANTRY BRIGADE ORDER No. 38.

| Serial Number. | UNIT. | FROM. | TO. | To pass Starting Point, MAZINGHEM CROSS-ROADS. | ROUTE. |
|---|---|---|---|---|---|
| 1 | 171st Bde H.Qrs. | COTTES. | RENESCURE. | 9. 0 a.m. | AIRE - WITTES - RACQUINGHEM - BELLE CROIX, thence by most direct road to Billets. |
| 2 | 2/8th K.L.R., | FONTES. | ,, | 9. 2 a.m. | |
| 3 | 2/6th ,, | ST HILAIRE. | WARDRECQUES. | 9.16 a.m. | |
| 4 | 2/5th ,, | COTTES. | RENESCURE. | 9.30 a.m. | |
| 5 | 171st L.T.M.B., | LESTHESSES. | ,, | 9.45 a.m. | |
| 6 | 171st M.G.Coy. | FONTES | ,, | 9.47 a.m. | |
| 7 | 421st Fd.Co RE. | LESPNESSES. | BANDRINGHEM. | 10. 6 a.m. | |
| 8 | 2/2nd Wessex Fd. Ambco. | BOURECQ. | ,, | 10.15 a.m. | |
| 9 | No.3 Coy, 57th Divl. Train. | ,, | RENESCURE. | 10.21 a.m. | |
| 10 | 2/7th K.L.R., | ESTREE BLANCHE | HEURINGHEM. | To be North of Railway Brigade, ESTREE BLANCHE, by 9 a.m. | THEROUANNE. |

AMENDMENTS

to

171st INFANTRY BRIGADE ORDER NO. 38.

------------------------------------------

The following amendments should be made to March Table attached to 171st Infantry Brigade Order No. 38:-

<u>Amendments to Column 4 "TO".</u>

| | | | | | |
|---|---|---|---|---|---|
| Serial No. | 2 | for | RENESCURE | read | COIN PERDU. North of FORET DE CLAIRMARAIS. |
| ,, ,, | 3 | ,, | WARDRECQUES | ,, | RENESCURE. |
| ,, ,, | 7 | ,, | BANDRINGHEM | ,, | CAMPAGNE. |
| ,, ,, | 8 | ,, | BANDRINGHEM | ,, | CAMPAGNE. |
| ,, ,, | 10 | ,, | HEURINGHEM | ,, | CAMPAGNE. |

<u>Amendments to Column 6 "ROUTE".</u>

Serial No. 10 - After THEROUANNE add BELLE CROIX.

Please ACKNOWLEDGE.

*[signature]*

B. H. Q.,
16.10.17.

Captain, Brigade Major,
171st Infantry Brigade.

ISSUED to all Recipients
of 171st Infantry
Brigade Order No. 38.

Copy No.16

## ADMINISTRATIVE ORDERS IN CONNECTION WITH
## 171st INFANTRY BRIGADE OPERATION ORDER NUMBER 38.

1. **BILLETS.** Units will be billeted during the night of 19th October as stated in March Table and Amendment of Brigade Operation Order No.38.

2. **MECHANICAL TRANSPORT.** Motor lorries are allotted as mentioned below for the two days of the move and will rendezvous as follows:-

| Unit. | Lorries allotted. | Rendezvous | Time. |
|---|---|---|---|
| 171st B.H.Q. | 1 | ) Reference Sheet | 8.0. am. Date 19/10/17 |
| 2/5th K.L.R. | 2 | ) Hazebrouck 5 A | |
| 2/6th K.L.R. | 2 | ) Cross Roads | |
| 421st Field Coy. | 1 | ) 6.E.85.80 S.E. | |
| 171st L.T.M.B. | 1 | ) of C in COTTES. | |
| 2/7th K.L.R. | 2 | Level Crossing on the RELY-ESTREE BLANCHE RD. | 7.0. am. |
| 2/8th K.L.R. | 2 | ) Cross Roads FONTES | 8.0. am. |
| 171st M.G.Coy. | 1 | ) near H.Q. 2/8th. | |

A guide from each Unit will report at rendezvous at time stated.
Loading parties of 4 men will be detailed for each lorry, and will proceed with lorry to destination.
Lorries will be loaded by 8.45.am. Motor lorries will move under orders of O.C. D.S.C.

3. **BAGGAGE WAGONS.** Baggage wagons will report to Units at 4.0.p.m. 18th October. These wagons will rendezvous and march under orders from O.C. No. 3 Coy, Divisional Train.

4. **TRANSPORT.** Transport will march in rear of Units on October 19th.

5. **BILLETING PARTIES.** Billeting parties for RENESCURE AREA will report at 5.30.pm. 18.10.17 to Units of 172nd Infantry Brigade at places stated below and will take over billets vacated by them on 19.10.17.

| Unit of 171st Brigade. | Strength. | Unit of 172nd Brigade. | PLACE. |
|---|---|---|---|
| 2/5th K.L.R. | 1 Off.4 N.C.Os. | 2/9th K.L.R. | Renescure (Chesel Rd.Area) |
| 2/6th K.L.R. | - do - | 2/5th S.L.R. | Renescure.-do- |
| 171st L.T.M.B. | 1 N.C.O. | 172nd LTMB. | Renescure |
| 171st M.G.Coy. | 1 N.C.O. | 172nd MGCoy. | ,, |
| No.3 Coy.Div.Tn. | 1 N.C.O. | No.4 Coy.DT. | ,, |
| 2/7th K.L.R. | 1 Off.4 N.C.Os. | 2/4th S.L.R. | Campagne. |
| 421st FieldCoy. | 2 N.C.Os. | 505 Coy.R.E. | ,, |
| 2/2 Wessex F.A. | 2 N.C.Os. | 2/3 Wessex FA. | ,, |
| 2/8th K.L.R. | 1 Off.4 N.C.Os. | 2/10th K.L.R. | Coin Perdu. |

Billeting parties for PROVEN AREA will report on 19.10.17 at times and places stated below. These parties will proceed direct to PROVEN AREA by motor bus.

| Unit. | Strength. | Rendezvous | Time. |
|---|---|---|---|
| 171st B.H.Q. | 1 N.C.O. Officer ) | | |
| 2/5th K.L.R. | 1 Off,4 N.C.Os) | At | |
| 2/6th K.L.R. | - do - ) | Headquarters | |
| 2/7th K.L.R. | - do - ) | 171st | 8.0.am. |
| 421st Coy.RE. | 1 Off.1 N.C.O.) | Infantry | |
| 171st LTMB. | 1 N.C.O. ) | Brigade. | |
| 2/2nd WessexFA. | -do- ) | | |
| 2/8th K.L.R. | 1 Off.4 N.C.Os) | At Headquarters | 8.10.am. |
| 171st MGCoy. | 1 N.C.O. ) | 2/8th KLR. FONTES. | |

- 2 -

6. REFILLING POINT. Refilling Point on 19.10.17 will be at the Square, Renescure. An N.C.O. from each Unit will report at the Refilling Point at 10.30.am on 19.10.17 for the purpose of drawing rations, and acting as guide to Mechanical Transport. *billetting party of*

7. MEDICAL ARRANGEMENTS. O.C. 2/2nd Wessex Field Ambulance will arrange to collect cases requiring evacuating from Units between 7.and 7.30.a.m. on 19.10.17. O.C. 2/ 2nd Wessex Field Ambulance will arrange to have the following roads traversed by motor ambulances under his own arrangements:-
Route taken from ST HILAIRE to RENESCURE and COIN PERU, also route taken by 2/7th K.L.R. from ESTREE BLANCHE to CAMPAGNE.

B.H.Q.
17.10.17.

Lieut.
A/Staff Captain,
171st Infantry Brigade.

Issued at 7.30.p.m. to:-

Copy No. 1. B.G.C.
2. Brigade Major.
3. 57th Division.
4. 172nd Brigade.
5. O.C.57th Divisional Train.
6. Area Commandant, Renescure.
7. 2/5th K.L.R.
8. 2/6th K.L.R.
9. 2/7th K.L.R.
10. 2/8th K.L.R.
11. 171st L.T.M.B.
12. 171st M.G.Coy.
13. 421st Field Coy.R.E.
14. 2/2nd Wessex Field A.
15. 507 Coy. A.S.C.
16. War Diary.
17. "
18. File.
19. File.
20. Spare.

SECRET.

COPY NO. 16

# 171st INFANTRY BRIGADE OPERATION ORDER NO.39.

......                                    October, 19th, 1917.

1. The 171st Brigade will move from RENESCURE AREA to PROVEN AREA tomorrow, October 20th, 1917.

2. Units will embus as under :-

(a) All Units of the Brigade except the 2/8th K.L.R. will embus on the ARQUES - EBLINGHEM - HAZEBROUCK Road at 8 a.m.
Units will be formed up by 7.45 a.m. in the following order, with head of column at the Road Junction immediately South of the N. in EBLINGHEM:-

    171st Infantry Brigade HdQrs.
    171st Machine Gun Coy.
    171st Light T.M.Battery.
    2/5th K.L.R.,
    2/6th K.L.R.,
    2/7th K.L.R.,
    421st Field Coy, R.E.,
    2/2nd Wessex Field Abce.

There will be 25 yds interval between each Unit, and 10 yds between each Company.

(b) The 2/8th K.L.R. on the CASSEL - ARQUES Road, at 7.45 a.m. Head of the Column will be at the Corss Roads, LE NIEPPE, facing S.W., When the Battalion has embussed, this Column will proceed to RENESCURE, to join remainder of column mentioned in (a).

3. The embussing will be carried out in accordance with 5th Army Memo, attached.

4. Billeting Parties will meet Battalions at Debussing Point, under arrangements to be made by Staff Captain.

ACKNOWLEDGE.

                                Captain, Brigade Major.
                                171st Infantry Brigade.

DISTRIBUTION :-

    Copy No. 1.  57th Division, "G".
            2.       "     "Q".
            3.  2/5th K.L.R.
            4.  2/6th  ,,
            5.  2/7th  ,,
            6.  2/8th  ,,
            7.  171st M.G.Co.
            8.  171st L.T.M.B.,
            9.  421st Field Co, R.E.
          10.  2/2nd Wessex Field Ambce.
          11.  No. 3 Coy, A.S.C.,
          12.  B.G.C.,
          13.  Brigade Major.
          14.  Staff Captain.
          15.  171st Brigade Signals.
          16.  War Diary.
          17.  ,,
          18.  Spare.

SECRET.

Copy No......16

## ADMINISTRATIVE ORDERS IN CONNECTION WITH
## 171st INFANTRY BRIGADE OPERATION ORDER NO. 2.

1. **ACCOMMODATION.** Units will be billeted in PROVEN No.4. Area on the 30/10/17.

2. **TRANSPORT.** Horse Transport will move according to attached March Table. No Horse Transport will enter WATOU until after 3.0.pm. 30/10/17.
Transport of 171st B.H.Q. will be attached to 2/8th K.L.R. for march.

3. **BAGGAGE.** Baggage will be stacked under Battalion arrangements and loading parties on scale of 4 men per lorry will be detailed.

4. **MECHANICAL TRANSPORT.** One motor lorry only will be allotted to 2/5th K.L.R. One extra lorry will be allotted to 171st L.T.M.B.
Motor Lorries will report at Units Headquarters at 9.0.am. to-morrow, 30/10/17. After loading they will rendezvous in the Square, Renescure at 10.0.am., and will move under orders of O.C. Convoy.

5. **REFILLING POINT.** Refilling Point and time for Guides will be notified later.

B.H.Q.
29/10/17.

Captain, Staff Captain,
171st Infantry Brigade.

ISSUED to:-

Copy No.1. 57th Division. "G"
2           "    "Q"
3  2/5th K.L.R.
4. 2/6th K.L.R.
5  2/7th K.L.R.
6  2/8th K.L.R.
7  171st M.G.Coy.
8  171st L.T.M.B.
9  431st Field Coy.R.E.
10 B/2nd Wessex Field A.
11 No.3.Coy.A.S.C.
12 B.O.O.
13 Brigade Major
14 Staff Captain.
15 171st Brigade Signals.
16 War Diary.
17     "
18 File.
19 Spare.

## 171st INFANTRY BRIGADE.

### MARCH TABLE FOR TRANSPORT 20/10/17.

| Unit. | From. | To. | Starting Point. Sheet Hazebrouck 5 A. | Time. | Route. |
|---|---|---|---|---|---|
| No.3 Coy.87th Divl.Tn. | Renescure | Proven Area. | Renescure-Cassel Rd. Cross Roads 800 yds South of "H" in HAEGDOEK. | 10.0.a.m. | Cassel-Steenvoorde Watou Rd. |
| 171st B.H.Q. 2/5th K.L.R. } | " | " | " | 10.10.a.m. | " |
| 2/6th K.L.R. | " | " | " | 10.17.a.m. | " |
| 2/7th K.L.R. | Campagne | " | " | 10.24.a.m. | " |
| 2/8th K.L.R. | Coin Perdu | " | " | 10.31.a.m. | " |
| 421st Field Coy.R.E. | Campagne | " | " | 10.38.a.m. | " |
| 171st M.G.Coy. | Renescure | " | " | 10.45.a.m. | " |
| 2/2nd Wessex F.A. | Campagne | " | " | 11.2.a.m. | " |

Intervals of 500 yds. will be kept between transport of each Unit.

B.H.Q.
19.10.17.

Captain, Staff Captain,
171st Infantry Brigade.

SECRET.                                              COPY NO. 16

171st INFANTRY BRIGADE ORDER NO. 40.
..................................
                                                23rd October, 1917.


1.      The 171st Infantry Brigade will move from PROVEN Area No. 4
to MALAKOFF Area to-morrow, October 24th.

2.      Moves will take place in accordance with the attached
Table "A".
        Transport will move under the command of the Brigade Transport
Officer as shewn in attached March Table "B".
        Units will entrain at PROVEN as shewn on attached Entraining
Table "C".

3.      Each Unit will send an Officer to PROVEN Station half an hour
in advance of the time detailed for the Unit to arrive to ascertain
from the R.T.O. where the train will be drawn up and how many vans
are available for his Unit.
        Blankets will be taken to the MALAKOFF Area.
        Lewis Guns will be taken on the train.

4.      200 yards distance will be maintained between Companies and
Units of similar length WEST of the YSER CANAL.
        There will be 100 yards between Companies on the march to
PROVEN STATION.
        Bicycles will go by road with the Transport.

5.      Brigade Headquarters will close at PENSHURST Camp at 10-0 a.m.
and will reopen on completion of move at ULM CAMP, B.23.c.6.8.


ACKNOWLEDGE.

                                R.W.Patterson
B. H. Q.,
23.10.17.                              Captain, Brigade Major,
                                       171st Infantry Brigade.



DISTRIBUTION :-

        1.   57th Division "G".       11.  B.G.C.
        2.   57th Division "Q".       12.  Brigade Major.
        3.   2/5th K.L.R.              13.  Staff Captain.
        4.   2/6th K.L.R.              14.  171st Brigade Signal Officer.
        5.   2/7th K.L.R.              15.  171st Brigade Transport Officer
        6.   2/8th K.L.R.              16.  War Diary.
        7.   171st M.G.Coy.            17.  War Diary.
        8.   171st L.T.M.B.            18.  Spare.
        9.   No. 3 Coy. A.S.C.         19.    ,,
        10.  170th Infantry Brigade.   20.    ,,

TABLE "A" - Attached to 171st Infantry Brigade Order No.40.
..........

| Serial No. | UNIT. | FROM. | TO. | ROUTE. | REPLACING. |
|---|---|---|---|---|---|
| 1. | 171st Inf.Bde HdQrs. | | ULM, B.23.c.6.5. | | 176th Inf.Bde H.Q. |
| 2. | 2/8th K.L.R., | | SOULT CAMP, B.23.a.I.I. | | 2/4th L.N.L.Regt., |
| 3. | 2/6th K.L.R., | | WOLFE CAMP, B.22.b.7.0. | By Train from PROVEN to ELVERDINGHE, thence via most direct Routes. | 2/5th L.N.L.Regt., |
| 4. | 2/5th K.L.R., | PROVEN AREA | BRIDGE CAMP, B.14.d. Central. | | |
| 5. | 2/7th K.L.R., | No.4. | BRIDGE CAMP, B.14.d. Central. | Guides will meet the Units at Detraining Point. | |
| 6. | 171st L.T.M.B., | | REDAN, B.22.d.3.8. | | |
| 7. | 171st M.G.Coy. | | SOLFERINO, B.22.b.9.0. | | |

Note:-  Map Reference, Sheet 28, N.W., Edition 6A.  1/20,000.

Ref. Maps.
HAZEBROUCK, 5A. 1/100,000.
BELGIUM. Sh.20. 1/40,000.
28. 1/40,000.
XIV. Corps Traffic Map.

TABLE "B" - Attached to 171st Infantry Brigade Order No.40.

| UNIT. | STARTING POINT. | TIME. | ROUTE. | DESTINATION. | REMARKS. |
|---|---|---|---|---|---|
| No.3 Coy, A.S.C., Baggage Section, and HdQrs. 171st Inf. Brigade. | Cross Roads, 850 yds. S. of Bde H.Q. on WATAU ROAD. | 10.30 am. | Cross Roadd N.W. of P. in PROVEN. NORTHERN CHEMIN MILITAIRE - TYRONE Cross Roads, 20.S.26.c.2.7. SANSIXT JUNCTION, 20.S.27.a.2.0. BRIDGE at 20.S.28.c.5.9. PLANK ROAD, 20.S.28.d.9.5. DE WIPPE CAMP. ONDAND CABARET, 28.A.12.a.0.7. WOESTEN SWITCH to 28.B.1.c.9.1 - ELVERDINGHE, thence by most direct route. | BRIDGE JUNCTION, 28.B.20.b.3.7. | Not to pass Cross-Road N.W. of P. in PROVEN before 11 am. |
| 2/7th K.L.R., | " | 10.35 am. | | | |
| 2/6th K.L.R., | " | 10.42 am. | | | Not to pass Bde H.Q. before 10.30 am. |
| 2/5th K.L.R., | " | 10.49 am. | | | Not to pass PLUM-STEAD CAMP before 10.30 a.m. |
| 2/8th K.L.R., | " | 10.57 am. | | | Not to leave PADDOCK WOOD before 10.40 am. |
| | | | A distance of 500 yds will be left between the transport of each Unit. | | |
| 171st M.G.Coy. | Cross Roads N.W. of P. in PROVEN. | 11-35 am. | -do- | -do- | Not to leave PECKWELL CAMP before 11 am & to follow Transport of 2/8th K.L.R. |

TABLE "C" - Attached to 171st INFANTRY BRIGADE ORDER No. 40.

Reference Map.
HAZEBROUCK, 5a.

| Serial No. | UNIT. | Time of arrival at Station. | Time of departure of Train. | REMARKS. |
|---|---|---|---|---|
| 1. | 171st Inf.Bde. Hd.Qrs. | 12 noon. | 12-30 pm. | |
| 2. | 2/7th K.L.R. | 12.5 pm. | 12-30 pm. | |
| 3. | 171st L.T.M.B. | 12.10 pm. | 12-30 pm. | To follow 2/7th K.L.R. and to join in rear of them at the Cross roads 850 yards S.E. by S. of 171st L.T.M.B. Headquarters. |
| 4. | 2/6th K.L.R., | 1.30 p.m. | 2. 0 pm. | |
| 5. | 2/8th K.L.R., | 1.40 p.m. | 2. 0 pm. | To follow 2/6th K.L.R., and move via Cross Roads on the WATOU ROAD, 550 yds S. of Brigade HdQrs. |
| 6. | 2/5th K.L.R., | 3.30 p.m. | 4. 0 pm. | |
| 7. | 171st M.G.Coy. | 3.35 p.m. | 4. 0 pm. | |

NOTE.  Units will entrain at PROVEN STATION at the 9 of 19 immediately N.W. of P. in PROVEN, and will detrain at ELVERDINGHE.

[WARDIARY]

To All Recipients of 171st Infantry Brigade
Order No.40.

***

Reference Table "C", attached to above order.

Serial No.2. Column 2. For 2/7th MLR read 2/6th MLR.
"       3.    "     2.  "  2/7th KIA   "  2/6th KIA.
"       4.    "     2.  "  2/6th KIA   "  2/7th KIA.
"       5.    "     2.  "  2/6th WIA   "  2/7th WIA.

ACKNOWLEDGE.

R W Salmon

Captain, Brigade Major,
171st Infantry Brigade.

Belle..
23.1.17

War Diary

TO ALL BATTALIONS OF 171st INFANTRY BRIGADE PRELIMINARY
INSTRUCTION NO. I.
* * * * * * * * * * * * * * * *

Please amend above as follows :-

Para. 2 (a) for 3-30 pm. read 4-30 pm.
Para. 2 (b)  „   4-30 pm.  „   3-30 pm.
Para. 2 (c)  „   3-30 pm.  „   4-30 pm.

ACKNOWLEDGE.

R W Patterson

B. H. Q.,
24.10.17.
Captain, Brigade Major,
171st Infantry Brigade.

BM/79?

SECRET.    171st INFANTRY BRIGADE PRELIMINARY INSTRUCTIONS No.1.    COPY NO. 17.

24th October, 1917.

**GENERAL DISPOSITION of TROOPS on Night of Oct.24th.**

1. The 171th Infantry Brigade is now holding the line which runs roughly from REQUETTE FARM - GRAVEL FARM - BROEMBELR RIVER, V.7.b.60.45.

There are 3 Battalions in the Line, and one Battalion in Support:-

RIGHT SECTION.
    2/5th L.N.L.    Battn.H.Q.,    FERDAN HOUSE, V.19.a.75.60.

CENTRE SECTION.
    2/4th L.N.L.R.    ,,    ,,    LOUIS FARM. U.24.c.50.95.

LEFT SECTION.
    2/5th L.N.L.R.    ,,    ,,    OLGA HOUSES. U.18.b.55.15.

SUPPORT BATTN.
    2/5th K.O.R.L.    ,,    ,,    DOUBLE COTTS. U.23.d.30.20.

171st Infantry Brigade is distributed in MALAKOFF AREA as shewn in Table "A" Attached to 171st Brigade Order No.40.

172nd Infantry Brigade is in PROVEN AREA No.I.

**MOVES on OCT.25th.**

2. On October 25th, the following moves will take place:-

(a) 2/8th K.L.R., will move into EAGLE TRENCH in U.23.B and D.    The head of the Battalion will cross the CANAL at BARD CAUSEWAY, B.18.d.9.3 at 3.30 p.m. and will proceed via Track B.

(b) 2/5th K.L.R. will move to HARSGUIN FARM AREA, C.8.B.    The head of the Battalion will cross the CANAL at BARD CAUSEWAY, B.18.d.9.3, at 4.30 p.m. and will proceed via "B" Track.

(c) 2/7th K.L.R. will move up to replace the 2/8th K.L.R. in SOULT CAMP, B.23.a.L.I.    The Battalion will not enter SOULT CAMP before 5.30 p.m.

All Units will move at 100 yds interval between Half-Platoons EAST of YSER CANAL.

3. (a) On Zero day at an hour which will be notified later, the 57th Division (170th Brigade) will attack on a three Battalion front;  the objectives of the attack are shewn on the Map issued under this Office No. INT/1./171.

(b) The 173rd Infantry Brigade, 58th Division, is attacking at the same time on the right, and the 149 Infantry Brigade, 50th Division, is attacking on the left.

(c) The 2/8th K.L.R., will be placed at the disposal of the G.O.C., 170th Infantry Brigade from zero hour onwards for use in case of emergency, but will not be used for purposes of relief except under instruct from Divisional Headquarters.

3. (a) On zero day, Units will be ready to move at one hour's notice from zero hour in fighting order.

On zero day, 2/5th K.L.R. and 2/6th K.L.R. will arrange to dump their greatcoats and packs in EAGLE TRENCH and MARSOUIN FARM AREA respectively.

(c) On zero plus one night, the 2/5th K.L.R. and 2/6th K.L.R will be prepared to take over the front line from the 170th Infantry Brigade - 2/5th K.L.R. on right, with HQrs at FERDAN HOUSE, and 2/6th K.L.R. on Left, with HQrs at OLGA HOUSES.

The 2/7th K.L.R. will move into Support in Area V.13.A. and C. with HQrs probably at LOUIS FARM.

The 2/8th K.L.R. will remain in Reserve in EAGLE HOUSE, and HQrs probably in DOUBLE CREES.

4. Pack Transport can be taken as far as RED HUTS and SHRIEBOOM, using roads as shown on Road Map issued to all Units. A Tramway runs as far forward as V.23.d.Central.

5. Battalions will arrange for Tracks "A" and "B" and LANDMARK TRACK to be thoroughly reconnoitred tomorrow morning, October 25th, by at least one Officer per Company and a proportion of N.C.Os, Signallers and Runners.

Units must be prepared to find their way up to the line without guides.

6. All Officers surplus to those laid down in my B.M.772 dated 22nd October, who have not gone to Corps Reinforcement Camp, will remain with their Transport Lines from October 25th onwards, until required.

7. The following are locations of Field Ambulance Aid Main Posts :-

| | | |
|---|---|---|
| FUSILIER, | C.13.c. | I. 3. |
| GALLIPOLI FARM. | C.8.a. | 8, 4. |
| PIG & WHISTLE. | U.28.b. | 4. 3. |
| HENLEY. | C.3.Central, | |
| LOUIS FARM. | U.24.a. | 5, 0. |
| FERDAN. | Y.19.a. | 7, 6. |
| EAGLE TRENCH. | U.23.b. | 4. 4. |

ACKNOWLEDGE.

R.W.Patterson
Captain, Brigade Major.
171st Infantry Brigade.

DISTRIBUTION:-

| | | | |
|---|---|---|---|
| Copy No. | 1. 57th Division. | Copy No. 11. | B.G.C., |
| | 2. 2/5th K.L.R. | 12. | Brigade Major. |
| | 3. 2/6th K.L.R. | 13. | Staff Captain. |
| | 4. 2/7th K.L.R. | 14. | 171st Bde Signals. |
| | 5. 2/8th K.L.R. | 15. | 171st Bde Transport. |
| | 6. 171st M.G.Co. | 16. | Bde I.O. |
| | 7. 171st L.T.M.B. | 17. | War Diary. |
| | 8. No.3. Coy, A.S.C. | 18. | '' |
| | 9. 170th Infantry Bde. | 19. | Spare. |
| | 10. 172nd Infantry Bde. | 20. | Spare. |

SECRET.                                                                                    COPY NO. 15

171st INFANTRY BRIGADE ORDER No. 41.

26th October, 1917.

1. The 171st Infantry Brigade will relieve the 174th Infantry Brigade in the Line tonight, Oct.26/27th.  Relief to commence as soon as possible.

2. The 2/8th K.L.R. will take over the front line from V.14.c.6.9. to V.7.b.8.5, with posts established in front at ROUTE HOUSE, HAMLIN FARM and RUBENS FARM and V.8.c.2.6.
   The line will be held by 3 Companies with 1 Company in Support.
   Right Company from V.14.c.6.9. to V.14.a.1.9.
   Centre Company from V.14.a.1.9 to WATERULLETBEEK. The Forward Posts mentioned above are inclusive to this Company.
   Left Company in from WATERULLETBEEK to V.7.b.8.5.
   Support Company in SENEGAL FARM and COLPROUILE FARM.
   Battalion HdQrs in LOUIS FARM.
   O.C. 2/8th K.L.R. will establish a forward Battalion Observation Station.

3. The 2/5th K.L.R. will move up from MARSOUIN FARM, and will take over the trenches vacated by 2/8th K.L.R. in EAGLE TRENCH, and will keep in close touch with the front line Battalion, and be prepared to reinforce, should the situation demand, on his own initiative.
   Battalion HdQrs - DOUBLET COPSE.

4. 2/6th K.L.R. and 2/7th K.L.R. will move up from MALAKOF AREA to MARSOUIN FARM, and will take over area vacated by 2/5th K.L.R.

5. 171st Machine Gun Company will choose positions for 2 guns near each of the following places :- GRAVEL FARM, HELLING FARM and BESACE FARM and REQUETTE FARM, with a view to covering the Brigade front with oblique fire.  He will keep in close touch with O.C. front line Battalion.
   The remaining 8 guns are under orders of the D.M.G.O. for S.O.S. barrage.

6. 171st L.T.M.B. will move up to BARD CAUSEWAY, where they will be held in readiness for use as Carrying Parties until the situation permits for them to take up positions in the line.

7. O.C. 2/8th K.L.R. will establish lateral communication with the flank Brigades.

8. The principle will be to hold the line in depth.  The front line covered by small posts at wide intervals, connections from front line to support line being maintained by small section posts.
   The Right Company will maintain touch with the Left of Brigade on Right, and if necessary put out an extra post on that flank. Left Battalion of Brigade on Right report having a post at V.14.c.XXX. 92.98. and a support post near V.14.c.82.72 (HETTES HOUSE).
   The Left Company will be responsible for keeping touch with the Right Battalion of the Brigade on Left, whose post is at V.7.b.6.8.   A post is reported South of VAN DYCK FARM at V.8.a.75.28, but situation not clear.
   The situation on flanks and at VAN DYCK FARM must be cleared up as soon as possible.

9. Pigeons will be kept with all Companies of the front line Battn. to be used to report any exceptional changes in the situation - and when communications are cut.

ACKNOWLEDGE.

*R W Patterson*
Captain, Brigade Major.
171st Infantry Brigade.

P.T.O.

DISTRIBUTION:-

Copy No. 1. H.Q. 57th Division, "G".
2. " "Q".
3. B.G.C., "
4. Brigade Major.
5. Staff Captain.
6. 171st Bde Signals.
7. OC. 2/5th K.L.R.
8. 2/6th ,,
9. 2/7th ,,
10. 2/8th ,,
11. 171st L.T.M.B.
12. 171st M.G.Coy.
13. H.Q. 170th Infantry Brigade.
14. 172nd ,, ,,
15. War Diary.
16. ,,
17.)
18.(
19.( Spare.
20.)

SECRET.                                                        COPY NO. 15

          171st INFANTRY BRIGADE ORDER  No. 42.
                    ........                       27th October, 1917.

1. The following inter-Brigade reliefs will take place tonight, October 27/28th.

(a) 2/5th K.L.R. will take over from 2/8th K.L.R. in the front line.
    There will be 3 Companies in the front line, and one Company in support, as laid down in 171st Infantry Brigade Order No.41, para.2., and will hold the line in a similar manner as it is now held by 2/8th K.L.R.,
    Guides from 2/8th K.L.R. will be arranged between Battalions concerned.
    On relief, the 2/8th K.L.R. will withdraw to HUDDLESTON CAMP, O.7.c.2.5.

(b) 2/6th K.L.R. will move forward and take over EAGLE TRENCH, evacuated by 2/5th K.L.R.
    They will move from MARSOUIN FARM at 4 p.m., moving by Track "B".

2. Attention is drawn to 171st Infantry Brigade Order No.41, para. 8.

ACKNOWLEDGE.

                                    Captain, Brigade Major.
                                    171st Infantry Brigade.


DISTRIBUTION :-

| Copy No. | | Copy No. | |
|---|---|---|---|
| 1. | H.Q. 57th Division, "G". | 11. | 171st L.T.M.B. |
| 2. | ,,      ,,      "Q". | 12. | 171st M.G.Co. |
| 3. | B.G.C., | 13. | 170th Inf.Bde. |
| 4. | Brigade Major. | 14. | 172nd    ,, |
| 5. | Staff Captain. | 15. | War Diary. |
| 6. | 171st Brigade Signals. | 16. |    ,, |
| 7. | 2/5th K.L.R. | 17) | |
| 8. | 2/6th   ,, | 18) | |
| 9. | 2/7th   ,, | 19) | Spare. |
| 10. | 2/8th   ,, | 20) | |

SECRET.

COPY NO. 16

171st INFANTRY BRIGADE ORDER No. 43.

28th October, 1917.

1. The following inter-Brigade reliefs will take place tonight, October 28/29th.

(a) 2/6th K.L.R. will take over from 2/5th K.L.R. in the front line.
    There will be 3 Companies in the front line and one Company in support, as laid down in 171st Infantry Brigade Order No.41, para.2, and will hold the line in a similar manner as it is now held by the 2/5th K.L.R.
    Guides from 2/5th K.L.R. will be arranged between Battalions concerned.
    On relief, the 2/5th K.L.R. will withdraw to HUDDLESTON CAMP, C.7.c.2.5.
    The relief may commence at 4.0 p.m.

(b) 2/7th K.L.R. will move forward and take over EAGLE TRENCH evacuated by 2/6th K.L.R. They will move from MARSOUIN FARM at 4 p.m. moving by Track "B".

(c) 2/8th K.L.R. will move forward from HUDDLESTON CAMP to MARSOUIN FARM, but should not arrive there before 4 p.m.

2. Completion of relief will be reported by wire by the code word "WOKING", or by runner.

ACKNOWLEDGE.

R W Patterson

Captain, Brigade Major.
171st Infantry Brigade.

DISTRIBUTION :-

Copy No. 1. 57th Division, "G",
        2.      ,,         "Q",
        3. B.G.C.,
        4. Brigade Major.
        5. Staff Captain.
        6. 171st Brigade Signals.
        7. 2/5th K.L.R.,
        8. 2/6th ,,
        9. 2/7th ,,
       10. 2/8th ,,

Copy No. 11. 171st L.T.M.B.
        12. 171st M.G.Co.
        13. 172nd Inf.Bde.
        14. 150th Bde - 50th Div
        15. 174th Bde - 58th Di
        16. War Diary.
        17.         ,,
        18)
        19) Spare.
        20)

SECRET.

```
O.C.,   2/5th K.L.R.
        2/6th   ,,
        2/7th   ,,
        2/8th   ,,
        171st L.T.M.B.
        171st M.G.Co.
H.Q. 57th Division.
```

H.Q.
171st
INFANTRY BRIGADE.
B.M./132.

.........

Reliefs will take place in accordance with my B.M./120 dated 28th instant, tonight.

2/7th K.L.R. and 2/8th K.L.R. will move forward to relieve at 4 p.m.

2/5th K.L.R. will move into MARSOUIN FARM CAMP at 4 p.m.

2/6th K.L.R. will on relief withdraw to HUDDLESTON CAMP, C.7.c.2.4.

ACKNOWLEDGE.

B.H.Q.
30.10.17

Captain, Brigade Major.
171st Infantry Brigade.

APPENDIX II.

MINOR OPERATIONS, etc.,

referred to in

171stn INFANTRY BRIGADE WAR DIARY,

1.10.1917

to

31.10.1917

...

Appendix B

Appendix A

APPENDIX III.

STATEMENT of CASUALTIES

in connection with

171st INFANTRY BRIGADE WAR DIARY,

1.10.1917

to

31.10.1917

....

# 171st INFANTRY BRIGADE.

## CASUALTIES from 1.10.17 to 31.10.17.

| DATE. 24 hours ending noon - | KILLED. Officers. | O.Ranks. | WOUNDED. Officers. | O.Ranks. | MISSING. Officers. | O.Ranks. |
|---|---|---|---|---|---|---|
| 1.10.17. | - | - | - | - | - | - |
| 2.10.17. | - | - | - | - | - | - |
| 3.10.17. | - | - | - | - | - | - |
| 4.10.17. | - | - | - | - | - | - |
| 5.10.17. | - | - | - | - | - | - |
| 6.10.17. | - | - | - | - | - | - |
| 7.10.17. | - | - | - | - | - | - |
| 8.10.17. | - | - | - | - | - | - |
| 9.10.17. | - | - | - | - | - | - |
| 10.10.17. | - | - | - | 3 | - | - |
| 11.10.17. | - | - | - | - | - | - |
| 12.10.17. | - | - | CAPT.W.J. OATFIELD. LIEUT.A.L. COWPER. | 3 | - | - |
| 13.10.17. | - | - | - | - | - | - |
| 14.10.17. | - | - | - | - | - | - |
| 15.10.17. | - | - | - | - | - | - |
| 16.10.17. | - | - | - | - | - | - |
| 17.10.17. | - | - | - | - | - | - |
| 18.10.17. | - | - | - | - | - | - |
| 19.10.17. | - | - | - | - | - | - |
| 20.10.17. | - | - | - | - | - | - |
| 21.10.17. | - | - | - | - | - | - |
| 22.10.17. | - | - | - | - | - | - |
| 23.10.17. | - | - | - | - | - | - |
| 24.10.17. | - | - | - | 3 | - | 3 |
| 25.10.17. | - | - | - | 20 | - | - |
| 26.10.17. | - | - | - | 15 | - | 1 |
| 27.10.17. | - | 5 | - | 30 | - | 8 |
| 28.10.17. | 2nd Lt.D. VAUGHEN. | 3 | CAPT.W.E. JONES. 2nd Lt.C. THORNE. 2nd Lt.C.W. CLARKE. | | | |
| 29.10.17. | - | 4 | 2nd Lt.T.J. HIGGINS. 2nd Lt.L.W.C. TODD. CAPT. J. MCWILLIAM. 2nd Lt. T. LEVER. 2nd Lt. L.T. PROFIT. | 114 | - | 1 |
| 30.10.17. | - | 11 | - | 62 | - | 6 |
| 31.10.17. | - | 11 | - | 57 | - | 4 |
| Total. | 1 | 34 | 10 | 307 | - | 23. |

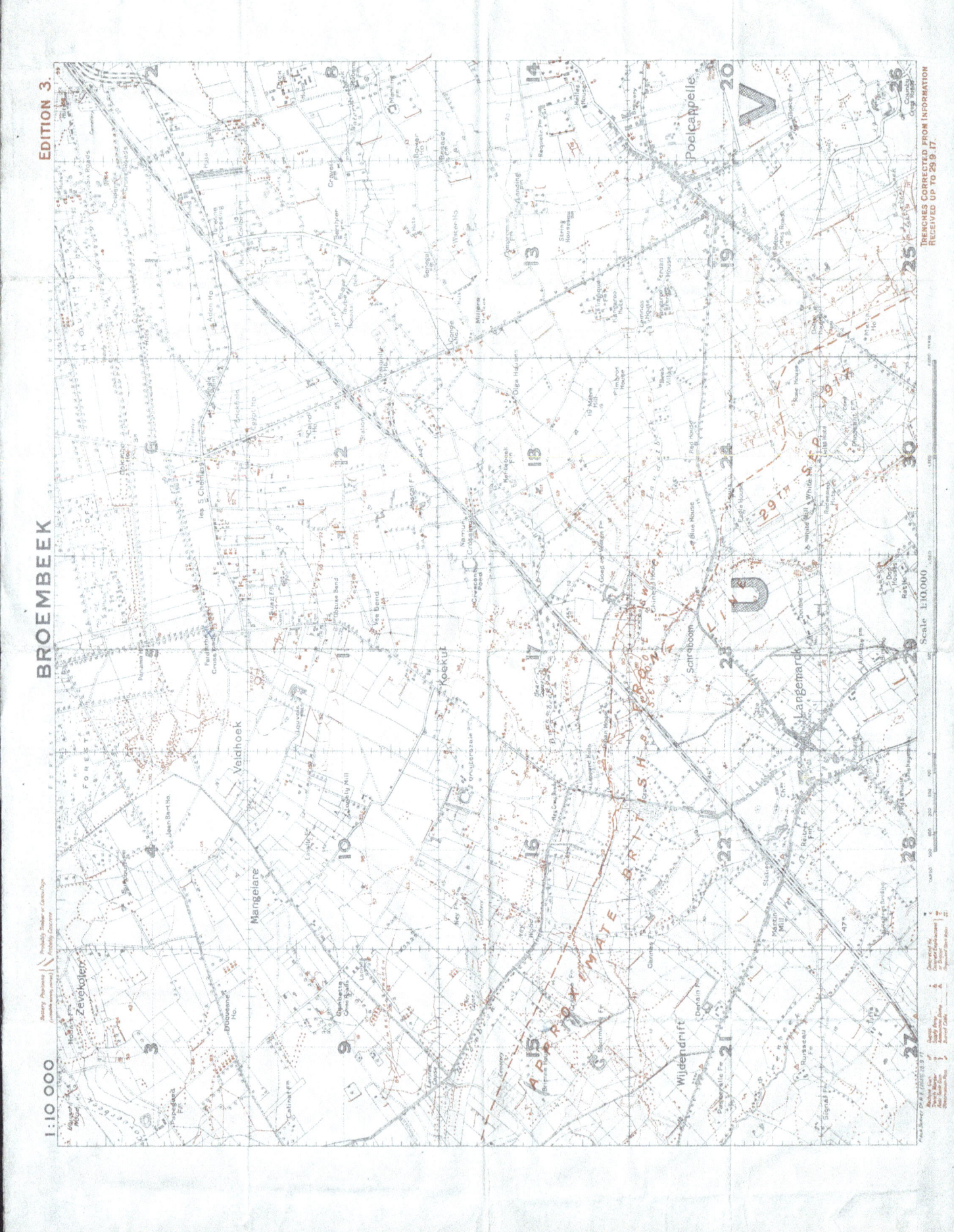

# GLOSSARY.

| | |
|---|---|
| Abbaye, Abbᵉ | Abbey. |
| Abreuvoir, Abʳ | Watering-place. |
| Abri de douaniers | Customs-shelter. |
| Aciérie | Steel works. |
| Aiguille | Pointe (Ry.) |
| Allée | Alley, Narrow road. |
| Ancien -ne, Ancⁿ⁻ⁿᵉ | Old. |
| Aqueduc | Aqueduct. |
| Arbre | Tree. |
| „ éventail | fan-shaped „ |
| „ décharné | bare „ |
| „ fourchu | forked „ |
| „ isolé | isolated „ |
| „ penché | leaning „ |
| Arbrisseau | Small tree. |
| Arc | Arch. |
| Ardoisière, Ardʳᵉ | Slate quarry. |
| Arrêt | Halt. |
| Asile | Asylum. |
| „ des aliénés | Lunatic asylum. |
| „ de charité | Asylum. |
| „ des pauvres | |
| „ de refuge | |
| Auberge, Aubᵉ | Inn. |
| Aune | Alder-tree. |
| Bac | Ferry. |
| „ à traille | „ |
| Bains | Baths. |
| Place aux bains | Bathing place. |
| Balise | Boom, Beacon. |
| Banc de sable | Sand-bank. |
| „ vase | Mud-bank. |
| Baraque | Hut. |
| Barrage | Dam. |
| Barrière | Gate, Stile. |
| (Machine à) Bascule | Weigh-bridge. |
| Bassin | Dock, Pond. |
| „ d'échouage | Tidal dock. |

| | |
|---|---|
| Bassin de radoub | Dry dock. |
| Bateau phare | Light-ship. |
| Blanchisserie | Laundry. |
| B.M. (borne militaire) | Mile stone. |
| Bⁿᵉ (borne kilométrique) | |
| Boulonnerie | |
| Fabᵉ de boulons | Bolt Factory. |
| Bouée | Buoy. |
| Brasserie, Brassᵉ | Brewery. |
| Briqueterie, Briqᵉ | Brickfield. |
| Brise-lames | Breakwater. |
| Bureau de poste | Post office. |
| „ de douane | Custom house. |
| Butte | Butt, Mound. |
| Cabane | Hut. |
| Cabaret, Cabᵗ | Inn. |
| Câble sous-marin | Submarine cable. |
| Calvaire, Calvᵉ | Calvary. |
| Canal de dessèchement | Drainage canal. |
| Canal d'irrigation | Irrigation canal. |
| Fabᵉ de caoutchouc | Rubber factory. |
| Carrière, Carrᵉ | Quarry. |
| „ de gravier | Gravel-pit. |
| Caserne | Barracks. |
| Champ de courses | Race course. |
| „ manœuvres | Drill-ground. |
| „ tir | Rifle range. |
| Chantier | Building yard. |
| „ | Ship yard. |
| „ | Dock yard. |
| Chantier de construction | Slip-way. |
| Chapelle, Chᵉˡˡᵉ | Chapel. |
| Charbonnage | Colliery. |
| Château d'eau | Water tower. |
| Chaussée | Causeway. |
| „ | Highway. |
| Chemin de fer | Railway. |
| Cheminée, Chᵉᵉ | Chimney. |
| Chêne | Oak tree. |
| Cimetière, Cimʳᵉ | Cemetery. |
| Clocher | Belfry. |
| Clouterie | Nail factory. |
| Colombier | Dove cot. |

| | |
|---|---|
| Coron | Workmen's dwellings. |
| Cour des marchandises | Goods yard. |
| Couvent | Convent. |
| Crassier | Slag heap. |
| Croix | Cross. |
| Dune | Inner dock. |
| Démoli -e | Destroyed. |
| Détruit -e, Détʳ⁻ᵗᵉ | |
| Déversoir | Weir. |
| Digue | Dyke, causeway. |
| Distillerie, Distᵉ | Distillery. |
| Douane | Custom-house. |
| Bureau de douane | |
| Entrepôt de douane | Custom warehouse. |
| Dynamitière, Dynamᵉ | Dynamite magazine. |
| „ | Dynamite factory. |
| Écluse | Sluice, Lock. |
| Écluzette, Eclᵗᵉ | Sluice. |
| École | School. |
| Écurie | Stable. |
| Église | Church. |
| Émaillerie | Enamel works. |
| Embarcadère, Embʳᵉ | Landing-place. |
| Estaminet, Estamᵗ | Inn. |
| Étang | Pond. |
| Fabrique, Fabᵉ | Factory. |
| Fabᵉ de produits chimiques | Chemical works. |
| Faïencerie | Pottery. |
| Ferme, Fᵐᵉ | Farm. |
| Filature, Filᵉ | Spinning mill. |
| Fonderie, Fondʳⁱᵉ | Foundry. |
| Fontaine, Fontⁿᵉ | Spring, fountain. |
| Forêt | Forest. |
| Forme de radoub | Dry dock. |
| Forge | Smithy. |
| Fosse | Mine, Pit. |
| Fossé | Moat, Ditch. |
| Four | Kiln. |
| „ à chaux | Lime-kiln. |

| | |
|---|---|
| Four à coke | Coke oven. |
| Ganterie | Glove Factory. |
| Gare | Station. |
| Garenne | Warren. |
| Garnison | Garrison. |
| Gazomètre | Gasometer. |
| Glacerie | |
| Fabᵉ de glaces | Mirror Factory. |
| Glacière | Ice factory. |
| Grue | Crane. |
| Gué | Ford. |
| Guérite | Sentry-box, Turret. |
| „ à signaux | Signal-box (Ry.) |
| Halte | Halt. |
| Hangar | Shed, Hangar. |
| Hôpital | Hospital. |
| Hôtel-de-Ville | Town hall. |
| Houillère | Colliery. |
| Huilerie | Oil factory. |
| Imprimerie, Imprⁱᵉ | Printing works. |
| Jetée | Pier. |
| Laminerie | Rolling mills. |
| Ligne de haute | High water mark. |
| „ „ marée | |
| „ de basse marée | Low „ |
| Maison Forestière Mon Fre | Forester's house. |
| Malterie | Malt-house. |
| Marbrerie | Marble works. |
| Marais | Marsh. |
| Marais salant | Saltern. |
| „ | Salt marsh. |
| Marché | Market. |
| Mare | Pool. |
| Meule | Rick. |
| Minière | Mine. |
| Monastère | Monastery. |
| Moulin, Mⁿ | Mill. |
| „ à vapeur | Steam mill. |
| Mur | Wall. |
| „ crénelé | Loop-holed wall. |

Vol. 10.

Headquarters
171st Inf. Bde.
(57th Div.)
November 1917.

WAR   DIARY,

of

HEADQUARTERS, 171st INFANTRY BRIGADE,

I.II.1917,

to

30.II.1917.

......

VOLUME   IX.

......

CONFIDENTIAL.

Headquarters,

    57th Division.

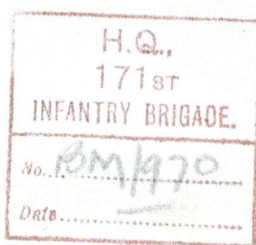

        Herewith War Diary of these Headquarters for period 1.11.1917 to 30.11.1917.

                              Brigadier-General,
                       Commanding 171st Infantry Brigade.

B. H. Q.,
1.12.17.

# WAR DIARY
## or
## INTELLIGENCE SUMMARY.

*(Erase heading not required.)*

Army Form C. 2118.

| Place | Date | Hour | Summary of Events and Information | Remarks and references to Appendices |
|---|---|---|---|---|
| LANGEMARCK area | 1.xi.17 | | Enemy displays his usual artillery activity shelling front and support lines intermittently throughout the 24 hours. LOUIS FARM - FERDAN HOUSE area to be shelled heavily. 2/8 K.L.R. returned to rest in front line FERDAN HOUSE area to be shelled heavily. 2/8 K.L.R. moved up to support EAGLE trench whilst 1/7 K.L.R. in Reserve to MALAKESTON Camp. 7.15 Both aeroplanes flew low above our front lines and remained up from 1.30 pm to 2.15 pm. Patrols reconnoitred RUBENS and 9 MEMLING farms which was found to be unoccupied by the enemy, but not in force - | Officer 3rd! |
| " | 2.xi.17 | | During the 24 hours the enemy shelled LOUIS FARM - AQUILE COTTS - EAGLE trench and our front line were very heavy. Shells in direct hit on LOUIS FARM which did considerable damage and several others fell in close proximity. Signallers 2/8 K.L.R. and R.V. HQrs personnel suffered casualties. Communication was cut during evening. During the evening MEMLING FARM was occupied by advance troops of 2/8 K.L.R. The Brigade Route Clearance 1/7 & 2/8 Bn. Relief night of 2/3. 1st relief being completed at 11.40 am. 3rd was completed by 9.43 Offrs/25 | Wounded! |
| MALAKOFF Area | 3.xi.17 | | Bde. H.Qrs. Camp at MINT FARM. 2/5 N.K. at WOLFE Camp, 2/6 K.L.R. at BRIDGE Camp, 2/7 K.L.R. at BRIDGE Camp, 2/8 K.L.R. at SOULT Camp, 171 & 172 M.G. Coy, and SOLFERINO Camp. | |

# WAR DIARY or INTELLIGENCE SUMMARY.

Army Form C. 2118.

(Erase heading not required.)

| Place | Date | Hour | Summary of Events and Information | Remarks and references to Appendices |
|---|---|---|---|---|
| MALAKOFF AREA | 4.XI.17 | | Brigade to billets - Day spent in cleaning, bathing, and issuing hospitals, kits said cleaning equipment. | |
| | 5.XI.17 | | Brigade halted. Cleaning, etc continued | |
| NOORDAUSQUES | 6.XI.17 | | Brigade left one route - (17 kils) moved to the NORDAUSQUES area. Straining started 12.15 p.m. for infantry from ELVERDINGHE - Transport moving from ROESINGHE by rail entraining by night. All the infantry were in billets by 10.0 pm | Appendix I |
| | 7.XI.17 & 8.XI.17 | | Brigade rested - Cleaning equipment, repairing billets etc carried out. | |
| | 9.XI.17 | | Training commenced. | |
| | 10.XI.17 | | First week's training programme commenced. Individual & collective training in Physical, Bayonet fighting, Musketry and Tactical Schemes | |
| | 11.XI.17 | | Sunday. Training suspended | |
| | 12.XI.17 | | Training continued - 75 & 96 KRR on range at NORDEVLINGHEM | |
| | 13.XI.17 | | Training continued in all units | |
| | 14.XI.17 | | 75 and 9/8 KRR. on range at NORDEVLINGHEM. Training continued in all units | |
| | 15.XI.17 | | Training continued by all units | |

Army Form C. 2118.

# WAR DIARY
## or
## INTELLIGENCE SUMMARY.
(Erase heading not required.)

III

Instructions regarding War Diaries and Intelligence
Summaries are contained in F. S. Regs., Part II.
and the Staff Manual respectively. Title pages
will be prepared in manuscript.

| Place | Date | Hour | Summary of Events and Information | Remarks and references to Appendices |
|---|---|---|---|---|
| NORDAUSQUES Area | 16.XI.17 | | Training continued - XVIII Corps Commander inspected troops during the morning | 60 J/A |
| | 17.XI.17 | | Training continued. 2/7 Bn. K.L.R. joined Bde in NORDAUSQUES area - under orders of | 60 J/A |
| | 18.XI.17 | | C.E. XVIII Corps - training suspended | 60 J/A |
| | 19.XI.17 | | Sunday - Training continued - | 60 J/A |
| | 20.XI.17 | | Conference at Brigade Hdrs. of Battn. Commanders & Company commanders | 60 J/A |
| | 21.XI.17 | | Lecture by XVIII Corps Commander | 60 J/A |
| | 22.XI.17 | | Training continued. All units | 60 J/A |
| | 23.XI.17 | | Training continued. | 60 J/A |
| | 24.XI.17 | | Training continued | 60 J/A |
| | 25.XI.17 | | Sunday. Training suspended | 60 J/A |
| | 26.XI.17 | | Training continued | 60 J/A |
| | 27.XI.17 | | | 60 J/A |
| | 28.XI.17 | | | 60 J/A |
| | 29.XI.17 | | | 60 J/A |
| | 30.XI.17 | | | 60 J/A |

Morgbourne

Statement of Casualties & officers
Brigade Insignia    Appendix II  60 J/A
Comdg 171st Inf Bde

APPENDIX I.

RELIEF ORDERS, etc.,

referred to in

171st INFANTRY BRIGADE WAR DIARY,

1.11.1917

to

30.11.1917.

....

SECRET.

COPY NO. 16

171st INFANTRY BRIGADE ORDER No. 44.

1st November, 1917.

1. The following inter-Brigade reliefs will take place tonight, November 1st/2nd.

(a) 2/8th K.L.R. will take over from 2/7th K.L.R., in the front line.
Guides from 2/7th K.L.R. will be arranged between Battalions concerned.
On relief, the 2/7th K.L.R. will withdraw to HUDDLESTON CAMP, C.7.d.2.5.
The relief may commence at 4 p.m.

(b) 2/5th K.L.R. will move forward and take over EAGLE TRENCH evacuated by 2/8th K.L.R., They will move from MARSOUIN FARM at 4 p.m.; moving by Track "B".

(c) 2/6th K.L.R. will move forward from HUDDLESTON CAMP to MARSOUIN FARM, but should not arrive there before 4 p.m.

2. Completion of relief will be reported by wire by the code word "RUM", or by runner.

ACKNOWLEDGE.

R W Patterson

Captain, Brigade Major.
171st Infantry Brigade.

DISTRIBUTION :-

| Copy No. | | Copy No. | |
|---|---|---|---|
| 1. | 57th Division, "G". | 11. | 171st L.T.M.B. |
| 2. | ,, "Q". | 12. | 171st M.G.Co. |
| 3. | B.G.C., | 13. | 172nd Infantry Bde. |
| 4. | Brigade Major. | 14. | 151st Bde - 50th Div. |
| 5. | Staff Captain. | 15. | 175th Bde - 58th Div. |
| 6. | 171st Bde Signals. | 16. | War Diary. |
| 7. | 2/5th K.L.R., | 17. | ,, |
| 8. | 2/6th ,, | 18.) | |
| 9. | 2/7th ,, | 19.) | Spare. |
| 10. | 2/8th ,, | 20.) | |

To all Recipients of 171st Infantry Brigade Order No.45.
...........

Reference Serial No.2, Column 7, of Table "A" attached to above Order.

ADD:- To be clear of MARSOUIN FARM and HUDDLESTON CAMP by 10 a.m.

NOTE:- East of CANAL interval of 200 yds between Platoons must be maintained.

for Captain, Brigade Major.
171st Infantry Brigade.

B.H.Q. 1.II.17

SECRET.　　　　　　　　　　　　　　　　　　　　　　COPY NO. 16

171st INFANTRY BRIGADE ORDER No. 45.

　　　　　　　　　　　　　　　　　　　　　　1st November, 1917.

1. The 172nd Infantry Brigade will relieve the 171st Infantry Brigade in the Line on the night of November 2nd/3rd.

2. The Relief will take place in accordance with attached Table of Moves, "A".

3. Guides will be detailed as laid down in Column 6 of Table "A". In order to facilitate the relief, further guides for Posts will be provided at Company HdQrs, under arrangements to be made between Battalion Commanders concerned.

4. Units will move by Tracks as under :-

"A" TRACK, and LANGEMARCK TRACK.
　　Left Front Coy, 2/9th K.L.R.,

"A" TRACK.
　　Centre Front Coy, 2/9th K.L.R.,
　　Support Coy, 2/9th K.L.R.,

"B" TRACK.
　　Right Front Coy, 2/9th K.L.R.,
　　Support Battn. 2/10th K.L.R.,

Troops relieved can use any Tracks.

5. Advanced 171st Brigade HdQrs will open at ULM FARM at 6 p.m.

6. The command of the Section will pass to G.O.C., 172nd Infantry Brigade on completion of relief.

7. Relief complete will be reported by wire by the code word "OXO", by or by runner.

ACKNOWLEDGE.

　　　　　　　　　　　　　　　　　R W Patterson
　　　　　　　　　　　　　　　　　Captain, Brigade Major.
　　　　　　　　　　　　　　　　　171st Infantry Brigade.

DISTRIBUTION :-

Copy No. 1. 57th Division, "G".　　Copy No. 11. 171st L.T.M.B.
　　　　 2.　　　　",　　 "Q".　　　　　　　12. 171st M.G.Co.
　　　　 3. B.G.C.,　　　　　　　　　　　　 13. 172nd Inf.Brigade.
　　　　 4. Brigade Major.　　　　　　　　　14. 151st Bde - 50th Divn.
　　　　 5. Staff Captain.　　　　　　　　　15. 175th Bde - 58th Div.
　　　　 6. 171st Bde Signals.　　　　　　　16. War Diary.
　　　　 7. 2/5th K.L.R.,　　　　　　　　　 17.　　",
　　　　 8. 2/6th　　",　　　　　　　　　　 18)
　　　　 9. 2/7th　　",　　　　　　　　　　 19) Spare.
　　　　10. 2/8th　　",　　　　　　　　　　 20)

TABLE OF MOVES "A" - Issued with 171st INFANTRY BRIGADE ORDER No. 45.

| Serial No. | UNIT. | RELIEVED BY:- | PRESENT LOCATION. | TO. | Guides, Times & Rendezvous, and by whom provided. | REMARKS. |
|---|---|---|---|---|---|---|
| 1. | 2/6th K.L.R. | 2/9th K.L.R. 2/10th KL.R. | MARSOUIN FARM. | BRIDGE CAMP, B.14.d.65.10. | No Guides; Incoming troops will arrive 9.30 a.m. | Dinners at WOLFE CAMP, which is to be clear by 2.30 p.m. NOT to enter BRIDGE CAMP before 2.30 p.m. |
| 2. | 2/7th K.L.R. | | HUDDLESTON CAMP. | BRIDGE CAMP, B.20.b.25.80. | | Dinners at SOULT CAMP, which is to be clear by 3 p.m. NOT to enter BRIDGE CAMP before 2.30 pm. |
| 3. | 2/9th K.L.R. | 2/8th S.L.R. | LOCATION I P.M., MARSOUIN FM. | Front Line. | 2/8th KLR - 4 guides per Coy. Junction "A" & "B" Tracks, C.3.c.20.45, at 3 p.m. | To leave MARSOUIN FARM, 3.30 p.m. |
| 4. | 2/10th K.L.R. | | LOCATION I P.M. MARSOUIN FM. | EAGLE TRENCH. | 2/5th KLR - 4 guides per Coy. Junction "A" & "B" Tracks, C.3.c.20.45, at 4 p.m. | To leave MARSOUIN FARM, 3.30 p.m. |
| 5. | 2/8th K.L.R. | 2/9th K.L.R. | Front Line. | SOULT CAMP. B.23.a.1.1. | Guides as detailed in Serial No.3 for 2/8th K.L.R. | |
| 6. | 2/5th K.L.R. | 2/10th KL.R. | EAGLE TRENCH. | WOLFE CAMP, B.22.b.7.0. | Guides as detailed in Serial No.4 for 2/10th K.L.R. | |
| 7. | 171st M.G.Co. | 172nd M.G.Co. | LINE. | SOLFERINO, B.22.b.9.0. | To be arranged between Os.C. Companies concerned. | All arrangements to be made by Os.C. Companies concerned. |
| 8. | 171st L.T.M.B. | 172nd L.T.M.B. | FUSILEER. | REDAN. B.22.d.3.8. | | All arrangements to be made between Os.C. Bns concerned. |
| 9. | 171st Bde H.Q. | 172nd Bde H.Q. | STRAY FARM. | ULM FARM, B.23.c.6.8. | | |

NOTES. (1) Serial Nos. 3 and 4 are 172nd Bde Moves.   (2) Map References - Sheet 28, N.W. 1/20.000.

SECRET.
                                                COPY NO. 18

                171st INFANTRY BRIGADE.

Map.Ref.
Sheet 5A        MOVE  -  WARNING ORDER.
HAZEBROUCK.              ......              5th November, 1917.

1. The 171st Infantry Brigade (less 2/7th K.L.R) will move from the MALAKOFF AREA to the NORDAUSQUES AREA tomorrow, November 6th.

2. Train arrangements, and the portion of Transport it will be necessary to move by road, will be notified later.

3. Troops moving by rail will entrain at ELVERDINGHE. Transport moving by rail will entrain at BOESINGHE. On arrival at the Detraining Point - AUDRUICQ - troops and transport will march by most direct routes to Billets (vide this Office A.1205 dated 4.11.1917).

4. Bicycles - Blankets and other articles of kit, will accompany personnel moving by train.

5. Transport proceeding by road - probably Train Baggage Wagons and 4 vehicles per Battalion - will rendezvous at a place and time to be notified later, and will march to BUYSSCHEURE, reaching WORMHOUDT at 1 p.m., and reporting to the Area Commandant, LEDERZEELE for accommodation. The move will occupy two days.

6. Intervals of 500 yds between Battalions, 100 yds between Companies and Light Trench Mortar Battery, and 200 yds between Battalion Transports and Machine Gun Company, will be maintained during all movements by road.

7. Brigade HdQrs will close at ULM FARM at 11 a.m., 6.11.17, and will reopen at NORDAUSQUES at 6.30 p.m., 6.11.17.

ACKNOWLEDGE.

                                                  Lieut. Acting Brigade Major.
                                                  171st Infantry Brigade.

DISTRIBUTION:-

| Copy No. | | Copy No. | |
|---|---|---|---|
| 1. | 57th Division, "G". | 11. | No.3 Coy, Divl.Train. |
| 2. | " "Q". | 12. | 172nd Inf.Bde. |
| 3. | 2/5th K.L.R., | 13. | B.G.C., |
| 4. | 2/6th " | 14. | Brigade Major. |
| 5. | 2/7th " | 15. | Staff Captain. |
| 6. | 2/8th " | 16. | 171st Bde Signals. |
| 7. | 171st L.T.M.B., | 17. | 171st Bde Transport Officer |
| 8. | 171st M.G.Coy. | 18. | War Diary. |
| 9. | 421st Field Co, RE. | 19. | " |
| 10. | 2/2nd Wessex Fd Ambce. | 20. | Spare. |

SECRET.                                                          COPY NO. 18

                    171st INFANTRY BRIGADE ORDER No. 46.
Sheet 28 NW.                          for
Hazebrouck 5A.           MOVE to NORDAUSQUES AREA.
                              ........                    5th November 1917.


1. One lorry each for 2/5th K.L.R., 2/8th K.L.R., 171st Inf.Bde HdQrs, 171st L.T.M.B., and 171st M.G.Coy, will report to M.D.S. at 28/B.23.c.0.3 at 10 a.m., 6.11.1917.   Baggage and stores to be loaded in the lorry are to be ready dumped by the roadside by 9.45 a.m.,
   One lorry for 2/6th K.L.R., will report at 28/B.20.b.3.7 at 9.45 a.m.
   The lorries are to rendezvous at DAWSON'S CORNER under the orders of Lieut.Tebbutt, 2/5th K.L.R., at 10.30 a.m., ready to move.

2. Horse Transport of Battalions (loss 2/7th K.L.R.), loss 3 Limbered Wagons, will entrain at BOESINGHE Railway Station at 9.15 p.m. 6.11.1917, in accordance with attached Move Table "B".

3. The remaining 4 Limbered Wagons of 2/5th, 2/6th and 2/8th K.L.R. will be ready to move in accordance with attached March Table "C", under the orders of an Officer to be detailed by O.C., 2/6th K.L.R.,   This Officer will report to Brigade HdQrs on arrival at the NORDAUSQUES AREA.

4. The two A.S.C. Baggage Wagons with each Battalion will report back to O.C., No.3 Coy, Divisional Train tonight, 5.11.1917. They will move under his orders, and be returned to Units on completion of the march, probably 48 hours later.

5. Personnel of Units at HOUNSLOW CAMP should be recalled forthwith if this has not already been done.

6. The entrainment at ELVERDINGHE will be carried out in accordance with attached Table "A".
   Units wishing to make Dumps at railhead will not do so before 7 a.m., 6.11.1917.   They will be made on the open ground on the south side of the Railway Station.   Guards and Loading Parties must be detailed for them.

7. Completion of Serial Number to be reported to Brigade HdQrs NORDAUSQUES AREA.

   ACKNOWLEDGE.                              Marshall

                                         Captain, A/Staff Captain,
                                            171st Infantry Brigade.
         DISTRIBUTION:-

Copy No.1. 57th Divn. "G".          No.11. No.3 Coy, Divl.Traing
     2.   ,,    ,,    "Q".             12. 172nd Inf.Bde.
     3.   2/5th K.L.R.,                13. B.G.C.,
     4.   2/6th  ,,                    14. Brigade Major.
     5.   2/7th  ,,                    15. Staff Captain.
     6.   2/8th  ,,                    16. 171st Bde Signals.
     7.   171st L.T.M.B.,              17. 171st Bde Transport Off.
     8.   171st M.G.Co.                18. War Diary.
     9.   C.R.E.  (for infn.)          19.    ,,
    10.   A.D.M.S. (for infn.)         20. Spare.

Ref.Map. HAZEBROUCK, 5A.  TABLE "A" - Issued with 171st INFANTRY BRIGADE ORDER No. 46.

| Serial No. | UNIT. | Time of Arrival at ELVERDINGHE STATION. | Time of Departure of Train. | REMARKS. |
|---|---|---|---|---|
| 1. | 171st Inf.Bde H.Q. and Signal Section. | 11.45 a.m. | 12.15 a.m. | To pass DAWSON CORNER, 10.45 a.m. |
| 2. | 2/5th K.L.R. less Transport. | 11.48 a.m. | 12.15 p.m. | To follow Brigade HdQrs. |
| 3. | 2/8th K.L.R. " " | 12.0 noon. | 12.15 p.m. | To follow 2/5th KLR - no halt at 11.50 a.m. |
| 4. | 2/6th K.L.R. " " | 12.45 p.m. | 1.15 p.m. | No restrictions. |
| 5. | 171st M.G.Coy. " " | 12.50 p.m. | 1.15 p.m. | No halt at 11.50 a.m. To pass DAWSON CORNER 11.50 a.m. |
| 6. | 171st L.T.M.B. " " | 12.52 p.m. | 1.15 p.m. | To follow 171st M.G.Coy. |

N.B. Os.C. Units will detail one Officer to report to Staff Officer, 171st Brigade, one hour before train is due to leave. These Officers should bring a means of marking coaches allotted to them, and an entraining state.

TABLE "B" - Issued with 171st INFANTRY BRIGADE ORDER No. 46.

The Transport of Units that is to be entrained will probably not have to leave the Transport lines before 4.0 p.m. Further details will be notified tomorrow morning.

TABLE "B" - Issued with 171st INFANTRY BRIGADE ORDER No. 46.

| Serial No. | UNIT. | Time of Arrival at BOESINGHE STN. | Time of Departure of Train. | Personnel. Offrs. | Personnel. O.R. | Horses. | G.S. Limbd. | 2 Whd. | REMARKS. |
|---|---|---|---|---|---|---|---|---|---|
| 1. | 171st Inf.Bde.H.Q. | Under arrangements by Bde.T.O. | 9-15 pm. 6.11.17. | 1 | 10 | 9 | 1 | 1 | Arriving AUDRUICQ 1-30 am 7.11.17. |
|  | Signal Section. | | | | 9 | 9 | 1 | 1 | |
|  | Transport for Lewis Guns. 4 Limbd.GS. Wagons per Battalion. | | | | 24 | 24 | 12 | | |
|  | 2 Cookers & 1 Mess Cart per Battalion. | | | | 15 | 15 | 6 | 3 | |
|  | Chargers & Pack Animals - 18 per Bn. | | | | 54 | 54 | | | |
|  | Medical Personnel with 1 Maltese Cart per Bn. | | | | 3 | 6 | 3 | | |
|  | 2/5th K.L.R.) To act as loading & 2/8th K.L.R.) unloading party. | | | 1 1 | 50 50 | 1 1 | 1 1 | 1 1 | |
| 2. | 171st M.G.Coy. | Under arrangements by Bde.T.O. | 12-15 mdnt. 6/7th Nov. 1917. | Whole personnel. | | 56 | 14 | 2 | Arriving AUDRUICQ 4-30 am. 7.11.17. |
|  | Tool Carts - 2 per Bn. | | | | 6 | 12 | 6 | 1 | |
|  | 2 Cookers & 2 Water Carts per Bn. | | | | 12 | 24 | 6 | 3 | |
|  | 171st L.T.M.B. incl. Handcarts & Lorries. | | | Whole personnel. | | 1 | 1 | 1 | |
|  | Loading Party - Whole personnel of L.T.M.B. & M.G.Coy. | | | | | | | | |

TABLE "C" - Issued with 171st INFANTRY BRIGADE ORDER No. 46.

| Serial No. | UNIT. | Time of Departure. | ROUTE. | REMARKS. |
|---|---|---|---|---|
| 1. | Limbered Wagons of 2/5th K.L.R., | 6.11.17 - 6 a.m. | ELVERDINGHE - POPERINGHE - HOUTKERKE - HERZEELE - NORDHOUDT - RUBROUCK - LEDERZEELE. | To be clear of NORDHOUDT by 1 p.m. Rendezvous, 28/B.14.b.99.05, under the orders of O.C. Convoy, who will report to Area Commandant, LEDERZEELE, on arrival, for accommodation on the night of 6/7th November, 1917. |
| 2. | Limbered Wagons of 2/6th K.L.R., | To follow 2/5th KLR. | | |
| 3. | Limbered Wagons of 2/8th K.L.R., | To follow 2/6th KLR. | | |

On 7th November, the Convoy will move to NORDAUSQUES AREA, by WATTEN - BAYENGHEM, under the orders of O.C. Convoy.

SECRET                                                    COPY NO. 18

ADMINISTRATIVE ORDERS in connection with

171st INFANTRY BRIGADE ORDER 46.

5th November, 1917.

1.  BILLETS.        Units will be billeted as follows :-

    2/5th K.L.R.,     LA FAXEE.
    2/6th    ",       LOUCHES.           Brigade HdQrs,
    2/8th    ",       ZOUAFQUES.         BOUDINGHEM.
    171st M.G.Co.     AUDINGHEM.
    171st L.T.M.B.,       ",

2.  REFILLING POINT.   Refilling Point will be notified later.
    In the meantime, supplies will be delivered by M.T. to
    Units' Headquarters.

3.  AREA STORES.    All Area Stores will be handed over to
    Relieving Units, and a receipt obtained.       Rear
    Parties of 1 N.C.O. and 3 men will be left behind for this
    purpose.
                These Rear Parties will then follow by
    omnibus train after relief.     A Movement Order for
    these Parties will be provided by Units.
                Receipts for the Stores will be forwarded to
    Brigade HdQrs on arrival at new Area.

4.  DIVISIONAL EMPLOY.      Divisional Details, and Infantry
    attached to 421st Field Co, R.E., will rejoin their Units
    on 7th November.

5.  MECHANICAL TRANSPORT.    Motor Lorries will probably meet
    trains on arrival.    Units will hold Loading Parties in
    readiness.

                                E. Marshall
                                Captain, A/Staff Captain,
                                171st Infantry Brigade.


            ISSUED to all Recipients of 171st INFANTRY
                    BRIGADE ORDER No. 46.

SECRET.  171st INFANTRY BRIGADE.  Copy No... 7

BRIGADE ORDER NO.47.

5th November 1917.

(1) The 2/7th K.L.R., will move from BRIDGE CAMP and occupy Camp at PARROY FARM, reference Sheet 28 N.W. B.16.D.O.5. on 6th November 1917.

(2) The 2/7th K.L.R., will be clear of BRIDGE CAMP by 12 noon.

(3) Advance parties should be sent to new camp.

(4) All Area Stores will be handed over to incoming Unit and a receipt obtained. A rear party of one N.C.O., and 3 men will be left for this purpose.
Receipt for Area Stores will be forwarded to Bde.H.Q.

(5) Camp and transport lines should be left scrupulously clean.

*J.J. Huntley*

Lieut.
A/Brigade Major,
171st Infantry Brigade.

Issued to:-

    Copy No. 1  B.G.C.
              2  Brigade Major,
              3  Staff Captain,
              4  57th Division "G"
              5        "    "Q"
              6  2/7th K.L.R.
              7  War Diary.
              8      "

APPENDIX II.

STATEMENT of CASUALTIES

in connection with

171st INFANTRY BRIGADE WAR DIARY,

1.11.1917

to

30.11.1917.

.....

## 171st INFANTRY BRIGADE.

### CASUALTIES from 1.11.17 to 30.11.17.

| DATE. 24 hours ending noon - | KILLED. | | WOUNDED. | | MISSING. | |
|---|---|---|---|---|---|---|
| | Officers. | O.Ranks. | Officers. | O.Ranks. | Officers. | O.Ranks. |
| 1.11.17. | - | 9 | Lieut. R.LEWIS. Lieut. AKH.NEALE. 2nd Lieut. G.FROUDE. | 34 | - | - |
| 2.11.17. | - | 3 | Lieut. W.A.KENNETT. | 18 | - | - |
| 3.11.17. | - | 2 | - | 17 | - | - |
| 4.11.17. | - | - | - | 1 | - | - |
| 9.11.17. | - | - | 2nd Lieut. N.D.A.FROST. | 1 | - | - |
| 10.11.17. | - | 1 | - | 3 | - | 1 |
| 11.11.17. | - | 1 | - | 11 | - | - |
| 14.11.17. | - | - | - | 2 | - | - |
| 16.11.17. | - | - | - | 4 | - | - |
| TOTAL - | - | 16 | 5 | 91 | - | 1 |

AQ 171/Inf Bn
(5th Div)
9/11
December 1917.

**On His Majesty's Service.**

R

171st Inf Bde

Confidential

Headquarters

51st (West Lancs) Div"

BM/1138

WAR DIARY

of

HEADQUARTERS, 171st INFANTRY BRIGADE,

1.12.1917,

to

31.12.1917.

...

VOLUME X.

...

**WAR DIARY**
or
**INTELLIGENCE SUMMARY**

(Erase heading not required.)

Army Form C. 2118

Instructions regarding War Diaries and Intelligence Summaries are contained in F.S. Regs., Part II. and the Staff Manual respectively. Title Pages will be prepared in manuscript.

| Place | Date 1917 | Hour | Summary of Events and Information | Remarks and references to Appendices |
|---|---|---|---|---|
| NORDAUSQUES | 1 Dec. | | Training continued. | 2o/ft |
| | 2 " | | Sunday. No work. | 2o/ft |
| | 3 " | | Training continued by all Units | 2o/ft |
| | 4 " | | do | 2o/ft |
| | 5 " | | do | 2o/ft |
| | 6 " | | do | 2o/ft |
| | 7 " | | Advance parties from all units reported to Area Comdt. PROOSDY Bde area PROVEN. | 2o/ft Appendix 1 |
| PROOSDY B. | 8 " | | All units moved by motor lorries to PROOSDY area. PROVEN. arriving at 4.0 p.m. Debussed and marched to respective camps - Nh units reported arrival by 6.0 p.m. | 2o/ft Appendix 1 Appendix 1 2o/ft |
| | 9 - 15 | | All units employed in improving camps, erecting NISSEN HUTS etc. A Labour Company hind part of IX Corps Works Batn. was formed on 9. XII. 17 personnel being drawn evenly from 2/5 2/6 2/7 & 2/6 KLR. | Appendix 1 2o/ft |

Army Form C. 2118

# WAR DIARY
## or
## INTELLIGENCE SUMMARY
(Erase heading not required.)

Instructions regarding War Diaries and Intelligence Summaries are contained in F.S. Regs., Part II. and the Staff Manual respectively. Title Pages will be prepared in manuscript.

II

| Place | Date 1917 | Hour | Summary of Events and Information | Remarks and references to Appendices |
|---|---|---|---|---|
| PROVEN. | DEC 9-15 (cont'd) | | The WIJDENDRIFT sector was reconnoitred on 14th & 15th Dec. | copy. |
| | 16 | | 2/5 & 2/6 K.L.R. moved to CANAL BANK near BOESINGHE (BOP) — 2 sections 171 M.G. Coy moved to SIGNAL FARM near the STEENBEEK — 2 sections 171 L.T.M.B. moved with M.G. Coy. | appendix copy. |
| FIFTEEN WOOD | 17 | | 171 Bde H.Q. moved to FIFTEEN WOOD — Reference Map 20 S.W.4. BIXSCHOOTE. U.25.C. 2.2. — 2/7 & 2/8 K.L.R. moved to CANAL BANK near BOESINGHE (BOP) — 1 section M.G. Coy. moved to SIGNAL FARM. 2/5 & 2/6 K.L.R. with M.G. Coy & L.T.M.B. moved to line. Front line SOUTHERN Boundary — BROEM BEEK at 20/V 7 B.4.7. through TURENNE CROSSING thence N.W. to V.5 B. 8. 9. 8. Front line is held by posts in two lines with 150 yards interval — each post distant from other posts by 50 yards. Two Companies from each line Battn in front line — One Company in support and one in Reserve. Weather very cold. Hard frost. Good going. Relief complete with no casualties, at 11.0 pm. Hostile aeroplane shot down and crashed near CANAL BANK, occupants killed. | appendix I copy. |

Army Form C. 2118

# WAR DIARY
## or
## INTELLIGENCE SUMMARY
*(Erase heading not required.)*

Instructions regarding War Diaries and Intelligence Summaries are contained in F. S. Regs., Part II. and the Staff Manual respectively. Title Pages will be prepared in manuscript.

| Place | Date 1917 | Hour | Summary of Events and Information | Remarks and references to Appendices |
|---|---|---|---|---|
| FIFTEEN WOOD | Dec 18 | | Activity confined to artillery fire - Frozen ground materially hindered by the severe frost which made it impossible to dig or to erect pickets for wire - | Byd. |
| | 19 | | With the exception of occasional bursts of artillery fire the period was quiet. Weather still exceedingly cold with thick mist - Working parties made slight progress. Wire was put up in front of our posts in the wood. Hostile artillery shelled the BROEN BEEK and STEEN BEEK valleys with H.E. & a few Gas shells. The shelling of our front line posts was only light and the situation remained quiet. | Byd. |
| | 20 | | During night of 19/20 wire in front of our posts was strengthened but work was still difficult owing to the continued frost. Visibility low owing to mist. Under cover of this carrying parties were employed in conveying material to the front line. Enemy machine guns reported to have been rather more active in harassing the area EGYPT HOUSE U.12.B.3.9 to the YPRES-STADEN Railway. BROEMBEEK and STEEN BEEK valleys were again shelled by H.E. and some Gas shells. Ground hard and dry - going good - No sign of any offensive action on the enemy's part - The entire 24 hours passed quietly | Byd. |

1875  Wt. W593/826  1,000,000  4/15  J.B.C. & A.  A.D.S.S./Forms/C. 2118.

Army Form C. 2118

# WAR DIARY
## or
## INTELLIGENCE SUMMARY

(Erase heading not required.)

Instructions regarding War Diaries and Intelligence Summaries are contained in F. S. Regs., Part II. and the Staff Manual respectively. Title Pages will be prepared in manuscript.

IV

| Place | Date 1917 | Hour | Summary of Events and Information | Remarks and references to Appendices |
|---|---|---|---|---|
| FIFTEEN WOOD | Dec 21 | | During night 20/21 the 2/8 KLR relieved 2/5 KLR on the right and the 2/9 KLR relieved 2/6 KLR on the left of sector. Weather cold and misty and the reliefs were accomplished without incident. Hostile artillery was quieter than normal and very few aeroplanes were up. | Appendix 1 2/9 |
| | 22 | | Bright clean day with frost. Going hard and dry. Artillery on both sides were active. Our aeroplanes were also up continuously. Enemy aircraft active during the morning. The enemy made a determined attack on our front at TURENNE CROSSING - his barrage descending at 4.20 p.m. Under cover of this he succeeded in rushing the post. Thirty nine of our men are unaccounted for. His barrage ceased at 5.15 p.m. and the situation was reported quiet at 5.40 p.m. After 4 hours artillery preparation a counter attack was launched at 8.15 p.m. by the counter attack company. This succeeded in advancing to within 50 yards of TURENNE CROSSING but were checked by enfilade M.G. fire. The officers leading the left 2/5 JOHNSON was killed and the attack broken up. A new line in rear of our old line was established and the posts on either | |

1875 Wt. W593/826 1,000,000 4/15 J.B.C. &A. A.D.S.S./Forms/C. 2118.

# WAR DIARY
## or
## INTELLIGENCE SUMMARY

Army Form C. 2118

V

(Erase heading not required.)

| Place | Date 1917 | Hour | Summary of Events and Information | Remarks and references to Appendices |
|---|---|---|---|---|
| FIFTEEN WOOD | Dec 22 (cont) | | Flanks brought back to conform to the general line. This new front approximately from ADEN HOUSE. V.I.c.9.9 to the BROEMBEEK at V.7.B.3.3. | Appendix III 9/Yorks |
| | 23. | | Artillery activity chiefly confined to the enemy's positions near TURENNE CROSSING and upon our new line. Back areas were singularly quiet. 2 Coys 2/5 K.L.R. were sent up after dark to reinforce right sector. Patrols were out endeavouring to obtain identification of the enemy but parties in No man's land were thick. | Appendix I. 9/Yorks |
| | 24 | | Normal artillery fire on both sides. A quiet day from an infantry point of view. Work on the front line posts was pushed on - advantage being taken of the thaw and warmth on the left of the sector was strengthened the wire being taken to tree stumps in the wood. Patrols were active particularly those sent out by 2/7 K.L.R. on the left. On the right the 7/8 K.L.R. sent out patrols but these were much hampered by the hard going and the state of the ground. 171 M.G.Coy was relieved by 172 M.G. Coy | Appendix I 9/Yorks |

# WAR DIARY or INTELLIGENCE SUMMARY

Army Form C. 2118

| Place | Date | Hour | Summary of Events and Information | Remarks and references to Appendices |
|---|---|---|---|---|
| FIFTEEN WOOD | 1917 Dec 25 | | The thaw continued but during the day occasional show showers fell which became heavier during the evening. Ground was consequently white and rather thin a bright moon the visibility during the evening was exceptionally good. Enemy displays no activity, his shelling of both advanced and back area being below normal. The 171 Inf Bde was relieved during the evening by 172 Inf Bde. The 7/8 K.R.R. were relieved on the right by 25 South Lanc. Regt and the 2/7 K.R.R. on the left by 2/9 K.R.R. Relief was complete by 9.0 pm & was accomplished without incident. The Brigade moved to BOESINGHE area No. 2. Headquarters being at ZONNEBEEK CAMP — 2/5 K.R.R — 2/6 K.R.R — 4/2/7 K.R.R at LARKY CAMP? 2/6 K.R.R at CANAL BANK BOESINGHE. | Appendix 1 |
| BOESINGHE area 2. | 26 | | Brigade halted. All units spent the day in cleaning equipment, baths etc | |
| | 27 | | Weather intensely cold. Snow froze. Brigade remained in reserve. | |
| | 28. | | Advance parties moved to CANADA area near PROVEN. | |

Army Form C. 2118

# WAR DIARY
or
# INTELLIGENCE SUMMARY VII

(Erase heading not required.)

Instructions regarding War Diaries and Intelligence Summaries are contained in F. S. Regs., Part II. and the Staff Manual respectively. Title Pages will be prepared in manuscript.

| Place | Date | Hour | Summary of Events and Information | Remarks and references to Appendices |
|---|---|---|---|---|
| CANADA area | Dec 1917 29 | | Brigade moved to CANADA area. Advance parties moved on to the GOEDWAERSVELDE area. | Appendix I 9/J/t. |
| GOEDWAER SVELDE | 30 | | Brigade moved to the GOEDWAERSVELDE area. Advance parties moved to the STEENWERCKE area. | Appendix I 9/J/t. |
| STEENWERCKE | 31 | | Brigade moved to STEENWERCKE. Advance parties moved to ARMENTIERES | Appendix I 9/J/t. |
| | | | List of casualties for period 1.XII.17 – 31.XII.17 attached. | Appendix IV 9/J/t. |

Montgomery Brig. Gen.
C.S.I. 171st Inf. Bde.

APPENDIX IV.

STATEMENT OF CASUALTIES

in connection with

171st INFANTRY BRIGADE WAR DIARY.

1.12.1917,

to

31.12.1917.

....

## 171st INFANTRY BRIGADE.

### CASUALTIES from 1.12.17 to 31.12.17.

| DATE. 24 hours ending noon. | KILLED. Officers. | O.Ranks. | WOUNDED. Officers | O.Ranks. | MISSING. Officers. | O.Ranks. |
|---|---|---|---|---|---|---|
| 12/12/17. | - | - | - | 1 | - | - |
| 19/12/17. | - | 7 | - | - | - | - |
| 20/12/17. | - | - | - | 2 | - | - |
| 21/12/17. | - | - | Lt.Col. M.I.G. Jenkins. | 6 | - | - |
| 22/12/17. | Lt.E.H. Johnson. | - | - | 5 | 2/Lt.J.A. Free. MC. 2/Lt.R.A. Davies. | - |
| 23/12/17. | - | 3 | - | 38 | - | 39. |
| 24/12/17. | Capt.C.A. Mackenzie. | 1 | - | 2 | - | 1. |
| 25/12/17. | - | - | - | 5 | - | - |
| 26/12/17. | - | - | 1 | 2 | - | - |
| 27/12/17. | - | - | - | 1 | - | - |
| 28/12/17. | - | - | 2/Lt.J.S.S. Mann. Lt.G.W. Wood. | - | - | - |
| T O T A L. | 2 | 11. | 3. | 62. | 2 | 40. |

APPENDIX III.

MINOR OPERATIONS

referred to in

171st INFANTRY BRIGADE WAR DIARY,

1.12.1917,

to

31.12.1917.

....

SECRET..

Headquarters,
    57th (West Lancs.) Division.

            .......

    With reference to attached report marked "A".

1. The enemy put down a hurricane bombardment from U.6.d. central - TURENNE CROSSROADS - COLIBRI FARM for about 5 or 10 minutes and then formed a box barrage round this line.
    The enemy appears to have attacked within 10 minutes from time of first opening fire with their artillery - and used bombs during their attack.

2. The Posts at V.1.c.45.40 beat off a fairly strong attack at about 4-40 pm. and two other attacks during the night; the latter were supported by enemy's M.G. and Trench Mortar fire.

3. (a) The failure of our counter-attack, which was made at 8 pm. from U.12.d.7.9. with 1½ platoons advancing on both sides of the RAILWAY in line of Sections with two Lewis Gun Sections in Support following in the 2nd line -, was due to direct M.G. fire from vicinity of TURENNE CROSSROADS and oblique fire from the North, the Lewis Gun Section on the Left flank being twice put out of action.
    The artillery fire had made the ground which was always difficult, worse.

    (b) Our 1¼ hour's bombardment prior to launching the counter-attack does not appear to have been sufficiently strong to have silenced the M.Gs. placed near TURENNE CROSSROADS, which were chiefly responsible for our casualties and failure to push the counter-attack home. On the other hand, it was sufficient to make the enemy thoroughly alert, and he put down a counter-barrage between the TURENNE CROSSROADS and V.7.c. Central.

4. The position of the Posts, which were held as handed over by the former Unit in the Line, were in nearly a straight line instead of chequerwise, and were therefore unsupported by fire from behind, which would have greatly strengthened the position against enemy attack. Owing to the frost and the consequent hard state of the ground the strengthening of existing posts in the outpost line was very difficult.

5. All Infantry wires North of the VEE BEND were cut by enemy bombardment, but messages were sent and received by Power Buzzer and Wireless, the latter being occasionally interfered with by enemy's instruments.

6. The delay of 3½ hours before the counter-attack was made on the 22nd instant, gave the enemy time to cover all approaches with Machine Guns and consolidate the position.
    From the above it would appear that time, together with reliable information of the situation, are the two most important factors in making a succesful counter-attack.
    (a) An Officer's patrol should go forward as soon as our line appears to be in difficulties. This patrol will find out the situation and best line of advance for the counter-attack from a previously selected position of assembly.
    (b) O.C. Counter-attack force will send out the patrol mentioned in (a) and at once move his troops to the selected point of assembly somewhere in the vicinity of our Front Line. O.C., Counter-Attack will then be well situated as soon as he receives his Patrol's report, to either make his counter-attack if the line has been pierced, or to reinforce any part of the Line as required.

B.H.Q.,                             Brigadier-General,
29.12.17.                   Commanding 171st Infantry Brigade.

SECRET.

## REPORT ON ENEMY'S ATTACK ON TURENNE CROSSING.
### 22nd Dec. 1917.

Map Ref.
BROEMBEEK.ED.3.
1/10,000.

**4.20 pm.** At 4-20 pm. hostile Artillery barrage of H.E. and shrapnel was placed along the front line from the BROEMBEEK U.7.b.3.5. to the Wood V.6.a.5.3. being particularly heavy around TURENNE CROSSING.
This part of the line was held by 2/8th Liverpool Regt.

**4.25 pm.** S.O.S. went up from the left of our line - held by 2/7th Liverpool Regt. and was immediately followed by S.O.S. all along our front.

**4.30 pm.** Our barrage opened.

**5.10 pm.** Enemy barrage lifted from front line to the line EGYPT HOUSE V.12.b.3.9. to junction road and railway V.12.d.7.9.

**5.20 pm.** Enemy barrage ceased - Our Artillery slackened.

**5.40 pm.** Situation reported fairly quiet.

Left Company 2/8th Liverpool Regt.)
Support Coy. 2/8th Liverpool Regt.) reported O.K.
Right Coy. 2/8th Liverpool Regt.- reported that group at TURENNE CROSSING V.1.d.2.4. was missing, and that he had ordered his support post to move up from V.7.a.2.8. but that otherwise the situation was quiet.

**6.30 pm.** Message received by 2/8th Liverpool Regt. that post at V.1.6.7.6. was holding out though hard pressed.

**7.47 pm.** Our Artillery placed $\frac{1}{2}$ hrs. barrage on V.1.d.5.6. and one Company "D" 2/8th Liverpool Regt. counter-attacked the posts at TURENNE CROSSING at 8.15 pm.

**8.15 pm.** Our troops advanced to within 50 yards of the Crossing but were met by Artillery barrage and enfilade M.G. fire. Forced to withdraw. Holding fresh line V.1.c.65.10. to V.7.b.00.60.

Germans in possession of posts TURENNE CROSSING to the BROEMBEEK formerly held by us.

APPENDIX II.

TACTICAL &

INTELLIGENCE SUMMARIES

in connection with

171st INFANTRY BRIGADE WAR DIARY,

1.12.1917,

to

31.12.1917.

....

CONFIDENTIAL.    NOT TO BE TAKEN INTO FRONT LINE TRENCHES.

## TA-CTICAL SITUATION REPORT.

171st INFANTRY BRIGADE.        PERIOD - 6 am. 17.12.17. to
                                        6 am. 18.12.17.

.......

A. OPERATIONS OUR OWN.

1. ARTILLERY. No report up to 6 pm. Very little activity during the night.
2. AIRCRAFT. Our Patrols crashed an enemy ALBATROSS Single-Seater Machine in B.6.b. 2.45 pm. Considerable activity was shown during the afternoon, the visibility being high.

B. ENEMY OPERATIONS & INTELLIGENCE.

1. ARTILLERY. LEW 5 CHEMINS was shelled at 9-15 am. with 77 mm. and again at 12-15 pm. with 10.5 cm.
   Very quiet night.
2. AIRCRAFT. An enemy patrol of 5 flying towards PILCKEM RIDGE was driven off by our AA fire at 2-40 pm.
3. MOVEMENT. Enemy at work on ridge V.17. central all the morning. (This has been reported before). Man seen at Pill Box V.2.d. 42.13.
II. GENERAL. The relief was succesfully carried out without casualties. The Right Battalion relief was complete by 10 pm. and the Left Battalion relief by midnight. Hostile Artillery activity during the relief was practically NIL. Visibility was high. The ground is very hard after the night's frost.

.......

Owing to the relief no Intelligence is available for the period up till 9 pm. last night. From 9 pm. to 6 am. the enemy's artillery, machine guns and trench mortars have been quiet.

Captain, Brigade Major,
171st Infantry Brigade.

.......

PATROL REPORT.....NIL.

CONFIDENTIAL.   NOT TO BE TAKEN INTO FRONT LINE TRENCHES.

TACTICAL SITUATION REPORT.
oOo

171st INFANTRY BRIGADE.    PERIOD - 6 am 18.12.17. to 6 am. 19.12.17.

A. OPERATIONS - OUR OWN.

 1. ARTILLERY.   Fairly quiet during the morning, but rather active from 4pm. to 6 pm. The Artillery of the flank Division displayed considerable activity at intervals during the day and night.
 5. SNIPERS.   Very little movement in enemy front line defences was observed and no targets presented themselves.
 6. PATROLS.   (See attached report).
 8. AIRCRAFT.   Our planes were very active from dawn to 8-30 am., and again throughout the day showed intermittent activity. Visibility was very high.
   One of our planes crashed in U.28.c. on the Sector on our right at about 11-0 am. The machine is a total wreck, both occupants being killed.

B. ENEMY OPERATIONS & INTELLIGENCE.

 1. ARTILLERY.   A normal day with desultory shelling of tracks, the BROEMBEEK - and the usual short bursts of fire on 5 CHEMINS, EGYPT HOUSE, SUEZ FARM, and other points in the forward area.
   NEY Cross Roads was shrapnelled at regular intervals from 8-15 am. - 9-30 am; and this area was again shelled about the same time at night.
   The front line was hardly shelled at all but J Post was shelled from 8am to noon with 5.9's.
   Back areas quiet.
 2. T.Ms.   COLOMBO HOUSE (U.6. central) was shelled at 7 am and at intervals during the day with medium Minnenwerfer.
 3. M.Gs.   The KOEKUIT Road and the 5 CHEMINS to COLOMBO House Road were fired on during the night.
 4. PATROLS.   No enemy patrols seen or heard.
 8. AIRCRAFT.   Less active than on the previous day.
 9. MOVEMENT.   Movement during day at Supply Dump O.36.central; also on two tracks running SW from Chateau (about 20 men in all - some wearing steel helmets, some caps, some equipment, some without equipment).
   Considerable movement observed on the road on the top of WESTROOSEBEKE Ridge.
 II. GENERAL.   A quiet day and a very quiet night. The absence of enemy patrols is remarkable, as the ground being hard is favourable for patrol work.
   Visibility was very high.

Captain, Brigade Major,
171st Infantry Brigade.

PATROL REPORT - 57th DIVISION - XIX CORPS.

| UNIT. | Strength of Patrol. | Time and Date. | Objective or Task. | REMARKS and INFORMATION. |
|---|---|---|---|---|
| 2/6th K.L.R. | 1 NCO (Corpl. F.Corkhill) and 5 men. | 6 pm - 8 p.m. 15.12.1917. | To reconnoitre LES CINQ CHEMINS - DIXMUDE RD. & try to locate enemy positions. | Patrol started out from No. 10 Lewis Gun Post (U.6.b.10.40) and proceeded parallel to and 30 yds distance from LES 5 CHEMINS DIXMUDE RD. for a distance of 350 yds. crossing two well defined ditches which were about 10' wide - depth unknown. On arriving 30 yds from road (U.6.b.20.80) sounds were heard of coughing and rattling so patrol lay up for 15 minutes during which period sounds of ice breaking were heard along and behind the road U.6.b.20.80. to U.6.a.80.70. Having ascertained that there was an enemy position patrol returned by same route. A double whistle was heard from left front as patrol started. N.M.L. is covered with water-logged shell holes. Going good owing to frost. No apparent obstacles on the road and none were encountered as shown on U.6.b.1.7. Visibility was very good owing to moon light. |

CONFIDENTIAL. NOT TO BE TAKEN INTO FRONT LINE TRENCHES.

## TACTICAL SITUATION REPORT.

171st INFANTRY BRIGADE.   PERIOD 6am. 19.12.17. to 6 am. 20.12.17.

A. OPERATIONS - OUR OWN.
  1. ARTILLERY. 18 pdrs. active at 7-30 a.m. on SCHAAP-BALIE Road in V.2. central and P.33.c. 4.5's Hows. active at 7-15 am. on SIX Cross Roads V.1.b. C.35.d. was shelled by 4.5's and 18 pdrs. at about 7 pm. and again at 10 pm.
  5. PATROLS. See report on reverse. An enemy post has previously been reported at U.5.b.99.99. Two patrols were out from Right Battn. but no report has yet been received.
  6. WIRE. Wiring of front line posts was carried out by right company of left battalion.
  8. AIRCRAFT. Owing to the mist it was difficult to see aeroplane movements. There was some activity from 2 - 3 pm. but otherwise it appeared to be normal.
  9. GENERAL. Liaison was established with right post of left brigade.

B. ENEMY OPERATIONS & INTELLIGENCE.
  1. ARTILLERY. Hostile Artillery activity was chiefly directed on BROEMBEEK and STEENBEEK Valleys, U.16.b, & d. A certain amount of Gas (Blue and Yellow Cross) was used about 2 - 6-30 pm. on our Batteries at this point, and again at about 11 pm. on the duckboard tracks in the vicinity.
  The NE wind was just strong enough to carry the gas for a considerable distance and sneezing was reported in back areas as far as BOESINGHE and the CANAL BANK, where the irritation was more violent than in the areas immediately East of the Canal.
  Seeing that the shelling was of inconsiderable quantity - probably 300 rounds on our area at the outside - this a long way for the gas to have carried.
  The firing seems to have been in retaliation to the shoots of the Artillery of our own and Left Division at 7 pm. and 10 pm.
  The enemy's activity on forward areas was normal - the usual shelling of 5 CHEMINS, KAJAK & EGYPT HOUSES, SULZ and PASCAL FARM being reported. A little gas was used at night in retaliation to our fire.
  2. T.Ms. Quiet.
  3. PATROLS. No enemy patrols reported.
  4. M.G. 3 guns reported firing. (1) V.1.d.6.2. on EGYPT HOUSE and STATION ROAD. (2) MARECHAL FARM on Road at U.5.d.8.1. (3) 0.35.d.8.2. on FAIDHERBE Cross Roads.
  8. AIRCRAFT. An enemy plane flying low passed over our lines flying toward the Forest at 3-20 pm., fired on by our AA Guns.
  9. MOVEMENT. Owing to the mist no movement was observed.
  II. GENERAL. A quiet day and, except for the gas shelling, a quiet night. There are no casualties reported from the gas shelling. Visibility was fairly high at midday, but otherwise low. A thick mist came down about midnight, and still prevails. The Company reliefs were successfully carried out, no casualties being reported.

Captain, Brigade Major,
171st Infantry Brigade.

P.T.O.

PATROL REPORT  -  57th DIVISION  -  XIX CORPS.

| Unit. | Strength of Patrol. | Time & Place. | Objective or Task. | Remarks & Information. |
|---|---|---|---|---|
| 2/6th K.L.R. | 2nd.Lt.R.L.MOON, 2 O.Ranks. | 5-30 p.m. to 7-30 p.m. 19.12.17. | To establish liaison between the left post (No.16) and the right post of the Battn. on our left. | Patrol left No.15 Post U.6.a.10.55. at 5-30 pm. and emerged on road at U.5.b.90.75. Here we heard coughing and knocking against wire coming from the direction of U.5.b.90.90. We crawled out in the open ground leaving a covering party and proceeded some 75 yards. Hearing nothing more and believing the left Battn's post to be on the road near U.5.b.7.7. We returned and advanced in a westerly direction along the road. This road was covered with obstacles such as fallen trees and also by a barricade of concertina wire at about U.5.b.85.75. From there we heard a rattling about 50 yds. further down the road, so we challenged and got a reply. Leaving the remainder of the patrol I went on and discovered the post of the other Battalion. We t.en laid a tape right back to our own post at U.5.b.95.75. which we came across on our way back. |

CONFIDENTIAL.

## 171st INFANTRY BRIGADE INTELLIGENCE SUMMARY.
### Period 24 hours ending 6 a.m., 21.12.1917.
### NOT TO BE TAKEN INTO FRONT LINE TRENCHES.

..........

A. OPERATIONS - OUR OWN.
  1. ARTILLERY.   The usual programme of harrassing fire was carried out.
  4. SNIPERS.    A Hit is claimed by the Right Battn. on a man of an enemy working party in V.I.Central.
  5. PATROLS.    See reverse.   Liaison was established with Left Left Battn of Right Brigade.   As the BROEMBEEK was frozen, it afforded no obstacle to the patrol as on a previous occasion.
  6. WIRE.       The wire in front of the front line Posts has been strengthened along the whole of our Section.
  8. AIRCRAFT.   No activity owing to mist.

B. ENEMY OPERATIONS & INTELLIGENCE.
  1. ARTILLERY.  Quiet on the whole.   Slight shelling of the BROEMBEEK and STEENBEEK at night, including some gas shells - Yellow Cross.   Very quiet from 2 a.m. to dawn.
     The following points were shelled by short bursts of 77mm. during the day - U.5.d.4.3.  U.6.c.95.40.  U.12.b.4.5.
     The KOEKUIT ROAD, HUNTERS STREET and CLARGES STREET in the forward area were occasionally shelled with 4.2s" and shrapnel.
  2. T.Ms.  A few rounds were fired on our line in the Forest, U.6.a.Central early in the morning, and on the vicinity of COLOMBO HOUSE - no damage was done.
  4. MACHINE GUNS.   A gun is reported active at V.I.a.4.4. traversing the road from EGYPT HOUSE to the RAILWAY during the night and early dawn.   This might be the gun located at V.I.a.1.2 or the one suspected at V.I.a.5.2.
  5. SNIPERS.   O.C. Right Battn. was wounded by an enemy sniper at dawn this morning on the RAILWAY near TURENNE CROSSING.
  6. PATROLS.   No enemy patrol activity except that mentioned in the patrol report.
  9. MOVEMENT.   Owing to the thick mist which lasted throughout the period, no movement was observed.
II. GENERAL.   The low visibility was taken advantage of to cover the movement of carrying parties bringing up R.E. material for the improvement of existing posts and for the clearing of salvage from the line.   Several shelters were got up to the wood on the extreme left of our front line for erection as soon as possible.   An old track was discovered and re-taped from Left Battn. HdQrs to No.14 Post.
     The situation remains quiet, and the enemy appears to take no offensive action of any sort.   No unusual activity in the way of working parties is reported and only one patrol has been reported in the last 4 days, in spite of the good going in NO MAN'S LAND.   There was no aircraft activity of any sort.

                                          Captain, Brigade Major,
                                               171st Infantry Brigade.


                              P.T.O.

PATROL REPORT - 57th DIVISION - XIX CORPS.

| UNIT. | Strength of Patrol. | Time and date. | Objective or Task. | Remarks and information. |
|---|---|---|---|---|
| 2/5th Bn. K. L. R. | Sgt. Bond. 2 O.Ranks. | 10-0 pm. 20.12.17. | To locate enemy posts on roads running N.E. from ANGLE POINT at approximately V.1.c. 1.6.65. | Patrol left No. 3 Post at V.1.c.2.6. at 10 pm. and moved towards the enemy's wire. The wire is about 18 inches high. Whide lying near road running N.E. from ANGLE POINT (U.6.d.6.4.) the patrol saw an enemy patrol between themselves and our own post, 13 men were counted in this enemy patrol which moved off in a northerly direction, shortly after being seen. The patrol returned at 12 midnight. The enemy wire was easy to detect owing to the hoarfrost. Talking and movement was heard but the exact point from which it came was hard to locate. |

CONFIDENTIAL.   NOT TO BE TAKEN INTO FRONT LINE TRENCHES.

TACTICAL SITUATION REPORT.

171st INFANTRY BRIGADE  -   PERIOD 6 am. 21.12.17. to 6 am. 22.12.17.

..........

A. OPERATIONS - OUR OWN.
1. ARTILLERY.  A shoot was postponed owing to the relief. Otherwise a very quiet day with little activity on either side on this Sector.
3. PATROLS.   3 Patrols were out. (1) to determine site of enemy post reported at U.6.b.2.7. (Aero Photo GB135), (2) to investigate enemy post at fork of roads V.I.c.18.83, (3) to locate suspected enemy post near V.1.d.6.4.   See attached report.   The first two were successful in locating the posts but no trace could be found of the third.
4. M.Gs.   Occasional bursts of fire about 4 pm.
9. GENERAL.  No aircraft and no movement is reported owing to the low visibility. The reliefs were successfully carried out by 8-30 pm. The relieved battalions reaching the CANAL BANK area by about 11 p The relief was started before dusk, the low visibility making this possible. Only one casualty is reported from a spent rifle bullet.

B. ENEMY OPERATIONS & INTELLIGENCE.
1. ARTILLERY. A very quiet day in this Section.
2. T.Ms.    A few minnies fell on COLUMBO HOUSE and at about U.6.a.0.7 No damage was done.
3. M.Gs.    The Roads from LES 5 CHEMINS West and to the railway crossing past EGYPT HOUSE were kept under ~~cover~~ fire at intervals
5. DEFENCES.   The enemy was heard at work in the neighbourhood of MARECHAL FARM, sounds of hammering being reported.
6. WIRE.    Enemy wiring party reported at V.1.d.7.4.
7. SIGNALS. Two white lights were fired at 8-15 am. from left of MARECHAL Farm. No action followed.
9. MOVEMENT.  10-50 am. Two Bosche in loose dress observed walking from O.36.c.90.95. to O.36.d.35.85. The mist lifted for about half an hour at this time and then came down thicker than before. No movement was observed accordingly with the exception of the above.
11. GENERAL.   Owing to the state of the ground, work at wiring was diffic and the period was again employed in bringing up R.E. material for the improvement of our defences and positions.
   The enemy is still at work near MARECHAL FARM, and also appears to be strengthening his defences in front of the HUTS, V.1.d.
   The period was very quiet owing to the mist and there is accordingly little to report.

Captain, Brigade Major,
171st Infantry Brigade.

PATROL REPORT - 57th DIVN. - XIX CORPS.

| Unit. | Patrol Strength. | Time. | Objective or Task. | Remarks and Information. |
|---|---|---|---|---|
| 2/8th Bn. K.L.R. | 1 N.C.O. 3 O.R. | 1 a.m. to 2.15 a.m. 22.12.17. | To locate enemy post at about P.1.d.6.4. | The patrol left our lines at 1 a.m. from V.1.d.18.37. and proceeded 85 yards along the SQHAAP-BALIE Road. They then left the Road and struck off about quarter right for 120 yards to the line of the ditch running from V.1.d.6.0. to V.1.d.52.44. An enemy wiring party of about 15 was then seen quiet close to the patrol engaged in putting out low wire. The patrol then moved NW across the Road and Railway and returned to our lines along the North side of the Railway about 25 yds from it and parallel to it. They found a trip wire at about V.1.d.38.60. but could see no sign of any enemy post. The wiring party was probably at work along the line of the ditch 70 yds. east of the Huts. REMARKS (There are known to be enemy posts just east of this d-itch. The machine gun previously reported at V.1.d.30.68. was probably not a permanent location.) |
| 2/8th Bn. K.L.R. | 1 N.C.O. 3 O.R. | 12 midnight to 1 a.m. 22.12.17. | To locate position of enemy post at V.1.c. 18.83. To find out strength of garrison. | The patrol reports more than a dozen men were seen in the fork of the roads at C.18.83. Two machine guns were active while the patrol was out firing from behind the trees on the road running East from V.1.a.0Q.05. (? Guns reported previously at V.1.a.1.2, V.1.a. 5.2.) A fallen tree covered by wire is also lying across the road South of the fork. The patrol encountered none of the enemy and saw none except those mentioned above. |
| 2/7th Bn. K.L.R. | 1 N.C.O. 5 O.R. | 8-30 pm. 21.1.17. | To reconnoitre enemy post at about U.6.b. 6.7. | Patrol left our post at U.6.b.15.40 at 9-50 pm. and proceeded along ditch on right of road for about 150 yards. They report an enemy post about 50 yards in rear of U.6.b.2.7. on the COLUMBO HOUSE - MARECHAL FARM. Work was heard in progress near MARECHAL FARM. The patrol returned to our lines without any incident by the same route. REMARKS (It is possible that the post at U.6.b.2.7. and the one reported by this patrol 50 yards in rear are alternatively used. This point will be kept under observation until the definite location of the enemy's permanent post is obtained. |

CONFIDENTIAL.

171st INF. BDE. TACTICAL SITUATION REPORT.
PERIOD - 6 am. 22.12.17. to 6 am. 23.12.17.
NOT TO BE TAKEN INTO FRONT LINE TRENCHES.

A. OPERATIONS - OUR OWN.
   I. ARTILLERY. Active during the day. The follow targets engaged:-
      18 pdrs. shelled active 77mm. Battery in V.5.b. at 10.30 a.m.
        "   "               road at V.12.c.2.7. at 11.20 a.m.
        "   "               vicinity of PUZZLE WOOD, V.17.B. at 12 noon.
        "   "               "      V.9.A. and road V.9.C.
      The heavy artillery engaged enemy batteries in the HOUTHULST FOREST.
      Our artillery fired on S.O.S. lines during the enemy's operation in
      the evening. A barrage was also put down at 7.47 p.m. for
      twenty minutes for our counter-attack.
   3. L.T.M.B. Co-operated in S.O.S. Barrage.
   4. M.Gs. Co-operated in S.O.S. Barrage. Enemy planes flying low
      over our lines were engaged by AA M.G.fire, but without success.
   5. WIRE. The road at U.6.D.95.70 was wired, and the wiring of the
      Right Posts of Left Battn. was continued.
   5. PATROLS. A patrol of 1 N.C.O. and 3 men was sent out again from
      U.6.b.18.40 at 1.30 am. to locate suspected enemy Post at U.6.b.2.7;
      The patrol moved across the field on the right of the road till they
      came to the line of trees on the road running East from U.6.b.2.7.
      Stopping short of this they observed a party of the enemy about 8 in
      number about 20 yds beyond the road moving about apparently in a
      ditch or trench. The patrol was unable to cross the road, and
      returned safely to our lines.
   6. AIRCRAFT. Eight aeroplanes flew over our lines at 1 p.m. and flew
      over the FOREST. They returned at 2.30 p.m. The enemy aircraft
      who were active during the morning patrolling our lines (apparently
      Artillery planes) then withdrew - and enemy fire lessened noticeably.
      Two enemy planes were flying high over our lines during the
      afternoon. Aerial activity on both sides was distinctly above
      normal.

B. ENEMY OPERATIONS & INTELLIGENCE.
   I. ARTILLERY. Enemy artillery was active during the morning, apparently
      employed in registration. LES 5 CHEMINS and the roads leading
      to it were shelled intermittently and fairly heavily through the
      day. For account of barrage see special report. During
      the operations a barrage was put down about 100 yds in front of VEE
      BEND and PASCAL FARM. A few H.V. shells fell near BABOON CAMP
      at about 12.30 p.m. RAILWAY STREET was shrapnelled at 20 minute
      intervals through the night.
   2. T.Ms. Co-operated in enemy barrage. A pineapple machine fired
      on LES 5 CHEMINS during the barrage; its position was not located.
   7. SIGNALS. During barrage:-
      4.30 p.m., 2 green lights from direction of MARECHAL FARM.
      4.50 p.m.,   "       "    some distance to left of MARECHAL FARM.
      4.55 p.m., 3 green lights from MARECHAL FARM.
      5.30 p.m., 4  "       "     "
      5.35 p.m., 4 white lights from near V.1.Central.
      8.45 p.m., a number of red lights bursting into two were put up on
      enemy front.
   8. AIRCRAFT. An enemy machine painted red flew over our lines at 7.45 a
   9. MOVEMENT. Two men (black caps, red bands, black leggings) were seen
      at O.36.b.45.40 at about 11 a.m. A collie dog was seen in the
      vicinity shortly afterwards.
   III. GENERAL. The day was very clear and observation was accordingly
      good. There was, however, no particular activity to report - and
      beyond the increased artillery and aeroplane activity, which might
      have been due to the improvement in weather conditions - there was
      no indication of the enemy's intentions.

                                                              Captain, Brigade Major.
                                                              171st Infantry Brigade.

PATROL PRO FORMA - NIL.

CONFIDENTIAL.

# 171st INFANTRY BRIGADE – INTELLIGENCE SUMMARY.

24 hours ending 6 a.m., 24.12.1917. – NOT TO BE TAKEN INTO FRONT LINE TRENCHES.

## A. OPERATIONS – OUR OWN.

1. **ARTILLERY.** Quiet during the morning but active during afternoon with harrassing fire on enemy's new position. Night was very quiet. Our heavy artillery was engaged in counter-battery work on batteries in HOUTHULST FOREST during the morning.
6. **WIRE.** The ground was still very hard, but wire was put out in the wood on the left flank of the Left Battn.
7. **WORK.** The mist by day and the moonlight by night were taken advantage of to clear tracks, to bring up R.E. material, and for clearing such salvage as was possible.
8. **AIRCRAFT.** Activity was normal during the day. At midnight two aeroplanes crossed our front line from the direction of the Forest carrying white navigation lights.
10. **GENERAL.** Visibility was low until about 10 a.m. when it cleared, but the mist started to settle again at about 2.30 – 3 p.m. The work of consolidation of our new line was carried on as far as possible under the circumstances, as the ground was very hard.

## B. ENEMY OPERATIONS & INTELLIGENCE.

1. **ARTILLERY.** Inactive on forward areas during the morning, but engaged our batteries in the BROEMBEEK VALLEY during the morning and early afternoon. Our new positions on the Right were shelled at about 4.45 p.m. LES 5 CHEMINS and EGYPT HOUSE were also shelled during the afternoon.
2. **T.Ms.** A few pineapples were fired on patrol which left our lines at U.6.b.6.40.
3. **M.Gs.** All the roads leading to LES 5 CHEMINS were kept under fire during the night, but most of the shots were rather high.
7. **SIGNALS.** Enemy sent up two rockets bursting into two red lights from near V.I.Central. No apparent action followed.
8. **AIRCRAFT.** An enemy plane patrolled our lines at 7 a.m. and 4 pm. and from 4.30 – 5 p.m. flying low, and firing white lights.
9. **MOVEMENT.** The mist in the morning and the early afternoon considerably hindered observation. No movement of any sort is reported, except a working party which was heard during the night in the direction of MARSHALL FARM.
11. **GENERAL.** There was no shelling of back areas during the day or night by the enemy. The period on the whole was quiet except for artillery activity on both sides near the new positions on our right flank.

    With reference to the enemy's operation on the night of the 22nd Dec., the enemy had roughly 4 four barrage lines, one, our front line positions, two, EGYPT HOUSE and CAIRO HOUSE, three, 100 yds in front of VEL BEND across HUNTERS and CLARGES STREET, and 100 yds in front of PASCAL FARM across RAILWAY STREET, and four, on our batteries in the BROEMBEEK VALLEY on the Northern side. Patrols were out last night to secure identification if possible from the enemy in the neighbourhood of TURENNE CROSSING, but this purpose was not achieved.

Captain, Brigade Major.
171st Infantry Brigade.

P.T.O.,

PATROL REPORT - 57th DIVISION. XIX CORPS.

| Unit. | Strength of Patrol. | Time and date. | Objective or Task. | Remarks and information. |
|---|---|---|---|---|
| GIDDY. | 2 N.C.Os. 6 O.Rs. | 2-30 am. 24.12.17. | To reconnoitre enemy Post about U.6.b.2.7. | After leaving our Post at U.6.b.20.45, patrol moved forward near road. A light was observed coming from U.6.b.3.7. as if a door were being opened and closed. Patrol was detected by the enemy and were subjected to "pineapple" fire. The patrol then withdrew. Time of return 4 am. |
| GILLY. | 1 Officer 1 O.R. | 10-30 pm. 23.12.17. | --- | Investigating disused bivouac 130 yds. in front of U.6 No.5 Post. Three bivouacs were found, two with entrances facing us, and uninhabitable, and one with entrance facing Bosche. In the last was found the body of a British soldier belonging to 4th (Res) Bn. CHESHIRE Regt., some old Hun equipment and a Respirator, but no identification on it. This bivouac is 130 yds from our Post, to the direct front. |

171st INFANTRY BRIGADE - INTELLIGENCE SUMMARY.
24 hrs ending 6 a.m. 25.12.1917.   NOT TO BE TAKEN INTO FRONT
                                    LINE TRENCHES.

A. OPERATIONS - OUR OWN.
   1. ARTILLERY.  A quiet day except for the usual harrassing fire
       on tracks and roads.
   4. M.Gs.    Carried out usual programme of indirect fire on roads
       & tracks.
   5. PATROLS.  Patrols were active on Left Sector but failed to secure
       identification.   2 patrols were operating on Right Sector
       as follows :-    (I) A patrol of I Sergt. & II O.R. GILT
       operated from midnight to 2 a.m. between YPRES - STADEN RY.
       and the BROMBEEK in front of our new position.  No enemy post
       was definitely located.  An enemy patrol of 30 men was seen
       but no contact was obtained.   (2) Another patrol of I Sergt.
       & IO O.R. GIRLIE operated along the ADEN HOUSE - TURENNE
       CROSSING ROAD.   The patrol report that they lay up for 40
       minutes within 50 yds of TURENNE CROSSING.  They however failed
       to locate any enemy post or to secure contact.
   6. WIRE.    The road at V.I.c.48.25 was wired with a thickxaxfixthink
       thick entanglement.  The wiring of our new posts near V.7.a.5.6
       was also carried out.   Wiring in the FOREST on our Left
       flank was carried out, the wire being wound from tree to tree.
   7. WORK.    The work of improvement of our posts was pressed on
       full advantage being taken of the thaw.  Elephant back shelters
       were erected at 4 posts.   A small O.P. was made at U.5.6 for
       2 men.   Track between Posts in the wood was also improved.
   8. AIRCRAFT.  No activity owing to unfavourable weather conditions.
   9. GENERAL.   Observation was impossible owing to mist.  Night was
       very quiet indeed.  The thaw is making the ground, especially
       in the FOREST, very difficult.

B. ENEMY OPERATIONS & INTELLIGENCE.
   1. ARTILLERY.  A H.V. gun fired a few rounds on BOESINGHE STN. between
       9 a.m. to I pm. and also on the vicinity of CLARGES ST. near
       GREEN MILL U.25.d.OI.OI between 2 - 3 p.m.   There is a branch
       of the DECAVILLE RY. leading to GREEN MILL, which may have
       been the cause of the shelling, as a dump may have been suspected
       at this point.
   2. T.MS.  Fired on U.6.d.9.3 occasionally.  Position could not be
       located.
   3. M.Gs.  Fired at intervals on roads leading to LES 5 CHEMINS.
       M.G. was located at U.6.a.20.75 - see Patrol Report.
   4. PATROLS.  An enemy patrol of 4 men near U.6.b.00.45 was dispersed
       by our rifle fire at about 8 p.m.
   6. DEFENCES.  Hammering was heard from direction of O.35.d.25.60.
   7. MOVEMENT.  Our snipers in V.I.c. fired on enemy movement during
       day, but without success.  Very few targets were presented.
       Singing and talking were heard throughout night from direction
       of MARECHAL FM.   A duckboard track runs E. from U.6.b.3.7.
       behind the road.  Movement has been observed on this track
       before by patrols - Summary of 23.12.1917 (A.5).
   II. GENERAL.   The period under review has been very quiet.  The
       thaw has made movement very difficult in forward areas.
       There was very little shelling of back areas (but see B.I)
       Visibility was very low and observation impossible.
       Our patrols were active on Left Sector but failed to secure
       identification.  Patrols on Right were much hampered by bad
       ground.  They failed to secure contact with enemy or
       definitely to locate any of his posts in the vicinity of our
       new positions.

                                       Captain, Brigade Major.
                                       171st Infantry Brigade.

                        P.T.O.

PATROL REPORT - 57th DIVISION - XIX CORPS.

| Unit. | Strength of Patrol. | Time and date. | Objective or Task. | Remarks and information. |
|---|---|---|---|---|
| GIDDY. | 1 N.C.O. & 3 men. | 9-30 pm. 24.12.17. | To investigate suspected M.G. position at U.6.b.5.5. | Patrol left by post U.6. No. 7, and proceeded to U.6.b.5.5. thence round to U.6.b.00.45. The suspected M.G. position was found to be unoccupied, and none of the enemy were encountered. The going was very difficult owing to broken nature of ground. |
| GIDDY. | 1 Officer, 1 N.C.O. & 5 men. | 10 pm. 24.12.17. | To investigate Pill Box 50 yds. in front of Post No. 5, U.6. | The patrol worked to within a few yards of the objective and to the right, when the garrison opened fire with a machine gun and three rifles from it. Capt. Colombie (i/c patrol) was badly hit and died. 1 N.C.O. was killed and 1 wounded. The N.C.O. with that patrol got back and got rifle fire to bear on the Pill Box, under cover of which Capt. N.C.O.'s name was brought in. Patrols went out for the two men but have not yet succeeded in bringing them in. |
| GIDDY. | 1 NCO. 7 O.R. | 5 pm 25/12/17. | To obtain identification from post reported at U.6.b.2.7. | Patrol went as for as previous patrol i.e., the road running West to East from COLUZO HOUS. & LARGHAI FAR Road, but no enemy movement could be heard or seen. A duckboard track was seen, 5 yds from the road running East to West, which bent round North towards the enemy lines. Patrol remained out 1 hr. 40 mins. in the hopes of seeing movements on duckboards and of waylaying someone on the duckboards but saw no movement. It returned to our lines at 3.10 am. At 5 am. another patrol went out to the same point but was not out long enough to report. This patrol returned about 1½ hrs. later reporting great activity on above-mentioned duckboards. Lowness and our shelling nearby prevented closer observation or action. Approach of daylight rendered further action impossible and patrol returned without having obtained identification. |

APPENDIX I.

RELIEF ORDERS, etc.,

referred to in

171st INFANTRY BRIGADE WAR DIARY,

1.12.1917,

to

31.12.1917.

....

SECRET.                                                          COPY NO. 23

## 171st INFANTRY BRIGADE ORDER NO. 49.

and 3/2nd West Lancs Field Amb<sup>ce</sup>

1. The transport of the 171st Infantry Brigade Group, together with H.Q., R.E., Divisional Signal Coy., 2/1st Mobile Veterinary Section and Divisional Train Headquarters, will move to LEDERZEELE on 7.12.17, as per attached march table "A". The convoy will move under the command of O.C. No.3 Coy. Divisional Train.

2. On the night of 7/8th December 1917, the convoy will be billeted at LEDERZEELE.
   Capt. P. Williams, 171st Brigade Transport Officer will proceed in advance to make necessary arrangements with Area Commandant for billets, horse lines etc.

3. Each Unit will detail a mounted N.C.O. to report to Capt. Williams, Area Commandant's Office, Lederzeele, two hours before transport arrives to guide Units to respective destinations.

4. Rations for personnel of convoy for 7th and 8th December will be carried by Units.
   Forage for 8th inst. for Battalions and M.G. Coy. will be carried by No. 3 Coy. Divisional Train, who will issue instructions for drawing.

5. The move from Lederzeele to Arneedy Brigade Area will be arranged by O.C. No. 3 Coy. Divisional Train on route shown in attached table "B".

6. Guides will be arranged by Units to meet transport on 8.12.17. at Cross Roads, HOUTKERQUE – POPERINGHE ROAD and WATOU – ROUSBRUGGE ROAD. (Reference Sheet Hazebrouck 5A – 2.H.45.45.)

7. Arrival at destination on 7th and 8th will be reported by each Unit to this Office.

                                                    [signature]
B.H.Q.                                              Captain, A/Staff Captain,
6.12.17.                                            171st Infantry Brigade.


Issued at    a.m. to:-     Copy No. 1. L.G.C.
                                    2. Brigade Major.
                                    3. Staff Captain.
                                    4. 57th Division "A"
                                    5. 57th Division "G"
                                    6. 2/5th K.L.R.
                                    7. 2/6th K.L.R.
                                    8. 2/7th K.L.R.
                                    9. 2/8th K.L.R.
                                   10. 171st L.T.M.B.
                                   11. 171st M.G.Coy.
                                   12. 421st Field Coy.R.E.
                                   13. 2/2nd Wessex Field A.
                                   14. No.3 Coy. Divisional Train.
Copy No. 23. War Diary.            15. 172nd Brigade.
         24.  "                    16. 170th Brigade.
         25. File.                 17. Brigade Transport Officer.
         26. Spare  arms           18. C.R.E.
         27. Spare                 19. Divisional Signal Coy.
                                   20. Brigade Signal Section.
                                   21. 2/1st Mobile Veterinary Sect.
                                   22. O.C. 57th Divl. Train.

TABLE "A".

MARCH TABLE FOR 171st BRIGADE GROUP TRANSPORT, NORDAUSQUES to LEDERCLIZE on 7.12.17.

| Serial no. | Unit. | Starting Point. | Time to pass Starting Point. | ROUTE. | REMARKS. |
|---|---|---|---|---|---|
| 1. | No.3 Coy.Divl.Tn. & 171st F.H.Q. | Shoot Hazebrouck 5 A. | 9.30.a.m. | MOULLE – SERQUES – ST.MOMELIN – WATTEN – HOUTKERQUE – LEDERCLIZE. | Not to enter WATTEN before 12 noon. |
| 2. | 2/5th K.L.R. | St.OMER – CALAIS RD. | 9.35.a.m. | ,, | |
| 3. | 2/6th K.L.R. | Junction of road | 9.40.a.m. | ,, | |
| 4. | 2/7th K.L.R. | immediately South of 2nd | 9.45.a.m. | ,, | |
| 5. | 2/8th K.L.R. | xg" in NORDAUSQUES. | 9.50.a.m. | ,, | |
| 6. | 171st M.G.Coy. | | 9.55.a.m. | ,, | |
| 7. | Divl.Signal Coy. | | 10.0. a.m. | ,, | |
| 8. | H.Q., R.E. | | 10.5. a.m. | ,, | |
| 9. | H.Q. Divl. Train. | | 10.8. a.m. | ,, | |
| 10. | 2/1st H.V.C. | | 10.11.a.m. | ,, | |
| 11. | 431st Field Coy.RE | | 10.16.a.m. | ,, | |
| 12. | 2/3rd Wessex F.A. | | 10.22.a.m. | ,, | |
| 13 | 3/2nd Welfare ? Ambce | | 10 27 am | ,, | |

Intervals of 200 yds. to be kept between Units.
In order to prevent blocking of main ST.OMER – CALAIS RD., starting point must not be reached before scheduled time.

----------

## TABLE "B".

MARCH TABLE FOR 171st BRIGADE GROUP TRANSPORT. LEDERZEELE to FROOSDY BRIGADE AREA. on 8.12.17.

| Serial No. | Unit. | Starting Point. | Time to Pass Starting Point. | ROUTE. | REMARKS. |
|---|---|---|---|---|---|
| | As in Table "A" Order of March to be arranged by O.C. No.3 Coy. Divl. Train. | To be arranged by O.C. No. 3. Coy. Divl. Train. | To be arranged by O.C. No. 3. Coy. Divl. Train. | ZEGGARS CAPPEL - WORMHOUDT - HERZEELE - HOUTKERQUE. | To reach WORMHOUDT at 1.0.pm. |

Copy No. 13

## 171st INFANTRY BRIGADE.

### ADMINISTRATIVE INSTRUCTIONS.

1. **BILLETING PARTIES.** Billeting Parties consisting of
   will proceed to new
   Area on 7.12.17. Train leaves ARDRUICK at 7.0.am.
   Parties to report to Officer i/c 172nd Brigade Train.
   Rations to be taken up to and including 8/12/17.

   New Area is allotted as follows:-

   Sheet 19. Portsmouth.)
   W.30.b.3.0.)
   Pitt.            )   2/5th K.L.R.
   W.30.d.2.2.)
   Portobello.  )
   W.30.d.7.9.)

   Sheet 19. Portsdown. )
   X.25.a.7.3.)         2/6th K.L.R.
   Privett    )
   X.25.c.8.5.)

   Petworth   )
   X.26.d.4.7.)         2/7th K.L.R.

   Sheet 27. Paddington )
   F.3.a.     )         2/8th K.L.R.

   Sheet 19. Putney, Camp,  X.26.b.4.6.    171st M.G.Coy.

   Sheet 19. Piccadilly,    X.20.d.6.3.    171st L.T.M.B.

   Sheet 19. Portland.      X.25.a.        481st Field Coy.R.E.

   Sheet 27. Portsea.       F.I.c.4.4.     2/2nd Wessex F.A.

   Sheet 27. Poplar.        F.2.a.6.2.     No.3 Coy. Divl. Train.

   Sheet 19. Penge.         X.27.a.4.7.    171st. B.H.Q.

   Billeting parties on arrival, will report to Area
   Commandant, Proeedy Brigade Area, Proven.
   Maps of Brigade Area will be issued to all concerned by
   7.0.pm. to-morrow night. 6/12/17.

2. **SUPPLIES.** Rations for 8/12/17 will be delivered to Units
   by M.T. Guides from each Unit will report at junction of
   Roads immediately South of "P" in PROVEN (Hazebrouck 5 A.)
   at 10.0.am. on 8/12/17 to guide lorries to respective Camps.

3. **GUIDES.** Debussing Points for Units will be notified
   later, also probable time of debussing. Guides for each
   Unit will be found from Billeting Parties. Guides for M.T.
   also required on 8/12/17. Transport route and also
   probable time of arrival will be notified later.

B.H.Q.
6/12/17.

Captain, A/Staff Captain,
171st Infantry Brigade.

*[Margin note: Billeting Parties. Units. 1 Off. 6 O.R. / L.T.M.B. 1 Off. 2 O.R. / 2/2 Wessex 1 Off. 3 O.R. / M.G.C. & R.E. / No. 3 Coy.A.S.C. 2 N.C.Os. / B.H.Q. 1 Off. 5 O.R.]*

ISSUED AT 11-0/-  TO:-

Copy No. 1. B.G.C.
2. B.M.
3. Staff Captain,
4. 2/5th K.L.R.
5. 2/6th K.L.R.
6. 2/7th K.L.R.
7. 2/8th K.L.R.
8. 171st L.T.M.B.
9. 171st M.G.Coy.
10. 421st Field Coy.R.E.
11. 2/2nd Wessex F.A.
12. No.3. Coy.Divl.Train.
13. Area Commandant, Proosdy Camp,
        Proven.
14. File.
15. War Diary.
16.    ,,
17. 172nd Brigade.
18. 57th Division.

Copy No.........

## 171st INFANTRY BRIGADE.

### ADMINISTRATIVE INSTRUCTIONS NO.2.

1. **MECHANICAL TRANSPORT.** Motor Lorries for baggage will be allotted as follows:-

   | | |
   |---|---|
   | 2/5th K.L.R. | 2 Lorries. |
   | 2/6th K.L.R. | 2 Lorries. |
   | 2/7th K.L.R. | 2 Lorries. |
   | 2/8th K.L.R. | 2 Lorries. |
   | 171st L.T.M.B. | 1 & a half Lorries. |
   | 171st M.G.Coy. | One half Lorry. |
   | 171st B.H.Q. | 1 Lorry. |

   A guide from each of the above Units will report to D.S.C. RECQUES at 7.0.am. on 8/12/17 to guide lorries to their respective Units.

2. **LOADING PARTIES.** Blankets, Baggage etc. will be stacked and loading parties of 3 or 4 other ranks detailed to each lorry. Loading will not take more than three quarters of an hour. Each loading party will be provided with a map of Brigade Area and name of Camp allotted to Unit.

3. **RENDEZVOUS FOR LORRIES.** Time and place will be notified later.

4. **DESTINATION OF LORRIES.** Each lorry driver will be provided with written orders stating Unit, name of Camp and Map reference in accordance with instructions issued under this Office Q.497 dated 5/10/17.

5. **AREA STORES.** All Area Stores, including wash bowls and paillasses will be returned by Units to Billet Warden and a receipt obtained.

6. **R.E. MATERIAL.** All surplus R.E. material will be collected and handed over to Brigade Area Commandant or Billet Warden on the site and a receipt obtained and forwarded to this Office.

7. **BILLETS.** The vicinity of billets and billets will be left scrupulously clean and certificate obtained from the Brigade Area Commandant to this effect.

8. **ACKNOWLEDGE.**

B.H.Q.
7/12/17.

Captain, A/Staff Captain,
171st Infantry Brigade.

Issued at 12 noon to:-  Copy No. 1. B.G.C.
2. Brigade Major.
3. Staff Captain.
4. 2/5th K.L.R.
5. 2/6th K.L.R.
6. 2/7th K.L.R.
7. 2/8th K.L.R.
8. 171st L.T.M.B.
9. 171st M.G.Coy.
10. 421st Field Coy.R.E.
11. 2/2nd Wessex Field A.
12. No.3. Coy.Divl.Train.
13. War Diary.
14. War Diary.
15. File.
16. Spare.

## 171st INFANTRY BRIGADE.

### Reference ADMINISTRATIVE ORDERS No.2.

1. **MECHANICAL TRANSPORT.** Para.1. Guides drawing lorries from 57th D.S.C. RECQUES at 7.0.am. 8/12/17 will be provided by Unit with authority to draw Lorries.

   Rendezvous for Motor Lorries will be at NORDAUSQUES, Main ST.OMER - CALAIS RD. (Reference HAZEBROUCK 5A) at 9.30.am. 8/12/17.

   Loading parties will travel on motor lorries.

**ACKNOWLEDGE.**

   Issued to all recipients of Administrative Instructions No.2 and D.S.C. and Brigade Signals Officer.

B.H.Q.
7/12/17.

Captain, A/Staff Captain,
171st Infantry Brigade.

SECRET.                                                      COPY NO. 15

             171st INFANTRY BRIGADE ORDER No. 49A.
             ........                        7th December, 1917.

1.   171st Infantry Brigade (less Transport) will move by bus
to PROOSDY AREA tomorrow, December 8th.

2.   Units will embus as under :-

(a) <u>Embussing Point.</u>
                    NORDAUSQUES.         Head of Column, Cross-
Roads immediately South of the second S in NORDAUSQUES facing
South-East. (HAZEBROUCK, Sheet 5A).
                        Units will be formed up by 8 a.m. in the
following order :-
          HdQrs, 171st Infantry Bde.
          2/7th K.L.R.,
          2/5th K.L.R.,
          421st Field Co, R.E.,
          2/8th K.L.R.,

(b) <u>Embussing Point.</u>
                    ARDRES - ZOUAFQUES Road.     Head of
Column fork of Road immediately North of the last E in
CREZEQUES facing South-East. (CALAIS, Sheet 13).
                        Units will be formed up by 7.30 a.m.,
in the following order :-
          2/6th K.L.R.,
          171st L.T.M.B.,
          171st M.G.Coy.
          2/2nd Wessex Field Ambce.

3.   O.C., 2/6th K.L.R. will detail an Officer to superintend the
embussing of the troops mentioned in para.2 (b) above.
Full details as to bus accommodation will be forwarded to him
as soon as available.

4.   Units will debus on the PROVEN - ROUSBRUGGE Road, just
North-West of PROVEN.

5.   Units should carry haversack rations with them.

6.   Units will be billeted on arrival in PROOSDY as detailed in
this Office No.A.1563 dated 5.12.1917.

7.   Guides from Advanced Parties will meet Units at the Debussing
Point to guide them to their Camps.

8.   ACKNOWLEDGE.
                                     R.W.Pattison
                                     Captain, Brigade Major.
                                     171st Infantry Brigade.

DISTRIBUTION:-

Copy No. 1.  2/5th K.L.R.,      Copy No.11.  B.G.C.,
         2.  2/6th    ,,                 12.  Brigade Major.
         3.  2/7th    ,,                 13.  Staff Captain.
         4.  2/8th    ,,                 14.  Signals, 171st Bde.
         5.  171st L.T.M.B.              15.  War Diary.
         6.  171st M.G.Co.,               16.    ,,    ,,
         7.  421st Field Co, R.E.,        17.)
         8.  2/2nd Wessex Fd Ambce.       18.) Spare.
         9.  57th Division, "G".          19.)
        10.    ,,      ,,    "Q".         20.)

SECRET.   COPY NO. 19

Ref. Map.  
Sheet 20. S.W.  
1/20,000.

171st INFANTRY BRIGADE ORDER No. 50.

15th December, 1917.

1. The 171st Infantry Brigade Group (less 2/2nd Wessex Field Ambulance and 421st Field Co, RE.), will relieve the 55th Infantry Brigade Group in the Line on 16th - 17th December 1917.
The Boundaries of the Sector are as follows :-
SOUTHERN.  20/ V,7,b,4.4 - River BROEMBEEK - 20/ U,17,c,5.8 - thence S.W. along Railway.
NORTHERN.  20/ U,10,d,2.9 - U,10,b,75.40 - U,11,a,0.4 - U,11,a,6.3 - U,5,d,8.3. - CLARGES STREET inclusive to Front Line, U,5,b,8.8.

2. All details of reliefs will be arranged between Os.C. Units concerned.

3. All Defence Schemes, Air Photographs, Maps and other documents, and information concerning the Area, will be taken over on Relief. Copies of Receipts will be forwarded to these Headquarters.

4. Personnel of Units will move in accordance with attached Move Table "A".
Transport of Units will move in accordance with attached Move Table "B".

5. Administrative Instructions are included in attached "C".

6. The following intervals will be maintained on March Routes:-
500 yds between Battalions.
100 yds between Companies, Infantry and any Transport, and between every 6 vehicles.

7. Brigade HdQrs will close at 9.30 a.m., 17th instant, at PENGE CAMP, and open on arrival at FIFTEEN WOOD.

8. Completion of Reliefs to be reported to this Office.

9. The Command of the Sector will pass to G.O.C., 171st Infantry Brigade, on completion of relief.

10. ACKNOWLEDGE.

R W Patteson

Captain, Brigade Major,
171st Infantry Brigade.

ISSUED TO :-

Copy No. 1. 2/5th K.L.R.,
2. 2/6th ,,
3. 2/7th ,,
4. 2/8th ,,
5. 171st L.T.M.B.,
6. 171st M.G.Coy.
7. 421st Field Co, RE.
8. 2/2nd Wessex Fd Ambce.
9. No.3 Coy, Divl.Train.
10. 55th Infantry Brigade.

Copy No. 11. 57th Division, "G".
12. ,, "Q".
13. B.G.C.
14. Brigade Major.
15. Staff Captain.
16. Brigade Intelligence Offr.
17. Brigade Transport Offr.
18. Signals, 171st Bde.
19. War Diary.
20. ,,

TABLE "A" - Issued with 171st INFANTRY BRIGADE ORDER No. 50.

| Serial Nos. | Date. | Unit. | From. | To. | Replacing. | Route. | REMARKS. |
|---|---|---|---|---|---|---|---|
| 1. | 16th. | 2/5th K.L.R., | PORTSMOUTH CAMP. | CANAL BANK, B.6.C. | 8th E.Surreys. | By Train, 10 am. from PROVEN to BOISINGHE. | Officer to report to Bde Entraining Offr. at PROVNNGE at 9.30 am. Units should be at STN. by 9.45 am. |
| 2. | 16th. | 2/6th ,, | PORTSDOWN CAMP. | BABOON CAMP, B.6.B. | 7th R.W.Kents. | - ditto - | - ditto - |
| 3. | 16th. | 171st L.T.M.B. | PICCADILLY CAMP. | SIGNAL FARM, U.21.C. | 55th L.T.M.B. | - ditto - | - ditto - |
| 4. | 16th. | 171st M.G.Coy. (3 Sections) | PUTNEY CAMP. | - ditto - | 55th M.G.Coy. | - ditto - | - ditto - |
| 5. | 17th. | 2/7th K.L.R. | PETWORTH CAMP. | CANAL BANK, B.6.C. | 2/6th K.L.R. | Time and place of Entrainment on 17th Dec. will be notified later. | - |
| 6. | 17th. | 2/8th ,, | PADDINGTON CAMP. | BABOON CAMP, B.6.B. | 2/5th L.L.R. | | - |
| 7. | 17th. | 171st Inf.Bde H.Q. | PINGA CAMP. | FIFTEEN WOOD,U.25.C. | 55th Bde H.Q. | | - |
| 8. | 17th. | 171st M.G.Coy. (1 Section). | PUTNEY CAMP. | SIGNAL FARM, U.21.C. | 55th M.G.Coy. (1 Section). | | - |
| 9. | 17th. | 2/5th K.L.R., | BABOON CAMP,B.6.B. | LINE - H.Q. EGYPT HOUSE, U.12.B. | 7th Queens. | - | Will move under orders of G.O.C. 55th Inf.Bde. |
| 10. | 17th. | 2/6th K.L.R. | CANAL BANK, B.6.C. | LINE - H.Q.AJAX HOUSE, U.6.c.8.3. | 7th Buffs. | - | |

NOTE:- On completion of Moves Serial Nos. 1, 2, 3, and 4, these Units will come under orders of G.O.C., 55th Infantry Brigade, until passing of Command.

TABLE "B" - Issued with 171st INFANTRY BRIGADE ORDER No. 50.

| Serial No. | Date. | Unit. | From. | To. | Replacing. | Route. | REMARKS. |
|---|---|---|---|---|---|---|---|
| 1. | 16th. | 2/6th K.L.R., | PROOSDY AREA. | BIRBECK and BLACKPOOL CAMPS. 20/A.II.B. | 7th R.W.Kents. | PROVEN NORTHERN MILITARY ROAD - ONDANK. | Will move under Bde Transport Officer, 171st Inf. Bde. |
| 2. | 15th. | 2/5th K.L.R., | | | 8th E.Surreys. | | 2/5th KLR. to be clear of 19/X.28.C, CRUCIFIX CORNER by 7.50 a.m. |
| 3. | 16th. | 171st M.G.Coy. (3 Sections). | | | 55th M.G.Coy. | | 2/6th KLR. by 7.55 a.m. 171st MG.Coy by 7.59 a.m. (3 Sections). |

NOTE :- Transport Orders Orders for the Remaining Units - who will move early on the 17th December - will be notified later.

## ADMINISTRATIVE INSTRUCTIONS IN CONNECTION WITH BRIGADE ORDER NO. 50.

### APPENDIX "C"

**MECHANICAL TRANSPORT.**    1. Motor lorries are allotted as follows and will report to Units H.Q. at 8.0.am. on 16.12.17:-

     2/5th K.L.R.      3 lorries.
     2/6th K.L.R.      3 lorries.
     171st M.G.Coy.      1 lorry.
     171st L.T.M.B.      2 lorries.

     All blankets and baggage should be stacked and usual loading party detailed to each lorry.
     Orders in writing stating name of unit and destination of lorry should be given to each driver.
     Q.M.Stores of each Unit will be located at Unit's TRANSPORT LINES.
     Lorries will be loaded immediately and will rendezvous at Ref. HAZEBROUCK 5.a. 2.I.35.74. at 9-30 am.

**BAGGAGE WAGGONS.**    2. Baggage Waggons will report to 2/5th K.L.R. and 2/6th K.L.R. at 5-30 am. to-morrow, 16/12/17. After loading they will rendezvous at HAZEBROUCK 5.a. 2.I.18.82. and march to destination under Officer detailed by O.C., No. 3 Coy. Divnl. Train.
     Units will send guides to No. 3 Coy. Divnl. Train Ref. Sheet 28, B.6.c.5.8. on arrival to guide baggage waggons to units' Q.M.Stores.

**DIVISIONAL TRAIN.**    3. Forage for consumption on 17th instant will be carried by No. 3 Coy. Divnl. Train.

**SUPPLIES.**    4. Supplies for consumption on 18th inst. will be drawn at refilling point Sheet 28, B.8.c.8.3. at 8-30 am. on 17/12/17. Units will arrange to send a guide to refilling point to guide supply waggons to Units' Q.M.Stores.
     Units moving into Line on 17th Inst. will indent for 2 days preserved rations to be carried up on 17th inst. for consumption on 18th & 19th insts.
     On the 18.12.17. another 2 days' preserved rations will be obtained by units in line for consumption on 20th and 21st insts.

**ADVANCE PARTIES.**    5. O.C., 2/7th K.L.R. and O.C., 2/8th K.L.R. will detail advance parties of 1 Officer and 6 O. anks to proceed by train leaving PROVEN at 10 am. to-morrow, 16.12.17. These parties will proceed to CANAL BANK CAMP and BABOON CAMP respectively.

**SALVAGE.**    6. Before leaving present Camps all salvage will be removed to Brigade Area Salvage Dump at Ref. HAZEBROUCK 5.a. 2.H.86.79.

**R.E. MATERIAL.**    7. All surplus R.E. material will be collected in camps and handed over to incoming Units. If no advance party arrives material will be handed over to Camp Warden and a receipt obtained.

**PETROL TINS.**    8. Every effort must be made to collect petrol tins which are not easy to obtain in forward areas.

**GUM BOOT STORES.**    9. Gum Boot Stores and Boots will be taken over by O.C., 2/6th K.L.R. List of Stores taken over will be forwarded to this Office. Personnel in charge of store, i.e., 1 N.C.O. & 2 O.R. will be provided by O.C., 2/6th K.L.R.

P.T.O.

- 2 -

TRENCH & AREA STORES.
10. All Area Stores will be handed over to incoming units, or to Camp Warden if advance party of unit is not available. Receipts will be forwarded to this office.

In accordance with 57th Divisional Administrative Instructions in connection with 57th Divisional Order No. 55 all Lists of Trench and Area Stores taken over will be forwarded to this Office.

CAMPS, BILLETS AND HORSE LINES.
11. Camps, Billets and Horse Lines will be left scrupulously clean and a certificate to that effect will be obtained from the Camp Warden and forwarded to this Office.

C. Marshall

Captain, .../Staff Capt.
171st Infantry Brigade.

ADDITION TO TABLE "B" issued with 171st INF. BDE. ORDER NO. 50.

| rial o. | Date. | Unit. | From. | To. | Replacing. | To be clear of CRUCIFIX CORNER, I9/X.28.C. by. | Remarks. |
|---|---|---|---|---|---|---|---|
| 4. | 17th. | 2/8th K.L.R., | | BIRBECK | 7th Queens. | 8.14 a.m. | Will move under orders of O.C. No.3 Coy, Divl. Train. |
| 5. | 17th. | No.3 Coy, Divl. Train. | PROOSDY | and | - Coy, 12th Divl.Train. | 8.20 a.m. | No.3 Coy, Divl. Train not to pass PADDINGTON C..P. - 2/8th K.L.R. until 8.5 a.m. |
| 6. | 17th. | 2/7th K.L.R., | ARLA. | BLACKPOOL CAMP. | 7th Buffs. | 8.26 a.m. | |
| 7. | 17th. | 171st M.G.Coy. (I Section) | | | 55th M.G.Coy. (I Section) | 8.27 a.m. | |
| 8. | 17th. | 171st Inf.Bde Hdqrs. | | 20/A.I.I.B. | 55th Inf.Bde Hdqrs. | 8.29 a.m. | |

B.H.Q. 16.12.1917.

ACKNOWLEDGE.

Captain, A/Staff Captain,
171st Infantry Brigade.

## 171st INFANTRY BRIGADE ORDER NO. 50.   B0/50/2.

Reference above order, Serials 5 to 8 inclusive.
Time of Train and Remarks of Serial Nos. 1 to 4 of
16/12/16 apply to Serials Nos. 5 to 8 of 17/12/17.

B. H. Q.,
16.12.17.

Captain, A/Staff Capt.
171st Infantry Brigade.

**SECRET**

Addition 1 to -
ADMINISTRATIVE INSTRUCTIONS IN CONNECTION WITH
BRIGADE ORDER NO.50.
"APPENDIX "C".

**MECHANICAL TRANSPORT.**   1. Motor lorries are allotted as follows and will report to Units' Headquarters at 8.0.am. on 17.12.17.
     171st B.H.Q.    2 lorries.
     2/7th K.L.R.    3  ,,
     2/8th K.L.R.    3  ,,
Instructions laid down in Administrative Instructions issued 16.12.17 will be adhered to.

**BAGGAGE WAGONS.**   2. Baggage wagons will be sent back to No. 3 Coy. Divisional Train after loading.
On arrival at destination, Units will send guides to No. 3 Coy. Divisional Train at Sheet 28 B.3.c.5.8. to guide baggage wagons to Units Q.M.Stores.

**SUPPLIES.**   3. Para. 4 is amended as follows:-
Refilling Point for 17.12.17 ELVERDINGHE STATION.
Time of Refilling will be 10.15.am.
When indenting for preserved Rations, Units will only indent for numbers actually going into the line. Fresh rations will be drawn for the remainder.

**ACKNOWLEDGE.**   4.

                                                  E. Marshall.

B.H.Q.                    Captain, A/Staff Captain,
16.12.17.              171st Infantry Brigade.

Issued to all recipients of Brigade Order No.50.

SECRET.                                                                 COPY NO. 19

171st INFANTRY BRIGADE ORDER NUMBER 51.

20th December 1917.

1.  2/8th K.L.R. and 2/7th K.L.R. will relieve the 2/5th K.L.R. and 2/6th K.L.R. in the Right and Left Battalion Sub-Sectors, respectively, on the night 21st/22nd December 1917.

2.  On relief, 2/5th K.L.R. will withdraw to BABOON CAMP and 2/6th K.L.R. to CANAL BANK.

3.  Relieving Units can leave their Camps at 3-0 pm.

    2/8th K.L.R. will relieve by RAILWAY STREET.
    2/7th K.L.R. will relieve by CLARGES STREET.

    HUNTER STREET will be kept clear for down traffic.
    The Company of the 2/6th K.L.R. at ABRI FARM and the Company of the 2/5th K.L.R. at TUFFS FARM and CAPTAIN'S FARM can be relieved earlier, under Battalion arrangements.

4.  O.C., 2/7th K.L.R. will arrange to take over the Left Front Line Sub-Sector with two companies of three platoons each, from the one Company at present holding it.

5.  S.O.S. relay posts will be taken over by relieving Battalions as follows :-

    1. At VEE BEND, 1 N.C.O. & 3 men by 2/7th K.L.R. from 2/6th K.L.R.
    2. At CANNES FARM, 1 N.C.O. & 3 men by 2/8th K.L.R. from 2/5th K.L.R.
    3. At U.26.d.6.8, 1 N.C.O. & 3 men by 2/8th K.L.R. from 2/5th K.L.R.

    No.1 will be taken over on relief; No. 2 and 3 by 12 noon December 21st. Relieving Battalions will send an Officer to ensure that reliefs fully understand their duties.

6.  Os.C. Relieving Bns will arrange to take over all surplus water bottles.

7.  All details of relief will be arranged between Battalion Commanders concerned.

8.  ACKNOWLEDGE.

                                                    R.W. Pattison
                                                    Captain, Brigade Major,
                                                    171st Infantry Brigade.

DISTRIBUTION .-
    Copy No. 1.   2/5th K.L.R.              Copy No. 12.  H.Q. 57th Divn.(G)
            2.   2/6th K.L.R.                       13.   ,,      ,,     (Q)
            3.   2/7th K.L.R.                       14.   Area Comdt.
            4.   2/8th K.L.R.                             BOESINGHE, No.1
            5.   171st L.T.M.B.                     15.   B.G.C.
            6.   171st M.G.Coy.                     17.   Staff Captain.
            7.   2/2nd Wessex F.A.                  18.   Bde.Signalling Off
            8.   No.3 Coy.Divl.Train.               19.   War Diary.
            9.   421st Fd.Coy.R.E.                  20.   ,,    ,,
           10.   H.Q. 170th Inf.Bde.
           11.   ,,  172nd    ,,
                                                    21.   Brigade Major.
                                                    22.   Brigade I.O.,
            27.  3rd Inf Bde                        23.   45 KLR (Rear)
            28.  175 Inf Bde                        24.   2/6 ,,   ,,
                                                    25.   285 Bde RFA
                                                    26.   286 Bde RFA

SECRET.                                                          COPY NO 16

## 171st INFANTRY BRIGADE ORDER No. 52.

1. On night 23/24th December, two Companies 2/5th K.L.R. will come under orders of O.C. 2/8th K.L.R.

2. These two Companies of 2/5th K.L.R. will be used by O.C. 2/8th K.L.R. to relieve the Front Line System.

3. (a) The Company taking over on the Right will take over with 4 Platoons :-
(1) Two Platoons taking over new Front Line Posts from V.I.C.5.4. to V.I.c.68.20 to V.7.a.8 5.90 to V.7.b.00.60. These Posts should be made chequerwise if possible.
(2) Two Platoons taking over a close Support Line from V.I.c.05.15 to V.7.a.35.70.
Dispositions of Lewis Guns for Right Company are shown on Disposition Map forwarded to 2/5th K.L.R.

(b) The Company taking over on the Left will take over with 3 Platoons in the same manner as the Left Company Front is now held.

4. (a) O.C. 2/8th K.L.R. will garrison ADEN HOUSE and Strong Points at U.6.D.45.40 and V.7.a.5,5. with a Platoon each. One Platoon of this Company will also be accommodated at CAIRO HOUSE and Pill Boxes at U.12.d.60.80 (at Support Company HdQrs).

(b) One Company, 2/8th K.L.R., will be accommodated for counter-attack purposes in PASCAL FARM Area.

(c) Remaining troops will be accommodated in ABRI WOOD.

5. Guides will be sent by O.C. 2/8th K.L.R. to BABOON CAMP as soon as possible.

6. O.C. 2/8th K.L.R. will keep two runners from Companies at ABRI WOOD at Right Group Artillery HdQrs at U.25.d.5.8. in order to keep in touch with those Companies. Messages bothen should be sent direct to Brigade HdQrs, who will ensure their correct delivery.

7. Relief complete will be reported by the Code word "HUNTER".

8. ACKNOWLEDGE.

for Captain, Brigade Major.
171st Infantry Brigade.

DISTRIBUTION :-

| Copy No. | | | Copy No. | |
|---|---|---|---|---|
| 1. | 2/5th K.L.R. | | 11. | Left Group, R.A. |
| 2. | 2/6th ,, | | 12. | B.G.C., |
| 3. | 2/7th ,, | | 13. | Brigade Major. |
| 4. | 2/8th ,, | | 14. | Brigade Signals. |
| 5. | 171st L.T.M.B. | | 15. | Staff Captain. |
| 6. | 171st M.G.Coy. | | 16. | War Diary. |
| 7. | 57th Div. "G" | | 17. | ,, |
| 8. | ,, "Q" | | 18.) | |
| 9. | 173rd Inf.Bde. | | 19.) | Spare. |
| 10. | Right Group, R.A. | | 20.) | |

SECRET.                                                                COPY NO. 16

### 171st INFANTRY BRIGADE ORDER NO. 53.

23rd December 1917.

1. 171st M.Guns and 170th M.Guns (attached 171st Infantry Brigade) will be relieved by 172nd Machine Gun Coy. on the night December 24th/25th.

   (a) The guns to be relieved are located at the following positions :-

   | | | | |
   |---|---|---|---|
   | 1. U.12.d.63.87. | | 7. U.5.d.93.28. | (2 guns). |
   | 2. U.12.b.90.20. | | 8. U.5.d.40.38. | |
   | 3. U.12.b.25.95. | | 9. U.5.d.95.25. | |
   | 4. U.6.d.18.12. | | 10. U.12.b.20.95. | |
   | 5. U.6.c.90.47. | | 11. VIEW BEND | (2 guns). |
   | 6. U.6.c.80.50. | | 12. PASCALL FARM | (2 guns). |

   TOTAL - 15 Guns.

   (b) 172nd Infantry Brigade is arranging to place 1 gun in a new position, approximately U.12.b.40.80. in the vicinity of EGYPT HOUSE.

   (c) The arrangements for the above relief will be made by Os.C. M.G. Companies concerned.

2. The gun of 171st M.G.Company now at U.10.d.10.10. will be relieved by two guns of 173rd M.G.Company on or before the night 25th/26th December. Arrangements for this relief will be made by Os.C. Units concerned.

3. Progress of relief will be reported to this office by code word "SIGNAL".

4. O.C., 2/6th K.L.R. will arrange to relieve the 2 Vickers Guns of 170th M.G.Company at CANNON FARM (C.1.c.7.4.) by 4-30 p.m. December 24th, with 2 L.G. These guns are required for anti-aircraft work.

5. 171st M.G.Company, on relief, will withdraw to camp at B.9.a.9.1.

6. Units concerned ACKNOWLEDGE.

                                                    Captain, Brigade Major,
                                                    171st Infantry Brigade.

B. G

### DISTRIBUTION.

| | |
|---|---|
| Copy No. 1. 2/5th K.L.R. | Copy No. 9. 170th Infantry Brigade. |
| 2. 2/6th  " | 10. 172nd        " |
| 3. 2/7th  " | 11. 170th M/Gun Company. (SIGNAL FARM) |
| 4. 2/8th  " | 12. B.G.C. |
| 5. 171st L.T.M.B. | 13. Brigade Major. |
| 6. 171st M.G.Coy. | 14. Staff Captain. |
| 7. 57th Division "G" | 15. Brigade Signals. |
| 8. D.M.G.O. | 16. War Diary. |
| | 17. War Diary. |
| | 18. File. |

SECRET.                                                           COPY NO. 18

171st INFANTRY BRIGADE ORDER NO. 54.
------------------------------------------

23rd December 1917.

1.   The 171st Infantry Brigade (less 171st M.G.Coy). will be relieved in the Line by 172nd Infantry Brigade on the night of the 25th/26th December.

2.   Relief will be carried out in accordance with attached relief table.

3.   A representative of each Platoon from 2/5th Bn. S.L.R. and 2/9th Bn. K.L.R. is being sent as an advanced party to the front line system on the night of 24th/25th December.
     Advanced parties of 2/4th S.L.R. and 2/10th K.L.R. will report to the Units whose camps they will be occupying on the night of December 25th/26th.

4.   Guides from 2/7th K.L.R. and 2/8th K.L.R. will be sent to report to 2/9th K.L.R. and 2/5th S.L.R. at CANAL BANK CAMP and BOESINGHE CAMPS respectively by 1 pm. on December 25th.
     Guides can be sent down on December 24th and will be accommodated by O.C., 2/8th K.L.R. for the night of 24th/25th December.

5.   2/5th S.L.R. and 2/9th K.L.R. will use RAILWAY STREET and CLARGES STREET respectively.   HUNTER STREET will be kept for down traffic.

6.   S.O.S. Posts will be taken over by the Relieving Battalions as follows :-
     Post at CANNES FARM, from 2/8th K.L.R. by 2/5th S.L.R.
     Post at VEE BEND        ,, 2/7th K.L.R. by 2/9th K.L.R.
     Post at U.26.d.6.8.     ,, 2/8th K.L.R. by 172nd Bde. Observers.

7.   All Defence Schemes, Aeroplane Photos, Maps and other documents concerning the Brigade Sector will be handed over on relief.   Copies of receipts will be forwarded to Brigade Headquarters.

8.   171st Bde. Headquarters will close at FIFTEEN WOOD at 6 pm. on December 25th and reopen at that hour at ZONNERBLOOM CABARET B.8.c.6.6.

9.   The Command of the Sector will pass to G.O.C., 172nd Inf. Brigade on completion of Relief .

10.  ACKNOWLEDGE.

                                                Captain, Brigade Major,
                                                171st Infantry Brigade.

DISTRIBUTION -

| Copy No. | | | |
|---|---|---|---|
| 1 | 2/5th K.L.R. | 11 | H.Q. 172nd Inf. Bde. |
| 2 | 2/6th K.L.R. | 12 | Area Comdt. BOESINGHE No.1. |
| 3 | 2/7th K.L.R. | 13 | ,, ,, ,, ,, ,,2. |
| 4 | 2/8th K.L.R. | 14 | B. G. C. |
| 5 | 171st L.T.M.B. | 15 | Brigade Major. |
| 6 | 171st M.G.Coy. | 16 | Staff Captain. |
| 7 | 57th Division (G). | 17 | Bde. Signalling Officer. |
| 8 | ,, ,, (Q). | 18 | War Diary. |
| 9 | 285th Bde.R.F.A. | 19 | War Diary. |
| 10 | 286th Bde.R.F.A. | 20 | Spare. |

Relief Table issued with 171st. INFANTRY BRIGADE ORDER No. 53.

| Serial No. | Unit. | Present Position | Relieved by:- | Proceed to:- | Vacated by:- | REMARKS. |
|---|---|---|---|---|---|---|
| 1. | 2/5th K.L.R., | CANAL BANK CAMP. | 2/9th K.L.R., | ELITH CAMP. | 2/9th K.L.R., | Relieving Troops reach CANAL BANK, 11.30 am. |
| 2. | 2/5th K.L.R., | BABOON CAMP. | 2/4th S.L.R., | LARRY CAMP. | 2/4th S.L.R., | Relieving Troops reach BABOON, 3 p.m. |
| 3. | 2/8th K.L.R., | RIGHT SUBSECTOR FRONT LINE. | 2/5th S.L.R., | BOESINGHE CAMP. | 2/5th S.L.R., | To leave Camps at 2.30 p.m. |
| 4. | 2/7th K.L.R., | LEFT SUBSECTOR FRONT LINE. | 2/9th K.L.R., | LARRY CAMP. | 2/10th K.L.R., | ,, |
| 5. | 171st LTMB., | LINE. | 172nd LTMB., | N.9.a.2.1. | 172nd LTMB., | ,, |

SECRET.                                                          COPY NO. 18

### 171st INFANTRY BRIGADE ORDER NO. 55.

                                                         27th December 1917.

1.    The 171st Infantry Brigade will move to the CANADA AREA on 28th December 1917.

2.    Moves will be carried out in accordance with attached table.

3.    The following intervals will be kept between units :-

       500 yds. between each Bn. & L.G.Coy.
       100 ,,     ,, Companies and between Units and their Transport
                         The 171st L.T.M.B. will be considered 1 Company.
        25 ,,     ,, each group of 6 vehicles.

4.    Transports will join in rear of their units at DE WIPPE Cross Roads.

5.    Advance parties will proceed by motor lorry to CANADA AREA on 28th December. Time and Starting Place will be notified later.

6.    Receipts for -
       (1) All Maps, documents, etc. connected with the Area, which are to be handed over.
       (2) That Camps are handed over in clean and sanitary condition.
will be obtained from advance parties of 53rd Infantry Brigade, who will arrive on the morning of 28th December.

7.    Arrangements which are being made for M.T. for each unit will be issued later.

8.    Completion of moves will be reported immediately to Brigade Hd.Qrs.

9.    Brigade Headquarters will close at ZONNEBLOOM CABT. at 9 am. and reopen at POUNDON F.15.d.1.6. upon arrival.

ACKNOWLEDGE.

                                          for Captain, Brigade Major,
                                                   171st Infantry Brigade.

### DISTRIBUTION -

| Copy No. 1 | 2/5th K. L. R.         | Copy No. 11 | Area Comdt. BOESINGHE. |
|------------|------------------------|-------------|-------------------------|
| 2          | 2/6th ,,               | 12          | ,,      ,,    CANADA.   |
| 3          | 2/7th ,,               | 13          | A.P.M. 57th Divn.       |
| 4          | 2/8th ,,               | 14          | B.G.C.                  |
| 5          | 171st L.T.M.B.         | 15          | Brigade Major.          |
| 6          | 171st M.G.Coy.         | 16          | Staff Captain.          |
| 7          | No.3 Coy. Divnl. Train.| 17          | Bde. Signalling Offcr.  |
| 8          | 57th Division 'G'.     | 18          | War Diary.              |
| 9          | 57th    ,,    'Q'.     | 19          |                         |
| 10         | 53rd Infantry Brigade. | 20          | File. (a & w)           |

21. Transport Off
22. Mons re Chauny
23. 2/5 Messes Manbee
24. File
25. 2OMS Bde

Map Ref.
Sheet 28 NW 1/40 000
27 Feb 2 3/10 000

## TRACE TABLE issued with
## 171st INFANTRY BRIGADE ORDER NO. 55.

| Serial No. | Unit. | To. | Camp vacated by | Route. | HEAD OF EACH COLUMN TO PASS - | | REMARKS. |
|---|---|---|---|---|---|---|---|
| | | | | | Starting Point, Road Junction, B.14.b.3.6. | D. YPRES. | |
| 1 | Bde. Hd. Qrs. | LOUDON F.15.d.1.6. | 53rd Inf. Bde Headquarters. | | 9-26 am. | 9-48 am. | |
| 2 | 2/5th M.L.R. | PLAISTON F.8.a.2.9. | 10th Essex Regt. | | 9-28 am. | 10-0 am. | |
| 3 | 2/6th M.L.R. | GOODWIN F.8.b.2.2. HITCHONT, F.9.c.8.8. | 8th SUFFOLK Regt. | | 9-45 am. | 10-15 am. | |
| 4 | 2/7th M.L.R. | FILCH F.15.b.8.9. PIMLOES F.10.a.5.1 | 8th NORFOLK Regt. | D. WIPPA SOUTHERN MILITARY ROAD. | 10-8 am. | 10-30 am. | |
| 5 | 2/8th M.L.R. | FOREZ F.12.d.2.8. | 6th R.BERKS. | | 10-23 am. | 10-45 am. | |
| 6 | 171st M.G.C. | PLAISTON F.9.d.2.9. | 53rd M.G.Coy. | | 10-38 am. | 11-10 am. | |
| 7 | 171st L.T.M.B. PRALD F.9.d.4.9. | | 53rd L.T.M.B. | | 10-47 am. | 11-19 am. | |
| 8 | No.3 Coy. A.S.C. | PARDO F.14.c.9.1. | 151st Coy. A.S.C. | | 11-0 am. | 11-21 am. | |

Copy No... 18...

## ADMINISTRATIVE INSTRUCTIONS

### ISSUED IN CONNECTION WITH 171st INFANTRY BRIGADE ORDER NO.55.

1. **ADVANCE PARTIES.** Advance parties as under will report at Brigade H.Q. at 10.30.a.m. on 28th and 29th inst. and proceed by motor lorry to CANADA Area on 28th inst and GODE Area on 29th respectively. Only sufficient kit for the night will be taken by Officers. As accommodation is limited Officers from 2/5th and 2/7th K.L.R. only will take batmen.

    | | | |
    |---|---|---|
    | 2/5th K.L.R. | 1 Off. | 2 O.R. |
    | 2/6th K.L.R. | 1 Off. | 2 O.R. |
    | 2/7th K.L.R. | 1 Off. | 2 O.R. |
    | 2/8th K.L.R. | 1 Off. | 2 O.R. |
    | 171st M.G.C. | - | 1 O.R. |
    | 171st L.T.M.B. | - | 1 O.R. |
    | No.3 Coy.A.S.C. | - | 1 O.R. |
    | No.2 Sec: Sigs: | - | 1 O.R. |
    | 171st B.H.Q. | - | 2 O.R. |

2. **TRANSPORT.** Motor Lorries on the following scale will report at Units' H.Q. at 8.0.am. on the 29th and 7.0.am on 30th inst. at the BOESINGHE and GODE Areas respectively.

    |  | CANADA |
    |---|---|
    | Each Battalion | 3. |
    | M.G.C. & T.M.B. (combined) | 2. |

    If necessary these lorries can make two journeys.
    An Officer is to be placed in charge of each Units' convoy to ensure the lorries reaching their destination and to avoid any unnecessary lorry journeys.

3. **CAMPS.** All camps and billets occupied will be left clean and a certificate to that effect obtained from the incoming Unit and a copy forwarded to this Office.

4. **AREA STORES.** Units will hand over all Area and Camp Stores to incoming Unit and forward list of stores handed over to this Office. All camp and area stores in the new camps etc. will be taken over and receipts given and copies forwarded to this Office.

5. **SUPPLIES.** Units will send guides to report to No.3 Coy.Divl. Train at 1.0.pm. on 28th inst to guide baggage wagons. The wagons should be loaded with surplus stores as they will proceed with Divl.Train.
    The wagons should be loaded and returned to No.3 Coy. Divl.Train by 6.0.pm. on 28th inst.
    Brigade refilling points on the march will be notified later.

B.H.Q.
27.12.17.

Captain, A/Staff Captain,
171st Infantry Brigade.

Issued to all recipients of Brigade Order No.55.

SECRET.

COPY NO. 18

28th December 1917.

ADDENDUM
to
171st INF. BRIGADE ORDER NO.55.
.........

Reference above order.

2/3rd Wessex Field Ambulance will move independently from CRO.BEKE to PIGEON CAMP F. 14. a. 2. 1. arriving at PIGEON CAMP at 3-30 pm. December 29th.

Billeting parties should proceed there to-night to take over from 56th Field Ambulance who will be vacating Camp to-morrow morning.

J C J Huntley Lt-

for Captain, Brigade Major,
171st Infantry Brigade.

Issued to all recipients of above Order.

SECRET.  COPY NO. 18

## AMENDMENT to
## 171st INF. BRIGADE ORDER NO. 55.

28.12.17.

Reference March Table issued with the above order, the times given for Head of March Column to pass Starting Point, Road Junction, B. 14. b. 3. 6, should be amended to read as follows :-

Serial No. 1 - 9-6 am.
          2 - 9-8 am.
          3 - 9-23 am.
          4 - 9-38 am.

Serial No. 5 - 10-3 am.
          6 - 10-18 am.
          7 - 10-27 am.
          8 - 10-31 am.

ACKNOWLEDGE.

for Captain, Brigade Major,
171st Infantry Brigade.

Issued to all Recipients of above Order.

ADDITIONAL ADMINISTRATIVE INSTRUCTIONS ISSUED WITH BRIGADE
ORDER NO.55.

SUPPLY WAGONS. The supply wagons for the 2/5th and 2/6th K.L.R.
will be on the PROVEN-POPERINGHE Rd. near PARDO CAMP
F.14.c.9.1. at 10.0.am. 30/12/17 and will join the 1st
line transport of these Battalions.
On reaching their destination in the GODEWAERSVELDE Area
the wagons must be off-loaded as quickly as possible
ready for the guides who will be sent from No.3 Coy.
Divl.Train to take wagons to Refilling Point.
The supply wagons of remaining Units will proceed with
No. 3 Coy. Divisional Train and Units will provide guides
to be at the fork roads, Sheet 27, Q.23.b.6.9. at 3.0.pm.
to conduct the supply wagons to their respective Units.

ADVANCE PARTIES. Advance parties as detailed in para No.1 of
of Brigade Order No.55 of 28/12/17 will rendezvous at
cross roads Sheet 27, F.21.a.3.6 (5) at 9.30.am. 30/12/17
where a lorry will be waiting to take them to the
STEENWERCK Area.

ACKNOWLEDGE.

B.H.Q.   C.J. Stewart
29/12/17.   Captain, A/Staff Captain,
   171st Infantry Brigade.

ISSUED TO ALL RECIPIENTS OF BRIGADE ORDER NO.55.

SECRET.

COPY NO. 22

28.12.17.

171st INFANTRY BRIGADE ORDER NUMBER 56.
----------------------------------------

1. 171st Infantry Brigade will move from CANADA Area to GODE Area on 30th December, and from GODE Area to STEENWERCK Area on 31st December.

2. Moves will take place in accordance with attached March Table.

3. Intervals similar to those ordered in Brigade Order No. 55 will be maintained.

4. Advance parties composed as under will proceed to the STEENWERCK Area on 30th December.

| | | |
|---|---|---|
| 2/5th K.L.R. | 1 Off. | 2 O.R. |
| 2/6th K.L.R. | 1 Off. | 2 O.R. |
| 2/7th K.L.R. | 1 Off. | 2 O.R. |
| 2/8th K.L.R. | 1 Off. | 2 O.R. |
| 171st L.T.M.B. | - | 1 O.R. |
| 171st M.G.Coy. | - | 1 O.R. |
| No.3 Coy ASC. | - | 1 O.R. |
| No.2 Sec: Sigs: | - | 1 O.R. |
| 171st B.H.Q. | | 2 O.R. |
| 2/3rd Wessex Fd.Amb. | - | 1 O.R. |

They will report to Bde.Hd.Qrs. at POUNDON at 8-30 am. on 30th December. Officers from 2/6th & 2/8th K.L.R. only will take batmen.

5. Completion of moves will be reported immediately to Bde.H.Q.

6. Brigade Headquarters will close at POUNDON at 9-30 am. on December 30th and re-open at GODEWAERSVELDE on arrival - closing at GODEWAERSVELDE at 10 am. on December 31st and re-opening at STEENWERCK at 3 pm.

ACKNOWLEDGE.

for          *F J Huntley Lt*

Captain, Brigade Major,
171st Infantry Brigade.

DISTRIBUTION -

| | | | | | |
|---|---|---|---|---|---|
| Copy No. | 1 | 2/5th K.L.R. | Copy No. | 13 | 53rd Inf. Brigade. |
| | 2 | 2/6th K.L.R. | | 14 | Area Comdt. BOESINGHE. |
| | 3 | 2/7th K.L.R. | | 15 | ,, ,, CANADA. |
| | 4 | 2/8th K.L.R. | | 16 | ,, ,, GODE. |
| | 5 | 171st L.T.M.B. | | 17 | A.P.M. 57th Divn. |
| | 6 | 171st M.G.Coy. | | 18 | B.G.C. |
| | 7 | No.3 Coy.Divnl.Train. | | 19 | Brigade Major. |
| | 8 | 2/3rd Wessex Fd.Amb. | | 20 | Staff Captain. |
| | 9 | 57th Division "G". | | 21 | Bde. Signalling Offr. |
| | 10 | 57th Division "Q". | | 22 | War Diary. |
| | 11 | 9th Australian Inf.Bde. | | 23 | ,, ,, |
| | 12 | 10th ,, ,, | | 24 | File. |
| | | | | 25. | Area Comdt. STEENWERCK |

Map. Ref. Sheet 27. 1/40,000.
and 28 N.W.I. 1/10,000.

MARCH TABLE issued with 171st INFANTRY BRIGADE ORDER No. 56.

| DATE. | Serial No. | UNIT. | FROM. | TO. | Column to pass Starting Point - Road Junction, L.4.B.6.2. | Guides from Road Advance Parties meet Units at:- | ROUTE. | REMARKS. |
|---|---|---|---|---|---|---|---|---|
| 30th Decr. 1917. | 1. | 2/5th K.L.R. | PANTON, F.8.d.2.9. | LES 4 FILS AYLON. | 10. 0 am. | SCHUERKEN, R.35.c.5.9. | POPERINGHE SWITCH Road to L.17.b.3.0, L.17.d.6.4. BOESCHEPE, BERTHEN. | Troops not allowed to halt on POPERINGHE SWITCH RD. |
| | 2. | 2/6th K.L.R. | POODLE, F.8.b.2.2. PITTOMON, F.9.c.8.8. | HASSCHLIOUCH, R.28.A. and B. | 10.15 am. | BERTHEN. | | |
| | 3. | 2/7th K.L.R. | PITCH, F.15.b.8.9. PLITIOUS, F.10.a.5.1. | Le ROUKLOSHILLE. | 10.30 am. | Le dos de PAILLE, R.31.d.7.1. | | |
| | 4. | 2/8th K.L.R. | PONEY, F.12.d.2.8. | THIBUSHOUK. | 10.45 am. | CROSS-ROADS, Q.30.c.2.5. | | |
| | 5. | 171st LTMB. | PRAND, F.9.a.4.3. | Q.30.c.1.5. | 11. 0 am. | CROSS ROADS, Q.30.c.2.5. | POPERINGHE SWITCH ROAD to ROUTE de CASSEL ABEELE, GODEWAERSVELDE. | Leading Bn. will not halt until just before entering ABEELE. |
| | 6. | 171st MG Co. | PLAISTO, F.9.d.2.9. | HUGADOORN, Q.23.a.4.4. | 11. 2 am. | CROSS ROADS, Q.23.c.4.2. | | |
| | 7. | No.3 Co, ASC. | PARDO, F.14.c.9.1. | Q.29.b.9.5. | 11.11 am. | CROSS ROADS, Q.23.c.4.2. | | |
| | 8. | 2/3rd Wessex Fd. Ambce. | PIGEON, F.14.a.2.1. | Q.23.c.6.5. | 11.15 am. | | | |
| | 9. | 171st BDE. | POUNDON, F.15.d.1.6 | GODEWAERSVELDE. | 11.24 am. | | | |

P.T.O.

| DATE. | Serial No. | UNIT. | FROM. | TO. | Column to pass Starting Point - CROSS ROADS, EEDERZEELE A.15.a.5.7. | Guides from Advanced Parties Meet Units at:- | Relieving:- | REMARKS. |
|---|---|---|---|---|---|---|---|---|
| 21st Decr. 1917. | 10. | 2/5th K.L.R. | LES 4 FILS SYMON. | WATERLANDS. | 10.30 am. | NIEPPE. | | |
| | 11. | 2/6th K.L.R. | MASSCHLIOUCH. | HOLLEBEKE. | 10.45 am. | PAPOT. | | |
| | 12. | 2/7th K.L.R. | Le ROUKLOSHILLE. | IRRECATE. | 11.10 am. | PAPOT. | Units of 10th Austln. Brigade. | |
| | 13. | 2/8th K.L.R. | THIEUSHOUK. | EL SUIE. | 11.25 am. | | | |
| | 14. | IVIst LTMB. | Q.30.c.5.1. | A.18.a.6.8. | 11.40 am. | PAPOT. | | Troops are not allowed to halt on roads in BAILLEUL. |
| | 15. | IVIst MG Coy. | HUETDOORN. | TROIS ARBRES. | 11.42 am. | PAPOT. | | |
| | 16. | No.3 Coy Divl. Train. | Q.29.c.5.9. | | 12.1 pm. | | | |
| | 17. | 2/3rd Wessex Field Ambce. | Q.23.c.6.5. | STEENWERCK. | 12.5 pm. | | 11th Austln. Fd. Ambce. | |
| | 18. | IVIst BHQ., | GODEWAERSVELDE. | A.17.a.0.1. | 12.16 pm. | | HQrs, 10th Aus.Inf.Bde. | |

SECRET. COPY NO. 17

### 171st INFANTRY BRIGADE ORDER NO. 57.    30.12.17.

1. The 171st Infantry Brigade will relieve the 9th Australian Infantry Brigade in the ARMENTIERES SECTOR on the night of 1st/2nd January, 1918 :-
   2/5th K.L.R. will be on the Right, and will take over from the 33rd Battalion, in the Line.
   2/6th K.L.R. will be on the Left, and will take over from the 36th Battalion, in the Line.
   2/7th K.L.R. will be in the Subsidiary Line, and will take over from the 35th Battalion.
   2/8th K.L.R. will be in the LAUNDRY H.5.a, and will take over from the 34th Battalion.
   171st M.G.Coy. will take over from the 9th Australian M.G.Coy. in the Line.
   171st L.T.M.Battery will take over from the 9th Australian L.T.M.B. in the Line.

2. Guides will meet the 2/5th K.L.R. at SANDBAG CORNER, I.1.d.7.3. at 4 pm. on the 1st January.
   Guides will meet the 2/6th K.L.R. at HOUPLINES Level Crossing, C.27.a.15.10, at 4-30 pm. on the 1st January.
   Guides will meet 2 Coys. of 2/7th K.L.R. for the Right Subsector at SANDBAG CORNER, and 2 Coys. of 2/7th K.L.R. for the Left Subsector at HOUPLINES Level Crossing at 5-30 pm. 1st January.
   2/8th K.L.R. will relieve by daylight, relief to be complete by 1 pm.

3. All Maps, Defence Schemes, Log Books, Trench Stores etc. will be taken over and receipts forwarded to this office by 12 noon 2nd January.

4. All details of relief will be arranged between Officers Commanding Units concerned.

5. O.C., 2/8th K.L.R. will make arrangements with the Staff Officer, ARMENTIERES Defences, to take over the following duties in connection with the defences:-
   (A) 24 O.R. to guide Reinforcing Battalions to their Battle positions.
   (B) 14 O.R.     ,,        ,,        M.G.Coy. to their Battle positions.
   (C) 2 platoons to furnish nucleus garrisons.
   (D) 24 O.R. for Guard duties on Weirs and Bridges.
   These duties will eventually be found by the Reserve Brigade.

6. ACKNOWLEDGE per BLADR.

                                        Captain, Brigade Major,
                                        171st Infantry Brigade.

### DISTRIBUTION -

| | |
|---|---|
| Copy No.1, 2/5th K.L.R. | Copy No.11, 9th Australian Bde. |
| 2, 2/6th ,, | 12, B.G.C. |
| 3, 2/7th ,, | 13, Brigade Major, |
| 4, 2/8th ,, | 14, Staff Captain, |
| 5, 171st L.T.M.B. | 15, Signalling Officer, |
| 6, 171st M.G.Coy. | 16, Bde. Transport Officer. |
| 7, 507 Coy. Divnl. Train. | 17, War Diary. |
| 8, 2/3rd Wessex F. Amb. | 18, ,, |
| 9, 57th Division 'G'. | 19, File. |
| 10, ,,         'Q'. | 20, ,, |

www.ingramcontent.com/pod-product-compliance
Lightning Source LLC
Chambersburg PA
CBHW081430300426
44108CB00016BA/2338